# LANGUAGE IN SOCIETY 14

## Sociolinguistics and
## Second Language Acquisition

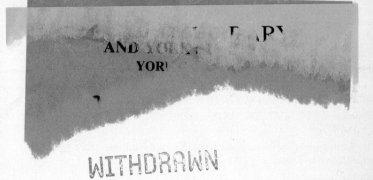

AND YORK
YOR

# Language in Society

GENERAL EDITOR
Peter Trudgill, Professor of Linguistic Science,
University of Reading

ADVISORY EDITORS
Ralph Fasold, Professor of Linguistics,
Georgetown University

William Labov, Professor of Linguistics,
University of Pennsylvania

# Sociolinguistics and Second Language Acquisition

DENNIS R. PRESTON

BASIL BLACKWELL

Copyright © Dennis R. Preston 1989

First published 1989

Basil Blackwell Ltd
108 Cowley Road, Oxford, OX4 1JF, UK

Basil Blackwell Inc.
432 Park Avenue South, Suite 1503
New York, NY 10016, USA

*British Library Cataloguing in Publication Data*

Preston, Dennis R.
  Sociolinguistics and second language
  acquisition. – (Language in society)
  1. Foreign language skills. Acquisition
Sociolinguistic aspects
  I. Title   II. Series
  401'.9
  ISBN 0–631–15245–8
  ISBN 0–631–15247–4 pbk

*Library of Congress Cataloging in Publication Data*

Preston, Dennis Richard.
  Sociolinguistics and second language acquisition / Dennis R. Preston.
    p.   cm. – (Language in society)
  Bibliography: p.
  Includes index.
  ISBN 0–631–15245–8 – ISBN 0–631–15247–4 (pbk.)
  1. Language and languages–Variation.   2. Second language acquisition.   3. Language and languages–Study and teaching.
I. Title.   II. Series.
P120.V37P74   1989
401'.9–dc19              88–37942
                         CIP

Typeset in 10/11½pt Times
by Joshua Associates Ltd, Oxford
Printed in Great Britain by Billing & Sons (Worcester) Ltd

# Contents

# Editor's preface

We often hear claims along the lines that a particular scholar is 'probably uniquely qualified' to speak or write on a particular topic. Given the intensive and specialized nature of academic activity, and given the current increasing narrowness of this specialization, such claims will often have some foundation. The author of this particular volume is himself probably uniquely qualified to write on the present topic, but his unique qualification is of a rather different and more impressive kind. It lies, not in narrow specialization, but rather in deep specialization in two separate topics which have traditionally had, within linguistics, two different literatures, two different sets of courses, and two different groups of practitioners. He is thus probably uniquely qualified to develop a synthesis and to provide an informed discussion of the relationship between second language acquisition studies and sociolinguistics. There can be few other scholars who have the necessary depth of knowledge in both fields. Dennis Preston has carried out important research and taught courses in sociolinguistics, and is very well-known, for example, for his work in perceptual dialectology. But he has also carried out significant research in second language acquisition, and acquired considerable practical experience in the field as a classroom teacher and as a foreign language teaching adviser.

It is perhaps surprising that Dennis Preston is unusual in this way, and it is certainly regrettable that so few have as yet been able to take advantage of the high degree of overlap between at least parts of the two areas. The amount of potential cross-pollination is considerable, and it is our hope that this book, which is the first to treat the relevance of the whole of sociolinguistics for the whole of second language acquisition, and vice versa, will inspire new research, new courses, and a new outlook. We would like to see, not only more cooperation between the fields, but also, where appropriate, a blending and a blurring of distinctions between them. That language acquisition takes place in a social context, that second language acquisition may help us understand some aspects of linguistic change, that variation occurs in the language of learners as well as of native speakers – these and many other phenomena need to be considered from the perspectives of both sociolinguistics and second language acquisition studies. The social matrix of language learning and language use is too central to language acquisition for it to be ignored. And the value of language acquisition as a proving ground for sociolinguistic theories is as yet relatively unexploited.

This book will be of interest to those who are familiar with the theory and practice of both second language acquisition and sociolinguistics, but it should also be of relevance to, for example, historical linguists and to students of first language acquisition. The book is based on original empirical and descriptive work, as well as on a wide knowledge of the literature, but it is also of clear theoretical significance. Variability in human language is a subject that is still poorly understood, and the innovative overall framework provided by *Sociolinguistics and Second Language Acquisition* takes us a step further along the road in our ability to analyze and comprehend it.

Peter Trudgill

# Acknowledgments

I wrote this book partly because I was encouraged to do so and partly because I have a split personal history of research in sociolinguistics, dialectology, and language attitudes on the one hand, and in foreign and second language learning and teaching on the other. That should be the right combination.

At the risk of sounding peevish, I confess that I also wrote this book to challenge the notion that theoretical linguistics is hard and sociolinguistics is easy. Though I hope not to make the latter arcane to disprove this, I want to show that the complexity of language and sociocultural facts stands behind a rich, intellectually rewarding field and that its findings are of considerable importance to all who look at language, regardless of perspective. I want to show here that interaction between sociolinguists and SLA researchers in particular can be (and has already been) rewarding.

Many people have been of great help in the coming of age of this book, not the least my first mentors in things linguistic – Fred Cassidy, Dave Maurer, and Marty Stevens. Charles Scott first attracted my attention to SLA when he assigned me an ESL class at the University of Wisconsin–Madison and trained me to do the job after the fact. I have always been grateful to him for that confidence.

At the University of Wisconsin–Milwaukee, Robert Roeming and Diana Bartley appointed me curriculum director for two summers (1969 and 1970) of the first large-scale teacher training efforts for ESL specialists in ABE. Much of what I learned about the importance of related fields to SLA came about as a result of that intensive training experience and the colleagues with whom I worked – Helene Aqua, Teresa Gomez, Carol Guagliardo (later Preston), Ralph Kite, Pat Mullen, Yvette Polcyn, Dan Rose, Jim and Jackie Stalker, Darnell Williams, and an exciting and skilled group of teachers who taught us more than we taught them.

From that same time, Gene Brière of the University of Southern California has tried to keep me psycholinguistically honest, and I have come more recently to appreciate his efforts.

Also at the same time I got to know Roger Shuy, then the leader of a Center for Applied Linguistics traveling sociolinguistic gang which included Joan Baratz, Ralph Fasold, Bill Stewart, and Walt Wolfram. What they had to say about language variation and the uses of that information in education had more than a little influence on me, and Roger, who collaborated with me on a United States Information Agency project to prepare materials on language variation for NNS ESL teachers, has continued to help my work along.

In 1972, Jacek Fisiak, Director of the Institute of English at Adam Mickiewicz University in Poznań, Poland, asked me to train several of his people in sociolinguistics, most of whom also had a considerable interest in SLA. I am grateful to him for that opportunity and for the Fulbright grant which took me there. Most importantly, I value the many hours of conversation with friends I made in Poland – Janusz Arabski, Jurek Bańczerowski, Karol Janicki, Tomek Krzeszowski, Waldek Marton, Kazik Polański, Jim Sehnert, Mike Sharwood Smith, Olek Szwedek, and others (friendly diminutives intended). My Polish days gave me an opportunity to work on and think about SLA as I had not done before.

Dick Day, Chairperson of the Department of English as a Second Language at the University of Hawaii at Manoa, invited me to spend 1980–1 as a visiting professor and run sociolinguistically amok among his faculty and students. Since Derek Bickerton was putting the finishing touches on *The Roots of Language* just then, it would be unnecessarily dishonest not to acknowledge his influence and the friendship he and Yvonne and Carol and I started and kept up.

In 1987 Sue Gass, Carolyn Madden, Larry Selinker, and I organized the XIth University of Michigan Conference on Applied Linguistics: Variation in Second Language Acquisition; their insights from SLA and the input from that conference have been especially welcome. Larry and John Swales, former and current Directors of the English Language Institute at the University of Michigan respectively, have talked about genre, discourse, and other matters with me and have each read and commented on the whole book; what advice of theirs I have followed has undoubtedly helped, what I have ignored I will likely come to regret.

Peter Trudgill, editor of this series, has taught me a great deal about language variation and change in his lectures, his writings, and in personal conversations; his comments on this book have been very helpful. I regret that in return I have been able to teach him only that language is a boat.

Much of this book was written while I held a faculty research fellowship from Eastern Michigan University. Without that, there would not have been time.

Penultimately, this book has grown out of respect for those students who have taught me the greater responsibility of educating teachers whose work takes them into immediate touch with people in need of a new language. It is good to know that some I have had a hand in educating have helped their students stay out of the clutches of loan sharks, get bargains in grocery stores, find work, and get to the bathroom in new languages.

Finally, as the dedication says, one who has always done what the previous paragraph suggests – as an ESL teacher here and abroad, as an ESL and bilingual teacher trainer, and as a bilingual program administrator – is my wife, Carol Guagliardo Preston. Her concern for those who need another language has inspired me, and her skill, hard work, and enthusiasm in providing language for those who need it most have kept me in awe. She is largely responsible for what little clarity this book may have, and it is dedicated to her and, through her, to the acquirers of new languages.

I am grateful to the following for permission to reproduce material already published elsewhere: Academic Press for figure 1.2 (from R. Fasold (1984), Variation theory and language learning, in P. Trudgill (ed.), *Applied Sociolinguistics*); Basil Blackwell for figures 3.7, 3.8 and 3.9 (from L. Milroy (1980), *Language and Social Networks*); Cambridge University Press for figure 1.5 (from D. Bickerton (1975), *Dynamics of a Creole System*), figures 2.1, 2.2, 2.10, and 2.11 (from J. K. Chambers and P. Trudgill (1980), *Dialectology*), figure 2.4 (from H. Giles (1979), Ethnicity markers in speech, in K. R. Scherer and H. Giles (eds), *Social Markers in Speech*) and figures 1.1, 2.12, and 2.14 (from P. Trudgill (1974), *The Social Differentiation of English in Norwich*); Center for Applied Linguistics for figure 2.3 (from W. Labov (1966), *The Social Stratification of English in New York City*); Edward Arnold for figure 3.6 (from E. B. Ryan, H. Giles, and R. J. Sebastian (1982), An integrative perspective for the study of attitudes toward language variation, in E. B. Ryan and H. Giles (eds), *Attitudes towards Language Variation*); *Language Learning* for figure 3.2 (from R. Kaplan (1966), Cultural thought patterns in inter-cultural education, *Language Learning*); MIT Press for figures 3.4 and 3.5 (from R. Brown and R. Gilman (1960), The pronouns of power and solidarity, in T. A. Sebeok (ed.), *Style in Language*); Mouton de Gruyter, A Division of Walter de Gruyter & Co., for figure 4.1 (from S. M. Ervin-Tripp (1971), Sociolinguistics, in J. Fishman (ed.), *Advances in the Sociology of Language*); Prentice Hall Inc. and the authors for figures 1.3 and 1.4 (from W. Wolfram and R. W. Fasold (1974), *The Study of Social Dialects in American English*); *Technology Review* for figure 3.1 (from B. L. Whorf (1940), Science and linguistics, *Technology Review*); University of Michigan Press for figure 2.6 (from H. Kurath (1949), *A Word Geography of the United States*); University of Pennsylvania Press for figure 2.13 (from W. Labov (1972a), *Sociolinguistic Patterns*), and figure 3.6 (from W. Labov (1972b), *Language in the Inner City*); University of Texas Press for figure 2.5 (from E. B. Atwood (1950), 'Grease' and 'greasy': a study of geographical variation, *Texas Studies in English*; *Word* for figure 2.9 (from U. Weinreich (1954), Is structural dialectology possible?, *Word*).

Superior Township,
Michigan, USA

# List of figures

# List of tables

# List of abbreviations

ABE     adult basic education
ESL     English as a second language
LSP     language for special purposes
L1      first (native) language, mother tongue
L2      second language, target language
NNS     nonnative speaker
NS      native speaker
SLA     second language acquisition (including foreign language learning)
TESOL   teachers of English to speakers of other languages

For Carol – the world's greatest
ESL/bilingual teacher, teacher trainer, and administrator

# Introduction

This book is about those matters which interest both sociolinguists and SLA specialists. The common ground might seem minimal, for a central concern of the latter is the description of *interlanguage*, the systems which develop during language acquisition. That should make psycholinguistics the essential partner discipline of SLA, and, although I will not deny that role, I will make two claims to help justify focusing on sociolinguistics as well.

First, there is a tradition in psycholinguistics, at least as old as the earliest generative grammars, which states that the best model of a language's mental representation is the best grammar of that language. Although that position has been challenged, according to it the details of grammatical description must have psycholinguistic relevance. Even if the rules of a grammar are not duplicates of mental operations, they should describe structures which are capable of being processed by such operations. From that point of view, all linguistic description is important to psycholinguistics; therefore, if sociolinguistics contributes hypotheses concerning linguistic structure, it too, by definition, contributes to psycholinguistics.

Second, there is a growing concern for external variables in SLA. In the past, SLA has been studied from a largely internal perspective, relying on an account of forces which are a part of the learner's mental states or processing abilities. For example, one version of an SLA hypothesis depends on accounting for the degree of influence of the structures of a learner's L1 on his or her L2. Studies of the attitudes, aptitude, personality, and motivations of learners are equally internal. Newer studies focus on the linguistic and nonlinguistic context of SLA and require extremely careful descriptions, classifications, and interpretations of the input to the learner. If, for example, a learner's interlanguage is simplified at a certain stage because of simplified input (for example, *foreigner talk*), researchers must have the grammatical machinery to show in just what way such input is simplified as well as the sociolinguistic and ethnographic skills to show how, when, where, with whom, and in what situations learners encounter such input. More broadly, if learners of languages are acquirers of rules of linguistic and social behavior which go beyond those associated with what might be called the sentence grammars of a language, then researchers must have the sociolinguistic and ethnographic skills to study the communicative competence of NSs and fluent bilinguals and the developing communicative competencies of interlanguages. Other justifications for looking at the common interests of sociolinguistics and SLA will be developed later.

In addition, this work seeks to inspire as well as instruct. A number of connections not yet made between the two fields and missed (or bungled) opportunities will be pointed out; for this reason I hope I have not simply catalogued the contributions sociolinguists have made to SLA research and vice versa. Professionals from both areas should find suggestions for work to do (and redo), and students of both will find an introduction to as well as a critique of work already done. Finally, teachers, teacher trainers, methodologists, curriculum specialists, textbook writers, and researchers in second and foreign language teaching and learning should profit from what is reviewed and suggested here.

It would be foolhardy to try to make this book completely self-contained, for that would require a thorough introduction to both sociolinguistics and SLA. Current surveys exist (e.g., Wardhaugh 1986 and Saville-Troike 1982 for sociolinguistics and Klein 1986 and Van Els et al. 1984 for SLA), and several anthologies provide illustrations of recent concerns and advances (e.g., Robinett and Schachter 1983, Gass and Selinker 1983, Felix 1980a, and Scarcella and Krashen 1980 for SLA and Baugh and Sherzer 1984 and Allen and Linn 1986 for sociolinguistics). In addition, such publications as *Language Learning*, *Interlanguage Studies Bulletin*, *Applied Linguistics*, *TESOL Quarterly*, *Studies in Second Language Acquisition*, and others focus on current work in SLA, and *Language in Society*, *Journal of the Social Psychology of Language*, *International Journal of the Sociology of Language*, and others publish recent work in sociolinguistics.

It is necessary, nevertheless, if for no other reason than to indicate something of the scope of this book, to survey briefly the major themes of sociolinguistics, particularly those of relevance to SLA. Though one might attempt a careful classificatory system in accomplishing such a task, it is carried out informally here; the concerns of the field represented in this book are determined from recent conference presentations, publications, communication among practitioners, and an assessment of their relevance to SLA.

In the broadest sense, this is a book about bilingual (or developing bilingual) sociolinguistics. Since there are probably more bi- and multilinguals than monolinguals in the world, it should be an idea especially abhorrent to sociolinguists that their special interest can be pursued adequately in ignorance of the messy data produced by such speakers. Many who are known as sociolinguists prefer to be called linguists, assuming that their perspective on language in its broader social context is necessary to any complete understanding not only of the interactional functions but also of the internal make-up of language systems. SLA researchers deserve the same status. While it is true that their work often feeds areas of applied or educational linguistics, in doing so it deals with the formation of normal, second language abilities. By offering a contrast to L1 acquisition data, to the abstracted, intuitive, or simplified data common to much so-called core linguistic research, to pathological and pidgin-creole data, and even to the complex but typically monolingual data sought by sociolinguists and ethnographers, SLA provides another perspective from which language and its structure may be investigated.

I will also use this book to oppose vigorously the notion that sociolinguistics is easier than so-called core linguistic research. Much of what passes for sociolinguistic inquiry is easy since it is only NS intuition. While there are areas of research where intuitions serve linguistics, one place where they serve nothing is the area of direct, objective language use. Even hard core generative grammarians do not ask people what they *do*; they may ask if certain constructions are possible, but these are not to be construed as questions about use. Curriculum specialists, textbook authors, methodologists, and teachers, NS or not, have little justification in making unsupported judgments about actual occurrences of language in context. The accompanying illustration from two recent texts will help make this point. To mention only the most obvious disagreement, why are the 'would' forms at the top of the formality scale in (a) but at the bottom in (b)?[1] Although it is easy to criticize those faced with the monstrous task of selecting that part of the whole complex truth which will produce a helpful lesson, the failure of intelligent, fluent speaker intuitions about formality (as the above examples surely exhibit) should be enough to show that the desire to provide authentic models and generalizations can be met only if applied linguists, textbook writers, methodologists, teacher trainers, and teachers take seriously the sociolinguistic and ethnographic complexity of locating, describing, and interpreting form–function correlations, not only as regards degrees of formality and/or politeness, but also in hundreds of other language tasks which face the learner. Similarly, the systems of developing interlanguage rules can be studied profitably only if both accurate NS (or fluent bilingual)[2] target language data and surrounding interlanguage data are available for contrast. If one compares natural learner data with intuited data, similar facts are not being compared. Only in a sentence grammar approach to interlanguage development might such contrasts be justified; one might not seek further than fluent speaker intuitions to see just what was wrong with 'I studied those book yesterday.' It is, however, dangerous to carry this contrast any further than the clearest situations, and even situations which seem clear must be carefully screened. Is 'I go downtown yesterday' a stage in the interlanguage which reveals something about tense formation, or is it just like a fluent speaker's casual, rapid style used to indicate excitement or involvement (the so-called *historical present*)? Finally, where will intuitions about

(a)

| | | |
|---|---|---|
| Would you be kind enough to ... | | |
| Would you (please) ... | **Formal** | lend me five dollars? |
| Could you (please) ... | | drive me to school? |
| Could you possibly ... | | help me with my homework? |
| Do you think you'd be able to ... | | repeat that question? |
| Will you (please) ... | **Informal** | go to the store for me? |
| Can you (please) ... | | |

(b)

| Polite $\longleftrightarrow$ | More polite | Most formal |
|---|---|---|
| May I ... | Might I ... | |
| Can I ... | Could I ... | |
| Will you ... | Would you ... | |
| Do you mind ... | Would you mind ... | Least formal |

Formal and informal requests: comparison of scales from two ESL textbooks (sources: (a) Coffey 1983: 108 (b) Marquez and Bowen 1983: 72)

various stages of the interlanguage (as opposed to the systems of L1 and L2) come from?

Many books hope to simplify; this one hopes to complexify, in part, by showing that intuitions are not worth much, at least with regard to language use. Quite a few years ago, I was training teachers of ESL for Spanish-speaking migrant, agricultural workers in the United States. The teachers, mostly regular public school teachers, were being treated to a quick ESL methods course. In one class I was making the point that the comprehension of casual, spoken English was an obvious goal, making my usual pitch against prescriptivism. I illustrated such allegro speech phenomena as 'gonna' and 'hafta' and closed the session. One of the trainees strode quickly to the front. 'I've been teaching English in the public schools for years. I have a great deal of respect for the language, and I try to instill that respect in my students,' the trainee declared. 'I cannot teach newcomers to the language to use such barbarous pronunciation, not after a life of trying to stamp out such sloppy usage; I just can't do it. I never use such forms myself, and I don't see why incorrect forms should be taught. I'VE NEVER DONE IT BEFORE AND I'M NOT GONNA START NOW.' With that, of course, the other trainees howled, and our prescriptivist looked at them as if they were silly. Finally, she asked, 'What in the world are all of you laughing at?' One told her, between chortles, that she had just said 'gonna.' 'Ridiculous,' she said; 'Never did; never will,' and she left, convinced of her accurate self-report.

It is always fun to make fun of Mr and Ms Fidditches, but the point of this tale has to do with the accuracy of reporting our own (and even others') language use. Since the usual concern in talking is with messages, not forms, reports on use are likely to be a long way off from the facts.[3] How those facts are collected and interpreted, how they change, how they covary with social facts about people and situations is precisely the hard stuff of sociolinguistics. The risk of misrepresentation of sociolinguistic facts is even greater than that of the misrepresentation of grammatical ones, for the symbolism of class, status, role, and so on attach themselves to just such items and processes.

In spite of these difficulties and others, I hope this book will guide those who want to help begin elaborating the sociolinguistic concerns of SLA.

# 1

# The sociolinguistic background

Sociolinguistic topics are more difficult to catalog than those of general linguistics, which might be organized on the basis of the size of the unit being considered – from smallest to largest: phonetics and phonology, morphology and lexical semantics, syntax and propositional semantics, and conversation and pragmatics. Although a list of general concerns (e.g., variability, switching, pidgin-creole studies) and specific social foci (e.g., age, formality) might be given for sociolinguistics as well, classification is often based on how data are collected and the type of speech community from which they are gathered.

## 1.1 Approaches to language variation

Getting the data for sociolinguistics should be an easy task; ordinary talk is always around, and the linguist need only go out and record it. What to collect from this richness and how to get it are the essentials.

The earliest collections of variable language focused on geographical variation, but not for its own sake; historical linguists investigated areal diversity in order to test the major tenet of the Neogrammarians – that sound change was without exception. If each region showed an exceptionless set of items for a sound change which had operated in its territory, the interpretation of sound changes as *laws* would be strengthened. After initial surveys found exceptions, proving the Neogrammarian view an exaggeration, dialect study continued to have a historical bias. Respondents were usually selected from older, less well-educated, rural segments of the population so that older forms could be located and recorded before they disappeared forever. What was collected was overwhelmingly the smaller aspects of language – phonology, morphology, and lexicon. Little attention was paid to syntax and none to text or discourse.

The early methods of dialectology varied, but, in general, two approaches persisted. First, nonprofessionals (schoolmasters, clergy) were mailed questionnaires and asked to translate forms into the local dialect. Second, fieldworkers (some trained linguists, some not) interviewed respondents, usually working from a questionnaire, though often collecting material in open or only partially guided conversational settings.

In some studies, different subgroups of the population were identified, but methods for reckoning social status, for example, were inconsistent with generally accepted social science procedures (as were the general methods of respondent selection). However insensitive dialect studies were to the procedures of the social sciences, they provided a wealth of information on regional language distribution and formed the foundation for much socio-linguistic work. Chambers and Trudgill (1980) shows how a sociolinguistic-ally sensitive dialectology may overcome many of the problems of earlier work; other recent reviews include Davis (1983), Francis (1983), and Petyt (1980).

Though sociolinguists now use more responsible methods in identifying respondents, they encounter the *observer's paradox* (Labov 1972a:113): the more aware respondents are that speech is being observed, the less natural their performances will be. The underlying assumption is that self-monitored speech is less casual and that less casual speech is also less systematic, and thus less revealing of the basic language system, or *vernacular*. Since surreptitious recording strikes most as unethical (but see Murray 1985), eliciting natural samples is a serious problem, but a number of investigators have devised techniques for acquiring and identifying casual speech.

In one approach, the familiarity of the collector and of his or her collection materials is made use of. The most extreme version of this approach uses only established members of groups as fieldworkers. While this might seem ideal, the nonlinguist may not be as effective in directing activities onto the focus of the investigation, and there is no assurance at all that the temporary collector status of a group member would not itself produce odd effects in the respondent performances. In addition, the unnaturalness of the respondent's telling a familiar, in-group fieldworker what he or she already knows is an obvious drawback (Jackson 1987:99–100). Nevertheless, when a professional linguist is (or becomes) a member of the group under investigation, there have been benefits. Milroy (1980) is an excellent account of how a field-worker who becomes a member of a social network not only insures more authentic and representative data but also acquires insights into the norms and values of the community which aid later interpretation.

The degree to which data recording equipment and activities (e.g., note-taking, tape recorders, cameras, and experimental settings) influence language behavior should not be minimized, but many investigators report that, after a brief period of nervousness and comment, instruments have little effect. Milroy goes so far as to suggest that '... the presence of the tape-recorder in itself ... seemed less likely to produce a shift away from the vernacular than did conversation with a higher-status participant ...' (1980:60).

Another general method for collecting natural data might be called contextual. During interviews, interaction among respondents as well as interaction between a respondent and the fieldworker may take place. In some cases, interaction between a respondent and another person not a part of the interview may occur, or there may be interaction between the fieldworker and the respondent which is not a part of the interview. In all these cases, respondents may change from an interview style (relatively formal) to a more relaxed style; in some cases, the shift is dramatic. Labov (1972a) records the following speech during an interview right before a break:

> If you're not careful, you will call a lot of them the same. There are a couple of them which are very similar; for instance, *width* and *with*. [What about *guard* and *god*?] That's another one you could very well pronounce the same, unless you give thought to it.

The following occurs during a break (while the respondent is opening a can of beer for the fieldworker):

> These things here – y'gotta do it the right way – otherwise [laughter] you'll need a pair of pliers with it . . . You see, what actually happened was, I pulled it over to there, and well . . . I don't really know *what* happened . . . Did it break off or get stuck or sump'm? . . . just the same as when you put one of these keys into a can of sardines or sump'm – and you're turning it, and you turn it lopsided, and in the end you break it off and you use the old fashioned opener . . . but I always have a spoon or a fork or a screw driver handy to wedge into the key to help you turn it . . . [laughter] I always have these things handy to make sure.

This last sample occurs after the interview resumes:

> [How do you make up your mind to rate these people?] Some people – I suppose perhaps it's the result of their training and the kind of job they have – they just talk in any slipshod manner. Others talk in a manner which has real finesse to it, but that would be the executive type. He cannot [sic] talk in a slipshod manner to a board of directors meeting. (Labov 1972a:87–8; All bracketed material in the original)

The contrast in formality between the two interview samples and the break sample comes across nicely even in this written transcription.

Another contextual way to reduce the formality of interview talk is related to change in topic. Such questions as 'Did you ever have a dream that really scared you?' or 'Were you ever in a situation where you were in serious danger of getting killed?' (Labov 1984:33) and those which ask about childhood games (Labov 1972a:91–2) have been effective in acquiring less carefully monitored speech.

In cases of standard to nonstandard grammatical change or increasing use of slang, the identification of a more casual style is simple. In the absence of such obvious keys, however, laughter and changes in tempo, pitch range, volume, and rate of breathing may be *channel cues* to style change (Labov 1972a:95).

Labov suggests that these collection and interpretive techniques allow identification of a *stylistic continuum* reaching from the most formal (carefully monitored, often elicited through written stimuli) to the most casual (unmonitored); the casual end of the continuum exemplifies vernacular style. This continuum has, however, been criticized from several points of view.

The special status of interview data, for example, may be suspect. Wolfson (1976) claims that role-relationships and genres determined by interviews severely limit the range of data obtained by such means (3.3.3). The break in interviewing illustrated above displays the radically different data which emerge when the identity of the situation alters. A continuum based on data derived from variation in that setting alone is suspect, therefore, as an indication of general conversational styles. A similar criticism of the operational distinctions used in determining the continuum addresses the problem of reading styles. Romaine (1980), for example, claims that one cannot assume that speaking (in whatever genre) and reading form a continuous dimension, and Milroy and Milroy (1977) note that in some speech communities skills in reading aloud might be so weak as to make the reading of a continuous passage require more attention than the reading of word lists.

Although one of the aims of this book is to characterize the richness of variables which influence performance, it does not take the radical position that the dimension of formality or 'style' looked at in much sociolinguistic work is vitiated by the fact that every potential variable has not been controlled for or identified. Nevertheless, such criticisms suggest a need for more careful consideration in the preparation and conduct of fieldwork of levels of *fluency* (2.2.4) in individuals and of types of fluency expected (and prized) by speech communities.

In some cases, the focus of a study may be so well-defined that surreptitious observation (not recording) may suffice. In a study of postvocalic [ɹ] deletion in New York City department stores, Labov determined what goods were located on the fourth floor and asked a clerk (whose ethnicity and approximate age he remembered) for directions – 'Excuse me, where are the women's shoes?' The clerk responded with a phrase which was sure to include the words 'fourth floor.' Then Labov leaned forward slightly and said 'Excuse me?' to elicit a more emphatic version of the same message (Labov 1966: chapter III).

Though the procedure was simple, it allowed investigation of the linguistic variable in preconsonantal ('fourth') and final ('floor') positions, in two ethnic groups, in two stylistic varieties (ordinary and emphatic), and in three different social status groups – inferred from the reputation of the stores where the survey was conducted.

In rare cases even recalled data may suffice when such large variants as clearly perceived language or variety shift are under consideration. Blom and Gumperz (1972) describe the social meaning of the use of local dialect (Ranamål) and standard (Bokmål) in Hemnesberget, northern Norway (425–6):

> The case of the local who, after finishing his business in the community office, turns to a clerk and asks him to step aside for a private chat . . . illustrates the contrast. . . . By their constant alternation between the standard and the dialect during their business transaction, they alluded to the dual relationship which exists between them. The event was terminated when the local asked the clerk in the dialect whether he had time to step aside to talk about private affairs, suggesting in effect that they shift to a purely personal, local relationship. The clerk looked around and said, 'Yes, we are not too busy.' The two of them stepped aside, although remaining in the same room, and their subsequent private discussion was appropriately carried on entirely in the dialect.

Only such general observations are appropriate from recalled data, and even they require considerable further substantiation in observation and, perhaps, recording.

In addition, to make the above observations, Blom and Gumperz must know what one speaker did and/or said in response to another, and, more subtly, they must have known what speakers in Hemnesberget believe about the status of the dialect and the standard, the symbolic importance of the varieties in interactions, and a host of other folk linguistic notions. Even the collection of massive amounts of authentic interactional data may not directly address such larger conversational, symbolic, and attitudinal interests; in fact, what is left to be collected may be quite broad:

> What is needed, then, is a general theory and body of knowledge within which diversity of speech, repertoires, ways of speaking, and choosing among them find a natural place. (Hymes 1974:32)

Although data for sociolinguistic analysis often provide plenty of 'diversity,' they contain no natural method for identifying 'repertoires, ways of speaking, and choosing among them.' What must be said, to whom, with what tone of voice and how the talk (or silence) of others is to be taken are some of the *communicative competence* aspects of language ability, and the field which discovers and analyzes such facts is the *ethnography of speaking* (or *communication*). If researchers want to utilize such concepts, they must collect more than authentic speech samples from respondents, for the identity, meaning, and structure of such concerns are part of the cultural understandings speakers have (whether consciously expressed or not) of their language.

Introspective answers to questions about communicative competence might be given, but the danger of idiosyncratic definition is large, and there is no reason to believe that answers to such ethnographic concerns are any more available to the conscious minds of respondents (even those who are aware of the goals and procedures of the research) than are answers to grammatical questions. How may the meanings, values, and types of talk in a community be investigated? All respondent information is not untrustworthy (and some of that which is may be the result of leading questions put by the fieldworker); interviews concerning language use, beliefs, and attitudes may provide clues to the organization of talk in a speech community, and respondent remarks on language should be supplemented with participant-observer information and quantitative attitude surveying to achieve a better understanding of nonlinguists' regard for language, its structure, and its use.

From another perspective, studies of conversations and texts seek at larger levels the same sorts of patterning sought in phonology, morphology, and syntax (e.g., Labov and Fanshel 1977, Halliday and Hasan 1976). Some such studies combine the formal interest of linguists in the grammar of larger units with the sociologist's interest in the reality being constructed by conversation itself. Those studies emphasize such patterns as turn-taking (e.g., Sacks, Schegloff, and Jefferson 1974) or conversational openings and closings (e.g., Schegloff 1968 and Schegloff and Sacks 1973, respectively).

Finally, some sociolinguistic data come from specifically experimental settings – in particular, attitudinal responses to language performances. Though originally developed to study attitudes to different languages (Lambert et al. 1960), the technique of voice sample ratings rapidly spread to monolingual studies. In such research, raters are asked to respond to voice samples along several dimensions, e.g. 'friendliness':


       friendly \_\_\_\_ \_\_\_\_ \_\_\_\_ \_\_\_\_ \_\_\_\_ \_\_\_\_ \_\_\_\_ unfriendly


The scales are derived from prior studies of the community and its concerns. Although only a mean score for each individual scale might be calculated, a factor analysis is normally run to determine which scales group together. A common grouping in language-centered research in educational settings results in the factors of 'confidence–eagerness' and 'ethnicity–nonstandardness' (Williams 1976). Some such studies are referred to as *matched guise* since among the voice samples used to obtain the ratings there are two (or more) performances by the same speaker in the different varieties being rated. In this way, that part of the response which might be said to result from the speaker's individual vocal characteristics is filtered out.

Other experimental work in sociolinguistics includes variety identification (e.g., Labov in progress, Preston in progress), modeling (e.g., Fasold 1972), and task performance or completion (e.g., Linde and Labov 1975, Ito 1980).

Early collections of SLA data were carried out primarily in classroom and testing situations. Even when respondents have not been in classrooms, data have often been gathered from tests or similar procedures. Newer emphases on communicative competence, discourse, and LSP have prompted the collection of more natural SLA data through interviews and participant observation. If a learner's interlanguage is a communication system, evidence of its structure and variability, following sociolinguistic prejudices, should come from the collection and observation of its use. Although a number of experimental and interview techniques have recently emerged, perhaps the healthiest influence of sociolinguistics on SLA research remains the emphasis on the collection of connected speech data in a variety of settings.

## 1.2 Accounts of language variation

Sociolinguists are concerned with language variation, but how that variation is to be described and interpreted is a continuing concern. To illustrate some varieties of descriptive and interpretative accounts, the simplification of final consonant clusters in English which end in /t/ and /d/ will be used. Words such as 'test' and 'missed' may be pronounced 'tes' and 'miss.' Table 1.1 shows the percentage of final t/d deletion under four different linguistic conditions

*Table 1.1*  t/d deletion in Detroit Black speech

|  | Social classes | | | |
|---|---|---|---|---|
| Environments | Upper middle | Lower middle | Upper working | Lower working |
| Following vowel: | | | | |
| t/d is past morpheme (e.g., 'missed in') | 0.07 | 0.13 | 0.24 | 0.34 |
| t/d is not past morpheme (e.g., 'mist in') | 0.28 | 0.43 | 0.65 | 0.72 |
| Following consonant: | | | | |
| t/d is past morpheme (e.g., 'missed by') | 0.49 | 0.62 | 0.73 | 0.76 |
| t/d is not past morpheme (e.g., 'mist by') | 0.79 | 0.87 | 0.94 | 0.97 |

*Source*: Wolfram and Fasold 1974:132

and for four social classes of Black speakers from Detroit. These data show patterned variability; both the linguistic facts (whether the cluster is followed by a vowel or a consonant and whether the final member of the cluster is itself the past tense morpheme) and social facts (here class) have an effect on deletion. Though there has been controversy about whether or not such patterned variability occurs at levels other than phonology (e.g., Lavandera 1977, Labov 1978), it is generally agreed that data such as those in table 1.1 are the stuff of quantitative sociolinguistics. Such tables, however, do not answer some interesting questions. Is the deletion of final t/d a stable (*stagnant*) variable, or is it increasing or decreasing? Has t/d deletion disappeared (or decreased in frequency) in other groups, or is it starting in this group with some likelihood of spreading to others? What is its original source – language and/or dialect contact, universal phonetic tendency? What is the source of its perseverance – community or in-group identification, prescriptive norm? What psycholinguistic mechanisms in the individual speaker allow such variation? The use of formal rules (with their implied psycholinguistic relevance) is an attempt to address that last question and is taken up in 1.2.1; the others are elaborated in later sections.

### 1.2.1   *The variable rule*

For many linguists, the psycholinguistic status of a linguistic fact is best expressed in a rule. The neater, more general, and more economical the rule, the more likely it will resemble the cognitive structures of linguistic competence which enable language use itself.[1] If only a weak form of that claim is accepted – that mental representations of language may be illuminated or better understood through rules, not necessarily duplicated by them – the motivation to write them is still understandably strong.

Normally, linguistic rules are *categorical* – they work everywhere.

$$X \rightarrow Y / \underline{\quad\quad} Z$$

X becomes (or 'is realized as') Y whenever Z follows. In my phonological system, this vowel raising rule is categorical.

$$/\varepsilon/ \rightarrow [\mathrm{I}] / \underline{\quad\quad} [+\mathrm{nas}]$$

/ε/ is realized as [I] if a nasal follows, causing 'pin' and 'pen' to be homophones. (I say 'ball-point' nowadays when I want something to write with rather than stick with.)

The t/d deletion data cited in table 1.1 are not so easily captured in such a rule. If the rule is written categorically,

$$\mathrm{t/d} \rightarrow \emptyset / C \underline{\quad\quad} \#\# \{V, C\}$$

t/d would be deleted every time it followed a consonant and appeared at the end of a word. The data in table 1.1 show that that is not the case; even when all the best conditions for deletion are met (lower working class, t/d is not the past tense morpheme, and the following word begins with a consonant), the deletion percentage, though 0.97, is still not categorical. One solution is to make such rules *optional*. The mechanism for this shows the product of the rule or any optional constraint in parentheses.

$$t/d \rightarrow (\varnothing) / C \, (\#) \underline{\quad} \#\# \, \{V,C\}$$

Here t/d *may* be deleted after a consonant (C), at the end of the word (##), before a vowel or a consonant {V,C} whether it (the t/d) is a separate morpheme or not (#). The product of the rule itself ($\varnothing$ = 'nothing') and the morpheme boundary are indicated as options by enclosing them in parentheses.

This solution, however, wipes out all the quantitative information about morpheme status, following segment, and social class. If class constituted the only source of variation, it might be justified to claim that variation should be represented in rules of language use or implementation (e.g., Kiparsky 1972). The data show, however, that the variation is as much influenced by morpheme status and following segment as it is by social class. A *variable rule* allows for the incorporation of the probabilistic information from table 1.1.

$$t/d \rightarrow \langle\varnothing\rangle / C \left\langle \begin{matrix} \varnothing \\ \# \end{matrix} \right\rangle \underline{\quad} \#\# \left\langle \begin{matrix} C \\ V \end{matrix} \right\rangle$$

Angle brackets ⟨ ⟩ replace parentheses and curly brackets around both the variable output of the rule (in this case $\varnothing$) and constraints on the rule. The latter are indicated by the variables ⟨$\varnothing$,#⟩ (the absence or presence of a morpheme boundary) and ⟨C,V⟩ (a following consonant or vowel).

How may the probabilistic information from table 1.1 be built into this variable t/d deletion rule? Imagine that there were exactly one hundred total tokens of each of the categories presented in table 1.1, yielding (for upper middle class speakers) the raw data of table 1.2. These data may serve as the basis for a statistical analysis program known as VARBRUL 2, one way of determining the probability each constraint contributes to the operation (or nonoperation) of the rule. In the most widely used version, the program calculates the probabilities for each factor and assigns it a value ranging from 0.00 to 1.00. A probability below 0.50 indicates that the factor inhibits the operation of the rule; a probability over 0.50 indicates that the factor promotes the rule.[2] The VARBRUL 2 program was run on the hypothetical raw data of table 1.2, and the probabilities assigned the constraints are shown in table 1.3. When a consonant follows and when t/d is not a separate morpheme, the rule operates more frequently; when a vowel follows and t/d

*Table 1.2*   t/d deletion in the speech of upper middle class Black Detroiters

| Environments | Total | Deleted | Nondeleted |
|---|---|---|---|
| Following vowel, t/d is past morpheme | 100 | 7 | 93 |
| Following consonant, t/d is past morpheme | 100 | 49 | 51 |
| Following vowel, t/d is not past morpheme | 100 | 28 | 72 |
| Following consonant, t/d is not past morpheme | 100 | 79 | 21 |

*Source*: Extrapolated from Wolfram and Fasold 1974:132

*Table 1.3*   VARBRUL 2 calculation of probabilities of constraints on t/d deletion in upper middle class Black Detroit speech (table 1.2)

| | |
|---|---|
| Following vowel | 0.23 |
| Following consonant | 0.77 |
| Morpheme | 0.33 |
| Nonmorpheme | 0.67 |
| | |
| Input probability | 0.37 |

| | Observed | Expected | Total | Error |
|---|---|---|---|---|
| Following vowel, morpheme | 7 | 7.97 | 100 | 0.128 |
| Following vowel, nonmorpheme | 28 | 27.08 | 100 | 0.043 |
| Following consonant, morpheme | 49 | 48.07 | 100 | 0.034 |
| Following consonant, nonmorpheme | 79 | 79.88 | 100 | 0.048 |

| | |
|---|---|
| Total chi-square | 0.254 |
| Average chi-square per cell | 0.063 |

is a morpheme, its operation is retarded, but there is now an exact estimate of each constraint's influence. In the lower part of table 1.3 the columns labeled 'Observed' and 'Total' reconfirm the raw data figures; the column labeled 'Expected' indicates the number of rule applications predicted by the analysis, and the column labeled 'Error' displays the degree to which the actual data and expected number of applications correspond. Error values below 1.5 (conservatively, 1.0) are good; they indicate that the statistical model produced by VARBRUL 2 fits the raw data. In this case, the worst error score, 0.128, is far below the upper limits of acceptability in even a conservative interpretation.

The 'Input probability' is the likelihood that this rule will operate independently; that is, there is a tendency for this rule to operate (0.37) aside from the factors considered here. The measurement of chi-square indicates the degree to which the elements in the analysis are independent of one another. Here a total chi-square of 3.8 would be necessary to show that the factors were not independent. The 0.254 score insures that the two constraints (morpheme status of t/d and following segment) are not somehow related. The average chi-square per cell indicates the degree to which the variables considered account for the data. The further from 1.0 this figure is, the surer one may be that additional variables need not be sought. The score here, 0.063, is very low, indicating that the following segment and morpheme status variables are nearly completely explanatory for the observed variation.

Although this analysis allows the elements of a rule to be associated with specific probabilities, it still might be objected that the variable influences on the operation of t/d simplification are exclusively linguistic. A variable rule may, however, include elements of the social surroundings as well. The results of a VARBRUL 2 run of the hypothetical raw data from table 1.1 for *all* social classes is shown in table 1.4. The error column shows that all the expected and observed scores were acceptable with the exception of the lower working class, following consonant, morpheme boundary category which showed an error of 1.662 (observed 76.0, predicted 81.05). This mismatch is not great, however, and the error score, though slightly outside the limits, should not cause great concern. Moreover, no other single category exceeds even the more conservative 1.0 limit. However, since a large error score might indicate that the factors are not independent, the total chi-square is a good further check on this possibility. A score of at least 16.90 would have been necessary to establish a relationship among the factors; the 4.981 score obtained here insures that the influences of social class, morpheme status, and following segment operate independently of one another. In addition, the low average chi-square per cell (0.311) again suggests that the most important factors governing this variation have been investigated.

This analysis allows a probability to be associated with class membership's influence on t/d simplification exactly as probabilities were associated with linguistic environments earlier. The variable rule for t/d deletion is repeated with appropriate places numbered to indicate the probability inputs derived from table 1.4.

$$\text{t/d} \rightarrow \emptyset \underset{(1,2)}{/} \left\langle \begin{array}{c} \emptyset(3) \\ \#(4) \end{array} \right\rangle \underline{\qquad} \#\# \left\langle \begin{array}{c} C(5) \\ V(6) \end{array} \right\rangle$$

The numbers (not technically part of the rule itself) indicate the probabilities which have been assigned the various factors:

*Table 1.4*   VARBRUL 2 results for t/d deletion by Black speakers from Detroit (all social classes)

| | | | | |
|---|---|---|---|---|
| Following vowel (V) | 0.25 | | | |
| Following consonant (C) | 0.75 | | | |
| Morpheme (M) | 0.31 | | | |
| Nonmorpheme (N) | 0.69 | | | |
| Upper middle class (UMC) | 0.29 | | | |
| Lower middle class (LMC) | 0.42 | | | |
| Upper working class (UWC) | 0.60 | | | |
| Lower working class (LWC) | 0.69 | | | |
| Input probability | 0.600 | | | |

| | Observed | Expected | Total | Error |
|---|---|---|---|---|
| VMUMC | 7 | 8.09 | 100 | 0.159 |
| VMLMC | 13 | 13.73 | 100 | 0.045 |
| VMUWC | 24 | 24.84 | 100 | 0.038 |
| VMLWC | 34 | 32.04 | 100 | 0.176 |
| VNUMC | 28 | 30.61 | 100 | 0.321 |
| VNLMC | 43 | 44.37 | 100 | 0.076 |
| VNUWC | 65 | 62.36 | 100 | 0.297 |
| VNLWC | 72 | 70.27 | 100 | 0.143 |
| CMUMC | 49 | 44.39 | 100 | 0.860 |
| CMLMC | 62 | 59.07 | 100 | 0.354 |
| CMUWC | 73 | 74.99 | 100 | 0.211 |
| CMLWC | 76 | 81.05 | 100 | 1.662 |
| CNUMC | 79 | 80.01 | 100 | 0.064 |
| CNLMC | 87 | 87.86 | 100 | 0.069 |
| CNUWC | 94 | 93.76 | 100 | 0.010 |
| CNLWC | 97 | 95.54 | 100 | 0.498 |
| Total chi-square | | 4.981 | | |
| Average chi-square per cell | | 0.311 | | |

1   Enter the probability 0.60, the input probability or tendency for the rule to work independently of the other factors considered here.
2   Enter the appropriate social class probability – 0.29 upper middle, 0.42 lower middle, 0.60 upper working, and 0.69 lower working.
3   Enter 0.69, the probability contributed by the fact that t/d is not the separate morpheme 'past tense.'
4   Enter 0.31, the probability contributed by t/d being 'past tense.'
5   Enter 0.75, the probability contributed by a following consonant.
6   Enter 0.25, the probability contributed by a following vowel.

The probability of deletion in a particular environment (social and linguistic) may be calculated by combining the appropriate probabilities associated with the various factors.[3]

VARBRUL 2 also allows a stepwise regression which identifies factors which do *not* contribute to the variability of the rule. When applied to the data from table 1.1 (all classes), the regression analysis did not suggest doing away with any of the factors (following segment, morpheme status, social class). Combining the results of the average chi-square per cell figure with the results of the regression analysis allows one to claim that (1) no factor which influences rule variability has been overlooked, and (2) factors which have little or no influence on variability have been excluded.

In the above examples, the probabilities given by the linguistic environments differ very little for all classes (table 1.4) from the probabilities given for just the upper middle class (table 1.3). That is a mathematical correlation to the idea that members of the same speech community share rules but differ in their degree of realization of them. Norwich speakers' variation between the velar [ŋ] and alveolar [n] in such words as 'walking' further illustrates this fact (figure 1.1). Norwich speakers all share a rule which realizes the velar nasal as alveolar, but lower social classes make greater use of it. The rule is also sensitive to style: the more attention paid to speech, the fewer alveolar realizations. The discovery of such patterns has led to the redefinition of *speech community*. Speakers who share norms are members of the same speech community even if their degree of rule implementation is radically different. That lower working class Norwich speakers use [n] categorically in casual speech and middle middle class speakers use it less than 40 percent of

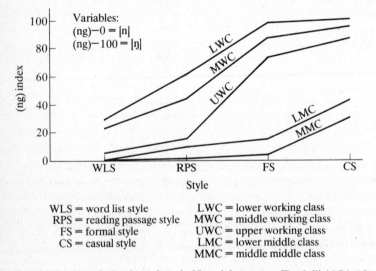

WLS = word list style      LWC = lower working class
RPS = reading passage style    MWC = middle working class
FS = formal style          UWC = upper working class
CS = casual style          LMC = lower middle class
                         MMC = middle middle class

*Figure 1.1* Alveolarization of -ng in Norwich (source: Trudgill 1974: 92)

the time in the same style makes their performances strikingly dissimilar, but the fact that velar varieties increase in more formal environments for both groups suggests that they are members of the same speech community, although many more variables would need to be investigated before that claim could be strongly made.

If linguistic rules have psycholinguistic significance, how might the probabilistic influences of a variable rule operate in language processing? It might be argued that the data reported so far are drawn from numbers of respondents and have social but not individual, psycholinguistic ramifications.

First, there is no evidence that probabilities themselves are too complex to play a role in human behavior. Studies outside linguistics have shown that probabilistic behavior occurs in individuals (Garner 1962, Sternberg 1963).

Second, a rule's probability influences each occasion of the variable element. It is not, as some have misunderstood (e.g., Bickerton 1971), the result of keeping track of the number of uses of each variant. For example, it is not the case that upper middle class Black speakers from Detroit, faced with the problem of a final t/d in a consonant cluster (nonmorphemic, before a vowel) must remember the number of deleted versus nondeleted forms used during the day and decide to delete or not delete on the basis of bringing the day's usage average closer to the rate predicted by the overall input (0.60), class (0.29), and linguistic environment (0.69, 0.25) probabilities. The likelihood of the rule's application is its probability of operating in each occurrence of its use by such a speaker and in such an environment. There is no requirement that a speaker review (or predict) performance. The application of these combined probabilities to a large number of opportunities will result in the rule's actual application percentage coming closer and closer to the percentage predicted by VARBRUL 2.

Imagine that categorical rules are represented by coins with the same thing on both sides.[4] As soon as my linguistic delivery system discovers that an /ε/ is about to be produced in front of a nasal segment, a coin with a raising rule on both sides is flipped into its processor. I am a victim of this categorical rule and cannot produce [ε] before nasals (unless I shift to another dialect or language, and I still have considerable interference).

How might variable rules be represented? For a t/d deletion rule, there are coins with DELETE written on one side and DON'T DELETE on the other. Before the coin is flipped and enters the processor with the appropriate instruction, an environmental scanner checks the linguistic surroundings and changes the coin from a fair one to a dishonest one.[5] One might imagine something like the attachment of those small weights put on automobile tire rims to balance the wheel. If the speaker is a Black Detroiter and if a vowel follows a t/d in a consonant cluster, a little weight changing the coin from honest (fifty-fifty) to 0.25 against deletion will be added. At the same time, however, the environmental scanner will discover that the t/d is not a morpheme and attach a corrective weight which will contribute 0.69 probability to the likelihood of the DELETE side of the coin coming up.

The input probability (the inclination for the rule to work at all) and the social status of the speaker have so far been left out of this picture. Imagine that the coin which is ready to be processed is already unfair – already contains the weights contributed by class and by input probability before the linguistic weights modify it. A coin weighted 0.29 DON'T DELETE (for an upper middle class Black Detroiter) and 0.60 DELETE (input probability), before it is flipped, has the additional linguistic environment weights added, perhaps 0.25 (following vowel), and 0.69 (nonmorpheme). The convergence of these probabilities, through an appropriate model (see note 3), yields the total probability for the coin before it is flipped; the resulting flip triggers an instruction (DELETE or DON'T DELETE) to the processor.

The psycholinguistic possibility for a variable rule does not seem so arcane. Variable items are unfair coins made so by appropriate weightings which derive from such characteristics of identity as age, sex, and social class and by such features of the environment as formality, solidarity with other speakers, and power and status relations among interlocutors. Last minute adjusters add additional weights to these already unfair coins as the specific linguistic environment is scanned. The coin is flipped, and the processor receives the information necessary for delivery.[6]

Variation in SLA performance and the application of VARBRUL analyses have only recently been carried out. Dickerson (1974) is the first attempt to analyze SLA performance in terms of variability, and she summarizes in Dickerson (1975) her study of Japanese learners' attempts to pronounce English /z/. The environments which seem to influence this performance are (1) following vowel, i.e., (___V) (2) following [θ], [ð], [t], [d], [ʧ], and [ʤ], i.e., (___T), (3) following silence, i.e., (___##), (4) following consonants other than those listed in 2, i.e., (___C). Figure 1.2 shows the percentage of correct English /z/ according to environment. Though there is no great difference between following vowels and consonants (other than those belonging to the group symbolized by 'T'), systematic variability according to other environments exists.

Variation due to linguistic environment is, perhaps, the area where the strongest explanatory parallelism exists between NNS and NS behavior. Many SLA researchers and sociolinguists would agree that, the markedness (or degree of naturalness or universality) of an item is a strong conditioning factor on its frequency. In table 1.1, for example, the consonants t/d are more likely to be deleted when another consonant follows. This situation is predictable from the more marked (in this case, phonetically unnatural) status of a V+C+C+C+V sequence as opposed to the less marked V+C+C+V, e.g., the pronunciation of *missed by* as [mɪsbaɪ] as opposed to [mɪstbaɪ]. Additionally, at the morpho-semantic level, one may assume that a meaningful feature is marked (more unnatural) if it has no phonetic realization. This

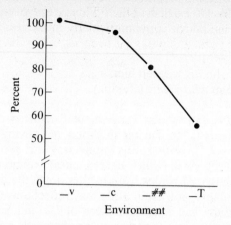

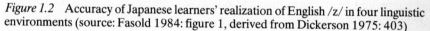

*Figure 1.2*    Accuracy of Japanese learners' realization of English /z/ in four linguistic environments (source: Fasold 1984: figure 1, derived from Dickerson 1975: 403)

explains why t/d deletion is more frequent in such forms as *mist by* where the t/d carries no past tense information than in such forms as *missed by* where it does.

Variation which may be attributed in part to markedness exists at the syntactic level as well. In many languages, not all nouns in a sentence may be relativized. Keenan and Comrie (1977: 66) argue that nouns in functions farther down on the following list are less open to relativization:

Subject
Direct object
Indirect object
Oblique object (e.g., John put the money *in the chest*)
Genitive
Object of comparison (e.g., John is taller than *the man*)

In Western Malayo-Polynesian languages, for example, only subjects may be relativized (Keenan and Comrie 1977:69); in Welsh, only subjects and direct objects (70). When items from farther down the list are relativized, other strategies may often be used. For example, a pronoun copy of the relativized noun may be retained as in Welsh for an oblique object:

Dyma 'r llyfr y darllenais y stori ynddo.
here-is the book that I-read the story in-it
Here's the book in which I read the story.
(Keenan and Comrie 1977:70)

Note that Welsh copies the relativized noun ('ynddo') as English does not. Even some varieties of English, which allows relativization on all noun functions, show pronominal copy, particularly in the less relativized ones (here the genitive):

I know the man who *his* wife left him.
(cf. I know the man *whose* wife left him.)

Hyaltenstam (1984) shows that learners of Swedish from a variety of language backgrounds (some having and some not having the pronominal copy rule in their L1 relativization strategies) use pronoun copies of relativized nouns in Swedish (which *never* copies) with greater frequency if the noun being relativized comes from further down the list. This suggests that syntactic variability, at least in SLA, may reflect universal markedness characteristics rather than only influences of L1 and L2. The place of syntactic and even larger unit variation in sociolinguistic work is considered further in 4.1.1.

Kroch (1976) suggests that NS use of marked forms is a reflex of the effort upper and middle class speakers make to set themselves apart from lower social strata. Though such class distinctions have no value in many SLA situations, the 'effort' to acquire relatively more marked forms of an L2 may reveal itself in other ways.

In particular, variation in SLA may be attributed to a stylistic dimension (exactly as was shown for NS data in figure 1.1). Though this dimension is often regarded as a cline of formality, it is much more frequently realized in research as varying *attention to form*, and it is in this sense that it is like the 'effort' of upper (and upwardly mobile) classes to distinguish themselves linguistically. On the other hand, it is claimed for SLA as well as for NS performance that the *vernacular* (here the variety which occurs when form is least attended to) is the variety which reveals the most systematic and rule-governed behavior of a speaker (e.g., Tarone 1979). It is generally well-agreed that SLA data display a continuum of styles ranging from the vernacular to the *careful* or *formal* (the variety in which the greatest attention is paid to form), and, in general, one finds the greatest number of not only L2 features in the careful style but also L1 features (*transfer*), particularly if the L1 features are prestigious (Tarone 1983). On the other hand, casual varieties often show the greatest percentage of forms which are unprecedented in the learner's L1 or in the L2 (e.g., Felix 1980b).

The focus on attention as one of the principal markers of language variation has led to the strikingly dichotomized interpretation of SLA as *learning* (where form is attended to) versus *acquisition* (where it is not) in Krashen's *monitor model* (e.g., Krashen 1981). From one sociolinguistic point of view, this position is easily criticized simply on the basis of the fact that in both NS and NNS performance the variation found in the continuum from the vernacular to the careful is precisely that – a continuum, not a cluster of greater or fewer occurrences around monitored and unmonitored SLA performances.

More seriously critical of the sociolinguistic style continuum supposed to exist in SLA behavior is the observation that attention to form is difficult to measure (Sato 1985) and that its locus is, essentially, internal. That is, it operationalizes itself, at least on one end of the continuum, through reading passages and word lists, thereby minimizing the explanatory value of social factors. Bell (1984) argues for a dimension of *audience design*, essentially the adjustment of the speaker's performance to the variation which exists between interlocutors along social lines, to explain so-called stylistic variation. This interpretation and attention to form as a representation of the cline *formal–informal* are discussed in 3.5.1.

More generally, attention to form (and therefore more careful varieties) is a by-product of greater *planning time* (e.g., Hulstijn and Hulstijn 1984). Of course, it remains to be seen which sociolinguistic environments allow (and demand) greater planning time, although the greater time generally allowed in writing as opposed to speech is obvious, and studies have reflected the greater accuracy of L2 forms in written tasks (e.g., Ellis 1987a). Attention to form, the vernacular, and the planned–unplanned dimension are given special attention in 5.1.

VARBRUL analyses of SLA data have only very recently been done. Adamson (1988) reanalyzes Schumann's (1978a) data from Alberto, a Spanish speaker whose rules for negation in English do not develop beyond 'don't + verb' – e.g., 'He don't understand.' Alberto alternates between this negation strategy and an even simpler one – 'no + VERB' – e.g., 'He no understand.' (It is assumed that the unanalyzed 'don't' strategy is a more complex construction than the 'no' one, even though the form must have been learned as a 'chunk.') Is there evidence that Alberto's use of 'no' and 'don't' are sensitive to environmental constraints? Adamson isolates the following environments: (1) the subject of the sentence is 'I' or another subject ('other'); (2) 'can,' 'like,' 'have,' and other verbs ('MV') are distinguished; (3) the complement of the sentence is a 'noun,' 'none,' 'pronoun,' or 'other' (the last including sentential complements and so on). VARBRUL 2 was run with applications of the rule resulting in the 'don't' strategy; table 1.5 shows that the influences of the above environments are relevant. Alberto's use of 'no' and 'don't' is not random but sensitive to the linguistic environment. 'I' subjects, for example, promote the 'don't' strategy (0.636) while other subjects retard it (0.364). Among the verbal environments, 'have' considerably retards the use of 'don't' (0.303) while 'like' promotes it (0.681). No complement after the verb is the greatest promoter of the 'don't' strategy (0.710) while complex complements ('other') retard it (0.327). A formal rule which expands sentence negation to 'no' and 'don't' lies behind this illustration, and a coin with 'no' on one side (− application) and 'don't' on the other

*Table 1.5*   VARBRUL 2 results for Alberto's use of the 'don't' negation strategy

| Subject | environment | Verb | environment | Complement | environment |
|---------|------------|------|-------------|------------|-------------|
| I | 0.636 | like | 0.681 | none | 0.710 |
| other | 0.364 | MV | 0.590 | noun | 0.541 |
| | | can | 0.429 | pronoun | 0.417 |
| | | have | 0.303 | other | 0.327 |

*Source*: Adapted from Adamson 1988:60, figure 6.4

(+ application) is flipped after the appropriate environmental weights are attached.

The use of variable rule analysis in SLA research is considered at greater length in 5.1.

### 1.2.2   *The dynamic paradigm*

The suggestion that generalizations about data such as those described in the preceding section might be a misleading by-product of looking at the performance of groups rather than individuals must be taken more seriously.

One criticism of the variable rule model (and of sociolinguistic research in general) is that results which are correlated to such factors as sex, age, and social class show the mean performance of groups and ignore individual behavior. It is true that much early research reported only group scores, often without a standard deviation or any other statistical indication that the mean was a realistic representation of individual performances. (Berdan 1975 is an extensive treatment of this difficulty.) The point is both a minor criticism of accuracy in data reporting and interpretation (which is easily resolved) and a broader criticism of how language variation is to be studied, represented, and interpreted. It is important precisely because it has psycholinguistic ramifications.

On the minor point, studies have shown patterned variability in individual as well as group scores. (This is elaborately and convincingly shown in Macaulay 1978, especially 137–9, but see Petyt 1980: 188–90 for an example of data where individual scores do not match group norms.) Additionally, sociolinguists have become considerably more sophisticated in their use of statistics, particularly after such complaints as those by Davis (1982).

The major issue raised above, however, is indicative of perhaps the most famous split in the history of linguistics: Is the object of research to be found in social groups or in individuals? Those who support variable rule analysis apparently hold to the former:

The grammars in which linguistic change occurs are grammars of the speech community. Because the variable structures contained in language are determined by social functions, idiolects do not provide the basis for self-contained or internally consistent grammars. (Weinreich, Labov, and Herzog 1968:188)

This perhaps surprising claim is not as patently silly as it might first seem. The structured variability (and, therefore, the coherent systematicity) of a grammar is subject to a wide variety of social facts. It is reasonable, then, to assert that the object of language study is a code's organization in a speech community, the only available source for such regularity. Though systematic variation is reflected in the speech of an individual, it is by definition not resident in the linguistic competence of any speaker. One principal source of this belief, one almost foundational to modern general linguistics, is de Saussure, who held that *langue* is just the sort of object which is resident in society rather than the individual and that instantiations of speech (*parole*) are insufficient clues to the overall patterned organization of language.

The opposite point of view (that linguistic structure is discoverable in the individual, or that *langue* is a cognitive rather than social entity, e.g., Chomsky's *competence*) has contributed to several related theoretical and historical perspectives on language structure. One is referred to as the *dynamic paradigm*. A principal difference between it and other sociolinguistic (and general linguistic) approaches is highlighted in the study of language change. Bailey (1973) summarizes, among other things, an approach to change known as *wave theory*. From this point of view, synchronic language variation is seen as a by-product of the spread of rule changes over time. Imagine a case in which an innovation (X) is introduced by one group of speakers, as at time 1 in figure 1.3. At a slightly later time, the inner circle group of figure 1.3 has introduced a second innovation, while a second group (the outer circle) has just picked up the first innovation. Since what identifies a group of speakers might be social similarity as well as

Time 1                                    Time 2

*Figure 1.3*   The innovation and spread of a feature in wave theory (source: Wolfram and Fasold 1974: 76)

geographical proximity, the diffusion of a rule occurs in social as well as geographical space and may be arrested by social or geographical barriers, as represented in figure 1.4. Waves could indicate the spread of a rule through different environments as well as the spread of an entire rule. If this picture of linguistic change is adopted, apparent variation might result from looking at the mean scores of groups of speakers who, taken individually, perform on the basis of slightly different rule configurations; that is, one speaker has already been encompassed by the wave of change as regards a particular rule or environment, and another has not. In some versions of the theory, the environments for spread of a change are lexical items themselves (*lexical diffusion*: Chen and Hsieh 1971, Chen and Wang 1975).

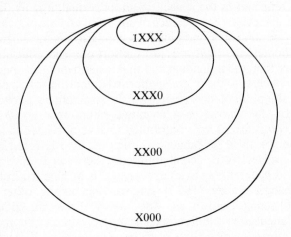

*Figure 1.4*   Interruption of spread in one direction (source: Wolfram and Fasold 1974: 77)

This view of language change and variation has been adopted to characterize the performance of speakers in creole language communities. Bickerton (1975) claims that such rule spread is easy to see there, first, because change (under pressure from a standard language) is often rapid, and, second, because forms which might have gone out of use are retained even by speakers who have learned new ones since they have symbolic, speech community membership value. One may see both a longer and a shorter history of language: shorter, since the change is so rapid; longer, since forms which might have died out in ordinary speech communities are retained for in-group value. Such a community ought to be an elaborate showplace for variation, but Bickerton argues that variable rules do not capture the psycholinguistic reality of its speakers. Table 1.6 shows how individual speakers align themselves along a continuum in the use of four variable Guyanese

*Table 1.6*   Distribution of 'a,' 'doz,' 'Ning,' and 'Ving' for
twenty-one Guyanese Creole speakers

| Speaker | Ving | Ning | doz | a |
|---------|------|------|-----|---|
| 1  | 0 | 0 | 0 | X |
| 2  | 0 | 0 | 0 | X |
| 3  | 0 | 0 | 0 | X |
| 4  | 0 | 0 | X | X |
| 5  | 0 | 0 | X | X |
| 6  | 0 | 0 | X | X |
| 7  | 0 | 0 | X | X |
| 8  | 0 | 0 | X | X |
| 9  | 0 | 0 | X | X |
| 10 | 0 | 0 | X | X |
| 11 | 0 | X | X | X |
| 12 | 0 | X | X | X |
| 13 | 0 | X | X | X |
| 14 | 0 | X | X | X |
| 15 | 0 | X | X | X |
| 16 | X | X | X | X |
| 17 | X | X | X | X |
| 18 | X | X | X | X |
| 19 | X | X | X | X |
| 20 | X | X | X | X |
| 21 | X | X | X | X |

X = occurs; 0 = does not occur
*Source*: Adapted from Bickerton 1975: 79

features: 'a,' a continuative-iterative marker; 'doz,' an iterative marker; 'Ning,' nominal -ing forms; and 'Ving,' a continuative marker.

Such variation may be apparent rather than real since speakers who differ by only one rule may be combined into the same social group; therefore, the variability of their collective performances would give the impression of variation even though there was none in the individual. Bickerton argues that individuals have relatively nonvariable (though changing) systems; variability is introduced when the data from several speakers, who are at different stages in the change, are lumped together.

In Guyanese Creole, movement in table 1.6 from right to left reflects a historical development from deepest creole features (*basilectal*), through middle-level features (*mesolectal*), to those most like Standard English (*acrolectal*). These data, however, show internal variation. Since some of the features may have the same function, cooccurrences in the same speaker indicate such variability. Bickerton claims, however, that this variability is, on the one hand, short-lived and, on the other, still only apparent.

As a rule moves through a speech community in waves, two forms compete with one another even in individual speakers, but such competition is brief – a sort of psycholinguistic disaster. Why should a system incorporate into itself some sort of grammatically unsystematic stuff? The few speakers who show real variation belong to that middle part of an *S-curve* (figure 1.5) which is flat at both ends – they occupy its short-lived vertical dimension. The categorical state is represented in the more or less horizontal parts of the curve, occupied by those speakers who are not yet taking part in the change (at the bottom) and those who have completed it (at the top). The occupation of the vertical by even a few speakers, however briefly, suggests the need for a psycholinguistically real variable grammar; no proponent of variable rules has ever suggested that *all* (or even a majority) of the rules of a grammar show systematic variability. Variation is likely to be most evident in those rules which are involved in change and at that moment when two rules are contending with one another.

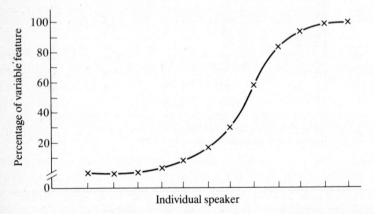

*Figure 1.5* S-curve displaying the smaller number of individuals who actually participate in variation between the 20 and 80 percent levels (source: Bickerton 1975: 65)

Granting even the limited status of variable rules, however, it is easy to see how apparent variation in a creole speech community might be exaggerated by the fact of long-term survivals which gain symbolic value. In creole, perhaps many varieties, change does not disallow the existence of more than one form at one time or within one individual. The coexistence of these systems is called the *creole continuum*, and societal facts explain why basilectal systems continue to exist alongside the more standardized acrolectal ones. The standard language carries with it, in addition to its representation of education and serious matters, the defect of social distance; the basilectal varieties carry with them, in spite of their associations with lack of education and backwardness, the advantage of familiar communication within closely knit communities.[7] It is socially advantageous, then, for one speaker to command a number of grammars along the basilectal to acrolectal creole continuum. To the extent that each is a separate grammar (a *lect* in the dynamic paradigm), an individual speaker needs no variable rules (with the possible exception of those few rules involved briefly in the *S-curve* vertical, and they might be unsystematic, representing only forms in *free variation* – honest coins). Instead, an individual shows considerable variation simply as a result of shifting from one lect to another as conditions demand.

This sort of language shift to meet social demands has come to be known as *code-switching*, particularly in bilingual environments, and will be discussed further in 1.2.4. From the point of view of the dynamic paradigm, code switching might be a particularly valid claim concerning creole communities. Aren't the basilectal, mesolectal, and acrolectal varieties three separate rule systems, more than one of which may be known to many speech community members? That would make the choices among acrolect, mesolect, and basilect very much like the choice between, say, Spanish and English in a Mexican-American community.

Unfortunately, the boundaries of the lectal varieties of a creole language are not as well-defined as those between Spanish and English. The creole continuum is a continuum exactly because the features from basilect to acrolect change in small increments, one by one. Though any number of scholars might agree that certain features are exclusively basilectal and certain others exclusively acrolectal, only those extremes could be agreed on. Middle-range features and the boundaries between mesolect and acrolect on the one hand and mesolect and basilect on the other are extremely fuzzy. Many speakers make use of much of the entire range and sensitively mix the levels of their production to match a wide range of personal and situational details. What is most unlikely is that each small increment represents a separate, psycholinguistically real lect and that  speakers are switching grammars rather than varying the selection or incidence of items within their overall competence. While a high incidence of acrolectal features or basilectal features may represent for creole speakers what they usually regard as a dichotomy, that folk opinion does not accurately reflect the actual continuum.

On the other hand, individuals do not randomly choose among features even within one of the three levels. An interesting fact about table 1.6 is its *implicational* character. Any X (presence of a feature) implies that any feature to the right will also be an X; any 0 (absence of a feature) implies that any feature to the left will be absent.

Where shift from one variety to another is even less linguistically dramatic than in creole varieties, it is difficult to see how a study of causes for switching could account for such rapid movement:

An' den like IF YOU MISS ONESIES, de OTHuh person shoot to skelly; ef he miss, den you go again. An' IF YOU GET IN, YOU SHOOT TO TWOSIES. An' IF YOU GET TWOSIES, YOU GO TO tthreesies. An' IF YOU MISS tthreesies, THEN THE PERSON THa' miss skelly shoot THE SKELLIES an' shoot in THE ONESIES: an' IF HE MISS, YOU GO fom tthreesies to foursies. (Labov 1972a:189)

Upper case is Standard English, and lower case is Black English Vernacular. Not all the phonological details which allowed the original investigator to determine which system is being used are shown in this transcript, but, even without those details, it is clear that a great deal of switching occurs in a very short time. More importantly, it appears to be impossible to motivate the switching on any systematic linguistic, personal, or environmental grounds. The conclusion from investigating such samples as these has been that shift from one grammar to another does not adequately characterize variation. That the entire message (according to genre, situation, interlocutors, and other factors) might have a probability which it contributes (represented in the input probability of VARBRUL 2) is imaginable but perhaps too complex to be of quantificational value.

In general, there does not seem to be any psycholinguistic advantage to the dynamic paradigm system. A speaker must control a very large number of separate grammars (lects) made up of categorical, nonvariable rules and must have mechanisms which trigger shifts among them in response to fluctuating social environments and to changing presentations of self.[8] What is apparently simpler in this system is the fact that weighted probabilities need not be used to represent the performance capacities of the individual. The implicational order of data, however, is not incompatible with the sort of patterned variability shown in table 1.1, particularly if three levels of features rather than two are recognized.[9] That is, features which are categorical might be marked 1, variable features X, and nonoccurring features 0. If features which occur with 10 percent frequency or less are interpreted as nonoccurring and those which occur with 90 percent frequency or more are interpreted as categorical, an implicational order of the data from table 1.1 might be represented as in table 1.7. The standard rule (no deletion) has established itself as categorical only for speakers of the highest social status and only in the linguistic environment least likely to cause deletion; on the other hand, only the lowest social status speakers have a categorical deletion rule and only in the linguistic environment most likely to cause deletion. In the dynamic paradigm, those environments which favor application of the rule are *heavy*, and those which retard it are *light*, or, in a wave theory approach to linguistic change, heavy environments are those in which the change first

*Table 1.7*  t/d deletion in Detroit Black speech

| Environments | Social classes | | | |
|---|---|---|---|---|
| | Upper middle | Lower middle | Upper working | Lower working |
| Following vowel: | | | | |
| Final member is -*ed* | 0 | X | X | X |
| Final member is not -*ed* | X | X | X | X |
| Following consonant: | | | | |
| Final member is -*ed* | X | X | X | X |
| Final member is not -*ed* | X | X | 1 | 1 |

0 = does not occur (categorical)
X = occurs variably (variable)
1 = occurs invariably (categorical)
*Source*: Adapted from Wolfram and Fasold 1974:132

appears, and light ones are those in which it operates last. It might seem that 'first' and 'most frequently' and 'last' and 'least frequently' are simply terminological differences between variable rule and wave theory analyses. The first highlights the psycholinguistic rule system of the individual; the second emphasizes the dynamic process of linguistic change. Although a greater amount of performance information is revealed in table 1.1 where the actual percentages are given, that representation less dramatically indicates change (i.e., the acquisition of a rule). A real psycholinguistic difference exists between the two systems, however, since variability is either the product of the operation of variable rules in individual performance or the reflection of lectal shifting.

Since implicational arrays are particularly well-suited to the display of change, SLA researchers have made use of them to show the development of interlanguage systems. Although Dickerson (1976) summarizes the application of wave theory and variable rules in SLA research in general, Gatbonton (1978) is the earliest study to make explicit use of an implicational array. Table 1.8 shows the variation between [ð] and [d] in French Canadian learners' pronunciation of English /ð/. Only six of twenty-eight respondents did not match any of the lects predicted, a statistically significant fit. Though no speakers use only [ð], one has variation in only the two lightest environments, and five have already achieved categorical performance in the heaviest environment. The pattern of variability for the acquisition of /ð/ is also similar to the socially stratified data of table 1.7. If one assumes that that table is a picture of linguistic change in the direction of no deletion, then the

*Table 1.8*  Implicational ordering of the acquisition of English ð in five different environments by French Canadians

| Lect | Heaviest V___ | VCT___ | VS___ | VLCT___ | Lightest VLS___ | Number of subjects N |
|---|---|---|---|---|---|---|
| 1 | 1 | 1 | 1 | 1 | 1 | 3 |
| 2 | 1,2 | 1 | 1 | 1 | 1 | 7 |
| 3 | 1,2 | 1,2 | 1 | 1 | 1 | 3 |
| 4 | 1,2 | 1,2 | 1,2 | 1 | 1 | 0 |
| 5 | 1,2 | 1,2 | 1,2 | 1,2 | 1 | 2 |
| 6 | 1,2 | 1,2 | 1,2 | 1,2 | 1,2 | 2 |
| 7 | 2 | 1,2 | 1,2 | 1,2 | 1,2 | 3 |
| 8 | 2 | 2 | 1,2 | 1,2 | 1,2 | 1 |
| 9 | 2 | 2 | 2 | 1,2 | 1,2 | 1 |
| 10 | 2 | 2 | 2 | 2 | 1,2 | 0 |
| 11 | 2 | 2 | 2 | 2 | 2 | 0 |

V___ = preceding vowel
VCT___ = preceding voiced continuant
VS___ = preceding voiced stop
VLCT___ = preceding voiceless continuant
VLS___ = preceding voiceless stop

1 = categorical presence of nonnative substitute for English
2 = categorical presence of native or native-like English
1,2 = variation of 1 and 2
*Source*: Adapted from Gatbonton 1978

heaviest environment is at the top, and the upper middle class has already acquired that rule categorically. The lightest environment is at the bottom, and the working class respondents show no instances of that rule yet. For the purposes of this illustration, the social classes of table 1.7 are like the groups of language learners in table 1.8. Other groupings of learners and users may be made in such arrays, and implicational orderings may be interpreted even more carefully within the SLA context. The parallelism of language change and SLA is more thoroughly explored in 5.1.

The difference between those who believe in a dynamic paradigm and others who hold to a variable rule account of noncategorical linguistic behavior appears to be dramatic. The apparent variation which arises from the use of a continuum of grammars is not, according to Bickerton, a result of language adjusting itself to social situations (1975). It is an indirect result of the development of form and function correlates in an emerging language system. Forms are acquired first, and their functions follow. These functions cause restructuring of the previous allocations of functions in the grammar. Basilectal Guyanese *na*, for example, is the exclusive negative marker. In the mesolectal variety, however, *en*, *doon(t)*, *di(d)n(t)*, and *neva* appear early. Though at first these forms are unanalyzed, they are among the features which cause the eventual restructuring of the acrolectal system into one which uses the English [+past] tense system as opposed to the Guyanese basilectal [+anterior] system (91–102). The variation which appears to exist in the speech community is, therefore, either the very short-lived (middle of S-curve) use of more than one negative form with the same function or the longer-lasting social use of the different lects of the continuum, essentially different subgrammars of a system unified by its diachronic development and preserved by its social symbolism.

The variability of an SLA system could be attributed to the emerging states of form-function correlations, and some research supports such a point of view. In particular, Huebner (1983a, b) shows how the variable interlanguage of a Hmong learner of English is, at least in part, due to the onset of new forms at first taken to be free variants of existing ones and later differentiated as new functional relationships emerge in the developing grammar. For example, his respondent reduces the role of *is(a)* as a topic marker (e.g., 'isa chiif tailaen' – 'There was a Thai chief,' Huebner 1983b:42) from a large range of constructions, drawing it closer and closer to its NS use in equative constructions (e.g., 'He's a driver'). Unlike forms in a creole continuum, however, interlanguage variants rarely have social significance for a group of learners, and earlier items disappear. The variation of emerging forms cannot, therefore, be explained by the sorts of social factors which stand behind much NS variation. Perhaps the lack of such obvious influences on variation is what leads Ellis (e.g., 1985b) to believe that much interlanguage variable data are 'unsystematic' (5.1.2), but it is important to show that all plausible determining environments have been exhausted before a variable is declared unsystematic (Schachter 1986).

Tarone distinguishes between *style-* and *register-*shifting (1983) and suggests that NNSs are monoregistral; their variability is exclusively determined by attention to form – style-shifting. Register-shift is an adjustment of the appropriateness of linguistic behavior by attending to the social relations among interlocutors. Although Tarone notes that what she calls style-shifting may eventually interact with register-shifting, the claim that NNSs only style-shift reduces the importance of sociolinguistic approaches to NNS variability, for it leaves exclusively linguistic reasons for variation (161). This is surely wrong on at least two counts. First, as Tarone admits, her concern is with classroom learners who may know only one register. Second, and more importantly, although the stylistic continuum is operationalized in experimental settings by reference to attention to form, it has always been intended to reflect greater and lesser degrees of *formality*, which Tarone says is a separate issue – namely *register*. If the continuum of SLA variability reflects only attention to form and not the social and interactional properties suggested by that attention, it is a much less satisfactory parallel to NS variable behavior. These and other models of variability in SLA are more thoroughly reviewed in 5.1.

Although variable rules on the one hand and extremely sensitive lect-switching mechanisms within a system of categorical rules on the other yield the same production results, the issue of the underlying psycholinguistic reality of variation is still unresolved. Dynamic paradigms have provided insights into the process of diffusion, the implicational nature of language data, and a functional basis for apparent sociolinguistic variability, but they have not resolved the issue of how to describe the psychological reality of variation once and for all.

### 1.2.3  Pidgin and creole

Although investigation of the origin, spread, and internal structure of pidgin and creole varieties would at first appear to be simply another branch of general, descriptive linguistics, the unique social settings in which these varieties have developed have always brought them to the attention of linguists concerned with the sociocultural aspects of language.

> Creole languages arose as a direct result of European colonial expansion. Between 1500 and 1900, there came into existence, on tropical islands and in isolated sections of tropical littorals, small, autocratic, rigidly stratified societies, mostly engaged in monoculture (usually of sugar), which consisted of a ruling minority from some European nation and a large mass of (mainly non-European) laborers, drawn in most cases from many different language groups. The early linguistic history of these enclaves is virtually unknown; it is generally assumed ... that speakers of different languages at first evolved some sort of auxiliary contact- language, native to none of them (known as a *pidgin*), and that this language, suitably expanded, eventually became the native (or *creole*) language of the community which exists today. (Bickerton 1981:2; italics in the original)

Even this account of the historical-social factors which gave rise to pidgin-creole varieties combined with the description of the symbolic continuum which develops during decreolization (1.2.2) does not exhaust the aspects of pidgin-creole studies which are of concern to this work. What psycho-linguistic processes are at work during the formation of pidgin-creole varieties? *Pidginization* and *creolization* are concepts derived from the study of such socially restricted language use and development which have been carried over to psycholinguistics. Pidginization is 'that complex process of sociolinguistic change comprising reduction in inner form, with convergence, in the context of restriction in use,' and creolization is 'that complex process of sociolinguistic change comprising expansion in inner form, with convergence, in the context of extension of use' (Hymes 1971:84).

The interpretation of the *simplification* and *complexification* processes in pidginization and creolization has not been consistent. What is the source of the simplifying tendencies of pidginization? Did the simplification come from the Europeans, who modified their own speech (the *superstrate*) by imitating NNS performances (Bloomfield 1933:472–5, Hall 1966:5), earlier known pidgins (Naro 1978:337–9), baby-talk, or the language use of some other linguistically distinct group, e.g., the deaf (Ferguson 1971:148)? Perhaps they called on some universal pattern of simplification, perhaps one like Naro's *factorization principle*: 'Express each invariant intuited element of meaning by at least one phonologically separate, stress-bearing form' (1978:340). On the other hand, simplification in the pidginization process may have its source in the learner-creator rather than in the superstrate language supplier. Perhaps simplification arises from use of the factorization principle by all those who find themselves in a situation where communication is required among speakers who share no common language, or from some universally based simplification procedure which allows the deepest categories of universal grammar to surface as the developing pidgin selects least-marked features from the various languages of the environment (Kay and Sankoff 1974). Perhaps elements of the L1s (*substrates*) of the non-superstrate speakers persist in the early stages of a pidgin (Bickerton and Odo 1976, Bickerton and Givón 1976, Bickerton 1977).

Whatever the source, there is considerable agreement that pidgins are simple in terms of missing features – 'consistent marking of tense, aspect, and modality; relative clauses; movement rules; embedded complements, particularly infinitival constructions; articles, especially indefinite' (Bickerton 1981:14).

A more controversial question concerns the sources of the complexifying characteristics of a creole. Bickerton's answer is most spectacular: since there are similar features in all (proper) creole languages, regardless of site of origin, and since there are features in creole languages which cannot be found in any of the languages which served as input (substrate or superstrate). creolization must have access to the universal, natural syntactic-semantic make-up of human beings (Bickerton 1981). Even if the more complex aspects of a developing creole do not come from such a deep source, it is clear that creolization refers to the creation of new, highly developed communicative systems in contrast to the impoverished systems of a pidgin. The attempt to discover the source of complexity in creole systems was a direct outgrowth of an older controversy – whether pidgin-creole varieties arose independently in each site or all developed from one source. Similarity of form and function in creoles based on different superstrates was obviously the source of this question, and such similarities are striking, as shown in table 1.9 for just a few Afro-American varieties based on English, French, and Portuguese-Spanish. Selection of 'm' forms for first person, of semantically similar completive markers for verbs ('don,' 'kabá,' and 'fin'), and even of similar metaphoric strategies for lexical specification ('man hog' and 'woman hog') suggests considerable similarity among these varieties. The search for the source of these similarities has moved from the older assertion of monogenesis, suggesting, principally, a Maritime Portuguese Pidgin (Neto

*Table 1.9*  Similar constructions in Afro-American creoles based on English, Spanish-Portuguese, and French

| Features | English (Guyanese, Jamaican, Krio) | Spanish-Portuguese (Papiamentu, Palenquero) | French (Haitian, Lesser Antillean) |
|---|---|---|---|
| Completive aspect: 'I have sung,' 'I am sick,' 'I know' | mi sing; mi siik; mi nuo | mi a kantá; mi ta malo; mi a sabé | mwẽ chãte; mwẽ malad; mwẽ sav |
| Completive aspect reinforced by 'finish' | mi don sing; mi don sick; mi don nuo | mi a kantá kabá; mi a sabé kabá | mwẽ fin chãte; mwẽ fin malad; mwẽ fin sav |
| Progressive | mi (d)a sing | mi ta kantá | mwẽ ape (or ka) chãte |
| Habitual | GY: same as progressive; JA: same as completive | same as progressive | HA: same as completive; LA: same as progressive |
| Conditional | GY: mi bin sa sing; KR: mi bin go sing | PAP: lo mi a kantá; PAL: mi tan ba kantá | HA: mwẽ te va chãte; LA: mwẽ te kai chãte |
| Past imperfect | mi bin a sing | PAP: mi ta ba kantá; PAL: mi ta kantá ba | HA: mwẽ tap (= te ape) chãte; LA: mwẽ te ka chãte |
| Noun plural: 'the men' | di man dem | homber nan | nom you |
| Genitive | mi dadi im buk | mi tatá su buki | liv papa mwẽ |
| Gender: 'boar,' and 'sow' | man hag; uman hag | porku homber; porku muhe | paper koshõ; mãmã koshõ |

*Source*: Adapted from Alleyne 1980: 11–13

1957:129–34, 1970:513–19), to polygenesis, dependent on innate linguistic universals as an explanation for likenesses in unrelated systems.

*Decreolization* (and the similar *depidginization*) have been adequately represented in the preceding section, which touches on the variability apparent in a creole continuum, itself a result of decreolization.

The language acquisition implications of pidgin-creole studies are many. Pidginization of an L2 as a result of ineffective personal integration into a new speech community is discussed at length in 2.1.3. Here the similarities of linguistic processes are reviewed.

Schumann (1978a) is a study of the acquisition of English by Alberto, a thirty-three year old Costa Rican (whose pattern of sentence negation is partially represented in table 1.5). Although he is careful to indicate that Alberto's interlanguage is not a pidgin, Schumann says it reflects pidginization processes, specifically 'simplifications and reductions' (1978a:71), a position first taken in Schumann (1974). Bickerton (1983) agrees with the interpretation of SLA as pidginization, noting that it 'promised striking new insights from the systematic comparison of language acquisition processes with processes of rapid, contact-induced linguistic change' (238–9). Later studies, however, call attention to the correlations between pidginization, depidginization, and decreolization on the one hand and SLA on the other.

Stauble (1978) studied the acquisition of negation in English by Spanish speakers and suggested that the developmental stages of an interlanguage could be called the *basilang*, *mesolang*, and *acrolang* to correspond to the varieties on the creole continuum. She suggested, therefore, that SLA was like decreolization, and showed parallels between SLA development of negation and the development of negation for Guyanese English as characterized in Bickerton (1975). Schumann (1978b) suggested, however, that the early stages of SLA were like pidginization since the basilect in a creole continuum is a fully developed variety while the basilang is a rudimentary, simplified system depending a great deal on transferred elements from an L1.

Andersen (1979 and elsewhere) has added to this argument by proposing a *nativization* hypothesis which seeks to elaborate a psycholinguistic perspective on pidgin-creole studies and language acquisition in general. Nativization is movement in the direction of underlying, universal, unmarked forms. These are presumably the ones creators of creole languages highlight as they construct their native language on the basis of extremely paucal input (from a pidgin), and those structures in interlanguage which have sources in neither the L2 nor L1 may have such origins. *Denativization*, in contrast, refers to movement away from such universal, unmarked structures. As a language decreolizes, it denativizes, and parallel events in SLA exist as, for example, early simplified structures give way to more complex forms. As has been shown, however, Bickerton in particular has been critical of any attempt to provide a general, unified account of pidgin-creole and SLA on these grounds, calling, instead, for a careful account of the precise similarities in form–function development and social setting (1983:239).

The study of the processes of simplification and elaboration in SLA as parallels to developments in pidgin-creole varieties continues, and Andersen (1983) provides a variety of positions and recent studies. The most recent general text on pidgin-creole studies to include an evaluation of the field's importance to SLA is Romaine (1988, especially chapter 6).

### 1.2.4   Language choice

Individuals in bi- and multilingual communities make language choices on the basis of both the linguistic and social environments. In some cases this context is so fluid and the interlocutors so comfortable with at least some aspects of either language that mixing may occur within units as small as a phrase. Some such cases come close to borrowing, and the entire topic is perhaps best thought of as a continuum from clear cases of language borrow- ing to those of total language change:

> Ah, this man William Bolger got his organization to contribute a lot of money to the Puerto Rican parade. He's very much for it. ¿Tú fuiste a la parada? (Fishman 1972a:38)

Such examples, in which a change in topic or some other variable seems to account clearly for the switch (4.2), strikingly contrast with the rapid shifting back and forth between Black and Standard English illustrated near the end of 1.2.2 in which perhaps neither extralinguistic nor linguistic variables could be isolated as causes.

Both the social and interactional structures help determine language choice. Gal (1979) shows how they interact in the Hungarian peasant culture of Oberwart (Felsöör), Austria in the selection of Hungarian or German. Data for female respondents are represented in table 1.10 in an implicational array (see tables 1.6 and 1.7 and the accompanying discussion). Since there are few exceptions to perfect implicational order, one must assume that language choice is not random. Though age is one determinant (older speakers preferring Hungarian), association with peasant culture (deter- mined by ascertaining if a respondent was from a household which owned pigs, cows, or both) was a very good predictor of Hungarian as well. A rank- order of individuals based on the percentage of their conversations over a period of a few weeks with members of the peasant culture compared with the order in table 1.10 yields a correlation of 0.78, only a little lower than the 0.82 correlation for age.

Other social factors and identities should correlate with language choice as well as such factors as topic and field of discourse. Fishman and Greenfield (1970) examined self-report data on the choice of Spanish or English among

*Table 1.10*  Implicational scale of Hungarian–German language choice for female speakers in Oberwart, Austria

| Speaker's age | Interlocutor | | | | | | | | | | | |
|---|---|---|---|---|---|---|---|---|---|---|---|---|
| | 1 | 2 | 3 | 4 | 5 | 6 | 7 | 8 | 9 | 10 | 11 | 12 |
| 14 | H | GH | | G | G | G | G | | | G | | G |
| 15 | H | GH | | G | G | G | G | | | G | | G |
| 25 | H | GH | GH | GH | G | G | G | G | G | G | | G |
| 27 | H | H | | GH | G | G | G | | | G | | G |
| 17 | H | H | | H | GH | G | G | | | G | | G |
| 13 | H | H | | GH | GH | GH | GH | | | G | | G |
| 43 | H | H | | GH | GH | | G* | GH | GH | G | | G |
| 39 | H | H | | H | GH | GH | G | G | G | G | | G |
| 23 | H | H | | H | GH | H* | G | | GH* | G | | G |
| 40 | H | H | | H | GH | | | GH | G | G | | G |
| 50 | H | H | | H | H | GH | GH | GH | G | G | G | G |
| 52 | H | H | H | GH* | H | | H | GH | G | G | G | G |
| 60 | H | H | H | H | H | H | H | GH | GH | G | G | H* |
| 40 | H | H | H | H | H | H | H | GH | GH | GH | | G |
| 35 | H | H | | H | H | H | H | H | GH | H* | | G |
| 61 | H | H | | H | H | H | H | H | GH* | H | | G |
| 50 | H | H | H | H | H | H | H | H | H | H | | G |
| 66 | H | H | | H | H | H | H | H | H | H | GH | G |
| 60 | H | H | | H | H | H | H | H | H | H | GH | G |
| 53 | H | H | | H | H | H | H | H | GH* | H | GH | G |
| 71 | H | H | | H | H | H | H | H | H | H | GH | G |
| 54 | H | H | H | H | H | H | H | H | H | H | | G |
| 69 | H | H | | H | H | H | H | H | H | H | GH | G |
| 63 | H | H | | H | H | H | H | H | H | H | GH | H* |
| 59 | H | H | H | H | H | H | H | H | H | H | | H |
| 60 | H | H | H | H | H | H | H | H | H | H | | H |
| 64 | H | H | | H | H | H | H | H | H | H | H | H |
| 71 | H | H | | H | H | H | H | H | H | H | H | H |

Interlocutors:

1 God
2 grandparents and their generation
3 black market clients
4 parents and their generations
5 age-mate pals, neighbors
6 brothers and sisters
7 salespeople
8 spouse
9 children and their generation
10 government officials
11 grandchildren and their generation
12 doctors

Languages: G = German; H = Hungarian
* These cells show exceptions to perfect implicational scaling
*Source*: Gal 1979:121

Puerto Ricans in New York City. A study of the community isolated five significant *domains* of social life – family, friendship, religion, education, and employment. The study then identified interlocutors, places, and topics which were congruent with these domains. For example, 'parent' (interlocutor), 'home' (place), and 'how to be a good son or daughter' (topic) were congruent with the domain of 'family.' Respondents were presented with two congruent elements and asked to supply a third. Additionally, they were asked to indicate whether they would choose Spanish or English (assuming their interlocutors knew both languages equally well) in such a situation. The choice of Spanish decreased as follows for the domains – family, friendship, religion, employment, education. Which element of the domain (interlocutor, place, or topic) had been omitted did not influence this order.

Though some scholars have tried to isolate single factors ('peasant culture' in the Hungarian–German study) and others have made use of high-level social constructs (domain), no well-agreed theory of language choice has emerged. A complex of social factors may impinge on even the apparently most open choice situations, and some seem to contradict the best possible predictors. Blom and Gumperz (1972) are careful to distinguish between *situational* switching and *metaphorical* switching. In the former, one chooses on the basis of governing norms – such details as topic, interlocutor, and setting. In the latter, one adds to a situation, enriching it with situationally unpredictable language choice, though such metaphoric shifts will have their larger social determiners as well. Imagine a young Oberwarter who used Hungarian with a doctor. Though unpredictable from the norms of the community, a specific situation (one, say, where the doctor demeaned local peasant culture) might bring about a metaphoric use of Hungarian – establishing for the listener the values and identity of the speaker.

In many cases language choice is made symbolic by virtue of the position of the varieties in a speech community. Those which support a radical differentiation of varieties are called *diglossic*. One variety is H ('high') and the other L ('low'), though the connotations of those words are unfortunate. Ferguson (1959) characterizes the likely functional differences assigned to H and L varieties (classical versus colloquial Arabic, in this case) as follows:

|                                                       | L | H |
|-------------------------------------------------------|---|---|
| Sermon in church or mosque                            |   | x |
| Instructions to servants, waiters, workmen, clerks    | x |   |
| Personal letter                                       |   | x |
| Speech in parliament, political speech                |   | x |
| University lecture                                    |   | x |
| Conversation with family, friends, colleagues         | x |   |
| News broadcast                                        |   | x |
| Radio 'soap opera'                                    | x |   |
| Newspaper editorial, news story, caption on picture   |   | x |

|  | L | H |
|---|---|---|
| Caption on political cartoon | x |  |
| Poetry |  | x |
| Folk literature | x |  |

Attempts to redefine creole continua and social dialect differences as diglossic have been popular, and the degree to which bilingual settings are also diglossic has been calculated. Fishman (1972a:93–106) suggests the following possibilities (with examples):

1  Diglossia and bilingualism: Paraguay (H = Spanish, L = Guarani)
2  Bilingualism without diglossia: immigrant languages and the language of the new environment (assuming rapid immigrant language loss)
3  Diglossia without bilingualism: nineteenth century Russian nobility (H = French, L = Russian)
4  Neither diglossia nor bilingualism: small, undifferentiated speech communities.

These approaches to language choice in social settings have provided a rich vocabulary and tradition of studies, but after the who, when, why, where, and what of choice is determined, the how still needs to be considered. What linguistic restrictions impinge on rapid intrasentential switching? Over the past few years, three major constraints have been suggested. The first is the *equivalence* constraint (Poplack 1980) – structures which exist in both languages are favored areas for language switch. German 'Ich habe Hunger' and English 'I am hungry' are more likely candidates for switching due to their NVA structure than English 'How much does that cost?' and German 'Wieviel kostet das?' since English uses do-support in questions and German does not. The second is the *phrase structure boundary* constraint – switches are likely to occur at boundaries of grammatical units rather than across them. For example, switching is more likely to occur at the indicated breaks in the following sentence than at other points: 'We / will try / to elect / a different president / next time.' Such reasoning has given rise to a corollary *size of constituent* constraint – the larger a linguistic element is (an entire sentence as opposed to a phrase or word), the more likely it is to be switched. An exception to this is the *noun* constraint – of elements smaller than sentences, nouns are more frequently switched than any other.[10] Third is the *free morpheme* constraint – code switching may not occur between a free and bound or bound and free morpheme. For example, the Hungarian plural (vowel+k) is never attached to an English noun (*book-ok) in United States Hungarian-English bilingual communities.[11]

Further studies of the sites for and precise linguistic mechanisms of language switching are likely to add to understandings of the psycholinguistic underpinnings of variable grammars, though, as yet, that connection has not been fully explored. For example, do privileged sites (or classes) for switching provide a richer environment for language transfer?

Some scholars suggest that the switching behavior of bilinguals is governed by a separate (third) grammar, not by an interplay of two separate NS-like grammars and the social and individual forces which contribute to their alternation.

Though apparently far from the concerns of variable monolingual linguistic behavior, language choice mechanisms may simply be at the end of the spectrum where the distinctiveness between two systems is linguistically though not necessarily socially dramatic. Since such mechanisms have been most often studied in relatively stable multilingual situations, they have not generally attracted scholars whose interests are in SLA. In the past switching was generally understood to indicate a weakness in the L2; speakers revert to their stronger language when lexical items, constructions, idioms, and so forth are not readily available in the weaker. Poplack (1980) argues, however, that intrasentential code-switching is an indicator of L2 proficiency. In a study of New York City Puerto Rican Spanish-English bilinguals, she shows that the speakers more proficient in English used intrasentential code-switches for 53 percent of all switches; the less proficient speakers used intrasentential strategies for only 31 percent of theirs, a difference significant at the 0.001 level on a chi-square test (Poplack 1980:609). A VARBRUL 2 test showed that language ability was, in fact, the greatest predictor of intrasentential code-switching (612–13). Such findings revitalize older interests in *compound* versus *coordinate* bilingualism, and, in the present context, continue to highlight the need for psycholinguistic sophistication in sociolinguistic concerns.

### 1.2.5 *Larger units*

The study of language units bigger than sentences is often explicitly associated with sociolinguistics:

> Sociolinguistics will ultimately have to be based, at least partly, on analyses of how people actually talk to each other in everyday settings, such as streets, pubs, shops, restaurants, buses, trains, schools, doctor's surgeries, factories and homes. Therefore, sociolinguistics will have to incorporate analyses of how conversation works: that is, how talk between people is organized; what makes it coherent and understandable; how people introduce and change topics; how they interrupt, ask questions, and give or evade answers; and, in general, how the conversational flow is maintained or disrupted. (Stubbs 1983:7)

Even this list does not exhaust the issues and concerns of discourse analysis and pragmatics, though it generally excludes the analysis of written texts even though some linguists have been interested in precisely that area (e.g., Chafe 1986). In the main, however, sociolinguistic concerns for larger units have focused on talk.[12]

Linguists have asked of discourse the same basic question asked of sentences: what are the rules which govern well-formed strings? For example, do parallel reasons exist for finding both (a) and (b) well-formed and (a)' and (b)' ill-formed?

(a)   DDT is an unhealthy substance.
(a)'  *Substance DDT an is unhealthy.
(b)   What did you have for dinner?
      Fish and chips.
(b)'  *What did you have for dinner?
      Your brother is a Conservative!

A clever reader can provide some context which will make putatively ill-formed discourse reasonable, but that should not stop the search for basic rules of conversational organization.[13] One difficulty in locating such patterns has been the mismatch between what is said (semantically and syntactically) and what is meant (conversationally and pragmatically). In the following coherent conversation, neither question is a question:

Could you pass the salt?
Don't you have high blood pressure?

The first utterance is a request and the second a temporary denial, a warning, a reminder, or a recrimination. Only when these questions are reinterpreted as requests, warnings, and so on is the exchange coherent.

Attempts to establish the units of conversation as something other than sentences borrow heavily from the work of John Austin and his theory of *speech acts* (1962). He suggests that sentences rarely explicitly describe what they accomplish in conversation; only a limited set of *performative* verbs are so precise. If one says 'I bet you five dollars some mammals lay eggs,' then he or she *has* bet you five dollars; nothing else is required. To say 'I bet you' is to accomplish a bet. Notice, however, that a speaker who says 'I will quit smoking' or 'Your grandfather didn't spit out his oatmeal when he was a little boy' has not accomplished any acts specified by the verbs 'quit' or 'spit.' To accomplish the first, one must actually not smoke; in the second, the speaker, even if he is your grandfather coyly using the third person to refer to himself, cannot accomplish his good table manners as a child by merely saying so. The first of these utterances may be a 'threat' or 'promise'; the second, a 'claim' or 'recollection.' Of course, performatives lurk in the backgrounds of such utterances: 'I hereby promise to quit smoking'; 'I state that your grandfather did not spit out his oatmeal when he was a little boy.' These performative speech act categories are attempts to describe utterances in terms which may be more useful in characterizing conversation. Illocutionary categories such as 'promise,' 'threaten,' 'bet,' 'state,' 'request,' and so on may be the basic units of the study of discourse rather than such grammatical categories as 'question' (interrogative) and 'statement' (declarative).

Speech act (and some other) approaches to discourse seek, in addition to the translation of a grammatical form into an appropriate illocutionary act, a set of sequencing rules which specify what sorts of combinations are allowed. There are difficulties with such rules, not the least being that there is no standard set of speech act types available for application, even though Austin's original suggestions have been elaborately expanded (e.g., Searle 1969, 1975, 1976, 1979, Hancher 1979, Stiles 1981). Equally troublesome is the fact that the illocutionary force of a speech act may be *indirect*. Although a speech act need not contain an explicit performative verb, it is constrained by its grammatical shape. The grammatical interpretation of 'It's cold in here' must be that it is a statement or assertion. In the following, however, a speech act interpretation must show that it is a request:

> It's cold in here.
> Oh, I'll close the window.

Indirect speech acts require a reinterpretation of the usual status of an utterance to one which better corresponds to its context.[14] Since indirectness is a likely feature of speech acts at any moment in conversation, a theory of sequencing for discourse may not rely on direct illocutionary acts alone.

Finally, it is the case that conversational turns may respond to *perlocutionary* as well as illocutionary (whether direct or indirect) acts. When one says 'You look nice tonight,' it might be taken as praise, though it would be difficult to suggest 'praise' as a basic illocutionary force. (*I hereby praise that you look nice. *I hereby praise you that you look nice.) The illocutionary act identity of 'You look nice tonight' is 'statement of personal belief' or some such category, but part of its intent and understanding can be interpreted as praise. Such utterance functions are perlocutionary – not a part of the grammar and semantics (the locution) or of the utterance's performative function (the illocution). Conversational moves may respond to that level rather than to the illocutionary; in fact, if perlocutionary praise is discerned, response to the illocutionary level might seem rude (or, in this case, egotistic):

> You look nice tonight.
> I think so too.

Contrast that with a normal, nonpraise interpretation:

> Mary looks nice tonight.
> I think so too.

Directness and indirectness and the perlocutionary level make the speech act increasingly suspect as the basic unit of discourse, though one philosophical approach to conversation in general makes indirectness more straight-forward. Grice (1975) suggests that a *cooperative principle* is followed in both forming and decoding discourse contributions. From this principle (actually a set of four maxims), it can be shown how nonliteral (but intended) meanings are accounted for:

Make your contribution such as is required, at the stage at which it occurs, by the accepted purpose or direction of the talk exchange in which you are engaged.

1  The maxim of quality: try to make your contribution one that is true, specifically:
   (a) do not say what you believe to be false
   (b) do not say that for which you lack adequate evidence.
2  The maxim of quantity:
   (a) make your contribution as informative as is required for the correct purposes of the exchange
   (b) do not make your contribution more informative than is required.
3  The maxim of relevance: make your contributions relevant.
4  The maxim of manner: be perspicuous, and specifically:
   (a) avoid obscurity
   (b) avoid ambiguity
   (c) be brief
   (d) be orderly.

This may seem simply a description of an ideal, but the point is more subtle. Imagine the following conversation:

Is Bill still a Republican?
Well, he's still giving money to the Contras.

The response appears to be uncooperative, breaking the maxims of relevance and quantity. Since one believes that speakers are obeying these maxims, however, the questioner will dig a little deeper. Why is 'giving money to the Contras' relevant to the question? Some readers may remember a Republican president of the United States in the 1980s who supported the Contra rebels in Nicaragua; therefore, the response has relevance and a *conversational implicature* (a principled understanding of a nonliteral message or indirect speech act) is achieved.

Though implicature allows a better understanding of indirect speech acts, it does not solve the problem of the diversity of speech act types, and it does not deal with perlocutions.

Speech act analyses and the associated conversational implicature have led directly to contrastive studies: do different languages and cultures share a list of basic speech acts, and are the maxims of conversation universal? The answer has been both yes and no. In an elaborate study of politeness, Brown and Levinson (1978) show that a number of face-saving devices (for both speaker and hearer) appear to have universal grammatical consequences (2.1.2), though one might question the speech act status of 'be polite.' In contrast, Keenan (1974) shows that that part of the maxim of quantity which requires a speaker to be as informative as required is not the norm, at least for men, in a Malagasy society (2.1.2).

Contrastive cultural studies of speech acts and related matters have led directly to SLA research and application. Schmidt and Richards (1980) review such concerns for language teaching specialists, though their scope is much broader than the matters outlined above. Studies of how to say no, be polite, apologize, request, and so on, popular in SLA literature, more often reflect the study of conversational routines and not, strictly speaking, speech acts. Even the functions of a language teaching *notional-functional* syllabus are only suggested by speech act theory (Wilkins 1976). Whether related to speech acts or conversational analysis, however, such concern for the acquisition of language functions rather than language structures is a further example of SLA specialists' interest in communicative competence.

Speech act (or philosophical) approaches to conversation (Hymes 1986) have not influenced sociolinguistics as profoundly as *conversational analysis* has. These studies adopt no ready-made units, for one leading principle is that the units of conversation are self-evident, revealing the speaker's own categories of organization. They are discovered (and labeled) as one does the analysis, usually from a transcription of actual conversation.

In a seminal study, Sacks, Schegloff, and Jefferson (1974) look at turn-taking in conversations. They reduce the linguistic problem by stating (after examining considerable data) that turns consist of sentential, clausal, phrasal, and lexical units. Listeners can project which unit is in progress and what is required for it to be completed, though the precise description of how the projection of units is done 'is an important question on which linguists can make major contributions' (703). The completion of a unit marks a *transition-relevance place* where the rules of turn-allocation apply:

1  For any turn, at the initial transition-relevance place of the initial turn-constructional unit:
   (a) If the turn-so-far is so constructed as to involve the use of a 'current speaker selects next' technique, then the party so selected has the right and is obliged to take next turn to speak; no others have such rights or obligations, and transfer occurs at that place.
   (b) If the turn-so-far is so constructed as not to involve the use of a 'current speaker selects next' technique, then self-selection for

next speakership may, but need not, be instituted; first starter acquires right to a turn, and transfer occurs at that place.

(c) If the turn-so-far is constructed as not to involve the use of a 'current speaker selects next' technique, then current speaker may, but need not continue, unless another self-selects.

2 If, at the initial transition-relevance place of an initial turn-constructional unit, neither 1(a) nor 1(b) has operated, and, following the provision of 1(c), current speaker has continued, then rule-set (a)–(c) applies at the next transition-relevance place, and recursively at each next transition-relevance place, until transfer is effected. (704)

Such rules help account for the fact that less than 5 percent of speech in conversations consists of overlaps and that gaps between speakers average only a few tenths of a second (Ervin-Tripp 1979:392).

Ironically, a second contribution of conversational analysts resembles speech act theory. *Adjacency pairs* are taken to be basic. Roughly, they consist of such pairs as greeting–greeting, offer–acceptance (refusal), question–answer, and so on.

*Adjacency pairs* are sequences of two utterances that are:
1 adjacent
2 produced by different speakers
3 ordered as a **first part** and a **second part**
4 typed, so that a particular first part requires a particular second (or range of second parts) – e.g. offers require acceptances or rejections, greetings require greetings and so on. (Schegloff and Sacks 1973)

Adjacency pairs also have a *sequencing rule*: 'Having produced a first part of some pair, current speaker must stop speaking, and next speaker must produce at that point a second part to the same pair.'

With this, however, conversational analysts (especially in proposing 'types') have come to the same problem faced by speech acts discourse analysts. Units of some sort must be classified to make sense of conversational organization. Though it is attractive to suggest that only those units derived from the observation of actual use will be identified, they are no more a conscious part of the speakers' repertoire than are verbs, passives, or low-front vowels; they require metalinguistic classification. Though it may be praiseworthy (and attractive to sociolinguists) to work with authentic data, that does not guarantee that the actual (i.e., psycholinguistically real) units may be extracted by common-sense procedures.[15]

Conversational analysis has also contributed accounts of overall organization by looking at fixed units of discourse and/or specific genres. Some of these studies have focused on the *scripts* or *routines* speakers follow when they engage in stretches of speech for which they have planned characteriza-tions (for example, Coulmas 1981). Schegloff (1979) suggests that the opening of telephone conversations requires the following parts:

| | |
|---|---|
| Summons | (Telephone ring) |
| Answer + display for recognition | Hello |
| Greetings first part | Hi |
| + claim that caller has recognized answerer | |
| + claim that answerer can recognize caller | |
| Greetings second part | Oh hi:: |
| + claim that answerer has recognized caller | |

The first 'hello' is not a part of the adjacency pair greeting-greeting, but the 'hi' and 'Oh hi::' are such a pair. Detailed conversational analyses of well-specified sections of talk often allow careful identification of linguistically similar but functionally dissimilar items. If the answerer had not recognized the caller, then the second 'hi::' would have been replaced by some sort of repair (which would have said, in effect, 'I don't recognize your voice though you have claimed that I should'), perhaps 'Who is this?' or 'Who's calling, please?'

Larger stretches of communication require reference to *topic* and gener-ate studies more like those within the framework of text linguistics with its entire array of terms and understandings (e.g., *new* versus *given* informa-tion). After the opening of telephone conversations, for example, the next move is the *first topic slot*, and it is up to the caller to select this turn and its content, which is limited to the reason for the call (Schegloff 1979). The precise informational structure of texts is rarely investigated by conversa-tional analysts.

The analysis of larger units of speech has attracted sociolinguists since it is set in social interaction. The degree to which it contributes to sociolinguistics in general depends very much on perspective. Those who consider its mainstream concerns to be the careful construction of implicational or variable rules for, particularly, phonological and morphosyntactic pheno-mena may not pay much attention to conversational interaction. Ethnographers of speaking, however, see the analysis of larger stretches of speech as one part of the total repertoire of language form, use, and regard which must be studied to provide a full account of a speech community.

SLA research in connected discourse, particularly in classroom settings, has been particularly active. Following research on first language acquisition (e.g., Scollon 1974), Wagner-Gough and Hatch (1975) and Hatch (1978) proposed that language acquisition was learning how to handle conversa-tions, acquiring first the functions of language and filling them in with the structures later on. Specific analysis of this trend is given in 2.1.1. Closely related to this perspective is the general claim that SLA is best approached from a functionalist point of view. How forms are related to function and vice versa in the development of an interlanguage require interactional data for analysis (Pfaff 1987). The development of so-called notional-functional syllabuses (e.g., Wilkins 1976) and the urging of communicative language teaching rather obviously have their parallels in such conversationalist and functionalist views.

Interest in the cross-cultural examination of classroom discourse resulted in a large anthology (Cazden, John, and Hymes 1972), and detailed analyses of how to collect and categorize classroom interaction shortly followed (e.g., Sinclair and Coulthard 1975). Such analytical models were specifically revised for SLA classroom study (e.g., Fanslowe 1977), though, in some cases, NNS–NNS and NS–NNS interactions have been studied for their general sociological and sociolinguistic interest with no particular focus on SLA.

Further impetus for the investigation of conversation in SLA comes from the interest in *input* (and *intake*). Ferguson (1971) calls the simplification of language addressed to NNSs *foreigner talk*, and Long (1980) suggested that such talk is not just an example of modified NS grammar and phonology but a reorganization of interaction, involving more checks on comprehension, requests for clarification, repetitions, and so on. Ultimately, such reasoning coincides with Krashen's *monitor theory* (e.g., 1981), one tenet of which is that learning does not occur unless there is access to *comprehensible input*. Obviously, simplification of input, whether in structure or conversational organization, is one way of making it comprehensible, and only the study of classroom and natural interactions can provide the data necessary for checking such hypotheses.

SLA research on conversational routines, ploys, or scripts has been mentioned above in connection with speech act analysis, although, as indicated there, many such studies fit better into the general framework of conversational analysis. All indicate the recent concern in SLA for discourse and function, often taken to be the entire content of so-called communicative competence.

Whatever the specific research aim, the collection of data from natural and classroom interaction is important in SLA, perhaps a necessary trend since *error analysis* showed the need for the examination of actual NNS data in addition to the abstract comparison of linguistic systems (*contrastive analysis*) to account for deviance from the L2 system and for a full account of the developing interlanguage system.

### 1.2.6  Language attitudes

Language variation has been treated thus far from the point of view of production. Though grammars in general tend to be silent on the question of production versus reception, there is a tendency to think of them as producers. In the discussion of the psycholinguistic reality of variable rules (1.2.1), the coin flipping analogy was devised on the basis of language production, though it should be clear that decoding problems must be solved as well.

There is another area of reception, however, which goes beyond decoding – even if decoding is taken to be a complex of locutionary, illocutionary, and even perlocutionary acts. Hearers of language respond to the personal, ethnic, national, gender, class, role, age and other identities of speakers. Such responses are *language attitudes*, and there is a considerable history of research and interest in this area, particularly among social psychologists. (Agheyisi and Fishman 1970 provides a definition and survey of methodological approaches; Ryan and Giles 1982 is a recent example of various settings and approaches.)

Language attitude research has its origins in bilingual settings; Lambert et al. (1960) wondered to what degree attitudes towards French and English differed in Francophone and Anglophone Canada (2.1.4). Direct questioning was an inappropriate way to elicit attitudes since respondents might not want to reveal prejudices. The techniques of a *semantic differential* rating (and subsequent factor analysis) and the *matched guise* presentation of voices (1.1) were employed to avoid this difficulty (an interesting social psychological corollary to the observer's paradox). After early studies of attitudes to French and English, interest in attitudes towards different dialects emerged. Tucker and Lambert (1969) investigated the attitudes of

Northern White ($N = 40$)
Southern White ($N = 68$)
Southern Black ($N = 150$)

male and female college students to taped samples of

1  'Network' English ('the typical mode of speaking of national newscasters')
2  College-educated White southern speakers
3  College-educated Black southern speakers
4  College-educated Black southern speakers currently enrolled at Howard University in Washington DC
5  Black southern college students (whose speech was similar to the group of Black raters)
6  Alumni of the college attended by the group of Black raters who lived in New York City at the time of the experiment.

The southern Black college students provided the semantic differential pairs; they were asked for traits which they considered important to 'friendship' and 'success' and for synonyms for these traits. Although the matched guise technique was not used, there were four speakers in each group, and each voice was heard reading the same, unemotional passage. The traits selected for responses were 'upbringing,' 'intelligence,' 'friendliness,' 'education,' 'disposition,' 'speech,' 'trustworthiness,' 'ambition,' 'faith (religious),' 'talent,' 'character,' 'determination,' 'honesty,' 'personality,' and 'considerateness.'

The results show that each group of judges clearly differentiated among the dialects. All three groups identified the 'Network' speakers as having the most desirable traits. The 'Black southern' group (3) was rated next best by the northern White and southern Black judges, though the Black judges barely distinguished between this group and the 'Howard' group. The southern White judges, however, rated their own peers ('White southern') second best and 'Black southern' (3) third. The Black judges rated the 'White southern' group worst on all traits, while the White judges rated the peer group (5) speakers worst and the alumni group (6) only slightly higher.

Such studies show that nonlinguists differentiate among varieties and have stereotyped attitudes towards them. In this particular study, although race was an important factor, it was not completely explanatory. The northern White judges, for example, guessed that the alumni group (all Black) was only 49 percent Black but rated it lower than the 'Howard' group which it believed to be 84 percent Black. Such findings opened a rich field of study; Howard Giles and his associates have continued matched guise, semantic differential studies of reactions to regional, social, and ethnic groups and have developed a more general theory of regard for language differences known as *accommodation* (Giles and Smith 1979; see also 2.1.3).

Sociolinguists have conducted similar experiments to determine precisely which linguistic element is responsible for an attitudinal response. Labov (1972a) asked New York City speakers to listen to tapes of local speakers, some repeated (matched guise). Only one linguistic variable was changed, however; in one place on the tape a speaker realized every postvocalic [ɹ] in the sentence 'He darted out about four feet before a car, and he got hit hard.' Later that same speaker said the same sentence but deleted postvocalic [ɹ] in only the last word. Another speaker read the sentence 'We didn't have the heart to play ball or cards all morning' twice, first with all postvocalic [ɹ]s, a second time with the [ɹ] in 'cards' deleted.

Labov asked his judges to indicate the highest professional rank they thought the taped speaker could hold. The ranks were, in descending order of speech prestige, (1) television personality, (2) executive secretary, (3) receptionist, (4) switchboard operator, (5) salesgirl, (6) factory worker, and (7) none of these. When the first speaker used all her [ɹ]s, she was rated 3 (receptionist), but when she deleted only one, she was lowered one rank to 4 (switchboard operator). Similarly, the second voice was rated 1 (television personality) for the version with all [ɹ]s but demoted two steps (to 3 – receptionist) for the version with the [ɹ] deleted in 'cards.' Interviews with the judges indicated that they could not say why they had lowered their ratings, but independent sociolinguistic studies of the production of postvocalic [ɹ] in New York City show that it is a prestige factor. Such experiments give a more precise linguistic character to attitude studies and provide further information about variables involved in language change and stratification.

Not all studies of language attitudes have been instrumental. There is a long history of questionnaires concerning language preference, some of it reviewed in 1.2.4, and data on attitudes towards language varieties have been collected in a more ethnographic framework by participant-observers (e.g., Scollon and Scollon 1979).

SLA researchers have not been particularly concerned with attitudes to varieties, though one would think the field of NNS and NS reactions to varieties of performances would be instructive. Eisenstein (1982) and Swacker (1977) are exceptions, and, more recently, a few studies have looked at both NS and NNS reactions to degrees of accentedness (2.1.3).

Social psychologists interested in SLA have, however, paid attention to the larger aspects of attitudes towards NNS performance, though many such studies use attitude questionnaires rather than experimental presentations of varieties (e.g., Gardner and Lambert 1972). More general social psychological approaches to SLA based on both surveys and voice sample attitudinal studies have been developed by Giles and his associates (2.1.3).

## 1.3  The ethnography of communication

Taken collectively, the concerns of this chapter (and surely more) provide some general account of language in its social context. Such a full characterization, as dependent on an account of low-level phonological variability (and attitudes towards it) as it is on rules for addressing a bereaved person, has come to be known as the ethnography of communication. The following chapters flesh out more fully the variety and scope of concerns that an ethnographic account of a speech community ought to touch on and try to relate those concerns to SLA.

# 2

# Individual characteristics

Beginning with individuals rather than interactions in an account of the sociolinguistic aspects of SLA is arbitrary. As interrelated variables multiply, it will become as difficult to refer back to some as it would have been to exclude them at an earlier stage of consideration. Perhaps only the fact that interactions are made up of individuals suggests this order.

## 2.1 Ascribed

Identity is both *ascribed* and *acquired*. Ascribed characteristics are those over which individuals have the least control. I might change my dialect, ethnicity, even gender but it is not expected by the surrounding culture, and when such changes are made, it is with considerable effort. Of course, there may be mismatches between an individual's 'actual' identity and the ascription of attributes by some or even all of the surrounding society. Those who are Black but light-skinned may be assigned the wrong slot in the culture by all but family and associates. Those who are dark-skinned may be classified as American Blacks in the United States or West Indians in Great Britain even if their own cultural backgrounds are very different from those groups. The list of ascribed individual characteristics includes, then, those factors most closely bound to identity, and it would be strange if such profoundly characterizing factors did not play a strong role in all behavior, including SLA.

### 2.1.1 *Age*

Most age related SLA studies touch on psycholinguistic issues – different success rates, the critical age hypothesis, and the similarities and differences between first and second language acquisition (with various emphases on general cognitive development, universals, parameters, bioprograms, and pragmatist-functionalist approaches). Hatch (1983) reviews the literature on age differences, particularly concerning variable rates, and Krashen, Scarcella, and Long (1982) is an entire volume devoted to just this topic.

In spite of the predominance of psycholinguistics here, a wedge for socio-linguistic interpretation exists. In a review of the research, Krashen (1982), referring to Krashen, Long, and Scarcella (1979), notes three general areas of agreement among researchers:

1   Adults proceed through the early stages of syntactic and morpho-logical development faster than children (when time and exposure are held constant).
2   Older children acquire faster than younger children (again, in the early stages of syntactic and morphological development where time and exposure are held constant).
3   Acquirers who begin natural exposure to second languages during childhood generally achieve higher second language proficiency than those beginning as adults. (202)

Krashen believes that the cerebral dominance theory is no longer supported by the evidence. Children do not acquire better because they have greater brain plasticity (a theory associated with Lenneberg 1967), for Krashen maintains that left-brain dominance is established well before puberty. Evidence from dichotic listening tests, motor skill observation, research with EEG and AER techniques, and the observation of morphological dif-ferences in the hemispheres even in prenatal brains leads to that conclusion. If it is true, that should cast considerable doubt on the strong position that the acquisition of cerebral dominance at puberty is the principal differentiating factor in child–adult SLA (Krashen 1982:205–7). Krashen prefers to believe that the older child and adult advantage in early language acquisition is a direct result of cognitive superiority.

If adults have an advantage in language acquisition due to some sort of formal operations superiority and children do not have an advantage due to greater brain plasticity, how may one explain the fact that eventual acquisi-tion success is much greater for those who begin SLA at a younger age?[1] Krashen agrees with Schumann (1975), who, after a review of literature on affective development, claims that 'language learning difficulties after puberty may be related to the social and psychological changes an individual undergoes at that age' (229). Specifically, according to Larsen and Smalley (1972):

As puberty approaches and the individual is concerned with the consolidation of his personality, it apparently becomes more difficult for him to submit to the new norms which a second language requires. As an individual's dependence on others gives way to his own independence in satisfying needs, there seems to be less pull toward the internalization of new norms required by a second language. (160)

Schumann (1975) cites findings which support the claim that adult and adolescent learners are more concerned with identity, less open to new people and customs, more suspicious of novelty, less malleable, and more threatened by situations in which they might appear ridiculous. Krashen (1982) takes all this to mean that adolescents and adults have an affective filter made up, at least in part, of suspiciousness and concern for identity; this filter removes *comprehensible input* from older learners' experiences and eventually causes them to lag behind the child, whose open and less ego-involved identity will ultimately lead to a more NS-like performance.[2]

Studies of the acquisition of second dialects (Payne 1976, 1980; reviewed, along with others, in Trudgill 1986) show that age at the beginning of accommodation is crucial to the degree of success. In Payne's work it was found that even children arriving in the Philadelphia area as early as eight years of age were still not young enough to master some fine phonetic details. Some SLA studies, as well, suggest early fossilization (e.g., Swain and Burnaby 1976).

Further age differences from a sociolinguistic perspective reflect two radically different processes. First, differences in generational speech may be indicators of language change. A strong claim in sociolinguistics is that change is not too slow to be observed. A new generation of speakers may reflect changes in the language, and historical linguistics may be done in living speech communities as well as in dusty tomes. Second, and this is tricky, age differences in a speech community may reflect *age-grading* rather than change.[3] If, for example, teenagers use certain slang items, and give them up when they become adults, such items are age-graded, not predictors of language change. If older people use certain forms only when they become old, such forms are age-graded, not even indicators of what the language used to be, for, without further evidence, one may assume equally that the next generation of older speakers will behave in the same way or that they will behave in a novel way appropriate to their age group and that their performances will not be the same as the last generation of older speakers. In neither case would such age-graded performance have any influence on general language change.

The differences between age-grading and change must be emphasized. Since studying speakers at long-term intervals is uneconomical, many sociolinguists have adopted the strategy of studying linguistic change in *apparent time* – a cross-section of different age groups in the speech community. In this format, the danger of interpreting age-grading as change is always a concern.

An example of linguistic change discovered through the investigation of apparent time data is the centralization of /ɛ/ in Norwich (East Anglia). In Norwich, (e)[4] has three phonetic values before /l/ – RP [ɛ], a more central [ɜ], and a central and lower [ʌ]. These variables may be identified as (e)-1, (e)-2, and (e)-3, respectively. To compute an *(e) score*, one examines a piece of recorded text (whether from natural speech, a reading passage, or even word lists) and counts occurrences of each variable. Imagine data such as the following from a putatively homogeneous group of respondents:

Instances of (e)

|  | (e)-1 | (e)-2 | (e)-3 |
|---|---|---|---|
| Speaker 1 | 3 | 4 | 2 |
| Speaker 2 | 3 | 6 | 8 |
| Speaker 3 | 1 | 0 | 10 |
| Total | 7 | 10 | 20 |

The total number of each variable observed in the data is multiplied by the value assigned each variable:

$$(e)\text{-}1 = 1 \times 7 \ = 7$$
$$(e)\text{-}2 = 2 \times 10 = 20$$
$$(e)\text{-}3 = 3 \times 20 = 60$$

The tokens and scores are summed:

$$7 + 10 + 20 = 37$$
$$7 + 20 + 60 = 87$$

The total score is divided by the total number of tokens:

$$87/37 = 2.35$$

And that score has 1 subtracted from it and is multiplied by 100 to avoid decimals and establish a base of zero:

$$2.35\text{-}1 \times 100 = 135$$

This is the (e) score for this sample, and may be contrasted with samples drawn from óther groups or other performances by this same group.[5] Such scores are convenient ways of representing the incidence of one or more variables from a large body of data. They do not, however, replace the necessity of treating raw data with such more sophisticated statistical means as VARBRUL 2.

Some actual (e) variable data from Norwich are shown in figure 2.1. The pattern in this figure is typical of linguistic change; the 10–19 age group has radically increased the instance of lowered and centralized (e) even in their most formal styles (3.5.1). It appears that RP-like [ɛ], in such words as 'bell' and 'tell,' is giving way to [ɜ] and even [ʌ].

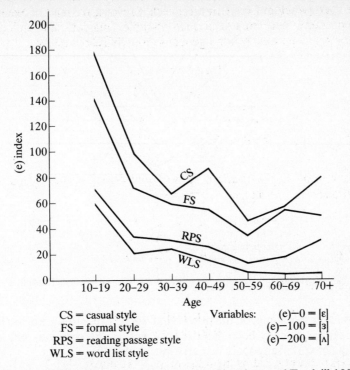

CS = casual style
FS = formal style
RPS = reading passage style
WLS = word list style

Variables:   (e)–0 = [ɛ]
(e)–100 = [ɜ]
(e)–200 = [ʌ]

*Figure 2.1*   Norwich (e) by age and style (source: Chambers and Trudgill 1980: 93)

In contrast, figure 2.2 displays the curvilinear pattern of age-grading. (ng) in Norwich varies between a velar [ŋ] and alveolar [n]. (ng)-1 is the standard velar, and (ng)-2 is the alveolar. Younger speakers have sharply reduced their use of the nonstandard variant (at least at the informal end of the style continuum) by the time they reach forty, though older speakers regain this usage, even for formal style, by the time they are seventy. Chambers and Trudgill explain this as follows:

We can probably account for this by supposing that for younger speakers the most important social pressures come from the peer group, and that linguistically they are more influenced by their friends than by anybody else. Influence from the standard language is relatively weak. Then, as speakers get older and begin working, they move into wider and less cohesive social networks, and are more influenced by mainstream societal values and, perhaps, by the need to impress, succeed, and make social and economic progress. They are, consequently, more influenced linguistically by the standard language. For

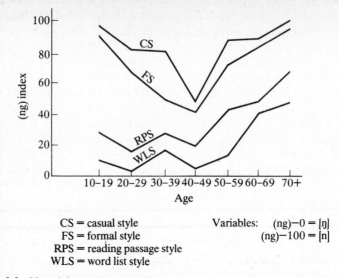

CS = casual style               Variables:   (ng)−0 = [ŋ]
FS = formal style                            (ng)−100 = [n]
RPS = reading passage style
WLS = word list style

*Figure 2.2*   Norwich (ng) by age and style (source: Chambers and Trudgill 1980: 91)

older, retired people, on the other hand, social pressures are again less, success has already been achieved (or not, as the case may be), and social networks may again be narrower. (1980:92)

Such sociolinguistic evidence allows even finer differentiation of the possible social influences on older children and adults in SLA. Recall that they succeed more rapidly than young children and that some scholars attribute this to their cognitive advantage. The ultimate greater success in SLA by younger children is attributed to their ability to accept external norms, perhaps a result of their as yet unformed stereotypes of their own identities. The sociolinguistic evidence suggests that adolescents and young adults match the pattern outlined in Schumann (1975); peer group influences are the principal input for their language behavior. In contrast, participation in SLA activities is usually not only not peer group in the general academic sense but also a threat to already established norms of behavior in its attempt to establish new linguistic skills. It is not unlikely to find adolescents' SLA, except for the advantage provided by cognitive superiority, lagging behind younger children's. On the other hand, why would younger children eventually surpass adults, as the evidence suggests? As Chambers and Trudgill make clear, adults are not freed from the sorts of socially conservative factors which restrained them as adolescents. They trade in their peer group oriented language behavior for the standard language of the wider community, and they are no less threatened by failure in the work place, in social and economic advancement, and in presentation of self than adolescents are by the embarrassment of exhibiting nongroup norms. In short, both groups have a solid front to put up against new or different language behavior, and SLA is the newest and most different that could be imagined.

It might be claimed that only L2s which demand considerable, long-lasting proficiency cause such fears in older learners, for they may carry with them the implication that L1 identity and language skill may be diminished or even lost. Although it may be true that such L2s are more likely to influence older learners internally, even short-term, restricted SLA may challenge the older learner's position in a group, or, at least, his or her perception of that position. That is certainly the correct interpretation of adolescent rejection of SLA in classroom situations. Only a few benefit (socially and/or individually) from multilingualism or the study of L2s (e.g., taxi drivers, tour guides, linguists, translators, actors).

Is there any clue in quantitative sociolinguistic research for a solution to resistance to SLA? After all, older children's and adults' difficulty in SLA is likened above to age-grading in sociolinguistic situations. How might change, as seen for some sociolinguistic facts (for example, figure 2.1), be encouraged?

To determine even a tentative answer to this, a deeper look at the types of language change will be required. Labov (1966) elegantly characterizes the relationships among types of language change, age groups, and social classes.[6] A primary distinction is that between *change from above* and *change from below*. Change from above involves linguistic responses to straightforward social pressures: forms are stigmatized on the one hand or prestigious on the other. The 'above' in 'change from above' refers, specifically, to the fact that such changes involve features which the speech community is aware of. When stigmatized features are involved in language change, the pattern for age and social class is as shown in table 2.1. If a

*Table 2.1*   Change from above for a stigmatized feature

|  | Social status | | | |
|---|---|---|---|---|
| Age | Lower class | Working class | Lower middle class | Upper middle class |
| Younger | (−) | −− | −− | − |
| Older | (++) | ++ | ++ | − |

++ = highest frequency of use
+ = moderately high frequency
− = moderately low frequency
−− = lowest frequency
(−) = a weaker tendency
*Source*: Adapted from Labov 1966:222

stigmatized item is not involved in change, the lower classes will show most extensive use of it, the higher classes almost no use at all, and the upper working or lower middle classes some slight decrease in its use as older speakers leave peer group dominated speech and come into some contact with standard community norms during their working years. As can be seen in table 2.1, however, the increasing stigmatization of a feature involved in linguistic change (eradication) results in its greatest frequency of occurrence in the oldest segments of the population and its lowest incidence among the younger groups, particularly those of the lower middle and working classes.

A prestige feature not involved in change shows nearly categorical use by the upper classes, little or no use by the lowest status groups, and some use by older middle status speakers. When a prestige feature is involved in change, however, the pattern in table 2.2 is more likely. The highest classes show the clearest evidence of change; the older speakers maintain the old prestige norm, but the younger speakers are beginning to adopt the new one. Older speakers from the middle classes, however, show the greatest linguistic malleability (perhaps as a result of linguistic insecurity) and begin to adopt the new norm while younger speakers maintain the form already learned.[7] The lowest groups show no evidence of the new prestige form.

*Table 2.2*  Change from above for a prestige feature

|  | Social status | | | |
| --- | --- | --- | --- | --- |
| Age | Lower class | Working class | Lower middle class | Upper middle class |
| Younger | – | – – | – – | + |
| Older | – | ++ | ++ | – |

Symbols as in table 2.1
*Source*: Labov 1966:223

In change from above, then, the lower status age groups must be distinguished when a stigmatized feature is involved in change but the upper status age groups must be singled out for change involving a prestige feature. Briefly, response to change involving a stigmatized feature can be seen first in younger, upper lower and lower middle status speakers, and response to change involving a prestige feature can be seen first in younger, upper status speakers.

Change from below is dramatically different. The linguistic features involved are neither prestigious nor stigmatized in ordinary senses, though

*Table 2.3*   Change from below

|  | Social status | | | |
|---|---|---|---|---|
| Age | Lower class | Working class | Lower middle class | Upper middle class |
| *Early stage* | | | | |
| Youngest | + | + | + | + |
| Young adults | 0 | + | 0 | − |
| Middle-aged | − | 0 | − | − |
| Oldest | − | − | − | − |
| *Late stages with correction from above* | | | | |
| Youngest | + | + | − | − |
| Young adults | + | + | + | 0 |
| Middle-aged | 0 | + | − | + |
| Oldest | − | 0 | − | 0 |

+ = most frequent use
0 = medium use
− = least frequent use
*Source*: Adapted from Labov 1966:225

they may have greater or lesser frequency of use by different social groups; that is, they may be socially stratified, but they are not consciously noted within the speech community.[8] Table 2.3 illustrates age and status related frequencies for change from below. Since the forms involved in change from below are, by definition, neither prestigious nor stigmatized since they are unnoticed, there is no distinction between the two types as there is in examples of change from above (tables 2.1 and 2.2). On the other hand, change from below usually arises in the lower classes, and table 2.3 exemplifies such a change on the basis of its arising in the working class.

Though this picture is idealized (not showing possible influences of sex or ethnic groups – 2.1.2 and 2.1.4), it is complicated by the fact that such changes are often stigmatized during their progress, that is *corrected from above*, and the second part of table 2.3 shows that possibility. In the early stage of the change, a feature which begins in the working class is seen spreading to the youngest members of the speech community, reflecting peer pressure acquisition of new norms of behavior. If this feature continues to develop unnoticed it will eventually spread throughout the speech community. Since, however, it is used by younger and lower status speakers, there is a considerable chance that it will be detected, become a stigmatized feature, and be subject to correction from above. In the bottom half of table

2.3, note that the youngest speakers of the highest social class are already responding to this correction.

Though change from below shows a different pattern of spread from change from above, what has been said about age need not be radically reinterpreted. Peer group influence on younger speakers (excepting standard language pressure on younger speakers of the higher social classes) and standard, community language pressure on older speakers (particularly middle and working classes) are principal factors.[9]

Assuming that SLA is a violent form of language change, sociolinguistic research suggests that the degree to which SLA contradicts or interferes with peer pressure norms would predict the degree to which it would be particularly unsuccessful with older children and adolescents. Under the same assumption, the degree to which SLA challenges or contradicts wider, standard community norms will predict the degree to which it may be particularly unsuccessful with adult learners.[10]

Minor adjustments to these generalizations may be required for oldest higher class speakers who do not respond to novel standard speech community norms (tenaciously hanging on to older ones) and, perhaps, for lower class speakers who seem not to respond to change from above when a prestige factor is involved. In general, however, the normalization of SLA activities through peer groups for adolescents and through acceptable, wider community norms for adults would appear to be strongly indicated by quantitative sociolinguistic research on age differences. A more general application of change from above and below to SLA settings is developed in 5.1.

More recent work in both sociolinguistics and SLA focuses on the acquisition of language through pragmatic and interactional forms and on the acquisition of the broader linguistic abilities known as communicative competence. Pragmatist and functionalist perspectives on SLA and first language acquisition are properly treated in psycholinguistically oriented surveys, and Pfaff (1987) is an excellent short review of the literature and at the same time an example of such research. On the other hand, discourse–interactionist research is so closely bound to sociolinguistics that it would not do to avoid comment on the relationship between these areas of research in sociolinguistics and SLA as they relate to the variable of age.

Studies of conversations between NSs and NNSs show that discourse rules vary according to the age of the NNS interlocutor. Hatch (1978) observes that conversational learning in L2 is very much like that in L1: SLA child acquirers use attention getters to open conversations, nominate or initiate topics, and so on. One of the more intriguing aspects of conversation which has been proposed in the psycholinguistic literature is that syntactic learning is a by-product of conversation. That is, the *vertical* combinations of turns in conversations are first language learners' early cues to the propositional (*horizontal*) structure of sentences.

*Brenda*: Kimby
*R*: What about Kimby?
*Brenda*: close
*R*: Closed; What did she close, hmmm?
(Scollon 1974)

Brenda's *topic nomination* ('Kimby') causes her adult interlocutor to try to find out more. Brenda responds with a predicate ('close'), but the object is lacking, so her interlocutor seeks it (What did she close, hmmm?'). The vertical construction of the dialog is such that it suggests the horizontal construction of some such more elaborate sentence as 'Kimby closed the door.' Such conversational syntactic learning goes on in child SLA as well.

*Paul*: This boat.
*J*: Mmhmm boat.
*Paul*: this my boat.
(Huang 1970)

In this conversation the NS interlocutor wants to know what the predicate of 'this boat' is. Paul's *horizontal* (syntactic) construction might have been 'This boat is mine,' revealing, again, that younger learners (of both first and second languages) may depend a great deal on the development of conversations for the acquisition of syntactic structure.

This sort of conversational analysis of NS and NNS interactions may help resolve the optimal age issue from another perspective. Scarcella and Higa (1981) use the conversational notion of *negotiation* in a comparison of NS interaction with older and younger SLA children. By negotiation they refer to the cooperative work interlocutors engage in to help along a conversation (Goffman 1974, Garfinkel 1967):

> Here we describe it [negotiation] in terms of the 'work' involved in helping one another communicate, for example, by jointly expressing messages, filling in lapses in the conversation, indicating gaps in understanding, and repairing communication breakdowns. (Scarcella and Higa 1981:410)

In their study, the adult NSs (1) used devices which secured and sustained the NNS child's attention much more frequently with younger than with older children, (2) repeated sentences more frequently with younger children, (3) used 'inclusive we' more frequently with younger children, (4) used imperative and interrogative (especially rhetorical questions) more frequently with younger children, (5) used 'frames' or 'utterance boundary markers' (for example, '*Yeah*, I think it's one of those, *isn't it*') more frequently with younger children, (6) provided more support or 'positive feedback' to younger children, (7) used more exaggerated intonation and nonverbal communication (for example, gestures) with younger children, (8) simplified the linguistic input considerably more to younger children, and (9) used more clarification devices (for example, 'right' and 'huh') with younger children (413–23).

The NNSs differed by age in their conversational strategies. The adolescent subjects (1) used more comprehension checking devices, (2) provided comments on NS introduced topics more frequently than younger children, (3) repeated utterances less frequently than younger children, (4) initiated new topics or shifted topics more frequently than younger children, and (5) used more conversational fillers (for example, 'let's see' and 'uhm') than younger children (425–8).

Scarcella and Higa conclude that such conversational work allows older NNSs to negotiate input which is at the right level for acquisition. The younger NNSs may not know how to negotiate around input which is too simple (and, therefore, already learned) or incomprehensible (and, therefore, useless for learning) (429–30).[11]

Research on L1 and L2 acquisition indicates that there may be a tendency for very young children to make up propositional strings or sentences from vertical conversational data. As in so many other areas of language teaching, this suggests that naturally occurring elliptical constructions are not only not errors but serve natural language acquisition purposes as well as functional, communicative ones. In addition, conversational studies suggest that very young children may lag behind adults and adolescents in the early stages of language acquisition because they have less interactional control over the sort of input they receive. This finding suggests more carefully programmed input in instruction for younger learners. Adults and adolescents will be able to negotiate appropriate levels of input in their instruction (except in situations where teachers of interlocutors are completely insensitive to the learner's negotiations). Such findings suggest, as well, that it is more crucial to discover the level of ability of younger learners so that input and teaching goals may be at an appropriate level, for the younger child's level of skill may not naturally emerge. Although all learners must acquire the rules of conversation and communicative competence, it seems that adults and adolescents may profit more from less carefully planned conversational activities while younger children require specific instruction and carefully planned activities which are explicitly related to learning goals.[12]

### 2.1.2  Sex

While concern for age differences is strong in both sociolinguistic and SLA research, the concern for male–female differences in the latter has been slight. In contrast, sociolinguistic accounts of sex differences have played an important role, particularly in exploring mechanisms of language change.

Other sex related sociolinguistic topics include, at least, (1) studies of language and language users' sexism, including evaluations of and reports on efforts to encourage change, (2) differential attitudes towards language and language use, (3) sex related differences in discourse rules and performance, (4) folk and anthropological linguistic studies of the concepts of women's language and language use, including cross-cultural accounts.[13]

A number of sociolinguistic studies show that variable features are distributed differently for men and women, and it is the case that women often seem to be in the forefront of linguistic change. This observation is at least as old as Gauchat (1905) who, in a survey of Charmey (Switzerland), found that women used newer linguistic forms more frequently than men. A good generalization is

> not that women lead in linguistic change, but rather that the sexual differentiation of speech often plays a role in the mechanism of linguistic evolution. (Labov 1972a:303)

A first step in determining what role gender may play in linguistic change is exposing the differential performance of men and women. Table 2.4 displays the distribution of the variable (ng) in Norwich, for class, style, and sex. Such scores are typical of male-female differences; in seventeen cases out of a possible twenty, the male scores are higher, representing a greater frequency of nonstandard or nonprestige alveolar (ng), that is, [n]. In the highest class,

*Table 2.4*  Norwich (ng) by class, style, and sex

| Class | Sex | Style | | | |
|-------|-----|-----|-----|-----|-----|
|       |     | WLS | RPS | FS | CS |
| MMC | M | 000 | 000 | 004 | 031 |
|     | F | 000 | 000 | 000 | 000 |
| LMC | M | 000 | 020 | 027 | 017 |
|     | F | 000 | 000 | 003 | 067 |
| UWC | M | 000 | 018 | 081 | 095 |
|     | F | 011 | 013 | 068 | 077 |
| MWC | M | 024 | 043 | 091 | 097 |
|     | F | 020 | 046 | 081 | 088 |
| LWC | M | 060 | 100 | 100 | 100 |
|     | F | 017 | 054 | 097 | 100 |

MMC = middle middle class    WLS = word list style
LMC = lower middle class    RPS = reading passage style
UWC = upper working class    FS = formal style
MWC = middle working class    CS = casual style
LWC = lower working class    *Source*: Trudgill 1983:171

female use of the prestige velar variant ([ŋ]) is categorical, and male use of the alveolar is nearly so in the lowest class.[14] Trudgill explains this differential performance as follows:

1   Women in our society are more status-conscious than men, generally speaking, and are therefore more aware of the social significance of linguistic variables. There are possibly two main reasons for this:

   (a) The social position of women in our society is less secure than that of men, and, generally speaking, subordinate to that of men. It is therefore more necessary for women to secure and signal their social status linguistically and in other ways, and they are more aware of the importance of this type of signal.

   (b) Men in our society can be rated socially by their occupation, their earning power, and perhaps by their other abilities: in other words, by what they *do*. For the most part, however, this is not possible for women, who have generally been rated on how they *appear*. Since they cannot be rated socially by their occupation, by what other people know about what they do in life, other signals of status, including speech, are correspondingly more important. This last point is perhaps the most important.

2   The second, related, factor, is that WC [Working Class] speech, like many other aspects of WC culture, has, in our society, connotations of masculinity, since it is associated with the roughness and toughness supposedly characteristic of WC life, which are, to a certain extent, considered to be desirable masculine attributes. They are not, on the other hand, considered to be desirable feminine characteristics. On the contrary, refinement and sophistication are much preferred. (1974:94–5; italics in the original)

With different emphases or subtleties, this interpretation appears again and again, female speech nearly always outstripping male in its degree of standardness or prestige. Recall, however, that the (ng) variable which Trudgill bases this discussion on was a stable, age-graded linguistic variable. What role will sex play in cases of ongoing linguistic change?

   Labov's (1966) account of the variable (eh) in New York City is a case of change from below with correction from above. Raised (eh) variants – [I³], [ɛ³], and [æ^] – are assigned the values (eh)-1, (eh)-2, and (eh)-3, respectively. The unraised vowel ([æ]) is assigned (eh)-4. The (eh) score in this case is computed by multiplying the average of the values by ten. For example, an average score of 2.5 would result in an (eh) score of 025, indicating a performance of nearly equal amounts of (eh)-2 and (eh)-3.[15] Table 2.5 summarizes sex differences for (eh). Of the thirty-one women who were mea-

*Table 2.5*   New York City (eh) by sex and style

| (eh) | Style | | | | | |
|---|---|---|---|---|---|---|
| | A | | B | | C | |
| | Men | Women | Men | Women | Men | Women |
| 010–013 | — | 1 | — | — | — | — |
| 014–018 | 1 | 4 | — | 2 | 2 | — |
| 019–021 | 3 | 10 | 3 | 9 | 1 | 2 |
| 022–026 | 4 | 6 | 7 | 9 | — | 5 |
| 027–032 | 3 | 4 | 11 | 12 | 8 | 9 |
| 033–039 | 4 | 4 | 3 | 5 | 4 | 14 |
| 040–042 | 1 | 2 | — | 6 | 4 | 16 |

A = casual speech        Variables:   (eh)–10 = [Iᵊ]
B = careful speech                        (eh)–20 = [Eᵊ]
C = word list                                (eh)–30 = [æ˙]
                                                    (eh)–40 = [æ:]

*Source*: Labov 1966:215

sured in casual style, twenty-five (0.81) score 032 or lower (predominantly raised variants). On the other hand, for the sixteen men who were measured in the same style, eleven (0.69) score in that range. When the most formal style (word lists) is examined, however, the pattern is reversed. Of the forty-six women investigated in that style, only sixteen (0.35) perform in the 032 and below range, but of the nineteen men studied, eleven (0.58) fall in the area of raised (eh).

With the sophistication of change from below with correction from above, it can be seen how women are leading change in apparently opposite directions. First, raised (eh) is an innovation from lower and working classes and is not noticed as a prestige or stigmatized feature (change from below). Women led that early change, and their leadership is still apparent in casual styles. Second, when (eh) raising became stigmatized, correction from above set in, and again women, in their more formal styles, can be detected as leaders of that change.

Men may lead in linguistic change if a variant is one which bears *covert prestige* – working class and local solidarity associations, toughness, and stereotyped masculinity. Trudgill (1983) detects such a change in a complex set of data related to the (o) variable in Norwich. (o)-1 is the rounded RP-like vowel [ɒ], and (o)-2 is any unrounded variant (local, nonprestigious, e.g., [a]). The data for this feature are shown in table 2.6. These data seem almost recalcitrant. Though it is true that the highest classes have nearly categorical use of the RP-like vowel and, as expected, women show higher use of this

*Table 2.6* Norwich (o) by class, style, and sex

| Class | Sex | Style | | | |
|---|---|---|---|---|---|
| | | WLS | RPS | FS | CS |
| MMC | M | 000 | 000 | 001 | 003 |
| | F | 000 | 000 | 000 | 000 |
| LMC | M | 004 | 014 | 011 | 055 |
| | F | 000 | 002 | 001 | 008 |
| UWC | M | 011 | 019 | 044 | 060 |
| | F | 023 | 027 | 068 | 077 |
| MWC | M | 029 | 026 | 064 | 078 |
| | F | 025 | 045 | 071 | 066 |
| LWC | M | 014 | 050 | 080 | 069 |
| | F | 037 | 062 | 083 | 090 |

| | |
|---|---|
| MMC = middle middle class | WLS = word list style |
| LMC = lower middle class | RPS = reading passage style |
| UWC = upper working class | FS = formal style |
| MWC = middle working class | CS = casual style |
| LWC = lower working class | *Source*: Trudgill 1983:179 |

prestige variant, the lower three classes are exactly reversed. In every case men rather than women show greater use of the prestige variant. The solution to this puzzle lies in the fact that, although it is possible to show that women lead in the upper classes' change to the RP-like vowel, the same vowel is also being introduced by geographical diffusion (1.2.2 and 2.1.5) as a non-standard, working class variant from Suffolk. It has the sort of masculine covert prestige described above, and change in its direction is being led by lower class men, particularly younger ones.

This example emphasizes the importance of Labov's insistence in the point that it is sex differentiation which plays a general role in language change, not just the leadership of women in establishing new norms.

In addition to their performance differences, men and women have different attitudes towards variables. Labov (1966) devised an *index of linguistic insecurity* to show how much speakers dislike their own perform-ance. Since outright questioning might elicit guarded responses, two variants of eighteen words were read to respondents; one variant was a prestige form, the other nonprestige, and they were numbered, randomly, one and two. The respondents were asked to circle the number of the item which they thought was pronounced correctly and then the number of the variant they normally used. The number of items circled differently was the index of linguistic inse-curity. The mean index score for women in the New York City study was 3.6, but men scored a much more secure 2.1. In a similar experiment, Trudgill

(1972) asked his respondents to report on their own usage of certain variables after he had determined whether they were typical users of that variable or not. The variable (ō) in Norwich (the vowel in 'road,' 'nose,' and 'moan') ranges from [ɐu] through [u:] to [ʊ], the first being the prestige, RP-like variant. Respondents who had scored at the fifty percent level or higher in a casual speech sample in the use of the RP-like variant were considered typical users of that variant; if, on the other hand, those whose use of the non-prestige variants was at the fifty percent level or higher in a casual speech sample were considered typical users of them. Subjects were then classified as over-reporters (those who claimed to use more of the prestige variety than they actually did), under-reporters (those who claimed to use more of the nonprestige variety than they actually did), and accurate reporters.

|  | Total | Male | Female |
|---|---|---|---|
| Over-reporting | 18 | 12 | 25 |
| Under-reporting | 36 | 54 | 18 |
| Accurate | 45 | 34 | 57 |

(Trudgill 1972:187)

Only 12 percent of the male subjects over-reported compared to 25 percent of the females. Conversely, 54 percent of the males under-reported compared to only 18 percent of the females. The nonprestige (ō) forms must have been attractive to men, who claim they use more of them than they actually do; on the other hand, considerably more women than men inaccurately claim to be users of the standard variant.

It would be strange if quantitative studies did not reveal some aspects of the changing status of women in modern society. Some women over-reported their use of the nonprestige variant of (ō), an indication that covert prestige may involve more than masculine traits. In Trondheim, Norway there is striking evidence that younger women may actually prefer local, nonprestige forms. In a study of men's and women's stress placement in certain loan words such as 'avis' (newspaper) and 'generasjon' (generation), the following differences emerged (Chambers and Trudgill 1980:100):

|  | Percent nonstandard forms | |
|---|---|---|
| Age | Male | Female |
| 18–36 | 64 | 59 |
| 37–62 | 63 | 24 |
| 63–82 | 64 | 7 |

Males of all ages prefer the nonstandard form, presumably for its covert prestige value; surprisingly, however, younger women prefer this same form at practically the same level as their male counterparts. Chambers and Trudgill suggest that these findings are best regarded not so much as language change but as a change in the linguistic behaviour of women which reflects a change in values and attitudes and which we may expect to see repeated in many other linguistic communities. (1980:100)

Milroy (1980) relates women's rarer use of local, nonprestige forms to the sorts of network associations they construct (3.3.2).

Finally, what has been said here about sex differences from the point of view of quantitative linguistics may be oriented to certain societies. Labov (1981) observes:

> Whenever there is style and class stratification, we can expect differences between men and women. For stable sociolinguistic markers [for example, Norwich (ng)], the mean values for women are shifted towards the upper end of the hierarchy. This effect can be large enough so that there is no overlap between men and women. But it's important to bear in mind that this shift of women towards the higher prestige forms (in the sense of national or standard prestige) is limited to those societies where women play a role in public life. The reverse tendency was found in Teheran by Modaressi (1978) and by Jain in India (1975).

What can be learned from quantitative sociolinguistics about sex differentiation in SLA? Although numerous quantitative studies have been carried out in SLA, almost none includes sex as a variable. From what is known of stylistic differentiation and language change in sociolinguistic studies, this is particularly surprising since many SLA studies model themselves on such research. In nearly every case, however, degree of formality (realized as attention to form) has been the principal focus (3.5.1, 5.1), although Selinker (1969) shows no difference in interlanguage word order for men and women.

If in general women show greater sensitivity to L2 (prestige?) forms than men do, SLA might be likened to change from above in which the L2 itself has overt prestige for the learner community. In at least one study (Hartford 1976), this has been shown to be the case, but the study is of indigenous, early bilingual subjects (Chicano males and females in the United States). Another possibility, that L1 prestige forms might be the source of greater transfer influence on women than men has not been investigated at all, though the carry-over of formality has (e.g., Schmidt 1977, Beebe 1980).

In some cases an L2 might have covert prestige, and a clue to that status might lie in the performance of younger, lower class men. In a study of Puerto Rican male adolescents in New York City, Wolfram (1973) shows that the degree to which Black English features are acquired corresponds to the learner's degree of contact with Blacks. Presumably those who acquire a higher percentage of Black English forms are responding to the covert prestige of that speech variety. The substitution of [f] for [θ] in morpheme-final positions (for example, 'both' pronounced as 'bof') is illustrated here (Wolfram and Fasold 1974:96):

| Number of informants | Occurrences of [f] | Occurrences of [θ] | Percent [f] |
|---|---|---|---|
| Black (10) | 36 | 8 | 81.8 |
| PR with extensive Black contacts (6) | 20 | 3 | 87.0 |
| PR with limited Black contacts (23) | 53 | 44 | 54.6 |

A contrastive analysis not sensitive to the two groups of Puerto Rican youths separated here might conflate the scores and note that [θ] does not exist in the (Caribbean) Spanish phonological system. That fact cannot explain the considerable use of the variable by the group with extensive Black contacts, a use which, by the way, is even greater than the NS base line figure.

In addition, accounts of differential male–female attitudes, derived from self-report studies, could be valuable supplements to variable data. Do men or women (or neither) over- or under-report their use of target language norms? Could an index of SLA insecurity be derived, and would it display such a large difference for men and women as it does in native language sociolinguistic studies?

Since so little quantitative work in SLA on sex differences has been done, it is difficult to generalize about learning perspectives. It may be important for women to be convinced that SLA is a prestige activity, although that might not be a correct strategy for younger female learners. Quantitative socio-linguistic data suggest that in many societies women lead linguistic change unless its source is covert prestige. Nevertheless, conscious change in the direction of a new, unestablished norm might challenge the peer group standards of younger women, with the possible exception of those in the highest classes. The appeal of SLA (if it is like language change) to younger women, as for men (excepting older men of higher classes), will not, then, derive greatest benefit from its associations with standardness and prestige. Since much classroom SLA, particularly foreign language teaching, has elitist overtones, the mismatch is obvious.

The practical dilemma which arises from prestigious versus nonprestigious models in SLA might be resolved in the following way. For some groups, perhaps the majority of adult learners, SLA activities should be divorced from the societal norms of the L1. Peer group norms and adult identities may simply be too strong for the challenge of SLA. Though sociolinguistic data will not allow further speculation in this direction, it may be that effective learners, those who have avoided the pitfalls of anomie and culture shock (e.g., H. D. Brown 1980:131–5) and/or early *fossilization* (e.g., Alberto as discussed in Schumann 1978a) are precisely those who, subconsciously, recognize the inherent inability of adults and adolescents to overcome the powerful inhibiting influences of peer norms and solidified identity. Such learners may construct new identities and a new set of norms of behavior for themselves in the new language, avoiding the clash between old identities and norms on the one hand and new demands in precisely such areas on the other. Discussion below of both *accommodation* and the *competent bilingual* develops these ideas further (2.1.3).

Observations of sex differences in language do not stop at the level of quantitative divergence. Recent work has investigated the conversational and discourse differences between the sexes. These larger, usually discoursal elements of gender specific language behavior are often the subject of folk linguistic belief and comment in the speech community.[16]

Even linguists have attributed gender specific language habits (particularly verbosity to women) without empirical study.[17] In fact, nearly every empirical study of this feature shows men to be more verbose. When Swacker (1975) asked respondents to describe three pictures, male subjects averaged 13.00 minutes per picture, females only 3.17. This pattern persists in conversation; in fifty-seven male–female student dyads, male subjects outtalked females in thirty-three of the pairs (Hilpert, Kramer, and Clark 1975).

Even greater differences exist in gender specific conversational behavior. In a study of eleven mixed-sex dyads, Zimmerman and West (1975) found that of forty-eight interruptions of the conversational partner's speech, fully forty-six were by men, though men failed to complete their interruptions at nearly twice the rate of women, and women objected to interruptions at twice the rate of men.[18]

When conversation goes on, one of its principal features is the topic. Participants who control the topic may be viewed as having greater control over the situation. In analyzing twelve hours of recordings of spontaneous conversations between couples, Fishman (1978) discovered that of seventy-six topics raised, forty-seven were by women and twenty-nine by men, but twenty-eight of the women's topics failed to be taken up in the subsequent conversation while only one of the men's topic nominations was unsuccessful. The net result was that of the forty-five topics actually sustained in the conversations, twenty-eight were instigated by men and only seventeen by women. Further investigation showed that women's topics failed simply because men ignored them.

The selection of topics may also vary by gender. In a study of college undergraduates, Aries (1976) showed that male groups talked about 'competition,' 'teasing,' 'sports,' 'physical aggression,' and 'doing things.' Female groups talked about 'self,' 'feelings,' 'affiliation with others,' 'home,' and 'family.' In mixed-sex groups, men initiated more of the talk, but both groups compromised on topics; males spoke less about competition and physical aggression and females less about home and family. Kipers (1987) shows that a mismatch between topic use and perceived importance is possible. Women talked more about World War II in her study, but men found it more significant.

There are also gender differences in lexical and grammatical areas of conversation. Fishman's (1980) study of male–female interaction (about twelve and one-half hours of conversation) shows that women asked 263 questions while men asked only 107, and in a study of ticket buyers' behavior in Amsterdam, Brouwer, Gerritsen, and Dettaan (1979) found that women asked more questions than men, particularly when the ticketseller was male.[19] Although the evidence from a number of studies is inconclusive, English-speaking women appear to use more tag questions than men. This is clearer, however, when the tags have a *facilitative* rather than interrogative function (Holmes 1984:54).

A number of these discoursal differences point to women's fulfilling certain cultural stereotypes in language use. Since women are caricaturistically thought to be less well-informed, frail, unsure, and beholden to men for information, their conversations may be interrupted and guided by men and full of questions and signals of self-doubt. O'Barr and Atkins (1980) catalogued ten features of *powerless* language (largely derived from Lakoff 1975) and transcribed 150 hours of trials in a North Carolina superior criminal court. The features were as follows:

1  Hedges, e.g., 'sort of,' 'kind of,' 'I guess'
2  (Super) polite forms, e.g., 'would you please . . . ,' 'I'd really appreciate it if . . .'
3  Tag questions
4  Speaking in italics, e.g., emphatic 'so' and 'very,' intonational emphasis equivalent to underlining words in written language
5  Empty adjectives, e.g., 'divine,' 'charming,' 'sweet,' 'adorable'
6  Hypercorrect grammar and pronunciation
7  Lack of a sense of humor, e.g., poor at telling jokes
8  Direct quotations
9  Special vocabulary, e.g., specialized color terms
10  Question intonation in declarative contexts.

Scores were assigned to each witness by dividing the total number of powerless features used by the number of utterances. Scores ranged from 1.39 (more than one such feature per utterance) to 0.18 (very infrequent use of such features). O'Barr and Atkins show that while powerless language is often a feature of women's speech, it is frequently the case that men earned high powerless language scores and that women earned low scores. They argue that social status and previous courtroom experience were much better predictors of scores than sex. They go on to reason that since, in North American and European societies, women are often less powerful than men, these language features show up more frequently in their speech and have become known as the defining characteristics of *women's language*. This 'relayed symbolism' is elaborated on in the description of the interaction of social features and linguistic frequencies in the *variety space* concept outlined in 5.1 and chapter 6.

Another feature often associated with so-called women's language is *politeness*. Brown and Levinson (1978) show that politeness may be specifically related to the degree to which interlocutors care for the *face wants* (derived from such expressions as 'save' or 'lose face') of one another. They characterize these wants as (1) *positive* – the need to be liked or admired, and (2) *negative* – the need to be left alone or not imposed on. One may be polite to others in recognizing their negative face wants, for example, by framing requests which apologize for imposing ('I'm sorry to bother you, but could you hand me the ketchup') or by using modal verbs (in the second clause of the previous example), which seem to make requests less demanding. One may be polite to others in recognizing their positive face wants by offering greetings and thanks and by praise ('You really look nice'). In a study of Tzeltal (a Mayan language of Mexico), which uses adverbial particles to strengthen or weaken the force of a statement, P. Brown (1980) discovered that these particles, assumed to emphasize the negative and positive politeness of utterances, were much more frequently used by women than by men, particularly in same-sex interactions.

Such studies, though they deal with putatively universal strategies of interaction, raise the interesting possibilities of anthropological and ethnographic investigations of gender-based differences across cultural and linguistic boundaries. Keenan (1974) casts doubt, for example, on the universality of the characterization of men's language as 'more straightforward,' 'less polite,' and 'more direct,' and women's language as 'more indirect,' 'less blunt,' and 'more circumlocutory.' In a Madagascar village, considerable value is placed on avoiding conflict and confrontation. As a result, criticism, disputes, and even orders and requests are carried out indirectly, even metaphorically. In contrast to many other cultures, however, it is the male speakers in the community who are especially constrained by these norms of indirect speech. Women are known as straightforward speakers, capable of expressing emotion, including anger, and criticism directly. This is so much the case that men often use women to settle disputes, bargain over prices, and make accusations – tasks which their own indirect style would make them especially ill-suited to carry out.

Such cross-cultural investigations support the earlier contention that men's and women's language features are reflections of the social roles assigned by the cultural environment, not biologically determined characteristics.[20] In cases of cross-cultural communications (with their obvious relevance to SLA), such differences may be especially subtle. Tannen (1982) discusses a misunderstanding between a wife (American native New Yorker of East European Jewish extraction) and her Greek husband. The reconstructed conversations which revealed the misunderstanding were the following:

Wife: John's having a party. Wanna go?
Husband: OK.
(Later)
Wife: Are you sure you want to go to the party?
Husband: OK, let's not go. I'm tired anyway.

In a discussion of the misunderstanding (both husband and wife claiming that they did not go to the party because the other did not want to), the wife indicated that she had simply been making sure that her husband wanted to go to the party and that she had intended to reveal nothing of her own preferences. The Greek husband maintained, however, that mention of the party in the first place indicated to him that his wife wanted to go, and he agreed; her second mention, however, suggested to him that she did not want to go, so he even invented a reason ('I'm tired anyway') to make her feel better about what he perceived as her 'changing her mind.' The Greek husband's 'OK' and 'anyway' were signals that he was agreeing with what he perceived as his wife's desires – that is, first to go and later not to. The wife, however, took the 'OK' to be, quite simply, a positive response to her question, not an indication that he was going along with what he took to be her wants. Earlier studies by Tannen (1979, 1981) suggest that the wife's ethnolinguistic background would require very little indirectness in interaction while the Greek husband's background (Tannen 1982) would suggest considerable reliance on indirectness, particularly concerning personal wants. In a related judgment study by respondents of such situations, Tannen determined that gender was not an important factor for the expectation of indirectness for Greeks but was strong for 'Americans' (well-educated adult Californians). The 'American' female respondents preferred indirect speech act interpretations of such conversations considerably more than male respondents did. In the specific conversation reported on, the preference for indirectness in American women is overcome by the specific ethnic and regional background of the wife. A few other cultural contact studies of sex related linguistic features have been carried out in bilingual communities, particularly Mexican-American (Patella and Kuvlesky 1979, Redlinger 1976, Rubin 1970, Sole 1976, Valdés-Fallis 1978).

Discourse strategies and general aspects of language behavior are especially revealing of the roles and functions allocated the sexes in different linguistic and cultural communities. The studies cited here should be enough to warn against caricatures of men's and women's language in general (though studies of folk caricatures are in themselves revealing).[21] It is disappointing to find that so little attention has been paid to sex differences in

SLA studies of interaction. An important exception is Gass and Varonis (1986), which investigates sex differences in conversational interactions among Japanese learners of English. Differences in four conversational areas are studied: (1) negotiation, (2) topic, (3) dominance, and (4) interpersonal phenomena. Gass and Varonis (1985) showed that negotiations in conversational interactions were more numerous in NNS interactions. In the 1986 study, they show that mixed-sex dyads show an even greater number of negotiations and that female interlocutors are responsible for double the male number of such negotiations. In topic selection (contrary to results in monolingual studies), male dyads exhibited the greatest number of personal topics. In conversational dominance, male interlocutors talked more in three out of four mixed-sex dyads while single-sex dyads were evenly distributed in amount of talk per interlocutor. Males also led in the number of conversational turns taken in the mixed-sex dyads, and men tended to lead the conversation in a picture-description task even when women were assigned the role of describing the picture to a male interlocutor who could not see it. Finally, men more often than women gained the floor after interruptions in the mixed-sex dyads. In interpersonal areas, there were considerably more encouraging remarks made in the single-sex dyads, a slight tendency (in one mixed-sex dyad only) for more apologies by women, and, finally, more hedges in single-sex than in mixed-sex dyads, though men used more hedges in mixed-sex dyads than women did.

Gender differences have also been explored in experimental settings, particularly in surveys of language attitudes, but only a few early studies considered male–female differences in either the samples to be judged or the respondents (Smith 1985:86). Elyan et al. (1978) and Giles and Marsh (1979) compared responses to male and female RP (British standard *Received Pronunciation*) and regional dialect voices and found, as in earlier work, that RP speakers were more attractive and competent than local dialect speakers. Surprisingly, however, female RP speakers were rated higher on both masculine and feminine stereotypes, and both male and female raters agreed on these evaluations, leading to the conclusion that competent or RP-speaking females might be perceived as androgynous. Giles et al. (1980), however, showed that masculine characteristics attributed to RP-speaking females could be construed as higher class traits, confounding the perception of sex differences with status. Berryman (1980) showed that both men and women were more *credible* (a group of factors which included, among others, reasonability, logic, correctness, organization, control, and meaningfulness) when they used so-called women's speech characteristics and that both sexes were more *extroverted* (a group of factors which included, among others, aggression, extroversion, leadership, assertiveness, activity, and superiority) when they used so-called men's speech characteristics. This further suggests that exclusively sex related interpretations of language use are likely to be misleading.

Gender-based attitudinal studies have not been conducted in SLA. Eisenstein (1982) shows that NNS females are better at recognizing dialect differences (373) but does not include sex as a variable in her study of NNS evaluations of four different varieties. Walters (1979) studied the reactions of male and female speakers of Spanish and English to various written requests and commands to determine their perceived degree of politeness. The difference between male and female English speakers, though not significant in a rank correlation test, revealed interesting distinctions. Women agreed more on which strategies were impolite or polite, but their mean ratings of strategies were more widely separated. Although the Spanish-speakers' politeness evaluations of English sentences agreed with the rankings of the NSs, they, like the female NS respondents, showed much greater agreement on which items were polite and which impolite. The temptation to call this categorical rather than incremental interpretation of politeness a learner characteristic must be rejected since the same tendency appears in NNSs and female NSs. In this same study, however, there was a low correlation between male and female Spanish-speakers' ratings of politeness in their own language, indicating that sex differences may exist for one language and cultural background in an area where there is little or no difference in another.

Sex determined perceptions of variety differences have not been extensively studied, but Oliveira do Canto (1982; summarized in Preston 1985) shows that men and women do not believe that the same distinct dialect areas exist locally. Even when male and female respondents agree that an area exists, they may not agree on its degree of difference from local speech. Faggion (1982; summarized in Preston 1985) shows how male and female ratings of language *correctness* and *pleasantness* do not agree. Brazilian female and younger respondents rated Rio de Janeiro fifth on a scale of one to ten for language correctness, while adult males rated it first. Male and younger raters rated the northeastern section of the country ninth for pleasant qualities of speech while adult females rated it fifth (again, on a scale of one to ten). Though ethnographic studies of language learners' classroom behaviors and beliefs have been done (e.g., Wong-Fillmore 1976), surveys of the general folk linguistic beliefs of language learners which highlight sex related differences have not.

Finally, the need for revision in language use and attitudes to conform to egalitarian principles is specifically related to gender. Studies of male–female interaction highlight their unequal status, and even more superficially observable linguistic facts could be pointed out – 'man' ('mankind,' 'men') and 'he' ('him,' 'his') as terms for both sexes, the use of insulting and/or unequal terms for women (e.g., 'ladies' when paired with 'men,' a host of slang terms such as 'skirt,' 'tomato,' and 'broad,' and the unnecessary sex-marking on such terms as 'male nurse' and 'poetess'). An extensive annotated, topical bibliography in Thorne, Kramarae, and Henley (1983) lists a number of descriptions, interpretations, and proposals concerning such usage and attitudes.

In the cross-cultural context of SLA, solutions to sexism in general and sexist language use and regard in particular are more complex. In an exclusively home culture setting, personal beliefs and professional activity are not at odds since, if that culture is one which an individual believes is in need of repair, membership in it empowers one to engage in activities which focus on bringing about awareness and change. On the other hand, the culturally relativistic position set forth by most anthropologically oriented sociolinguists (including those who have paid a great deal of attention to SLA, e.g., Saville-Troike 1982) seems to deny or call into question personal involvement in social change activities when one is in contact with other cultures, including ones in which sexual (or other) inequalities play a central role.

Judd (1983) is a careful consideration of the rights and responsibilities of language teaching professionals faced with language and social change brought about by the changing roles of women in Western societies, particularly when teachers of those languages face students from cultures in which such change is not evident. The problems are not easy to solve, but knowledge of the facts of gender related linguistic differences and of the folk beliefs concerning such facts should help inform those who must make such decisions. Studies of sexism in language teaching texts confirm the need for such information (e.g., Hellinger 1980, Porreca 1984).

In general, SLA work on gender specific language lags behind work in sociolinguistics, and it is disappointing to find that the majority of large SLA research projects have not included sex as a variable.

## 2.1.3 Nativeness

From a psycholinguistic point of view, nativeness is almost the entire question of SLA. The route through stages of the interlanguage from no ability to fluency is what must be accounted for,[22] and at least two major sociolinguistic issues arise. First, what are the attitudinal outcomes of learners' achievements along the scale of nativeness? Second, who are the learners' models and what are their language characteristics? This second concern is taken up in 2.1.5 where the question of varieties of English is discussed.

The first concern, essentially a social psychological one, may be divided into two parts – outcomes for the learner and outcomes for the surrounding speech community. From the learner's perspective, one wants to know the impact of identification with and accommodation to the new speech community. From the speech community's perspective, one needs to assess the reception of the learner's efforts to identify with and accommodate to a new set of linguistic norms. Much more has been said about the former, and three approaches to the study of an individual's social psychological approach to the acquisition of a second language (or variety) are examined here.

First, the *social psychological model*, summarized in Gardner and Lambert (1972), focuses on the affective factors of attitude and motivation in SLA. A successful learner

> must be both able and willing to adopt various aspects of behaviour, including verbal behaviour, which characterize members of the other linguistic-cultural group. (Lambert 1967:102)

Three main concerns emerge from that contention: how much does the learner risk losing his or her own linguistic-cultural heritage; does the learner have sufficient motivation to risk that loss; and, is the target culture an attractive one?

When learners gain proficiency in another language, perhaps to the point of being assimilated, they may experience *anomie*, a feeling of alienation, often coupled with confusion of identity. If the surrounding speech community does not pressure learners to replace their first language, the result is *additive* bilingualism, and the learners overcome negative reactions, though change in identity is bound to occur. If, on the other hand, the surrounding speech community expects learners to replace native languages (and general behavior), the result is *subtractive* bilingualism – the strongest setting for anomie, alienation, and loss of cultural identity.

Learners appear to have two principal orientations to SLA. The first, in which they want to associate with and find out about members of the target culture, is called an *integrative* motivation; the second, in which they have a specific, often utilitarian reason for learning a second language, is called *instrumental*. Some early studies indicated that an integrative orientation was optimal (Gardner and Lambert 1959), but more recent studies (Lambert 1974) indicate that situational variables may make an instrumental orientation (e.g., minority group members faced with the task of learning a prestige language) effective. Generally, however, a learner's positive evaluation of a target culture should promote integrative orientation and lessen the fear of cultural loss and resultant anomie.

Second, in an extension and elaboration of parts of the social psychological model, Schumann (particularly Schumann 1978b and c) has characterized SLA as an *acculturation* (earlier *pidginization*) process.[23] SLA

> is just one aspect of acculturation and the degree to which a learner acculturates to the TL (target language) group will control the degree to which he acquires the second language. (Schumann 1978b:34)

Acculturation may be blocked by social psychological impediments at the level of the two speech communities (L1 and L2) and at the level of the individual learner. The L1 or L2 community may be socially dominating, may offer or have no reasonable assimilation opportunities or strategies, may be so self-enclosed in social networks that contact with others is extremely limited, may be so bounded in group membership requirements that access (or departure) seems impossible, may be so different from the other that contact is difficult, and may have strong negative attitudes towards the other. All these factors impede acculturation. At the level of the individual learner, the factors of language shock (fear of being seen as comic), cultural shock (disorientation on entering a new culture), motivation (integrative or instrumental), and ego-permeability (the degree to which one's language boundaries can be overcome) are the main deterrents to acculturation and, hence, effective SLA (Schumann 1978b:29–34).

Third, Giles and Byrne (1982) summarize an *intergroup* model of SLA. Its major principle is the maintenance of a strong positive self-concept by the learner. Ball and Giles (1982:5) identify five propositions which explain an individual's inability to maintain self-concept in the face of the SLA task:

Some individuals
1 See themselves strongly as members of a group with language an important dimension of its identity
2 Regard their group's relative status as changeable
3 Perceive their ingroup's ethnolinguistic vitality as high
4 Perceive their intergroup boundaries as hard
5 Identify with few other social groups, and ones which offer unfavourable social comparisons.

Individuals for whom these five propositions are true fear or reject assimilation and are poor language learners. Although the model was designed to characterize minority group acquisition of majority languages, it is likely that it is of sufficient generality to cover many other cases of SLA (Gardner 1985:142). This approach stresses the importance of integrative motivation and further details those factors which would impede an individual's SLA.[24]

From the speech community's point of view, attitudes towards learner varieties have been caricatured by ample anecdotal evidence. The French of Paris, for example, are reported to be unforgiving to language learners who do not live up to exacting local norms. Unfortunately, such folk beliefs have not been carefully studied and catalogued, though a number of recent studies of *error gravity* (the degree of seriousness of a learner's error) have been conducted for French (and other languages) and are summarized in Eisenstein (1983). Such studies, however, focus on grammatical and phonological factors which affect intelligibility rather than the listener's attitude towards NNS speech.

A number of social psychological models of the reception of NNS performance have been advanced. I noted (Preston 1981a) that NS-like fluency is not always admired and offered an explanation for this through Goffman's suggestion that instances of language may be characterized on the basis of their attempts to control the environment:

1  Unwitting moves – those which the speaker performs with no intent that they will be evaluated by the hearer; unself- conscious behavior
2  Naive moves – those which respond to unwitting moves; responses which show that the hearer does not believe that the previous move was oriented to assessment
3  Control moves – those which the performer arranges for the observer, presumably to benefit the performer
4  Uncovering moves – those which the observer makes in response to controlling moves; attempts to 'get behind' the performer's real intention
5  Counter-uncovering moves – those which a performer makes when a controlling move has been detected (or when an unwitting move has been misinterpreted as a control move); an attempt to convince an observer that a previous move was unwitting. (Goffman 1969)

I further suggested that especially fluent (or particularly marked) NS-like performances may be received as control moves precisely because the performance of a known NNS has aroused suspicion due to its nativeness. I added this social distance corollary to Goffman's schema: 'The more socially distant the observer from the performer, the more likely the observer will interpret the performer's moves as controlling' (Preston 1981a:112). This corollary is partly based on the fact that failure to establish early common ground in an interaction may be due to dissimilarity (Berger and Bradac 1982). This does not doom all NS–NNS interaction (or interaction with any unknown interlocutor) to distrust, for a simple rule which supports the reduction of uncertainty might be added:

Social distance is decreased as participants have more and more information about one another, often through the confirmation of information (perhaps stereotyped) they assume they already possess. (Preston 1981a:112)

Various scenarios for NS–NNS interaction can now be examined. When an NS–NNS interaction begins, there is likely to be a great deal of social distance (less, of course, for interlocutors familiar with such situations); some of that distance may be reduced by the employment of stereotypes. In particular, NS stereotypes of NNSs may be partially confirmed by an NNS linguistic performance. If, however, the NNS performance is especially native, NSs may be confused, puzzled, perhaps even angry since a mechanism for confirming information about the NNS was blocked, and the first step towards the reduction of social distance could not be taken. Perhaps NNSs, sensitive to the need for knowledge about others in interactions, unconsciously acquire an optimally received variety, purposefully distinct from that of the NS. Educational interference with the construction of such a system, through, for example, insistence on NS norms at every level of performance, is counterproductive. On the other hand, discovery of the structure of such systems and the means with which they were acquired might lead to appropriate applied linguistics solutions.

Research in *accommodation* in monolingual settings shows that such reactions to similarity and dissimilarity are common:

> There is a dyad consisting of speakers A and B. Assume that A wishes to gain B's approval. A then
> 1   Samples B's speech and
>     (a)  draws inferences as to the personality characteristics of B (or at least the characteristics which B wishes to project as being his)
>     (b)  assumes that B values and approves of such characteristics
>     (c)  assumes that B will approve of him (A) to the extent that he (A) displays similar characteristics
> 2   Chooses from his speech-repertoire patterns of speech which project characteristics of which B is assumed to approve. (Giles and Powesland 1975:158)

If that held in every case, then the closer A (the NNS) got to B (the NS), the better impression the NS would have of the NNS. There is a point, however, beyond which accommodation produces negative rather than positive results:

> Accommodation . . . seems to depend for its effectiveness upon its *not* [emphasis in the original] being recognized as such by the receiver. Such 'covert' accommodation, of which the speaker himself may have little or no consciousness, would probably include changes in speech rate, pauses, grammatical complexity, accent etc. made by way of convergence towards the speech characteristics of the receiver. Detection by the listener of accommodation in this category would possibly tend to discredit the speaker. In the case of accent convergence, for example, the listener might feel that he was being mimicked or patronized and this would not enhance the approval of the speaker.
>
> Even in the case of overt accommodation there may be an optimum degree of accommodation so that it is not seen as a too-obvious act of ingratiation. Jones and Jones (1964) have shown that there is an optimum level of agreement with another whose esteem one values, and Jones (1964) points out that part of the ingratiation tactic is that we do

not agree too indiscriminately lest we be too obvious. So it would seem important to determine in different contexts and with different partici- pants what constitutes optimal speech accommodation. (Giles and Powesland 1975:169–70)

Giles and Smith (1979) studied British speakers' reactions to a Canadian who recorded eight versions of the same text. On the completely Canadian English version, the respondents did not find the speaker particularly attractive. The remaining versions contained a variety of convergent and nonconvergent strategies. The raters, however, found the speaker less attractive when he converged phonologically, though convergence in speech rate and certain message characteristics were appreciated. Speaker and audience identity as well as topic and other situational variables are, there- fore, important factors in determining the degree of accommodation appre- ciated by hearers.

SLA provides a laboratory of interactional contexts which display a wide range of accommodation strategies. Such considerations have led me to suggest (Preston 1981a, b, 1983, 1984, 1986b) that the *competent bilingual* is the most effective model for the language learner. NNSs must escape the double bind of rousing suspicion and affective distaste as a result of their foreign status on the one hand and as a result of their perceived overaccom- modation on the other. Numbers of successful learners have apparently acquired the ability (however subconsciously) to walk this tightrope. The investigation of successful NNS output must study those characteristics which make it effective, not just catalog its differences from NS behavior and assume that corrective measures are always in order when differences are discerned. The forces of self-concept, accommodation, and other social psychological mechanisms suggest that competent bilinguals have constructed efficient but divergent systems for themselves. That reasoning links characteristics of the learner and the environment even more closely. The learner's language ego and previous identity is less threatened by a divergent, competent bilingual system, and the speech community's expecta- tions of behavior are better satisfied, though, of course, it is an empirical mat- ter to determine the level (and linguistic type) of accommodation which is optimal for any given speech community.

This suggestion of competent bilingualism may seem cynical, even undemocratic. Shouldn't it be the aim to produce NS-like learners, letting the stereotypical impressions fall where they may? Perhaps not. The treatment of NNSs as equals would surely encourage competent bilingual strategies. In such an environment of mutual respect, the NS would not overtly demand perfect accommodation and then covertly resent its accomplishment. Similarly, the NNS would feel neither the external pressure for total assimila- tion nor the internal fear of loss of identity.

Though the structures of competent bilingual systems may vary, their realization is not entirely theoretical. The following journal entry by an NNS on the verge of competent bilingualism shows an unusual overt awareness of both the internal and external social psychological pressures which impinge on a learner's decisions about nativeness:

I just don't know what to do right now. I might have been *wrong* since I began to learn English. I always tried to be better and wanted to be a good speaker. But it was *wrong, absolutely wrong*! When I got to California, I started imitating Americans and picked up the words I heard. So, my English became just like Americans. I couldn't help it. I must have been funny to them, because I am a Japanese and have my own culture and background. I think I almost lost the most important thing I should not have. I got California English including intonation, pronunciation, the way they act, which *are not* mine. I have to have *my own* English, be myself when I speak English. Why was it hard for me to make friends in California? Why was I unhappy? Because I faked! I pretended to be like an American just like an awful actress. Others must have noticed that. But nobody told me the truth. Everybody said I talked like an American but something was wrong with me. I shouldn't have been that way. I tried too hard to improve English, but in the wrong way. At that time, I thought it was the best way and the only way to learn how to speak English. I watched TV, listened to the radio, read the newspaper as hard as I could. I didn't think about how others think about that. I believed that I would be able to think in English and talk naturally. I think I made it. But in the wrong way. I don't have to be like Americans. The most important thing is to be myself and communicate with people. I don't have to be good. It doesn't matter how others don't like me and think I am not good. It doesn't matter if I make a mistake not only in English but also in life itself. If I pretend to be like an American, nobody will like me and talk to me. If we just imitate others' way of speaking, I can never talk and communicate with people. Because it's not *me*, the words coming out of my mouth are not my own words. They are the words that I imitated and stole from Americans. If I really want to speak *good* English, I have to speak my own English, which might not be worse than the English I got in California. But that's the real English for me. Don't try to be good too hard. If I am too eager, my English will become worse and worse. I am at the top of the peak. It might take long to speak in my way. But I'll try. (HELP 1979; cited in Preston 1981a, b)

It would be difficult to find research which more expressively encapsulates the question of nativeness. The focus on SLA as a social as well as psychological process has led to a great deal of reflective and experimental work in the general area of assimilation, here taken to mean the effective linguistic integration of a speaker into a new speech community, not the loss of an earlier linguistic or cultural heritage.

Empirical research has been done on NS reaction to NNS speech (2.1.4), but little of it has addressed degree of nativeness or competent bilingual performance. Rey (1977) asked potential employers to rate White, Black, and Cuban accented American English speakers for employment suitability. The Cubans were divided into groups of heavy, medium, and minimally accented speakers. The White speakers were preferred; the Black and minimally accented speakers were next best rated, and the medium and heavily accented speakers were rated lowest. Brennan, Ryan and Dawson (1975) found that raters recognized degrees of accentedness of Spanish-English bilinguals' speech and that non-Hispanic raters attributed more negative characteristics to the more heavily accented speakers. On the other hand, Ryan, Carranza, and Moffie (1975) showed that foreign born Mexican-Americans rated more heavily accented speech favorably while American born Mexican-Americans agreed with non-Hispanic raters in downgrading the more accented varieties. A thorough review of studies of NS reactions to NNS varieties, including several which do include degree of nativeness as a variable, is given in Eisenstein (1983).

Janicki (1985) is an ambitious program for research on the status and reception of NNS linguistic behavior, what he calls the *foreigner's language*. In particular, he recommends research on the particular elements of NNS performance which elicit negative and positive responses from the surrounding NS speech community. In a pilot study (Janicki 1987), he shows that an English learner of Polish was rated higher on several dimensions (acceptability, approbation, irritation) when the sample involved only pronunciation errors rather than pronunciation errors along with errors of grammar (morphology and syntax). Further work on specific features should shed even more light on the sorts of NNS performances which are most admired by NSs.

Quite a number of studies have included assessments of NS and NNS abilities to understand one another's speech. In general, NNSs believe that NS speech is easier to comprehend, though Berkowitz (1979) found that beginners claimed that NNSs would be more easily understood. In nearly every study conducted, NS varieties have been more easily understood by NNSs (Eisenstein 1983). The intelligibility of NNS varieties to NSs has a more complex history of study; some researchers have tried to tease out the specific linguistic elements which have rendered the speech unintelligible, though there are variables of listener age, sex, and experience which have been taken into account as well (Eisenstein 1983:168–70). In general, though NSs understand more advanced learners better, more detailed questions concerning structural causes of unintelligibility have not yet been answered conclusively.

Such social psychological studies detail the reactions to the sociolinguistic continuum between NS and NNS performance and help determine the degree of nativeness which is effective, particularly at advanced stages of SLA. A thorough consideration of social psychological forces in SLA, pertinent to the following section as well, is forthcoming (Beebe To appear).

### 2.1.4 *Ethnicity*

Much early quantitative sociolinguistic work in the United States focused on Black English, and the earliest language attitude research was devoted to determining the regard the French and English ethnolinguistic communities of Canada had for one another. Though one research focus touched on ethnicity and two languages and the other on ethnicity and varieties of one, the strategies developed in both were widely applied to bilingual and multi-lingual communities and to social differences other than ethnolinguistic background.

In Labov's (1966) work on the social stratification of English in New York City, differences among ethnic groups were found to be significant. For example, the variable (eh) (computed on a scale of ten to forty) has values as follows:

$$10 = [\text{I}^\text{ə}]$$
$$20 = [\varepsilon^\text{ə}]$$
$$30 = [æ^\wedge]$$
$$40 = [æ:]$$

An average score in the teens would represent considerable low-front vowel raising, in the twenties to thirties moderate, and in the forties none. Figure 2.3 shows the distribution of (eh) for Jewish and Italian respondents in three styles. In the more casual styles (A and B), the Italian respondents lead in the raising of (eh). In Style A fewer than 5 percent of the Jewish respondents fall into the ten-to-eighteen (heavy raising) category while 45 percent of the Italian respondents perform in that range. In Style B there are nearly no Italian respondents in the ten-to-eighteen category, but they are still ahead of Jews in raising, particularly in the nineteen-to-twenty-one range. In Style D, the most formal, the two groups have nearly coincided. Blacks showed little or no sensitivity to style for (eh), centering their performances in the twenty-seven-to-thirty-two category with no occurrences in either extreme, and, in the most casual style (A), none even below twenty-two.

In attitudinal surveys of the same populations, Labov discovered that Italians downgrade raised (eh) more than Jews when presented with matched guise recordings changing only that variable. Similarly, Jewish respondents exhibit greater raising of the (oh) variable (the lower mid-back rounded vowel, 'open o') than Italians and display greater negative reactions to raised versions of it in matched guise presentations (1966:293). In a more general

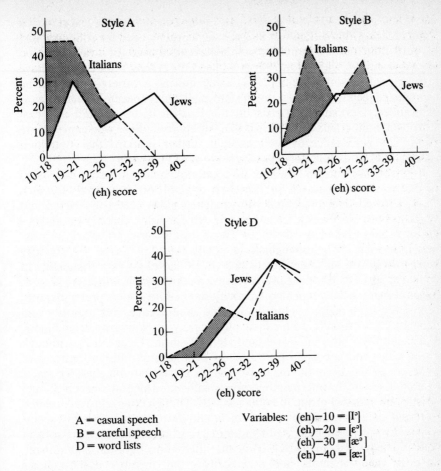

A = casual speech
B = careful speech
D = word lists

Variables:  (eh)—10 = [Iə]
(eh)—20 = [εə]
(eh)—30 = [æə]
(eh)—40 = [æ:]

*Figure 2.3*  New York City (eh) in Jewish and Italian groups (source: Labov 1966: 203–4)

measure of linguistic insecurity, Italians expressed the greatest overt insecurity and Blacks the least, though Jews showed a slightly greater tendency to believe that non New Yorkers disliked New York City speech (351), and Blacks felt that non New Yorkers did not downgrade local speech at all (352).

Quantitative sociolinguistic research which has focused on ethnic groups shows that such identity plays a lasting role in accounting for speech variety. Where immigrant communities are replenished by new arrivals and the stigma against ethnic varieties is not debilitating, subtle differences among groups may persist. Where such differences appear to be nonnative, teachers should not insist on putative NS patterns which contradict the solidary effects of ethnic speech. On the other hand, when such patterns cause social stigmatization, it is difficult to balance the learner's need for solidarity and identity in the new environment with the eventual need for a well-regarded language variety. Male Puerto Rican adolescents in New York City who have greater contact with Blacks (2.1.2) are acquiring a variety which will be stigmatized locally, but that is not the fate of all ethnic speech. In such cities as Milwaukee, Germanisms persist in the English of even south and east European immigrants who learned that variety from those who came before them. The persistence of such varieties further supports the contention (2.1.3) that successful bilinguals may serve as SLA models.

In-group and out-group responses to ethnolinguistic varieties have been the focus of numerous studies. Lambert et al. (1960), the model for such work, showed that, presented with matched guise voices in French and English, both NS French Canadian and NS English Canadian raters gave higher ratings to the English voices. Those results were particularly surprising since even the ethnolinguistic minority raters preferred the majority voices, and even on some dimensions which had to do with friendship. In many replications of this study, involving a considerable variety of groups, the pattern is partially repeated. Minority and majority raters prefer majority voices for leadership, responsibility, and competence, but minority and majority raters usually prefer their own variety for solidarity, friendliness, and likeability (Giles, and Powesland 1975, Ryan and Giles 1982). Although Ryan, Giles and Sebastian (1982) show how several different patterns of preferences may exist, the majority group is always rated highest for status characteristics by its own members and usually rated highest for such characteristics by minority group members as well. Though not exclusively related to ethnic identity, a pattern of *convergent* and *divergent* speech habits seems to explain both performance and attitudinal responses. There are two sorts of convergence. First, in formal contexts, interaction between a dominant, majority group member and a minority group member usually shows convergence towards the majority variety or language. Second, in some cases when assimilation with a minority group is desired, convergence in that direction may occur (Wolfram 1973). In contrast, divergence occurs in interactions in which members of one group wish to distinguish themselves from another (Giles, Bourhis, and Taylor 1977). Recent claims that Black and White vernaculars in urban northern American cities are diverging relates linguistic evidence to this social psychological claim (*American Speech* 1987). Beebe (1985) reviews a large number of alternative dialect and SLA situations and shows that a complex set of both social and situational factors on the one hand and feelings and motivations on the other help determine the learner's choice of target model (table 3.1).

Studies of ethnic attitudinal changes in SLA have not been conclusive. Lambert and Tucker (1972), found that very young (ages 6 and 7) English-speaking Canadians improved their attitudes towards French-speaking people after a French immersion program, but it was also determined that these changes were not maintained in later years. Other studies, including those of older students, have found conflicting or even negative results in attitude changes towards ethnic groups as a result of language study (Reynolds, Flagg, and Kennedy 1974, Halpern et al. 1976).

Giles (1979) has characterized interethnic contacts as *language choice*, *accommodation*, or *assimilation* situations. Figure 2.4 shows the possibilities. In a language choice situation, what is to be determined is which language is chosen from the shared repertoires of the groups. In accommodation situations (additive bilingualism), a dominated group (here B) learns the language of the dominant group (A), but preserves its own language for (some) intraethnic contact. Finally, in assimilation situations (subtractive bilingualism), the minority group loses its language. Though the focus of such research has been on naturalistic settings, understandings gained here may

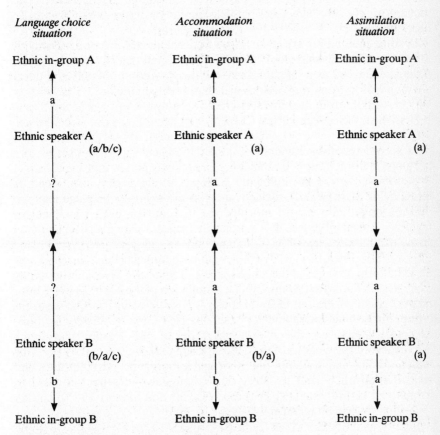

*Figure 2.4*  Language use in interethnic contact situations (source: Giles 1979: 255)

have wider implications for educational practices in formal settings. This discussion of ethnicity converges in many places with the immediately preceding discussion of nativeness, but the focus there was on degree; here the emphasis is on identity.

What sociolinguistic findings emerge from the three interethnic communication situations characterized above? Pidgin communication systems, which may result from early interethnic contact, could exist only in language choice situations, but fully developed creole languages could be one of the B codes in any of the situations shown in figure 2.4. Language choice situations are not limited, however, to pidgins. In some areas the matter of language choice is filled with symbolic potential. In Kenya, a multiethnic society, there are two lingua francas – Swahili and English. Scotton (1976) notes that when, for example, a Luo communicates with a Kikuyu, the choice of Swahili would symbolize the speaker's Africanness and traditionalism while the choice of English would reflect education and authority. This metaphoric choice of languages parallels the choice of varieties of Norwegian described in 1.1.

In some multiethnic areas the lingua franca itself may take on a distinctly local character. In Singapore, where Malay, Tamil, and Chinese speakers often use English as a lingua franca, the incorporation of loans and usage characteristics from those languages has created *Singlish*. This sort of variety, distinct from the pidgin-to-creole development (whether rapid as in Hawaii or slow as in Papua New Guinea), has been called a *creoloid* (Trudgill 1983).

In accommodation situations, a dominated language group uses its own language in intraethnic communication, and it may persist in using a distinctive ethnic accent in the dominant language, a fact already mentioned. A minority or SLA group's distinctiveness in the majority language may not depend on ethnic accent, morphology, lexicon, or even paralinguistic features. The maintenance of a more formal, distant style may be a common signal of a minority use of the dominant code (Segalowitz 1976, Brown and Fraser 1979, Preston 1981b). The common complaint that learners know only the formal ranges of the language (e.g., Troike 1971) must be carefully evaluated. A bookish style may not be a limitation of the learner's range but a natural result of the tendency to make a stylistic distinction between in-group, intraethnic communication and out-group, interethnic communication. An attack on the overformal style of the learner may be a disenfranchisement of one of the natural, distinguishing characteristics of the varieties being acquired. On the other hand, mutual negative attitudes and lack of motivation lead to intergroup communication's being limited to formal and institutionalized situations (Taylor and Simard 1975), and all such situations might qualify as *diglossic* (1.2.4).

Finally, assimilation, which leads to language loss (or even language death, e.g., Dorian 1980), is the most extreme form of pressure on new speech community members. In some areas the pressure has been institutionalized; as early as 1896 authorities in New Mexico 'in their enthusiasm for the English language have gone so far as to forbid the use of Spanish by the Spanish children during their play' (Espinosa 1917:411). The ups and downs of the bilingual education movement and the efforts to create national languages (and dispose of some) are related to patterns of interethnic communication and may be seen as desirable or undesirable in speech communities and political entities. Classic studies of multilingualism and language maintenance and shift include Fishman (1966), Fishman, Ferguson, and Das Gupta (1968), Fishman, et al. (1971), Haugen (1956), and Weinreich (1953). Such studies, however, focus on the sociology of language and its applications, concerns not fully treated in this book.

Although ethnic group membership is often a larger concern of national or region-wide educational and social planning, it is important at individual levels as well, and interactional factors of group membership which play a role in SLA are discussed in several sections in chapter 3.

## 2.1.5 Region

Dialectology, the grandparent of sociolinguistics (1.1), might seem to have little to do with SLA, but both the subject matter and its methodology are relevant.

From the largest perspective, dialectology divides; it shows where one variety stops and another begins, doing so by drawing *isoglosses*. Figure 2.5 shows the isogloss for the [gris] and [gri:z] pronunciations of the verb 'grease.' Though there is a small area of overlap, a rather sharp division of the eastern United States into north versus midland and south can be made on the basis of this boundary. It would not do, however, to determine the dialect areas of the United States with only a single variable. Dialectologists have, therefore, looked for *bundles* of isoglosses – the cooccurrence of a number of isoglosses in roughly the same territory. Figure 2.6 shows three isoglosses for the southernmost extent of three northern words. These three lexical isoglosses correspond to the pronunciation isogloss for 'grease,' suggesting that a boundary in this area is important in United States dialect geography.[25] Isoglosses may be based on phonetic, phonological, morphological, lexical, syntactic, and semantic information, though the first four levels have received much more attention.

The results of traditional dialectology have not been of great interest to SLA, though Allen (1973) correctly points out that many textbooks focus on achieving pronunciation contrasts which do not exist in the speech of literally millions of well-educated speakers.[26] In American English the contrast between /ɑ/ and /ɔ/ is no longer present for many speakers, particularly younger ones in the west of Canada and the United States. In spite of this, a book as sophisticated as Bowen (1975) presents the contrast (18) with no

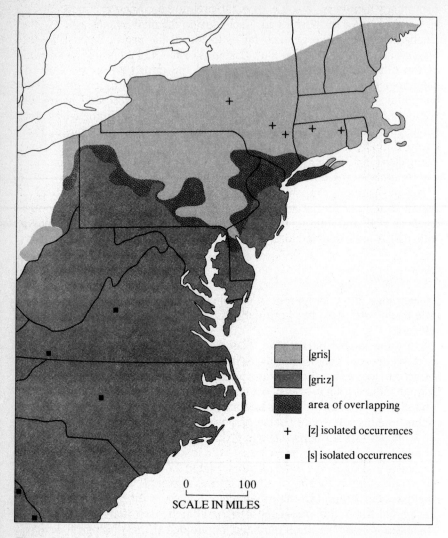

*Figure 2.5* [gris] vs [griːz] pronunciations of the verb 'grease' in the eastern United States (source: Atwood 1950)

comment on its regional limitations. Dialect realities should guide language teaching practices; teachers and materials preparation specialists in particular should know the distribution of current, standard forms so that they will not assume that their own educated usage is the unique model. Speakers naturally and unconsciously prefer educated forms from their own areas.

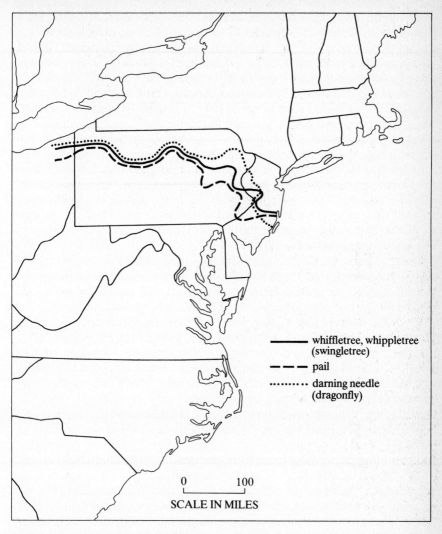

*Figure 2.6* Three isoglosses dividing the north from the north midland in the eastern United States (source: Kurath 1949: figure 5a)

When United States southerners first notice 'sick to my stomach,' their reaction is that the speaker is nonnative or uneducated. That form, however, is not at all stigmatized in its own territory. The usual southern form, 'sick at my stomach,' is also used by the best-educated speakers, though northerners might find it quaint, uneducated, even nonnative. In everyday conversation even linguists are not concerned with form, and if a form is not caricatured or made fun of, it may last unnoticed in a speaker's repertoire. A linguist from northwestern Ohio was surprised to learn that such constructions as 'my clothes need washed' or 'my hair needs cut' were very restricted. He had always assumed (until age forty or so) that such constructions were usual in English. Although they are indeed a part of a regional standard English, they are not widely distributed, and many nonlocals would be surprised to learn that such constructions exist in any variety of English. As indicated earlier, language users do not normally attend to form; message getting and sending are their preoccupations. Only if form is highlighted through careful speech (monitoring), valued expression (e.g., poetry), unexpected qualities (e.g., drunken speech, muttering), or caricatured or noticeable variety difference (e.g., dialect, nonnativeness) will speakers attend to it. An awareness of standard regional varieties is important, then, so SLA is not made more difficult than necessary through forced attention to forms and distinctions which the learner does not need, particularly if educated native speakers may be taken as appropriate models.[27]

Dialects carry with them sets of attitudes. In considerable research on local versus RP varieties of English, Giles and his associates have found the general pattern of greater feelings of comfort and amiability expressed toward local speech but assessments of greater intelligence and industry are made of RP samples (2.1.4). Regions may evoke even more specific caricatures. In the United States, southern voices awaken stereotypes of racist, barefoot, poorly educated, Protestant, illegal whiskey drinking, skilled woodsmen, good ol' boys while urban northern voices strike some listeners as those of people who are fast-talking, unfriendly, Jewish or Catholic, time-conscious, impersonal, harried, and dishonest.

Additionally, nonlinguists may not be in agreement about the physical boundaries of regional varieties. I asked (Preston 1986c) respondents to outline regional speech areas on a blank map. Figure 2.7 is a map generalized from a number of drawings made by respondents from southern Indiana, and figure 2.8 is a similar map constructed from drawing by respondents from southeastern Michigan; the differences are striking. Such taxonomies of the location of regional voices are ethnographically interesting, and their correlation with attitudes towards regional speech (and the ability to identify voices with regions) could provide even greater detail about regionalism and language.

More attention than necessary has been paid to the question of which world variety a learner of English ought to learn. Area traditions, proximity, availability of native instructors, and so on ought to be sufficient guides, and, again, such questions are more carefully dealt with in considerations of the sociology of language in SLA. Admittedly, however, some silly proposals have been made, recommending for all learners such varieties as American, partly due to its simpler vowel system (Powell 1966).

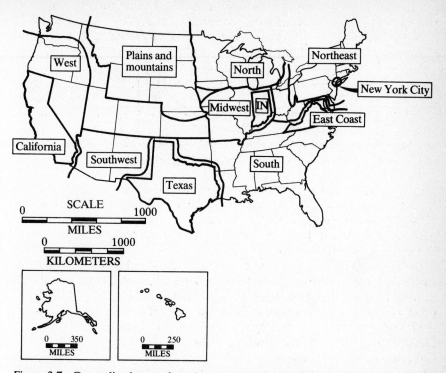

*Figure 2.7*   Generalized map of southern Indiana respondents' hand-drawn maps of the speech areas of the United States

Regionalism and ethnicity combine, however, in a more recent concern. Colonialism has resulted in large territories which depend on English, French, and Spanish for communication among groups of disparate ethno-linguistic varieties that found themselves in communication due to political union or contact among groups in a single area. Post colonial needs and the spread of English as an international language have fostered new varieties of English. This development was criticized by Prator (1968) in 'The British heresy in TESL.' Former British dominated colonial areas were developing their own nativized varieties; French-speaking colonies always had the model of Paris to live up to. Prator argued that NNS Englishes and their deterioration from one generation to the next would lead to a mass of mutually unintelligible varieties, appropriate only for local use.

Roughly 33 percent of the world's English speakers turn out to be NNSs, counting only schooled populations – actual numbers are much greater (Kachru 1982a:36). Whatever Prator feared has already happened, and NS teachers armed with stringent pedagogical devices for renativizing this recalcitrant mass will face an undoable job. Even if the purely linguistic task

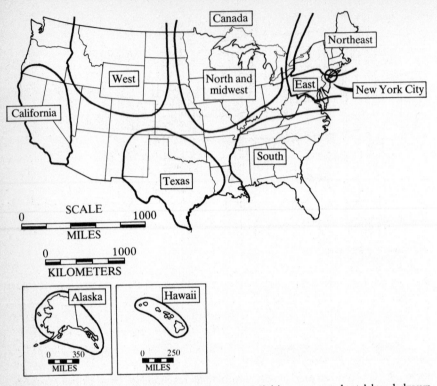

*Figure 2.8* Generalized map of southeastern Michigan respondents' hand-drawn maps of the speech areas of the United States

of making these Englishes conform to some native variety were imaginable, their developing value as ethnic varieties would make the task impossible. Kachru (1982b) provides a survey of linguistic and social factors in several of the world's NNS Englishes. Applied linguists will have to take these developing standards into consideration as they go about the task of preparing materials, training teachers, and carrying out instruction in second and foreign languages. Such new varieties are an interesting large-scale corroboration of the success of the competent bilingual as a SLA model.

Interesting parallels to SLA arise in dialect methodology and theory. A classic problem in dialectology has been that of system. When dialects differ, how can the systematic facts which relate one to another be displayed? Weinreich (1954) imagines a region in which the word 'man' is pronounced [man] in areas 1 and 2 and [mån] in areas 3 and 4. 1 and 2 should belong to one zone and areas 3 and 4 to another (figure 2.9a). Suppose, however, that in 1, vowel length is significant; therefore, [man] contrasts with [ma:n], and there are two phonemes – /a/ and /a:/. In 2, there is no such contrast of vowel

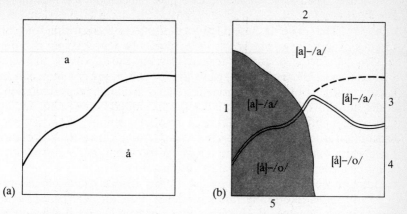

*Figure 2.9*  Dialect boundaries based on (a) phonetic and (b) structural (phonemic) contrasts (source: Weinreich 1954)

length, and the [a] of [man] is simply /a/. In 3 the [å] of [mån] is a positional variant of [a] (occurring only between [m] and [n]) and belongs to the phoneme /a/. Finally, in 4, the [å] is not a positional variant of /a/ but belongs to /o/. From a phonemic or structural point of view, 2 and 3 have the most in common. Although they show the different phonetic elements [a] and [å], those phones are instantiations of the same structurally contrastive element – /a/. Though one is tempted to classify 1 along with them, that cannot be done since /a/ contrasts with /a:/ there. In a map based on structural distribution rather than phonetic form (figure 2.9b) Weinreich imagines a fifth area in which [å] is a positional variant of /o/ and in which /o/, unlike /o/ in 4, contrasts with /o:/. One major dialect boundary separates 1 and 5 (shaded) from the others since they phonemically differentiate between long and short vowels. Another major boundary, however, separates 1, 2, and 3 where [a] and [å] belong to the phoneme /a/ (whether or not it contrasts with /a:/) from 4 and 5 where [å] is a variant of /o/ (whether or not it contrasts with /o:/). Finally, the fact that /a/ has a variant [å] between [m] and [n] cannot be as important as the boundaries which separate the phonemic differences shown between the two shaded areas (vowel length) or between the two large areas separated by a double line (vowel quality).

The *diasystems* which are used to represent such facts show how the phonemic inventories of dialects are related. For example, the following diasystematic rule shows how the five areas above might be represented:

$$
\big/\big/ \quad \frac{\begin{array}{cc} 1 & \text{/a: } \sim \text{a/} \\ \hline 2,3 & \text{a} \\ \hline 4 & \text{o} \\ \hline 5 & \text{/o: } \sim \text{o/} \end{array}} \quad \sim \quad e \quad \sim \quad i \quad \big/\big/
$$

The double slashes and tildes indicate phonemic contrasts. It is imagined here that the complex of /a/ and /o/ variation discussed above contrasts with /e/ and /i/. The single slashes and tildes indicate contrasts within some of the varieties of the diasystem. In this case, phonemic vowel length is differentiated in 1 and 5 for /a/ and /o/ respectively, and the /a/ vowels characterize 1, 2 and 3 (regardless of length) while the /o/ vowels are common in 4 and 5 (again, regardless of length). Phonetic detail is lost in this representation, for it does not show that the /a/ in 3 has the variant [å] between [m] and [n] or that /o/ in 4 and 5 is realized (at least in some positions) as [å]. Worse, this distribution is based only on the form /man/ (/mon/). Investigation of further lexical items in these related varieties might show that /a/ contrasts with /o/, requiring a complete restatement of the diasystem.

Although deeper relationships are shown in diasystems, their greater generality hides interesting phonetic detail. Phonological processes have proved more capable of characterizing synchronic and diachronic facts about dialects and their relations to one another. Most varieties of English have a rule which lengthens vowels before voiced consonants. The word 'mad,' therefore, is phonetically [mæ:d], but the word 'mat' is [mæt]. Some varieties of English have a flapping rule which changes intervocalic [t] and [d] to [ɾ]. Therefore, for many speakers, [mætɹ] ('matter') becomes [mæɾɹ]. Is its vowel to be long or short? Since the alveolar flap is voiced, the [æ] of 'matter' ought to be [æ:]. In American English, however, it occurs as both [mæ:ɾɹ] and [mæɾɹ]. Either the vowel lengthening rule is wrong, or some other principle is at work. If one is not committed to a static, phonemic inventory, the answer may lie in the ordering of such processes as vowel lengthening and flapping in different varieties:

| Variety A | | Variety B | |
|-----------|----------|-----------|----------|
| /mætɹ/ | | /mætɹ/ | |
| Lengthening | [mætɹ] | Flapping | [mæɾɹ] |
| Flapping | [mæɾɹ] | Lengthening | [mæ:ɾɹ] |

In A the vowel lengthening rule applied before the flapping rule and could not work since the appropriate voiced consonant did not follow the vowel. In B, the flapping rule preceded the vowel lengthening rule and provided the proper environment. If 'madder' were the input to either variety, the output would be [mæɾɹ] in both since the input form – /mædɹ/ – would have a voiced consonant for A to work on; B would still lengthen [æ] on the basis of the following voiced flap. Will these rules work for some varieties of English English, where the output is [matʰə]? At first it would seem that an entirely different inventory of sounds would be required for the input, but adding and subtracting phonological processes will do as well:

Variety C (English)
/mætɾ/

| | |
|---|---|
| r-loss | [matə] |
| Aspiration | [matʰə] |
| Vowel lengthening | does not apply |

First, an r-loss rule, lacking in many varieties of American English, applies. Second, a rule which aspirates voiceless consonants in syllable initial positions applies. That rule works in American English as well in such items as 'pat' [pʰæt] and 'depose' [dIpʰoːz], but it is ordered *after* flapping and cannot apply since the flap is voiced. Third, the flapping rule does not exist in most varieties of English English (exactly as the r-loss rule does not exist in many of American English).

A nonphonemic account allows portraying apparently disparate varieties of a language as similar at some deeper or underlying level and deriving superficially different forms by means of different or differently ordered phonological processes. Such processes seem well-motivated by universal laws of phonetic economy, though social pressures might instigate a process or even series of processes which would go against natural tendencies. These explanations have led to the heady assumption that *all* varieties of a language might eventually be derived from one set of underlying forms – a *panlectal* grammar (Bailey 1972). Whether that ambitious goal is realizable or not, many of the difficulties with Weinreich's structural account are solved in this approach. Varieties which share underlying forms may be only distantly related; those which share processes (flapping, r-loss) are more closely related; those which share most processes and most orderings are closest. A diasystem is not a static statement of the relationship of various phonemic contrasts (with added internal allophonic niceties). It is a complex of processes and orderings distributed over varieties which share a large number (not necessarily all) of underlying forms.[28]

Unfortunately, sociolinguists find difficulty even with this neat solution. Figure 2.5 displays the distribution of the [z] and [s] pronunciations of the verb 'grease' in the eastern United States. Though the area where both forms occur is small, it exists. What rules characterize individual performances in such a transitional area? Does each individual there use only one form or both? If the latter, in what proportion? Figure 2.10, a map of the variable (u) in the east of England (the pronunciation of the stressed vowel in items such as 'brother' and 'us' as [ʊ] or [ʌ]), shows that the area between 100 percent occurrences of [ʊ] (to the north) and 0 percent (to the south) contains a considerable number of individuals whose performance varies, ranging, in fact, from 2 percent use of [ʊ] all the way to 97 percent. Transition areas, then, may be made up of individuals who use both forms.

Applying alternative accounts of variable linguistic data from chapter 1 to this situation would provide either a variable rule format, if the focus were on

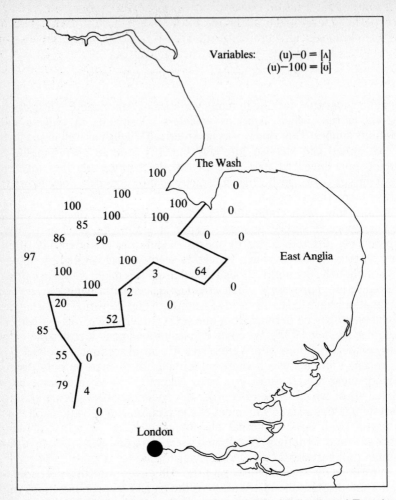

*Figure 2.10* Distribution of the variable (u) in the East Midlands and East Anglia (source: Chambers and Trudgill 1980: 130)

the synchronic psycholinguistic status of the rule and the linguistic and social environments which promoted and demoted the occurrences of forms, or an implicational array, if the focus were on the position of individuals in a network of linguistic change.[29] Neither account would solve the dialecto-logist's problem of how to draw an isogloss or mapped representation of the facts. Chambers and Trudgill suggest that the transition area may be marked by two different sorts of speakers, some involved in a form of *hyperadapta-tion*. A more careful look at the individuals represented in figure 2.10 shows that some of the transition area speakers mix northern and southern forms, an expected finding, but it is also the case that some mix either a northern or a southern form with an intermediate phone – [ɤ] – a central, unrounded vowel like [ʌ], but higher, closer to [u]. Varieties which mix the two regional forms are called *mixed*; ones which mix a regional and intermediate one are called *fudged*. Figure 2.11 shows the distribution of individuals in just these terms, and there is clearly a geographical pattern to the varieties within the transition zone. Fudged southern varieties predominate in the area just south

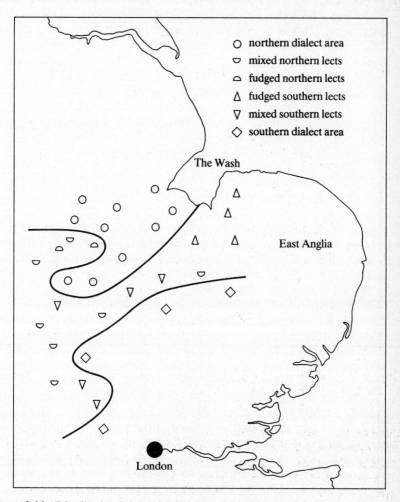

*Figure 2.11* Distribution of northern, southern, mixed, and fudged lects for the variable (u) in the East Midlands and East Anglia (source: Chambers and Trudgill 1980: 136)

of the Wash, and fudged northern varieties occur in the far northwest of the area studied. Mixed northern and southern varieties occur elsewhere in the transition area, though mixed northern lects seem to predominate in the west except for the southernmost part of the entire transition area. The immediate benefit to dialectology of such sophistication is a better representation of the status of forms for individual speakers in a transition zone.

More importantly, especially for the purposes of this book, is the fact that this approach to regional distribution offers a more satisfactory account of the processes of language change. The /ʌ/ forms (southern) are standard (RP) and are advancing. The line just below 100 percent /ʊ/ use is, to use Chambers and Trudgill's terminology, a *beach head*, and they order the pure, mixed, and fudged lects on a continuous north to south scale as follows (1980:135):

| Index | Type | Phonemic structure | Phonetics |
|---|---|---|---|
| 100 | Pure | /ʊ/ | [ʊ] |
| | Mixed | /ʊ/ | [ʊ, ʌ] |
| | Fudged | /ʊ/ | [ʊ, ɤ] |
| 50 | — — — — — — — — — — — — — — — — |  |  |
| | Fudged | /ʌ/ | [ʌ, ɤ] |
| | Mixed | /ʌ/ | [ʌ, ʊ] |
| 0 | Pure | /ʌ/ | [ʌ] |

This is odd since the fudged form is phonetically closer to the pure form in both cases. Moreover, in a discussion of a *scrambled* lect (where both mixed and fudged forms cooccur), Chambers and Trudgill provide an intuitively more satisfying order of existing forms (from one end of the scale only) – pure, fudged, scrambled, mixed (1980:141).

With this reinterpretation of the order, an imaginary history of the RP invasion of /ʊ/ can be written. The initial contact with a new form results in its use if it exists in the native variety (mixed) or in an attempt to use a form like it if it does not (fudged). In order of acquisition, then, one would expect [ɤ], not [ʌ] to occur in the earliest contact since the north did not have an [ʌ], even as an allophone of another phoneme (Wells 1982:351–3). That is, fudging should precede mixing. In the later history of the contact, the acquirers of the new form should begin to mix rather than fudge, and, later, change categorically. How does this scenario coincide with the facts? From it, one would expect fudged northern lects at the beach head, mixed northern lects a little farther south in the transition zone and, farthest south, mixed southern lects. In fact, the only two occurrences of fudged northern lects are at the northwestern extremity of the transition zone, and the mixed southern lects, especially those in the southwest, are farthest from the beach head, though they are interspersed with mixed northern lects here and there. So far, so good, but this interpretation excludes fudged southern lects, and SLA researchers will already have seen the danger of the above procedure. It was a simple exercise in dialect contrastive analysis – a prediction of which forms would occur and how they would be distributed on the basis of a comparison of systems. The tradition of *error analysis* or the study of interlanguage phonology in SLA has shown that predictions of learner errors do not always follow directly from a contrastive study of the two linguistic systems involved, and the account above is embarrassed by the existence of fudged southern lects.[30]

An approach to dialect forms which resembles those taken to phonological systems in a developing interlanguage is lacking because so much dialect study has taken place within a static framework. That is particularly ironic since dialectology had its origins in historical linguistics, but even the study of the history of a language may be made static if each stage is considered a categorical system. Trudgill (1983), however, discusses a number of statistical models, some borrowed from cultural geography, which focus on change.

A recent attempt to incorporate SLA understandings into dialect research (Trudgill 1986) regards the appearance of certain forms (e.g., fudged lects) as instances of *interdialect* – after *interlanguage*, the term introduced by Selinker (1972) to cover a wide range of phenomena which occur in the process of SLA. Trudgill notes that dialect contact may lead to intermediate forms (e.g., the [ɜ] of the Norfolk area) but that there are other possibilities as well. Forms may be *reallocated* to another part of the system. In Oslo Norwegian some such words as 'brøyt' (broke) contain a diphthong which has no historical precedent and seems to compromise between the upper class urban monophthong /øː/ and rural /æu/. This is reallocation rather than fudging since Oslo speech already has a phoneme /øy/ in such words as /gøy/ (fun) (62–3). Other interdialectal forms arise in dialect contact, in particular, *hyperadaptation*, a result of the learner's faulty category assignment. (In geographical linguistics, hyperadaptations might be called *hyperdialectisms*.) In the northern advance of RP, speakers in areas where /ʌ/ forms are not yet under control may assign words to the wrong phoneme class, e.g., /bʌʧr/ ('butcher') (Trudgill 1986:66). In such cases, hyperdialectisms are cases of *hypercorrection* (2.2.3) since the unprecedented form is an attempt to accommodate towards the encroaching standard. *Hypocorrection* (2.2.3), or resistance to the standard, is also possible. In East Anglia an older phonemic distinction between /eː/ ('name') and /æi/ ('nail') still has repercussions. The RP forms (/æi/) have rather thoroughly replaced the older /eː/ forms, though Trudgill (1974) reported that in Norwich in 1968, for example, even young speakers who consistently used only the RP phoneme were able to assign words to the correct phoneme on the basis of the older split. Now, however, young working class males, leading a sort of local pride rebellion against the encroaching RP forms (presumably another example of covert prestige), use the older /eː/ in items where it did not originally occur, e.g., /neːl/ (Trudgill 1986:67–8).

Dialect contact, therefore, does not always result in the eventual loss of an older form in the face of an encroaching one. Interdialectal forms may stabilize, and if enough such forms succeed in one area, a new dialect or a relatively stable dialect continuum (e.g., a creole continuum – 1.2.2) may arise. The concentration of fudged lects in the Norfolk area (right hand side of figure 2.11) makes one suspect that an intermediate form may be well on its way to stabilizing there, though, of course, one successful form might not result in a new system.

That dialectology is now concerned with such dynamic matters should make it more relevant to SLA. The acquisition problem in dialect change, whether rapid through personal dislocation or slow through areal spread, is of greater potential relevance to SLA researchers than the problem of static distribution of forms. A number of terms other than interlanguage itself might, in fact, be applied to dialect contact phenomena. *Fossilization,* the arresting of progress, is like the creation of a new variety. *Backsliding*, the use of older forms after evidence that a new rule has already been learned, is like some hyper- and hypocorrections, though their source is more clearly in the general psycholinguistic area of *overgeneralization*.

Such low-level psycholinguistic accounts of processes, however, do not explain why interdialectal forms should have a greater chance of stabilizing in one area than another. Trudgill (1986) offers two explanations, one – accommodation – already familiar. Accommodation, it should be recalled, must be finely tuned to its reception. Total accommodation may arouse suspicion in the NS community if, for some reason, the acquirers are not expected to use the native forms. Total accommodation from the point of view of the NNS may result in anomie, low self-concept, or loss of identity. Those factors may be complicated, of course, by the reception of new forms in the old community; the earliest learners of the new form may be seen as people 'putting on airs' if the change is in the direction of an external standard or prestige variety. From these interpersonal perspectives, then, one might expect subtle accommodation in some cases – namely, the invention and possible retention of interdialectal forms.

Trudgill generalizes further, however, about the larger social context within which such unprecedented forms may arise and persist. Le Page and Tabouret-Keller (1985), concerned particularly with creole-speaking areas, characterize speech communities as *diffuse* or *focused*. The latter is one in which the speakers regard their language norms as unique, not connected to any other variety. In accommodation terms, such speech community members would 'perceive their ingroup's ethnolinguistic vitality as high' (2.1.3). A diffuse speech community does not feel it controls a unique linguistic variety; it regards its language facility as a part, and usually a negatively regarded part, of some other bona fide system. Such diffuse systems may, however, become focused through the so-called covert prestige (2.1.2) which sometimes attaches itself to prejudiced-against varieties or usage.

Such complicating personal and social factors help explain why non-standard and regional varieties are not simply devoured by an advancing standard (and, by extension, why some interlanguages are not replaced by L2 forms). A local compact front against the attacking variety and/or social psychological fears of acquiring it may prevent acquisition, or, more likely, conspire to subtly alter an existing variety. Such understandings help explain unexpected elements (perhaps even fudged southern lects around Norfolk!) or entire varieties in the path of linguistic change; however, in drawing parallels with SLA, one must be careful to consider the total range of dynamics involved in a learner's selection of a target model (Beebe 1985, figure 3.1).

More specifically, the learner's interlanguage as a system of rules (variable or not) has been characterized as significantly different from all other language systems due to its *permeability* (Adjemian 1976). That is, it is easily influenced by its speakers' L1 forms (*transfer*) and by the overgeneralization and incorporation of L2 forms. In terms developed in this book, principally social rather than psychological, an interlanguage is permeable precisely because its speech community is diffuse. The great majority of learners do not belong to groups who feel that their interlanguage variety is a distinct, autonomous communication medium. It follows, then, that such a variety is open to alteration. On the other hand, developing nonnative varieties such as Indian and West African Englishes, though their source is partly in interlanguage forms, have developed such a history of use that the communities which support them have become focused. From the study of dialects and varieties in contact, it would appear that the uniqueness of interlanguage's permeability is a fiction. Other varieties (nonstandard and local dialects, creoles, and so on) may also exhibit lesser or greater degrees of permeability related, at least in part, to the degree of compactness or diffusion of the speech community. It should be as reasonable to speak of greater or lesser permeability of varieties (including interlanguages) as it is to speak of greater or lesser degrees of diffusion and compactness. From this point of view, fossilization may be negative (an individual's reaction to the danger of loss of identity) or positive (a community's emerging compactness).

There have been few studies of regional variety intelligibility in SLA, though a number of studies of the intelligibility of NNS versus NS varieties (2.1.3) and of social varieties have been conducted (2.2.3). Strother and Alford (1987) have shown that there is no correlation between NNSs' pronunciation ability and their ability to recognize regional varieties of American English.

If the learning of a nearby dialect is at the close end and the learning of an (unrelated) language at the far end of a language and variety acquisition scale, then linguistic, social, and social psychological issues previously associated uniquely with dialect study on the one hand and SLA research on the other may find a common ground.

## 2.2 Acquired

Although ascribed characteristics constitute the more or less static identity of an individual in social settings, acquired characteristics make up his or her dynamic interaction with society itself. Though prejudice, often against ascribed features, may prevent individuals from acquiring some characteristics, the following identifying factors are those which generally come to members of communities as a result of experience and are not attributed to them on the basis of identity alone.

### 2.2.1 *Role*

The roles an individual plays as a member of a community reach from short-term interpersonal interaction (buyer and seller) to long-term functions often fulfilled by specific members of the group (priest–parishioner, parent–child). Even in the latter, however, members of the society in general understand, at least in part, the expected behavior for many roles they do not typically play themselves. In societies where gender partly determines the function of parents, a father, for example, might say 'I'll have to be mother while your mom is in the hospital.' In a society where only certain religious authorities are empowered to hear confessions, a close friend might nevertheless suggest that he or she could act as a confessor.

Roles are sometimes understood as the more-or-less permanent characteristics of ascribed identity and sometimes as conversationally determined speech act types, e.g., request, demand, offer, promise, state. Here role is taken to mean what has been labeled *actional* role (Littlewood 1975:202) – such situationally determined social behavioral complexes as buyer, seller, patient, learner, offerer, and so on. These are both qualitatively and quantitatively distinct from other more lasting acquired roles such as specialization. Salespersons, for example, would be expected to play the role of sellers more often than others and would be expected to have a wider and subtler range of behaviors when involved in selling. Some actional roles are not, however, so easily separated from so-called speech act functions of language (1.2.5). If I want to appear to have promised something sincerely, that is, be an effective 'promiser,' I will certainly need to know the speech act rules for promising and have a suitable repertoire of appropriate linguistic acts. For convenience, such short-term behavioral complexes might be called *speech act roles*. Many such linguistically specified roles are the focus of work in notional-functional syllabuses (e.g., Wilkins 1976), and language teaching practices based on such syllabuses usually make specific use of role-playing (Wilkins 1976:80–1). Other actional roles (e.g., 'customer'), however, cannot be so easily related to speech act notions. In fact, such behavioral complexes imply the knowledge of a number of alternative moves (or speech acts) in a given speech situation, but they are not necessarily as specified as those one finds in a typical situational language learning syllabus. The customer, 'a buyer of goods and services,' for example, is an essential role in shops, supermarkets, restaurants, travel agencies, and a host of other environments, but to focus on one highly situationally specified setting ignores the common role element all share. On the other hand, even if one takes a liberal view of speech acts, regarding them as lists of language functions, much actional role behavior still requires more specification. For example, a customer might easily need to employ all the following language functions in a given interaction – 'asking,' 'identifying,' 'expressing whether something is considered possible or impossible,' and ' inquiring how certain others are of something' (Van Ek 1976:37). Such functions, then (borrowed here from a notional-functional syllabus,) are only the item-by-item content of a role and do not predict how and when to play it. The scripts and routines found in discourse analysis are more likely to fill out the linguistic behavior expected in an actional role. If one is a seller or buyer, what turns can be expected, what language functions are likely to occur at a certain point in the interaction, how may such interactions be opened, closed, cut short, and so on? The study of such larger conversational frameworks, closer to the concept of actional role, has not been extensive in SLA in either teaching or research. Studies of NNS conversation have usually focused on the type of communicative act employed (request, command, clarification, etc.) and the situation in which it was used (most often a classroom setting) rather than on the role being played by the speaker (e.g., Day 1986). Of course, classroom interaction studies have observed the usage of 'teachers' and 'learners,' but more often globally rather than in those role specific terms (e.g., Seliger and Long 1983).

From a more formal point of view, sociolinguistic research has made extensive use of the concept of role (Preston 1987). Fishman and Greenfield (1970) – and much subsequent work by Fishman – make use of the concept *domain*, one component of which is clearly role (1.2.4). Fishman notes that 'each domain can be differentiated into role-relations that are specifically crucial or typical of it' (1972b:251). Since roles are part of the necessary defining characteristics of domains, one wonders why the latter, global term has been used in place of the more accurate components of the congruent elements that Fishman has sought among places (3.1.2), roles, and topics (3.2.2) and that he might have sought among a much larger number of interactional categories (summarized in chapter 3). Some SLA researchers have tried to account for interlanguage variability on the basis of *discourse domains*. Selinker and Douglas (1985) suggest that such domains are related to important activities in a person's general experience, and, more importantly, that the interlanguage in each domain may support unique (or a unique set) of rules. They cite the example of a Polish linguist whose interlanguage varies when he is 'being an international professor who lectures in English' or 'telling stories about Poland in English after drinking several vodkas.' Unfortunately, while such overly-specified fields of subject activity may, indeed, yield a great deal of variable linguistic data, it is difficult to generalize from such observations (or generalizations may be inaccurate). While *domain* in Fishman's research may be treated as a handy operational cover term for the interaction of place, topic, and participant identity or role, the discourse domains of the Polish linguist are rather more complex. Which variables in the activity (vodka, topic, unmentioned interlocutors) contribute to specific linguistic variables, and how may they be generalized for replication? There is no doubt that speakers have performances rather carefully laid out for specific environments, but the bulk of previous research in quantitative sociolinguistics has shown that such lower-level variables as topic, interlocutor identity, and so on are both better predictors of variation and more generalizable to a variety of users and situations.

Quantitative studies of role have shown specific tendencies to use more or less of a variable. In a series of studies of Black street gangs, Labov (1972b) identifies lames as marginal members of the street culture, youths who may be associated with specific groups but who do not fully participate in the activities and beliefs as do the core members. Table 2.7 shows the differences in the frequency of the use of unmarked third person indicative singulars of selected verb forms by lame and core members of several gangs. With the exception of *say* (where nonstandard use by both groups is nearly categorical), the lames always use a higher percentage of standard forms. Of course, one learns that lames are lames by investigating their position in a *network* of individuals (3.3.2), but nowhere in this work is there a pretense that any category would not benefit from cross-classification with numerous others.

*Table 2.7* Percentage of lame and core gang member use of standard third person indicative markers on selected verb forms

| Verb forms | Percentage use | |
| --- | --- | --- |
| | Lames | Core members |
| has | 60 | 19 |
| doesn't | 36 | 03 |
| was | 83 | 14 |
| does | 13 | 00 |
| says | 04 | 00 |

*Source*: Adapted from Labov 1972b:273

SLA research has not used role in accounting for interlanguage variability in quantitative studies of traditionally short-range factors – phonology, morphology, and so on. SLA use of *task*, however, comes very close to role in some interactional settings, and a number of larger discourse concerns have been studied in terms of the task a learner has been assigned. Duff (1986), for example, reports on discourse performances by Chinese and Japanese learners of English when they are assigned *problem-solving* (PS) and *debate* (D) tasks. Though the latter task might be better classified as a *genre* (3.2.3), the two could be thought of as generating the roles *problem-solver* and *debater*. The following general findings emerged from the study:

1  The number of words did not differ according to task.
2  The number of turns was greater for PS.
3  The number of words per turn was greater for D.
4  There are a larger number of communication units in PS.
5  There are more words per communication unit in D.
6  There is greater syntactic complexity in D.

Such findings show that task (role) has a clear effect on the performance of discourse structure, and one might expect similar results if NSs were assigned the same tasks. Further studies of the contribution of specific roles to inter-language variability and/or degree of correctness which isolate other linguistic factors might prove interesting. The roles imposed (or strongly suggested) by specialization are the subject of the next section.

### 2.2.2 Specialization

There is perhaps no other sociolinguistic area in which more of the basic descriptive research has been carried out by SLA and language teaching specialists. The need to tailor language teaching to professional needs has led to such research leadership. Although it would be unfair to suggest that general sociolinguists have not looked at the language performances of specialized groups, general linguistics, at least traditionally, paid little attention to this sort of variation: 'different kinds of craftsmen, merchants, engineers, lawyers, physicians, scientists, artists, and so on, differ somewhat in speech' (Bloomfield 1933:49). It is almost certainly the case that the productive investigation of specialized or professional language (above the level of vocabulary) awaited the introduction of techniques for the study of discourse – elements larger than the sentence.

Early SLA studies looked at the frequency of grammatical and lexical categories in NS specialized varieties. Chiu (1972:136–7) shows that in administrative correspondence the frequency of certain verb forms is rather different from that in popular magazines:

| Rank | Administrative correspondence | Popular magazines |
|------|------------------------------|-------------------|
| 1 | make | go |
| 2 | attach | ask |
| 3 | enclose | say |
| 4 | receive | come |
| 5 | require | make |
| 6 | appreciate | know |
| 7 | provide | get |
| 8 | refer | see |
| 9 | forward | take |
| 10 | find | like |
| 11 | request | think |
| 12 | advise | look |
| 13 | send | want |
| 14 | take | give |
| 15 | give | find |

In grammatical rather than lexical territory, White (1974:406) shows that the frequency of verb types is different for general prose and scientific laboratory reports:

| | Percentage | |
|-----------|--------------|-------------------|
| Verb type | General prose | Laboratory report |
| Simple | 58 | 25 |
| Complex | 10 | 2 |
| Catenative | 7 | 12 |
| Passive | 25 | 63 |

Though both these studies go on to make recommendations concerning the use of such information in second language classrooms, both reveal ordinary sociolinguistic information concerning the distribution of lexical and grammatical features in specialized language use. Most importantly, such early research efforts show dramatically the need for empirical, descriptive research in establishing actual rather than imagined frequencies in language use, though that need is surely not restricted to specialist course and materials design.

Since such a descriptive research tradition has been productive in language teaching (leading, for example, to the special interest area of *LSP*), there is no need here or in what follows to cite separate sociolinguistic work which is unrelated to SLA.

Discourse perspectives on specialist language, as suggested above, have been the focus of attention in more recent work. Candlin, Leather, and

Bruton (1976) report on a study of the conversational routines carried out by doctors in emergency rooms and develop a rationale for integrating this specialist language use into a course for NNS doctors. The sorts of categories which they established for the study of the specialist activity they observed may be exemplified by the following selection:

1   *Greet*
    *D*: 'Hullo.'
    *D*: 'Good morning.'
    *D*: 'Mrs. Jones?'
2   *Elicit* (to get broad description of accident with some circum-
    stantial detail):
    *D*: 'Can you tell me what happened?'
3   *Interrogate* (to probe circumstances of trauma relevant to diag-
    nosis):
    *D*: 'Do you remember if your whole weight was on the foot?'
    *D*: 'Did you bend right back when you fell?'
4   *Question* (to get information during examination):
    *D*: 'Does this hurt?'
    *D*: 'Can you bend it?'
5   *Make sure* (to make sure that what *D* understands is what *P*
    meant):
    *D*: 'Does it hurt here?'
    *P*: 'No, not really.'
    *D*: 'It doesn't hurt?'
    *P*: 'No.'
(Candlin, Leather, and Bruton 1976: 269–71)

Though it might be possible to criticize these categories as ad hoc, the ethno-grapher or ethnomethodologist would respond that that is just the point of such research – the linguistically important categories in discourse emerge as the discourse is studied and are based, presumably, on the structure created by the participants in such interaction. On the other hand, surely routines, scripts, conventions, chains, and so on of discourse will not have to be discovered anew in every effort. If structure exists in connected talk, some of the exchanges represented here might belong to the parts of a more general analysis. That criticism, however, does not limit at all the usefulness of the categories derived here for applied linguistics purposes; nevertheless, in a general study of specialist language, the general patterns and functions of talk ought to be distinguished from the specific.

Using the categories derived above and performing analyses of a number of interactions, Candlin, Leather, and Bruton are able to derive general principles and make recommendations for instruction:

1   *Cycles*   The doctor's task 'cycles' at work are highly predictable; we suggest that some learning procedures could be modeled on these cycles – thus maintaining a convincing degree of pedagogical and psychological 'contextuality'.

2   *Chains*   Alongside and determined by the sequence of work cycles which characterize a doctor's spell of duty, are varying sequences/series of language skills and operational speech functions. The relative predictability of the serial ordering of these chains can be handled as a variable in teaching/learning materials.

3   *Variation*   The doctor's language needs to vary according to (among other things) interlocutor. This entails selection along two principal dimensions which are quite largely correlated – technical-lay, and cognitive-affective. Appropriate choice of language in these respects will be one of the main objectives for doctor-learners in a course.

4   *Task-oriented and Meta-communicative functions*   The Casualty doctor's speech FUNCTIONS might be graded in terms of both their indispensability to the work in hand and their value, from a pedagogical point of view, in learning materials. In the latter, the main criteria would be valency, task centrality, and communication management.

5   *Multiple functions*   As one utterance may fulfill in different discoursal contexts a number of different speech functions, so one utterance in one discoursal context may realize two or more speech functions simultaneously. The problem of speech function analysis is thus no less for the learner than for the linguist – though some system might be developed for the specification of such multiple function articulations.

6   *Networks*   The various communicative networks in which the doctor carries out his work cycles entail different roles in medical and communication management. Since the doctor as 'medical leader' may not always be the doctor as 'communication leader', and since there is generally a rather complex but predictable co-variation of task, role, setting and channel use, these networks must be considered in course materials.

7   *Transmediation and recoding*   Of particular importance in the work of the casualty doctor are the (largely correlated) skills of transmediation, i.e. the conversion from, say, speech to writing of the language medium in which a proposition is expressed, and recoding, i.e. the conversion from say, 'technical' to 'lay' of the code in which a proposition is expressed. Course work might include regular and graded exercises to develop this proficiency in 'switching' skills. The implications overall are that a course should approach lexical syntactic and phonetic variation in code from a speech function base. (1976:267–8)

A variety of similarly complex studies of the linguistic correlates of specialist speech and writing and their relevance to SLA are collected and evaluated in Swales (1983). As might be guessed from earlier remarks, it is recommended here that the speech practices of competent bilingual specialists be investigated to determine any significant differences in their use and that of NS specialists as well as to uncover any important clues for effective acquisition and/or teaching.

From the above recommendations for the education of emergency room doctors, it should be even further obvious that the sociolinguistic categories explored here are overlapping. Though the focus in the emergency room study is on specialist language, the concepts of *actional role* (doctor as 'leader'), *vehicle* (speech versus writing), *speech act role* ('reassurer,' 'acceptor,' etc.), *discourse routines or scripts* ('chains'), *network*, *status*, and many others are integral parts of the description and analysis of this one focus. It would be unusual if this were not the case in the study of language in use, and all the categories introduced and discussed here have similarly complex interrelationships with one another.

## 2.2.3  *Status*

Social status or class is with age (2.1.1), sex (2.1.2) and style (here *distance* – 3.5.1) one of the big four of quantitative sociolinguistics. In the simplest case, the use of a linguistic feature or the frequency of its use distinguishes one social rank from another. In such cases the frequency is not sensitive to the degree of formality since there is no pressure to use one form or the other, though respondents to voice sample tests would be able to characterize accurately the social status of voices on the basis of the frequency of such features; of course, they would not be able to say how they performed the task. Labov calls such features *indicators* (1972a:237), and their typical distribution is like that of Norwich (a:) shown in figure 2.12. In contrast, some features not only distinguish among social classes but also show sensitivity to the degree of formality. Figure 1.1, the distribution of (ng) in Norwich, shows the typical pattern of such a sociolinguistic *marker* (Labov 1972a:237).

Variables may be *sharply* stratified, as in figure 1.1, where there is a dramatic break between the use of one social class and another, or they may be *gradiently* stratified, as in figure 2.12, where all groups remain fairly equidistant from one another (Labov 1972a:242). Markers as well as indicators may be gradiently stratified, as, for example, the data in table 1.1 for t/d deletion show; indicators, on the other hand, could not, by definition, be sharply stratified. Sharp stratification provides in some cases the single most dramatic distinction between one social rank and another, particularly since language-independent means of reckoning social class (education, income, taste, profession, and so on) lead to a social class continuum in which the breaks are often arbitrary (Labov 1966: chapters 7 and 8; Trudgill 1972: chapter 5).

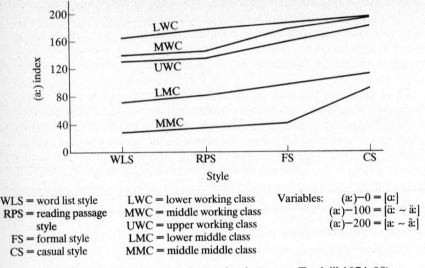

WLS = word list style    LWC = lower working class    Variables:   (a:)—0 = [ɑ:]
RPS = reading passage    MWC = middle working class             (a:)—100 = [ɑ̈: ~ ä:]
      style             UWC = upper working class             (a:)—200 = [a: ~ ã:]
FS = formal style        LMC = lower middle class
CS = casual style       MMC = middle middle class

*Figure 2.12*   Norwich (a:) by class and style (source: Trudgill 1974: 98)

In fact, it has been impossible to come this far without reference to class, and the function of class membership in two types of change (from above and below) is exemplified in tables 2.1, 2.2, and 2.3 and discussed in 2.1.1. In summary, in change from above for stigmatized features (table 2.1), it is younger, lower middle and working class speakers who show the greatest tendency to avoid prejudiced-against items, while in change from above for prestige features, early, extensive use by younger high status and older middle and upper working status groups is characteristic. In change from below (table 2.3), younger speakers from the working or lower middle classes show the earliest evidence of extensive use, though younger upper middle class speakers are influenced by the change. (Of course, if the change is interrupted by attention from the upper class groups, an odd pattern of class and age stratified use may emerge, as is shown in the bottom half of table 2.3.)

One theory of social interaction and symbolism which helps explain such linguistic stratification is Kroch's (1976) assertion that susceptibility to linguistic change in vernacular use is natural in working class speech but that elite groups set themselves off by attending to unnatural phonological distinctions. Put the other way around, lower status groups are not required to monitor their speech so elaborately to keep up with those phonologically less natural forms which symbolically separate one group from another (344–5). In change from above, forms characteristic of lower class use (*stigmatized* ones, table 2.2), may be eradicated. Such forms should, under normal circumstances, display more natural (*unmarked*) phonological characteristics. In change from above when the forms are characteristic of upper class use (*prestigious* ones, table 2.2), one would expect them to display abnormal (*marked*) phonological characteristics. Quantitative sociolinguistic studies have found the source of the more subtle change from below (table 2.3, top half) almost always in lower social strata, and such change should evidence more regular and unmarked phonological forms. When such change is corrected from above (table 2.3, bottom half), the normal phonological process is arrested by some more marked form which, presumably, carries with it the requirement for greater self-monitoring in performance. For simple examples, one might point out that such pronunciations as *libary* for *library* arise from normal, phonological simplification and that they are noticed (change from above) and eradicated (in all but the lowest social classes). Postvocalic /r/ in New York City, however, is a complicating (marked) phonological feature which carries prestige and is on the increase (again, change from above). Similar features might be listed for the more subtle change from below patterns. This relationship between change from above and below and marked versus unmarked forms is related more carefully to interlanguage development in 5.1.

In the dynamic interaction of class and change, some class patterns are unusual. Figure 2.13 shows the typical lower middle class *hypercorrection*[31]

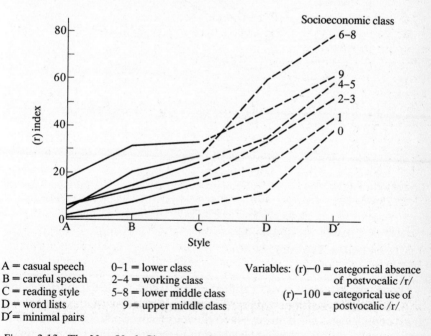

| | | |
|---|---|---|
| A = casual speech | 0–1 = lower class | Variables: (r)–0 = categorical absence |
| B = careful speech | 2–4 = working class | of postvocalic /r/ |
| C = reading style | 5–8 = lower middle class | (r)–100 = categorical use of |
| D = word lists | 9 = upper middle class | postvocalic /r/ |
| D' = minimal pairs | | |

*Figure 2.13* The New York City pattern for (r) by class and style, showing the lower middle class crossover typical of hypercorrection (source: Labov 1972a: 114)

often found when linguistic change is in progress (Labov 1972a:115). This pattern of the second highest social class outstripping even the highest class in its use of a new prestige feature is extremely common. It has already been noted that overachievement may occur in conjunction with covertly prestigious forms as well (table 2.6), a phenomenon known as *hypocorrection*. Finally, when change is from below and an emerging norm is not part of the speech community's awareness, the crossover phenomenon may involve the second lowest class as may be seen in figure 2.14. There the middle working class uses more of the nonstandard variant (at least in the reading styles) than does the lower working class (Trudgill 1974:110).

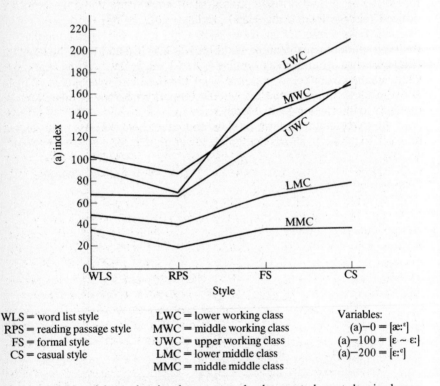

WLS = word list style      LWC = lower working class      Variables:
RPS = reading passage style      MWC = middle working class      (a)–0 = [æː$^\varepsilon$]
FS = formal style      UWC = upper working class      (a)–100 = [ɛ ~ ɛː]
CS = casual style      LMC = lower middle class      (a)–200 = [ɛː$^c$]
     MMC = middle middle class

*Figure 2.14*   Norwich (a), showing the crossover by the next to lowest class in change from below (source: Trudgill 1974: 10)

Though at first social class stratification may seem to have importance for SLA only within the framework of the sociology of language, the parallelism in psycholinguistic mechanisms is too obvious to overlook. If one regards a new language as a developing new norm in language change, then many of these parallels fall into place.

1  Perhaps most obviously, hypercorrection in sociolinguistics is like *over-generalization* (or *analogical* error) in SLA – 'He swimmed across the river,' 'Many womens have tried that,' etc.
2  Hypocorrection, retention of an old norm, is like *negative transfer*, the influence of the native on the target language – 'Ich bin hungrig' (literally 'I am hungry') from the English construction instead of the correct German 'Ich habe Hunger' (literally, 'I have hunger').
3  An indicator, a form not involved in change, is like *fossilization*, the persistence of an incorrect form in the emerging interlanguage (Selinker 1972).
4  Change from above is like conscious or *monitored* SLA (e.g., Krashen 1981), and change from below is like unmonitored SLA.

In some cases, since the motivation is so different (e.g., hypercorrection and overgeneralization) it is worth saying only, perhaps, that the similar psycho-linguistic mechanisms involved in monolingual and SLA settings ought to be investigated. In others, however, where much has been made of the parallel-ism (e.g., Krashen's monitor model of SLA), a great deal more will be said (5.1). It is interesting to note here, at least, that Kroch (1976) appears to believe that greater degree of attention or monitoring naturally accompanies language use which requires more marked forms. Although markedness may characterize the phonological systems of upper classes, it is rather obviously a variable consideration in SLA.

SLA researchers have paid little attention to social class as a variable. Since their work has been seen as predominantly psychological rather than social, that is not surprising. When certain individual traits (e.g., self-concept) have been related to class, however, there has been some interest in the relationship between language learning ánd such aspects of individual personality (2.2.5). On the other hand, when groups of language learners are seen as those who must accommodate to a new norm, a great deal of work has been done in SLA studies, and has already been commented on here, particu-larly in 1.2.4, 1.2.6, 2.1.4, and 2.1.5. Much of this work has focused on low-status immigrant workers in Europe and has generated a multinational SLA research effort (Perdue 1984).

In studies of the intelligibility of nonstandard as opposed to standard English varieties, Eisenstein and Verdi (1985) and Eisenstein and Berkowitz (1981) show that middle class learners found the standard variety more intelligible but that working class learners found both varieties equally intelligible, although the working class respondents did find nonstandard Black English less intelligible than nonstandard English without ethnic marking. Goldstein (1987) shows that contact with a nonstandard language group is a necessary but not sufficient condition for selecting it as a target model. She states further that studies of so-called *reference groups* for learners do not expose the further variables necessary for selection of a target model, though, admittedly, the instruments used to determine such groups may be invalid (430).

Perhaps findings from these and other ongoing studies will make some of the parallelism suggested above between social stratification and SLA more explicit.

## 2.2.4 *Fluency*

Fluency is often simply misunderstood as nativeness (2.1.3), the command of a second language equal to or very like that of an NS. Though different labels may be used to make the distinction, sociolinguistic studies separate the accident of ethnolinguistic mother-tongue from linguistic ability. There are any number of disfluent NSs – those who cannot read effectively aloud, those who cannot speak well in public, those who do not appear to listen well, those who cannot inspire confidence, and so on. These aspects of *communicative competence* are, in fact, not prejudiced as to NS or NNS status; an NS may be illiterate, an NNS a fluent reader. What is important for SLA is to know which fluencies may be especially important for learners from specialized groups (2.2.2) and, more generally, what fluencies are expected in everyday speech community performance. The latter suggests that ethnographic research in speech communities about the expectations of what competent speaker/hearers and reader/writers can do will be important in developing goals for language teaching.

Recent work in cross-cultural communicative competence has shown that the fluencies expected of a speaker in one ethnolinguistic speech community may not be the same as those expected in another. That is painfully obvious in the following ethnocentric definition of fluency, in which a speaker is said to be maximally gifted if he or she has the ability

1   to talk at length, fill time with talk, e.g. disk jockeys
2   to talk in coherent, reasoned and semantically dense sentences, mastering the syntactic/semantic resources of the language
3   to have the appropriate things to say in a wide range of contexts;
4   to be creative and imaginative in language use. (Fillmore 1979:93)[32]

Imagine the community judgment on the fluency of a speaker who followed the advice of 1 in Paliyan (south India) culture where all speakers 'communicate very little at all times and become almost silent by the age of 40. Verbal, communicative persons are regarded as abnormal and often as offensive' (Gardner 1966:398). On the other hand, 1 above might be insufficient for Rotinese culture:

For a Rotinese, the pleasure of life is talk – not simply an idle chatter that passes time, but the more formal taking of sides in endless dispute, argument, and repartee or the rivaling of one another in eloquent and balanced phrases on ceremonial occasions. ... Rotinese repeatedly explain that if their 'hearts' are confused or dejected, they keep silent. Contrarily, to be involved with someone requires active verbal encounter and this often leads to a form of litigation that is conducted more, it would seem, for the sake of argument than for any possible gain. (Fox 1974:65)

As a result of the growing interest of cultural anthropologists in the *ethnography of speaking* (or *communication*), there are abundant descriptions of how to perform linguistically in any number of non-Western cultures; it is only recently, however, that such ethnomethodological discovery procedures have begun to be applied to the ways of speaking in the native speech communities of some of the most commonly learned and taught languages in the world, English included. As a result, a textbook writer for Yakan, Turkish, or Koya might find good descriptions of how to conduct litigation (Frake 1972), perform verbal duels (Dundes, Leach, and Özkök 1972), and reckon kinship (Tyler 1972), respectively, but have to look hard for empirical studies of authentic speech behavior in French, Spanish, German, and English. With the growing awareness that nonexotic peoples are bound by the same sorts of covert conventions regarding daily life (language use included), it is now, in fact, possible to read professional accounts of such activities in those less esoteric languages and cultures as well.

In characterizing fluency for SLA, as in so many other areas, researchers with a sociolinguistic intent will have to study norms of actual language behavior and the speech community's reported norms for behavior (*folk linguistics*) to be able to make recommendations for materials, teacher education, and the like. Again, the fluencies of successful NNSs should not be ignored in such research.

## 2.2.5 Individuality

From one point of view, individuality is not an important sociolinguistic consideration since social reality is always a collection of individual behaviors (or, for Durkheimians, even a separate reality from that collection). If, on the other hand, one seeks explanation as well as description in sociolinguistics (short of psychiatric detail), then one must be prepared to give an account for the variable production and reception of linguistic items by the individual members of a speech community. I hope that the collection of concerns in chapters 2 and 3 helps provide such an account, and an illustration of an ambitious application is given in chapter 4.

Many apparently individual characteristics are really no more than a careful characterization of the complex of social identities which obtain in a given case. In the discussion of Labov's description of *lames* (peripheral gang

members or even associated nonmembers) in 2.2.1, it was shown that an individual's position in even a small-group network was a powerful predictor of
language performance. In another study, Labov showed that positive attitude
towards the local area (Martha's Vineyard, MA) provided the highest
correlation with the centralization of the first element in the diphthongs /ay/
and /aw/ (Labov 1972a:39):

| Number of respondents | Orientation toward Martha's Vineyard | (ay) | (aw) |
|---|---|---|---|
| 40 | Positive | 63 | 62 |
| 19 | Neutral | 32 | 42 |
| 6 | Negative | 09 | 08 |

The higher variable ratings indicate a greater tendency to centralize. The
association of this centralization with local values is obviously strong, and the
correlation with this attitude was, in fact, stronger than with any other social
characteristic of the respondents. In some cases, then, the researcher will
have to be sensitive to local norms, history, competing value systems,
changing attitudes, and other factors. It will be important to investigate these
factors first in   connection with regular linguistic variation rather than
appealing to some mysterious and poorly defined individual factors.

On the other hand, SLA literature offers numbers of studies and speculations about individual differences, particularly as predictors of success and
failure in language learning. Taking almost at random a list of such characteristics from a well-known study of SLA (H. D. Brown 1980) one finds
*inductive* versus *deductive*, *field-independent* versus *dependent*, *reflective*
versus *impulsive*, *tolerance* versus *intolerance of ambiguity*, *skeletonization*
versus *embroidery*, *self-esteem*, *inhibition*, *empathy*, *extroversion* versus
*introversion*, *aggression*, *instrumental* versus *integrative motivation* (2.1.3),
and *needs* and *drives* (86–115).[33] The first items in this list are characteristic
of what have come to be known as *cognitive* or *learning styles*; the ones from
*self-esteem* on are often grouped together as social psychological or *affective*
variables. Both areas are rich for sociolinguistic and SLA cooperation.
Neurological studies of SLA also focus on highly individualistic matters (e.g.,
Obler to appear)

What in monolingual and/or monocultural situations one often regards as
*cognitive* style may, in fact, emerge as a *cultural* learning style. One emerging
redefinition, for example, concerns literacy. Heath asserts that the functions
of reading and writing must be sought in every speech community. Her *Ways
with Words* (1983) is a model of ethnographic investigation of how different
cultural groups value, acquire, and use literacy. Not implicit or explicit in her
study, however, is the notion that limitations on the uses of literacy are
limitations on the communicative potential of individuals. In fact, her work
goes on to show how the uncovering of community uses of literacy may

bolster local educational programs. While it may be the case that there is a random distribution of some learning style characteristics throughout the individuals of the world's cultures, it will be important for ethnographers to determine the ways of knowing, using, learning, and regarding language in a variety of speech communities before such a conclusion is reached or used as a commonplace in explaining variation in SLA.

Individuality brings this second chapter full round to its beginning: the individual may seem an arbitrary place to begin the consideration of the social aspects of language as they have importance to SLA. It has been the purpose of this chapter, however, to show that the social identity of the individual is the constitutive, human background of sociolinguistics and the ethnography of communication. Roles, regional affiliations, and identities of every sort all guide speakers' performances and the performances of those who interact with them. The structure of those interactional relationships is the subject of the next chapter.

# 3

# Interactional factors

The components of interaction include the relationships among individuals whose characteristics were the subject matter of chapter 2. Interactions, however, are made up of more than the identities of and connections among participants. They happen in space and time; they have content (beyond the so-called linguistic content of their semantic meaning) and purposes. In the least conservative ethnomethodological interpretation, such facts are the very product of social interaction. The 'work' interactants do to make social life correspond to rational and reportable constructs is the focus of such studies (e.g., Garfinkel 1967:vii).

Points already made will not be reiterated for every subcategory introduced here. It is still assumed, for example, that an important sociocultural model for language learning and teaching (and a subject of interest in its own right) is the *competent bilingual*. How such individuals interact in different settings, including the human environments of NSs, other NNSs, and mixed groups is a strongly recommended theme of research for all the interactional variables surveyed here.

Additionally, emphasis on the collection and analysis of authentic data continues in this chapter; respondents, even if they are trained linguists, are no better at introspection concerning interaction than they are at self-reports of individual variation. The variables of interaction must be observed, recorded, and analyzed if they are to be of value.

## 3.1 Setting

The temporal and physical aspects of an interaction range from the inevitable, general time and some ubiquitous home or public locale at which the discourse took place all the way to carefully prescribed settings and moments which demand (and are demanded for) certain language acts.

### 3.1.1  *Time*

What time it is determines a wide range of speech behaviors. In Standard Modern Polish, one must know if it is daytime or evening to choose between the greetings *dzień dobry* ('good day') and *dobry wieczor* ('good evening'). In one Brazilian Polish speaker's system, however, *dzień dobry* is the greeting for the morning only and *dobry wieczor* serves for all afternoon and evening greetings. Perhaps the source of this rearrangement of Polish time is the result of the distribution of greetings in Brazilian Portuguese – *bom dia* ('good morning, good day'), *boa tarde* ('good afternoon'), and *boa noite* ('good evening'). The Brazilian Polish system does not add a third term to imitate the Portuguese system, but moves its change boundary from between morning and afternoon to between afternoon and evening, perhaps a more salient boundary in the new environment.

Time may have a significant effect on complexes of other variables. In Fishman and Greenfield (1970; see1.2.4) the factors considered part of a domain were interlocutor, topic, and setting. If one selected the domain of *education* and specified the congruent factors as *teacher*, *how to do an algebra problem*, and *school*, time might still play a large role if the distinction *in-class, during school time* were differentiated from *after school, extra help time*. The discourse or 'floor rights' of the teacher and an individual or small group of students after school would be different from such rights during an ordinary classroom session – e.g., length of turn (3.1.3), frequency of interruption, and so on. Additionally, a more private presentational style by the teacher might emerge, including, perhaps, modification of the degree of formality (3.5.1) and the manner of delivery (3.5.2, 4.1.3). Some sorts of talk are so closely related to a specific time that the name of the genre N itself reflects it, e.g., bedtime story, after-dinner speech.

The embedding of sociocultural time into the grammatical system (or vice versa) is subtle. The linguistic marking of time and time related concepts (tense and aspect) and the cultural regard for time and temporal activities are not universals. This topic provides a good illustration of the opinion of some linguists that speakers are prisoners of their grammatical systems. In Hopi, for example, 'validity' is a much more important basis for the tense–aspect system than time. Figure 3.1 displays how situations 1a, 1b, and 2 all take the Hopi verb *wari* since the validity of the act of running is very high: the running was either seen by both interlocutors (1b) or is being seen by one or both (1a and 2). A report of what one interlocutor (but not both) saw has less validity (even though it shares past time characteristics with 1b) and must be marked differently – *era wari* (Whorf 1940:213).

Different cultural uses of and regard for time do not have to reflect radically different markings on the verb or any other part of the grammatical system, but they may emerge in other aspects of communicative competence. In German universities, lectures scheduled for 10:00 a.m. begin

| Objective field | Speaker (sender) | Hearer (receiver) | Handling of topic: running of third person | |
|---|---|---|---|---|
| 1a |  | | English | he is running |
| | | | Hopi | wari (running, statement of fact) |
| 1b objective field blank devoid of running | 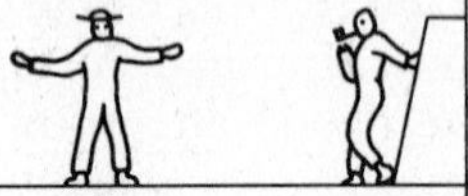 | | English | he ran |
| | | | Hopi | wari (running, statement of fact) |
| 2 |  | | English | he is running |
| | | | Hopi | wari (running, statement of fact) |
| 3 Blank | 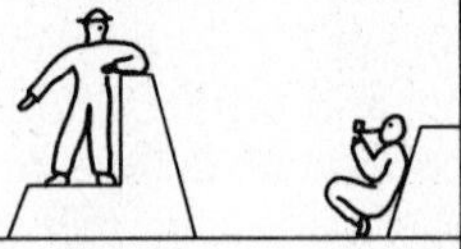 | | English | he ran |
| | | | Hopi | era wari (running, statement of fact from memory) |
| 4 Blank | 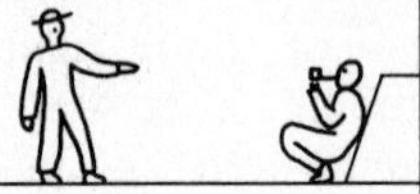 | | English | he will run |
| | | | Hopi | warikni (running, statement of expectation) |
| 5 Blank |  | | English | he runs (e.g., on the track team) |
| | | | Hopi | warikngwe (running, statement of law) |

*Figure 3.1*  Hopi verb forms (source: Whorf 1940)

promptly at 10:15. Imagine several different North Americans encountering this custom:

*Report 1*   The Germans are always late. I go to a lecture that's supposed to start at 10:00, and I always end up waiting around for a quarter of an hour or so for things to start.

*Report 2*   The Germans are incredibly erratic; I agreed to meet a friend downtown at 6:00 p.m. and was ten minutes late; he asked me what had kept me; I went to a lecture the next day at 10:00 a.m. and the speaker and over two-thirds of the audience didn't get there until almost ten after, and it didn't start for another five minutes or so. I don't get it.

*Report 3*   The Germans are really odd. They say there's going to be a lecture at 10:00, but they always start it fifteen minutes late. Why don't they just say 10:15 if that's what they mean?

Hall (1959) classifies North American (European) *sets*, *isolates*, and *patterns* of *formal* (as opposed to *technical* and *informal*) time. Sets include such concepts as day and night, the days of the week, hours and minutes, months, and seasons. Hall argues that the five minute period has recently crossed over from being an isolate (one of the units that made up a quarter of an hour) into a set (distinct from ten minutes, fifteen minutes, a half hour, and so on). Only recently will people in European culture apologize for being only five minutes late (168).

Isolates are more difficult to determine since they are cultural abstractions, but Hall identifies *ordering, cyclicity, synthesisity, valuation, tangibility, duration,* and *depth* as important in the European tradition. A week with any seven days would not be a week; they must come in a particular order. Cycles are limited – sixties (seconds and minutes), sevens (weeks), twelves (months), and so on. The valuation of time in European culture is obvious in such proverbs as 'Time is money.' That time is tangible may be seen in references to it as *lost, made up, saved, wasted,* and so on (170–1). Duration would seem basic to time since it implies that an amount of time has passed between two points, but there is variation even in this.

> For instance, the Hopi are separated from us by a tremendous cultural gulf. Time, for example, is not duration but many different things for them. It is not fixed or measurable as we think of it, nor is it a quantity. It is what happens when the corn matures or a sheep grows up – a characteristic sequence of events. It is a natural process that takes place while living substance acts out its life drama. (171)

Additionally, European time assumes a synthesis – that is, time adds up because it is part of an orderly universe. And, finally, European time assumes depth: there is a past on which the present rests, though mention of this historicity of time may be more elaborate in other cultures. Teachers of ESL composition often wonder why Arab students often begin compositions on simple or even technical matters with references to a historical background, but such a practice reveals a considerable valuation and awareness of the depth aspect of time (172).

The patterns of formal time in many ways follow from the sets and isolates. Europeans make plans, assuming that quantifiable time should fit a schedule. It is important to be at certain places at a certain time, and there are severe penalties for violations. Perhaps even more important is the European tradition of linking events with time – *post hoc, ergo propter hoc*. Events too far separated in time make it difficult to assign cause and effect relations between them (172–3).

One could, of course, distinguish sets, patterns, and isolates of time in a more technical or in a more informal way, the latter showing the greatest variation. Even such simple expressions as *next Tuesday*, for example, do not always find one interpretation. If it is Sunday, is the Tuesday which immediately follows *next Tuesday*, or is it the Tuesday which follows the next Sunday? My wife and I, though both from the Midwest of the United States, disagree on just this rule, and the existence of such expressions as *this coming Tuesday* substantiate the need for disambiguating devices.

Those who treat time differently will not only need to acquire the new concepts but also need to be allowed the use of older notions for some period, particularly in language learning and teaching situations. Perdue (1984) reports on a large European SLA research program which includes extensive treatment of temporal reference.

Pidgin-creole and first language acquisition studies have raised one further issue about time, tense, and aspect which must be considered here. If there is an underlying tendency to utilize basic or universal distinctions in language acquisition, then the sorts of systems which emerge in pidgin-creole and child language varieties might also be in evidence in SLA, particularly in the early stages. Forms which are not attested in either L1 or L2 might be attributed to an innate predisposition to structure human language in certain ways (e.g., Chomsky 1981, 1982, 1986, Bickerton 1981). For time, in particular, Bickerton notes that one of the imperatives of the *bioprogram* which informs language acquisition processes (more completely, of course, in the absence of adequate input) is that which states: 'Make sure that punctuals and non-punctuals are adequately differentiated' (1981:177). Bickerton evidences the realization of this injunction from Hawaiian Creole English, which has a nonpunctual marker (*stei*) which it, according to him, could not have derived from any of the input varieties. In addition, Bickerton reviews data from first language acquisition and suggests that children first attend to the punctual versus nonpunctual distinction, a position supported by Berman (1986:434) but denied by Weist (1986:364). In looking at parallels in the order of acquisition of morphemes between first language acquisition and SLA (for English), researchers have discovered that the morpheme *-ing*, principally functioning as a nonpunctual marker, is acquired very early (e.g., Bailey, Madden, and Krashen 1973). If it can be predicted that certain distinctions are sought early by the learner as a result of cognitive language universals, then materials and teaching strategies could be modified accordingly.

The sociolinguistics of time, therefore, reveals not only contrastive cultural attitudes and concepts but also basic form–function correlations in a grammar, ones particularly useful in the study of rapidly emerging and changing systems.[1]

### 3.1.2 *Place*

Place, perhaps even more dramatically than time, is a determiner of language choice. It is one of the components of Fishman's domains (1.2.4), and respondents immediately recognized the congruence of place (e.g., church) with topic (e.g., living a good life) and interlocutor (e.g., priest). In some cases, place is so intimately connected with speech, that it serves to identify a type – locker room talk, dinner table conversation, and so on.

Like time, however, place is a variable cross-cultural concept. Distances, sites, boundaries, areas, and so on differ in detail and conceptualization, and though such differentiations have not been written about as extensively as those for time, they are no less interesting. Condon and Yousef (1975) identify two sorts of *homes* in the United States. In the first, the *authority-centered home*, some standard (a person or persons, a religion, education) is the controlling guide to behavior. The family area and the guest areas are clearly distinguished; the family dines together, often with parents quizzing children about school or other activities; closed doors are unusual, arousing suspicion, though the parents' bedroom is often off-limits to children; the kitchen is often a place for negotiation of differences. The *social-centered home*, by contrast, is one prepared for interaction and is marked by considerable informality. No room is private, and any may serve for communication; the house is generally occupied by many people who do not live there, and the treatment of guests as members of the family ('get yourself a drink,' 'answer the door, would you') strikes members of other cultures as odd or even rude.

Not all variation in place is so beset with symbolic meaning; simply how to refer to place may be problematic. Schegloff (1972) points out that, given proper circumstances, any one of the following answers to the question where his notes were at the time of writing might be 'correct': right in front of me, next to the telephone, on the desk, in my office, in Room 213, in Lewison Hall, on campus, at school, at Columbia, in Morningside Heights, on the upper West Side, in Manhattan, in New York City, in New York State, in the Northeast, on the Eastern Seaboard, in the United States (97). Common-sense geography in the United States lets one know, for example, that a New Yorker who went to Philadelphia and was asked by a friend if he or she got to Boston on the trip would be properly bemused; a San Franciscan might consider it a reasonable question about what happened while he or she was *back East* (104).[2]

There is considerable variation in the verbal description of place. Linde and Labov (1975: 929–30) characterize three different strategies for describing apartments:

1   *Map*: I'd say it's laid out in in a huge square pattern, broken down in four units.
    If you were looking down at this apartment from a height, it would be like – like I said before, a huge square with two lines drawn through the center to make like four smaller squares.
    Now, on the ends – uh – in the two boxes facing out in the street you have the living room and a bedroom.

In between these two boxes you have a bathroom.
Etc.

2   *Existential*: The entrance is into the kitchen.
And through an archway is the living room, and then off through a separate doorway, a closing doorway, is the bedroom.
I'd say the bedroom is just a little bit smaller than the living room.
Etc.

3   *Tour*: As you open the door, you are in a small five-by-five room which is a small closet.
When you get past there, you're in what we call the foyer which is about a twelve-by-twelve room which has a telephone and a desk.
If you keep walking in that same direction, you're confronted by two rooms in front of you . . . large living room which is about twelve by twenty on the left side.
Etc.

The map style of description is extremely rare (accounting for fewer than 3 percent of all the descriptions they collected), and the tour format, the most popular, is especially effective when it is considered that its essential intent is to 'provide a minimal set of paths by which each room could be entered' (930).

K. Ito (1980) showed that route instructions from Japanese as opposed to Hawaiian residents in Honolulu contained a much greater number of essential *route markers* (e.g., 'pass the tall building on your left,' 'go until you see the Star Market,' 'turn right at the church'). Hawaiian residents found less need for such reassuring landmarks, and made much more use of *distance and direction indicators* (e.g., 'go three blocks and turn left,' 'go four blocks *makai* [toward the ocean] and turn left,' 'go a little further and turn right').

Such discourse strategies for talking about place could provide interesting exercises in language teaching materials, and they constitute another rich field for bilingual sociolinguistic inquiry. As with *time*, Perdue (1984) summarizes the linguistic backgrounds of spatial reference for a large SLA research program.

### 3.1.3  *Length*

How long one may talk when it is his or her turn, how long different sorts of talk are supposed to take, how talk may be interrupted and terminated are principally discourse concerns. Recently, a candidate for a position at a university in the United States was almost not made an offer because the interview speech went on beyond the time limit. Nonspeech behavior is also governed by such factors: in some places, it is understandable for members of an audience to get up and leave a presentation which goes over its allotted time; in others, it is not.

The responsibilities for determining reasonable length of turn in inter-actions when no single participant has special rights lies with both the speaker and the listener(s). This is particularly important in ordinary conversation since one of its defining characteristics is unspecified turn length (Sacks, Schegloff, and Jefferson 1974). The listeners indicate to speakers that they are to go on by a series of cues, and speakers seek confirmation of their right to go on with a series of checks. Such cues are called *back-channel* behaviors. Verbal signals are such items as 'Mmmm,' 'Surely,' 'Quite,' 'I see,' 'Yeah,' and 'OK' (Wardhaugh 1985:135) and do not interrupt the speaker's flow of conversation at all. *Shadowing* (completing the speaker's sentences) may also indicate attentiveness and invite the speaker to go on, but it may, as well, indicate a desire to interrupt (Wardhaugh 1985:135). Speakers who do not get back-channel cues from listeners may need to elicit such behavior by interjecting their discourse with such checks as 'see,' 'you know,' 'you understand,' 'get it,' and so on. On the other hand, speakers' rights to continue rest on their ability to maintain their turn through clarity, interest, and relevance. Speakers may, therefore, restate and paraphrase or may try to gain (or regain) the attention of listeners by referring to them – 'And you know what I said?,' 'Can you guess what I did?,' 'Let's suppose,' 'If you ask me,' and so on (Wardhaugh 1985:132). Similarly, the speaker may check on the listeners' comprehension – 'OK, so far?,' 'Are you with me?,' 'Do you get what I mean?,' 'Got it?,' 'Right?,' 'Am I making myself clear?,' and so on (Wardhaugh 1985:133). Finally, speakers may simply lengthen their utterances through repetition, paraphrase, or *repair*, the last a term not exclusively applied to devices used to correct errors in what has been said (Goodwin 1981:140–2). In the following discourse, for example, Ralph lengthens his turn by phonological means (: indicates a lengthened sound) and by repair (rephrasing).

*Ralph*: Somebody said looking at my:, son m y oldest son.

*Chil*: _____ , ,      .    X_____

The need for turn-lengthening arose from Chil's signal (by averting gaze – the break in the solid line) that attention was not focused on the speaker. Ralph lengthens and repairs to regain the listener's attention, indicated here by the X and bracket [ (Goodwin 1981:142). Duration of turn, then, may play a functional role in the speaker's and listener's negotiation of attention.

Talk must be cut off as well as go on, and listeners must develop strategies both to become speakers and to end conversations, though in successful conversational closure, there is a cooperative routine or negotiation among interlocutors which results in an inabrupt and polite cessation of talk (Schegloff and Sacks 1973). Interruption of turn has been perceived as more appropriate at clause and sentence breaks, however, regardless of the length of the utterance interrupted, suggesting at least a partial linguistic or structural control of conversational organization (Argyle, Furnham, and Graham 1981:148).

Duration of talk itself may be a cultural or subcultural marker or caricature. The putative talkativeness of women has been discussed in 2.1.2, and the cultural functions of taciturnity as opposed to verbosity for Paliyan and Rotinese speakers respectively was mentioned in 2.2.4. Even how much talk is expected within specific *channels* may be culturally different. In France, for example, when a telephone caller reaches a known answerer, he or she must spend some time with the answerer rather than immediately asking for the person actually called (Godard 1977). Additionally, talk is bound by genre (3.2.3) – a *debate* imposes strict time limits on turns; a *chat* does not. Finally, at the level of attitude and perception, the degree to which turn lengths are dissimilar in an interaction apparently contributes to participants' and observers' favorable reactions (Putnam and Street 1984).

Cross-cultural studies have focused on length in specific tasks. Blum-Kulka and Olshtain (1986) have found that NNSs often use a larger number of words to accomplish a similar act. A pair of samples (from their study of requests) illustrates this tendency:

> *Hebrew speaker of English*: I went over the material we will study in the next weeks and I rather like to have your lecture next week, if it's possible and if you can be ready.
> *NS of American English*: Look, your presentation would be perfect for next week's session. Do you think you could have it ready?

By investing more verbal effort in elaborating the speech act, the NNSs risk being harshly judged on Grice's maxim of relevance (175). If NNSs are guilty of unnecessarily formal speech, these findings may reflect other studies which suggest that increasingly informal speech is more abbreviated (Berger and Bradac 1982). Gumperz relates this issue to Bernstein's comparison of *elaborated* and *restricted* codes:

> Elaborated messages are messages where the maximum communication load is carried by words; restricted messages, on the other hand, rely on other nonlexical communicative devices (e.g., code switching, stress, intonation, etc.). The greater the reliance on words, the more accessible the message is to others who do not share similar speakers' knowledge or personal background. (1972:23)

From this one would predict fewer words between ethnically similar interlocutors, but it is important to distinguish between absolute amount of speech (per turn or conversation, for example) and amount of speech involved in the completion of a verbal task, the latter the focus of Gumperz's interpretation of elaborated and restricted codes. Beebe (1981) found that Puerto Rican learners of English took longer turns when their interlocutors were ethnically similar. That tendency was repeated in Duff (1986), though there ethnicity of speaker alone (Chinese over Japanese) was the best predictor of the amount of speech. On the other hand, Ervin-Tripp (1973b) and Takahashi (to appear) found that Japanese speakers used fewer words per turn when their interlocutors were Japanese; their respondents thought it odd to use a foreign language with an interlocutor who shared L1. It has already been noted (2.2.1) that Duff's NNS respondents used more words per turn when they were debating than problem-solving; such findings will, of course, be important to *genre* (3.2.3).

In general, NSs use shorter T-units (roughly, independent clauses) when talking with NNSs, perhaps part of their effort to make sure that their message is understood (Long 1983a), but their total contribution, at least in an NS–NNS dyad, is much greater than the NNSs' (Porter 1986), indicating that the Blum-Kulka and Olshtain findings and Gumperz's interpretation are related to message units and not to overall performance. In classrooms, NNS–NNS interactions apparently promote a greater quantity of learner talk than teacher directed activities (Long et al. 1976).

Further studies of language amount, perhaps especially turn-length and ways of turn-length management in NS and NNS performance, will shed light on bilingual sociolinguistics and perhaps provide a background for L2 instructional materials and procedures.

### 3.1.4 *Size*

When hundreds are gathered in one place, there must be different rules for the management of talk than when two or three people converse. Although students of social interaction have characterized the roles taken by members of groups of different sizes (e.g., Argyle, Furnham, and Graham 1981:174–6), little work has been done on other effects of group size on interaction.

Cross-culturally, similar group size does not demand similar linguistic behavior. Blacks and Whites in the United States exhibit different behavior in audiences. Blacks are physically active, particularly if they are interested in or moved by the presentation. They make attempts to assess the opinions of their fellow audience members and express their own feelings to them. In some cases they may even respond verbally to the presentation. Whites, on the other hand, keep their eyes directed towards the speaker, are physically inactive (except for applause), and communicate little (perhaps in whispers) or not at all with fellow audience members (Williams 1972).

In characterizing NS stylistic varieties (3.5.1), Joos (1962) suggests that smaller groups promote less formal performance. His *intimate* level, for example, is usually restricted to dyads (30).

Since most SLA studies have taken place in dyads (experimental) and classrooms (observational), it is difficult to assess the influence of size on bilingual performance. NNSs may use more speech in very small groups and dyads in informal situations but more in situations where learner input is requested (classrooms) in formal, larger groups. The base line work on NS variability for this component has, in fact, not been carried out,[3] and investigation of the influence of group size on language use by NSs and NNSs is highly recommended.


## 3.2 Content

Section 3.1 dealt with the principally physical characteristics of the environment; here the cognitive dimensions of the environment are studied.


### 3.2.1 *Situation*

Situations are an open-ended list of bounded event types which happen in a culture. They may completely overlap with the kind of speech (*genre* 3.2.3) which goes on in them (e.g., bull-session, after-dinner conversation) or describe an event type which may appropriately include any number of speech activities (e.g., a cocktail party, a wedding). One may note the distinction between situation and genre in the following:

Did you go to the lecture last night?
Yeah, but I couldn't hear it.

The 'lecture' referred to by the first speaker was the situation and included the site, time, physical arrangements, question and answer period, and so on as well as the presentation by the lecturer. The second speaker, however, refers to the genre exclusively. Though one might choose to refer to such situations which highlight language as *speech situations* (Hymes 1974), doing so probably contributes more to confusion of terminology than clarification of components.

Argyle, Furnham, and Graham (1981) call a situation 'a type of social encounter with which members of a culture or subculture are familiar' (4). Though situations may have universal components (appropriateness of place, number of participants, and so on), their labels, functions, and components are to be discovered in every separate cultural group. Some situations may be so ubiquitous in human behavior that comparisons might start with them, but even those must be carefully examined for different boundaries, meanings, and uses. From an ethnomethodological perspective, behavior (including talk) within situations creates them. That is, if interaction may be taken to be the neutral term which includes the more bounded and specified situation, then both are the products of the cooperative work of the participants involved in them; they are not abstract entities which wait for participants to perform them. On the other hand, the ability of performers to behave in situations in ways which match the expectations of other inter-actants indicates that tropes, roles, scripts, and stretches of all sorts are ready for use as the identity of a situation emerges.

Situation is a more *emic* than *etic* concept than perhaps any of the other categories yet discussed. It so completely overlaps with its *topics* (3.2.2), *genres* (3.2.3), *setting* (3.1), *relations* (3.3), *functions* (3.4), *tenor* (3.5), and so on that it might be said to have no existence at all beyond its components. On the other hand, intuitive folk linguistic evidence is strong against that position. Although every situation may not have a folk name, members of speech communities are aware of such a set of familiar social encounters and of the behavior (including language) appropriate to them. Social psycho-logists have conducted surveys to determine the existence, label, and structure of some of the most common situations for certain groups. Forgas (1976), for example, determined the twenty-five most common situations for Oxford psychology students:

> Morning coffee, drink in a pub, discussing essay in a tutorial, meeting acquaintance while checking mail, walk with a friend, shopping with a friend, acting as a subject in a psychology experiment, going to the pictures, having a short chat with shop-assistant, dinner in Hall, etc.

Once determined, the structure of common situations may be used for further observational and/or experimental study, and the base line data derived from them may be used comparatively across cultures, across NNS – NS boundaries, or across different stages of the developing interlanguages of NNSs.

In SLA the use of situational syllabuses was attacked by the developers of notional-functional ones in particular, but their notion of situation appears to be limited to what has been called *setting* (3.1) here:

> It seems best, therefore, to retain the term *situation* [emphasis in the original] for the sum of the observable and independently describable features of the context in which a language even occurs. (Wilkins 1976:17)

Such a limitation of situation excludes those features of interaction which are of considerable importance in SLA. Is 'At the post office' (Wilkins 1976:16) really a situation? If it is, is there any principled reason not to use it as a basis for investigating the variety of linguistic behaviors (and their functions) which take place there, even if the approach to language study had a so-called notional orientation? From a nonspecialist's point of view, one would expect to find a great deal more folk reality in situations (a visit to a friend's home, an evening walk with a lover, a chat over morning coffee) than in so-called notions (reckoning time and duration, indicating degree, characterizing specificity) and functions (requesting, demanding, informing). Notions and functions seem as abstract as the categories of a grammar. Sentences are made up of nouns, verbs, and such stuff, and situations are made up of acts of informing, requesting, demanding, and so on. That situations may be analyzed into the notions and functions which they are composed of does not qualify those units automatically as the ones to be focused on by the teacher or learner of another language. One might argue, in fact, that the cultural utility of the situation (defined so as to include its cognitive as well as physical content), with its contrastive features to similar situations in the L1 of the learner, is an excellent vehicle for language learning and instruction, particularly learning which hopes to include communicative as well as linguistic competence.

In practical applications of notional-functional approaches to language teaching, in fact, the situation, as described here, plays an important role:

> In a functional/notional approach, 'situational teaching' ... is not merely a presentation device for achieving a limited objective, but describes the sum total of all the aspects of communication which occur within any given context. It is used to cover not only grammar and lexis, but functions, notions and their exponents, settings and topics, social and psychological roles, and style and range of expression. (Alexander 1976:157)

In other words, the components of interaction are complexly interrelated. Once a situation is identified (whether, optimally, through observation or from intuition or introspection), its components will need to be detailed. What speech acts (functions) are likely to occur in it? What are some likely discourse plans or scripts for it? What roles are required? Are some settings more likely (or even required)? Research, teacher training, materials development, or a language lesson might begin by highlighting any of the categories of language variation. Determining which are the more effective organizers of experience for language learners (either self-determined as in untutored language learning or imposed as in classrooms) is one of the principal goals of a sociolinguistically sensitive SLA research and applied linguistics program.

Such generalizations should not weaken the specificity of the cultural identity of situations. Though they predict and are predicted by other components studied here, they are cognitively real elements of social structure. That those situations which are highly predictive of language behaviors probably play a large role in acquisition seems undeniable, and even proponents of notional-functional syllabuses note the utility of teaching programs designed around such highly specific linguistic needs (e.g., Wilkins 1976:18).

Situations seem to have been overlooked in recent SLA research (excepting, of course, LSP). The assumed inconsistency of highly specified situations with the goals of communicative teaching may be partly responsible for this, but it may be that persons in SLA have rejected situations since they found them no more sophisticated than such dialogue titles as 'At the post office' would indicate. In fact, the study of contextualized events has a great deal to teach any who would learn about human interaction.

### 3.2.2  *Topic*

Topic is at once the most complex and simplest of variables. What is being talked about is the topic. Though its linguistic reality (relation to pronominal-ization, syntactic position, opposition to *comment*, and so on) will not be discussed here, that reality is well-established (Li 1976). Its sociolinguistic importance falls in the general area of discourse and conversational analysis.

Topic is one of the most important contributors to discourse organization, but the more formal identification of a discourse or text topic as a proposition (e.g., van Dijk 1977:50, Keenan and Schieffelin 1976) is not dealt with here.[4] When an analyst wants to divide a discourse into units, where people stop talking about one thing (say, food) and start talking about another (say, sex), topic is a notion that is often appealed to. Discourse topic itself, however, is often ill-defined or admitted as a given or pretheoretical notion. For this reason, there may be disagreement over what the topic of a given stretch of speech might be. To help avoid associating topic with *title*, possibly limiting it to one correct answer (Bransford and Johnson 1973), Tyler (1978) proposes defining topic as 'one possible paraphrase.' Ethnomethodologists, as one might suppose, see topic as one of the aspects created by the negotiation and work which go on in an interaction; a topic is not static (or monolithic) but is made up by the participants as they go along (e.g., Schegloff 1972).

One way of characterizing the strategies conversationalists use in creating topic is to refer to the pool of shared knowledge of the interlocutors. General and shared knowledge plus information introduced in the conversation (including such contextual matters as time, setting, participant roles and identities) provide what Brown and Yule (1983:78–9) call a *topic frame-work*. Appealing then to Grice's *maxim of relevance* (1.2.5), it is possible to say that interlocutors are *speaking topically* when their contributions are relevant to the current topic framework (84). Less formally, the *newsworthi-ness* of a topic is analyzed when it is introduced, and participants constantly inquire *why that now and to me* (Coulthard 1977). Since these views of topic identity are so closely related to participant identity and background knowl-edge, it is not difficult to see how the route of a topic through NNS–NS or NNS–NNS conversations might be significantly different from one through typical NS–NS interactions.

A speaker often takes his or her last statement to be more relevant than another speaker's even more recent statement. From this point of view, a conversation may have a topic structure in which all participants might be said to be speaking topically with relevance to the topic framework, but each individual may be more involved with a *speaker's topic*, an entity more closely related to the speaker's own previous contribution (85).

Whether a formal or common-sense notion of topic is used, a number of studies related to conversational coherence based on topic have been carried out. Such studies often focus on topic nomination (or *initiation*), *maintenance*, and *shift*.

The tendency for women to nominate more topics than men and for men's nominated topics to be taken up more was reported in 2.1.2, and the tendency for adolescent SLA subjects to introduce and shift topics more than younger subjects was reported in 2.1.1. Topic nomination and shift in general, however, must be justified by relevance as suggested above, though conversation opening topic initiators ('How you doing?') may derive from the physical and/or social environments of the interlocutors (Planalp and Tracy 1980). The *topic bounding devices* which indicate topic shift are often *pre-acts* – 'Oh say,' 'I'll tell you what,' 'By the way,' and 'Before I forget,' for example. Topics may be shifted, however, by less clear-cut devices; that is, they may change through so-called *topic shading*. In such cases, the new topic is related to the (or a) previous one. Crow (1983: 143–4) provides examples of different levels of NS topic introduction and shift in couples' conversations:

1   \*M:  I tell you what love, if we eat any more of those potato chips, I won't be able to eat my dinner
    F:  Yeah, no more

2   M:  And there was something so incredibly strange about that place, y'know
    F:  Uh huh
       [[
    M:  Here's some guy singing ((sings)) 'Tiny bubbles, in the wa-' y'know it was so incredibly – strange sitting out there in the middle of the water
  \*F:  Speaking of that I heard a strange song today that I haven't heard since I was a little kid and used to listen to Arthur Godfrey on the radio with my mother
       [
    M:  Oh yeah

3   M:  I gotta go to the community auction, – check it out
    F:  And may- maybe I'll go with you
    M:  Mm hm, then we'd just walk down
       Don't take our purse or wallets along
    F:  heh
       \**That* Henry, I-
       *I* don't know, I think he – maybe did take my purse, y'know

*M*:   Mm *hm*

4    *F*:   Well, –
        (4.0)
        *I just hope Pam handled it alright
     *M*:   Oh, the card reminds you of Pat
     *F*:   Mm hm, – yeah
    **M*:   That is *such* a beautiful card
     *F*:   I love it it's my favorite one

*Notes*
* = Topic shift or initiation
[(|) = Simultaneous talk
Italics = loader or stressed segments
(X.X) = seconds of silence

These conversations are arranged in descending order of the *coherence* of their topic initiations or shifts. The less clearly the device indicates the change, the less coherent it is. In example 1, there is a pre-act of the sort already mentioned above ('I tell you what') and the use of a form of address as a second pre-act. The topic introduction is thus well-announced and taken up by the second speaker. In example 2, however, the topic bounding device ('Speaking of that') is what Jefferson (1978) calls an *embedded repetition*, one which anchors what is to follow in what has preceded. The topics are related but not identical since M had been talking about a song in a strange situation and F initiates a discussion of a strange song. In example 3, the shift is even less coherent, for F and M must share the knowledge that F has lost her purse, or the conversation would be incoherent. In this case, the *That* anchors the identity of Henry for both speakers, but the repetition of purse (from M's previous topic) does not make the shift unintelligible. In example 4, however, the reference to Pat and 'handling it alright' must refer to a previous topic shared by M and F, and M justifies the otherwise puzzling topic initiation by noticing a card and connecting it with Pat. M does not, however, take up F's topic and proposes one of his own (the card) which is then taken up by F.

Although these examples highlight topic change, perhaps exaggeratedly at the less coherent level, they show, nevertheless, the liquidity and apparent ease of conversational management in NS interactions. Studies of NNS (including both NNS–NNS and NS–NNS dyads) reveal some much less elegant topic transitions.

*Miyuki*: Are you going to attend today's party?
*Akiko*: I don't know yet, but probably I'll attend. (long pause, with
    intermittent 'hm's). So, when will you go back Japan?
(Gass and Varonis 1986:337)

Although 'awkward pauses' with such abrupt shifts are not unknown in NS conversation, they appear much more frequently in interactions involving NNSs (Long 1983b, Scarcella 1983), but NSs appear willing to accept numerous abrupt changes in topic when conversing with NNSs. Gass and Varonis (1986:339) suggest this may result from the NSs' desire to avoid the greater discomfort which arises from conversational silence (Coulthard 1977).

Classroom discourse is another area of SLA research which has highlighted abrupt topic shift:

> T: Yeah. Or to make an accusation. OK. You say he he did, he killed that man. OK. You claim that, but you, if you can't prove it, it's only a claim, Yeah?
>
> S: It's to say something louder?
>
> T: No. That would be *ex* claim. To to make shout, say something loud, it's exclaim.
>
> S: He claims ...
>
> T:     Yeah.
>
> S: I think they'd better produce electric machine for car to use.
>
> T: For, for to to end the pollution problem?
>
> S:                     Yeah.
>
> S: Yeah.
>
> T: Yeah. OK. What does this mean? 'Get to'? Uh.
>
> SS: XX
>
> T: OK. It says the group has been trying to get the government, the city government, to help uhm draw special lanes, lanes like this (draws on board) on the street. OK. These are for cars. These are for bikes ... (pointing to blackboard)
>
> S: You know in Moscow they reproduce all all cab.
>
> T: Uhm?
>
> S: They reproduced all cabs XX
>
> T: They produce?
>
> S: *Re* produce
>
> T: D'you mean uh they use old cabs, old taxis?
>
> S: No, no, no. They reproduced all A L L cabs.
>
> T: All the cabs?
>
> S: Yeah, all the cabs for electric (electric you know) electric points.
>
> T: Cab. Oh you mean they made the cabs in down in downtown areas uh uh use electric uh motors?
>
> S:     Yeah, no downtown, all cabs in Moscow.
>
> T:                              Where?
>
> S: In Moscow.
>
> T: Oh. And it's successful?
>
> S: Yeah.

*T*:  OK. Uhm. Just a second, Igor. Let's what does this mean? If you get someone to do something. Uhm.

(Allwright 1980:180–1)

*Notes*
XX = unintelligible
SS = simultaneous contributions from several participants
Indented line = overlap with previous line

In this piece of transcribed classroom discourse, the teacher (T) is, first, trying to explain the meaning of 'claim' and, later, 'get to' (as in 'get someone to do something'). The student (S) who appears to be providing a model of 'claim' by beginning a sentence ('He claims . . .') in fact initiates a topic with his next sentence 'I think they'd better . . . .' This topic is ignored by the teacher who initiates yet another topic ('get to') only to have the same student return to the electric motor topic he tried to introduce earlier. He is successful this time, and he and the teacher have a short conversation about electric taxis in Moscow before the teacher returns to 'get to.' Though this interaction might seem hopelessly flawed with abrupt topic transitions, it is important to remember that language classroom discourse often involves two topics – the pedagogical one (here the items 'claim' and 'get to') and the content or real topic (here city traffic). In a language classroom setting, then, though these shifts might upset the teacher's plan (focus on the pedagogical topic), they seem unavoidable if authentic language is to occur at all. Those who believe most strongly in communicative approaches would, of course, be delighted by the students' use of the content rather than the pedagogical topic.

Finally, topic shift may be dramatic in another way; it may be the key to registral, stylistic, dialect, or even language shift. Fischer (1958) shows that variation of [n] and [ŋ] in -ing endings may have a topical orientation. The less formal variant is preferred in such everyday words as *fishing*, *swimming*, and *playing*; the more formal variant in such items as *reading*, *studying*, and *writing*. The English–Spanish shift quoted in 1.2.4 is often cited as an example of total language shift due to topic change, although an analysis of this same shift in 4.2 suggests that a much larger number of variables must be considered. Fishman's suggestion that topic shift (from business to Puerto Rican community affairs) is the source of language shift (English to Spanish) is an idea obviously in keeping with his analysis of *domains* (1.2.4, 3.2.1).[5]

In SLA topic is a relatively well-explored concept in conversational interaction analysis (particularly in experimental dyads and in classroom settings) and in language shift. It has not been the focus of quantitative studies of lower-level variability (at, for example, the morphological and phonological levels) in NNS production. Perhaps extension (or reinterpretation) of those studies which have focused on linguistic environment (e.g., Dickerson 1974) or on stylistic levels (e.g., Sato 1985) to include topic would reveal interesting variation.

### 3.2.3 *Genre*

Genres are to the identity of longer stretches of language what situations are to events. An inventory of types of talk exists for every culture (and subculture), and an entire set of behaviors (by the senders and the receivers) is appropriate to such genres as 'quiet chats,' 'rap sessions,' 'lectures,' 'essays,' 'novels,' and so on. The fact that some genres are embedded in others has misled some researchers to propose two levels. Hymes (1972) suggests that a conversation (his *speech event*) could contain a joke (his *speech act*). First, there is a terminological problem; *speech act* is surely best restricted to the general theory of illocutionary and perlocutionary acts (1.2.5). Second, there is no logical reason to assign 'joke' a different label from that given 'conversation' because it is embedded in it since the reverse could as well be true – a joke which contained a conversation would not seem strange at all. In formulating rules for the two genres, researchers may show that conversations are at a higher level or less restricted (less marked, perhaps) though surely not dissimilar.[6] Up to a point, then, Hymes' definition of *speech event* corresponds to what is meant here by *genre*:

> The term *speech event* will be restricted to activities, or aspects of activities, that are directly governed by rules or norms for the use of speech. An event may consist of a single speech act, but will often comprise several. (1972:56)

The fact that some genres are closely identified with times, places, and situations has already been noticed, and that fact may cause some unavoidable confusion in terminology. Hymes (1972) errs again in suggesting that events and genres must be kept separate when he surely means situations and genres must be kept apart.

> Genres often coincide with speech events, but must be treated as analytically independent of them. They may occur in (or as) different events. The sermon as a genre is typically identical with a certain place in a church service, but its properties may be invoked, for serious or humorous effect, in other situations. (65)

Some confusion about any genre versus 'conversation' stems from the ambiguity of the latter term. In one sense *a* conversation is a high-level genre and suggests the very general rules that obtain where that genre (or *proto-genre*) label is appropriate. Since conversation in a more general sense is basic to all face-to-face interaction, however, it may refer to such a general level of speech performance that one would hardly want to call it a genre. Perhaps *talk* is a more appropriate term for this sense, reserving 'conversation' for the proto-genre. To exemplify all these levels, one might note that an *argument* (surely a genre) takes place in *talk*, but it is not at all clear that every argument is *a* conversation. One cannot tell a joke except through talk, but a raconteur who is asked to recite a joke at a party might not have *a* conversation with any of the hearers after or before the telling, and the telling itself could hardly be called a conversation, even if the joke itself contained a quoted conversation.[7]

A better definition of genre focuses on both the purposes and aims of the event and its structure.

> [A genre is] a recognized communicative event with a shared public purpose and with aims mutually understood by the participants within that event; [it is] ... a structured and standardized communication event with constraints on allowable contributions in terms of the positioning, form and intent. (Swales 1985:4)

Perhaps the most productive work on genres has focused on the specific structures which arise in genres well-defined by the specificity of such aims and purposes. In anthropologically oriented studies, the focus has often been on ritualized genres from non-Western cultures, though, more recently, ethnographers and folklorists have concentrated on such genres in cultures closer to home, though there, as well, the focus has been on minority or non-mainstream groups. There is, therefore, no wealth of information about the most commonplace of speech genres. As a result, a learner of Koya (a language of India) may be well informed about sexual joking in courting encounters (Brukman 1975), and a learner of urban United States Black English vernacular might readily discover the rules for the *dozens* (a ritualized insult game played, principally, by male adolescents) (Labov 1972b), but a learner of English (or a teacher or textbook writer) might have difficulty finding a description and interpretation of the structure and meaning of a *sales negotiation*, a *reproach to an employee*, a *condolence on the death of a family member*, a *job interview*, and so on in English, Russian, or Spanish. Set in the framework of cross-cultural research, however, there are some interesting analyses of ordinary speech genres, though their focus is often on why miscommunication or failed affective response patterns arose.

Akinnaso and Ajirotutu (1982) investigate the job interview, hoping to discover why some ethnic minorities in the United States have failed to succeed in them. Their description of the genre includes accounting for its structural and linguistic differences from ordinary conversational inter-action. It structurally differs by being held at an appointed time, and, although the outcome is unknown, its purpose – 'to settle future decisions about an issue known prior to the commencement of talk' (Silverman 1973:39) – is known to all participants (Akinnaso and Ajirotutu 1982:121). In addition, some sort of agenda or program guides the interaction, and there is generally some record kept of it (121). Most important structurally are the fixed rights and obligations of interviewer and interviewee; the interviewer is especially powerful in topic, questioning, personal information, and talk initiation and termination rights (121–2). These interviewer rights predict many of the linguistic differences between a job interview and ordinary talk. For example, interruption or the shift of the responsibility for answering to another speaker are linguistic examples of the powerful role occupied by the interviewer. In addition, an interviewer will often use a powerful *we* in contrast to the interviewee's weaker *I* (122). At an even deeper level, Akinnaso and Ajirotutu suggest that an interviewee must be especially sensitive to indirectness in the interviewer's questions. They cite (124) the following example of an interviewee's failure to see the intent behind a question:

> *Interviewer*: What about the library interests you most?
> *Interviewee*: What about the library in terms of the books? or the whole building?
> *Interviewer*: Any point that you'd like to . . .
> *Interviewee*: Oh, the children's books, because I have a child, and the children .. you know there's so many you know books for them to read you know, and little things that would interest them would interest me too.

The authors interpret the interviewer's question to mean 'What is there about *working in the library* which interests you and which you think you could do well?' [emphases in the original]. They go on to claim that the interviewee's failure to interpret this indirectness correctly led her to perform a damaging response about children's books, not a strong emphasis in most university libraries (125).

Questions in a job interview serve a particularly different set of functions from those used in ordinary talk: in addition to their being often indirect, obviously evaluative, and the general prerogative of the interviewer, they are, in fact, the focus of the communicative activity (127). This example shows how detailed study of a specific instance of a genre leads to deeper understandings of structure and content; even if elegant generalizations do not emerge, authentic examples for applied linguistic reference are made available.

Linguists who have had an eye on the future practical use of their investigations have carefully investigated a number of written genres. Concern over the inability of NNSs to write research articles, for example, has led to detailed analyses. Jingfu (1987:81) lists the knowledge a writer would need to produce such an article:

1   The conventional patterns of organization found in a research article e.g. in an experimental RA [research article], there would be an Introduction, a Method, and Results and Discussion sections, and there is likely to be an Abstract.

2 The purpose and content of each section e.g. the Introduction consists of a survey of past literature and a statement of purpose.
3 The possible choices of lexis and structure conventionally used to express each 'move' used in different sections.
4 A background knowledge of the specialized content area.

Apparently the most detailed work on a subsection of the research article has been done on the introduction. Swales (1981) suggests that the following discourse units make up that section:

>Move 1: Establishing the field
>(a) Showing centrality
>  (i) by interest
>  (ii) by importance
>  (iii) by topic-prominence
>  (iv) by standard procedure
>(b) Stating current knowledge
>(c) Ascribing key characteristics
>
>Move 2: Summarizing previous research
>(a) Strong author-orientation
>(b) Weak author-orientation
>(c) Subject orientations
>
>Move 3: Preparing for present research
>(a) Indicating a gap
>(b) Question-raising
>(c) Extending a finding
>
>Move 4: Introducing present research
>(a) Giving the purpose
>(b) Describing present research
>  (i) by this/the present signals
>  (ii) by move 3 take-up
>  (iii) by switching to the first person pronoun

Although specific studies of other genres have shown that the sequence proposed by Swales is not always strictly adhered to or that parts of it may be omitted (e.g., Cooper 1985) and there is criticism, as well, of the sampling and analysis (Bley-Vroman and Selinker 1984), such work provides generalizations based on samples drawn from professional, written work (forty-eight in the Swales study) and offers teachers, textbook writers, and learners guidance in linguistic structure where, before, only the study of individual samples existed. The connection of such genre study with the interests of specialized language use, whether with instructional aims or not, is obvious (2.2.2).

Some research has been done on the degree to which NNSs use (or fail to use) NS-like genres or organizational patterns. Kaplan (1966) studied paragraph organization in the *essay*, the written genre most often inflicted on United States college students, NNS and NS alike. In an early and informal look at a few samples, he concluded that the principles of organization were strikingly different from one language (or language group) to another; figure 3.2 is an attempt at a visual representation of the organizational patterns for several different linguistic groups. The English paragraph shows linear development; a topic is stated (or concluded at the end), and every other piece of fact or opinion in the paragraph is explicitly related to it. Semitic organization shows development through parallelism, a use of appositional and comparative statements to further the discussion of the main idea. The Oriental method of development looks at a topic from a number of different outside perspectives. Romance writers digress from the main topic, and Russian organization allows even more loosely connected parenthetical expansions of a minor subtopic or digression. Kaplan retracts the strong form of his contrastive claims about organization (1986), but conscious copying of an L1 composition style in an L2 writing task is reported in Stalker and Stalker (to appear).

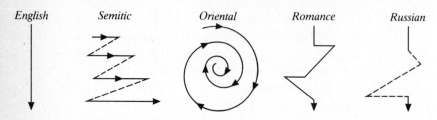

*Figure 3.2*   Paragraph organization strategies (source: Kaplan 1966)

Specific claims about NNS distinct performance in spoken genres have also been made. In some of the literature this work is referred to under the general rubric of *task*, but in many cases such verbal tasks may be thought of as genres.[8] A study of variation among NNSs from different language background groups in *debate* and *problem-solving* tasks was provided in 2.2.1. Additionally, studies of NS language directed to NNSs, though done for the specific purpose of studying NS modification of output when the interlocutor is an NNS, have often focused on one particular genre (e.g., the *lecturette* in Long 1985).

Woken and Swales (to appear) show that some patterns of typical NNS–NS discourse may be modified by the assignment of specialist roles in a specific generic setting. In a computer tutorial, for example, they show that an NNS, if he or she is the instructor rather than the student, gains and uses all the rights assigned that role by the genre. Attributions of reticence, lesser amount of speech, unwillingness to interrupt, and so on to the NNS in earlier studies may only indicate that the NNS is in a genre (e.g., *lesson*) in which the role assigned (*student*) is one of lesser power, predicting a less aggressive linguistic posture. A genre analysis may help elaborate and correct the predictions of a simple discourse analysis. Recall that in a study of *courtroom testimony*, experience in the genre proved to be an important factor in predicting a number of powerful speech characteristics, calling into question previous interpretations of gender specific powerlessness (2.1.2).

Though genre analysis seems to have its biggest influence in the study of texts in language for special purposes, the extension of such analysis to a greater variety of everyday speech genres may help sharpen researchers' and practitioners' awareness of larger units of language variety which fluent speakers and writers must have under both receptive and productive control. Additionally, the investigation of the structure and development of interlanguage genres, along with the investigation of interlanguage discourse in general, will both aid teaching and learning programs and sharpen the ability to characterize monolingual genres.

## 3.3 Relations

The connections between interlocutors may be characterized in three ways: how closely connected are they (*solidarity*), who has more or less *power*, and what is the pattern of communication between and among them (*network*)?

### 3.3.1 *Solidarity*

Brown and Gilman (1960) account for diachronic and synchronic variation in second person pronominal usage in a number of Western European languages on the basis of solidarity and *power* (3.3.2).

Such languages as German, Polish, Spanish, and so on have 'formal' or 'polite' second person forms (Sie, Vous, Usted, etc. – the *V* forms) and 'familiar' forms (Du, Tu, etc. – the *T* forms). Traditionally, the interlocutor with the greatest power used the *T* form to address others of lesser power and received the *V* form from them. Figure 3.3 shows the system as it once was: superiors giving *T* and receiving *V*. When equals in terms of power are considered, however, the dimension of the solidarity or closeness of the relationship between interlocutors must be considered to resolve pronoun selection. As figure 3.3 shows, when equals are in a solidary relationship, the *T* form is used by both; when the relationship is not solidary, the *V* is used. Though solidarity is important, the basics of the system may be said to be power generated.

The use of solidarity as a basis for pronoun selection, however, introduced tension into the system (figure 3.4), and solidarity began to be a consideration

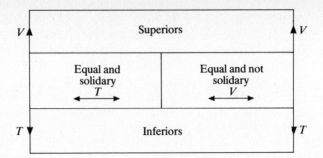

*Figure 3.3* The power dominated *T–V* pronoun system (source: Brown and Gilman 1960: 259)

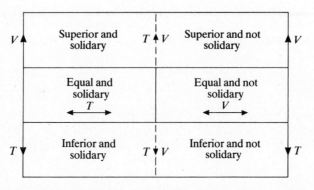

*Figure 3.4* The power dominated *T–V* pronoun system under tension from the influence of solidarity (source: Brown and Gilman 1960: 259)

even when power was not shared. The change is represented in the upper left and lower right areas of figure 3.4. Following the use of *T* in solidary and equal relationships, increasing uses of *T* to superior but solidary interlocutors occur. Similarly, following the use of *V* among equal but not solidary interlocutors, the uses of *V* to nonsolidary inferiors increases. Brown and Gilman claim that this tension is resolved by a new system in which solidarity rather than power is the dominating concern. Figure 3.5a shows a number of conflicts which result from the unstable system of figure 3.4, and 3.5b shows their resolution in the new, solidarity-based system. A customer might address a nonsolidary but inferior waiter with either *T* or *V* in the unstable system (figure 3.5a). Since the resolution is towards solidarity, the newer, invariant use is *V* (figure 3.5b). The other role relationships displayed in figures 3.5a and b show the domination of the solidarity relationship over the old power system.

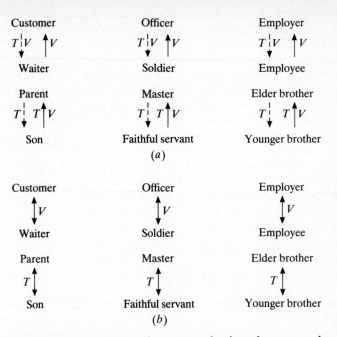

*Figure 3.5* (a) Situations of *T–V* use in a power dominated system under tension from solidarity (b) tensions resolved in the direction of solidarity (source: Brown and Gilman 1960: 260)

Such a study at the pronominal level parallels the work done in modern quantitative sociolinguistics, particularly for phonological and morphological matters; a stable rule system is intruded on, and variation is introduced. Although Brown and Gilman do not (and perhaps cannot) show the demographic details of this change (gender and class differences, for example), one may imagine that there was leadership and resistance in its progress exactly as there would be for units more typically studied in quantitative research.

Friedrich (1972), in a survey of a large number of factors guiding the selection of the *T* and *V* forms in Russian, isolates as one important variable 'emotional solidarity  the sympathy and antipathy between two speakers' (276), and he finds  the usage he studied more complex in just that area than the system outlined by Brown and Gilman:

Emotional distance and certain negative feelings went together with the formal pronoun. Contrariwise, close friends, lovers, and persons joined in some common purpose would tend to use *ty*, and *ty* in some contexts could symbolize the dislike or deprecation bred of familiarity. In brief, the correlation between pronouns and solidarity was complicated, and difficult to predict in terms of a simple continuum between the *ty* of 'like-mindedness' (Brown and Gilman 1960) and the *vy* of weak solidarity. (278)

In some cases, solidarity seems to be the foundation of a *network*, the notion taken up in 3.3.2. In describing how networks were determined in her study of linguistic variables in Belfast, Northern Ireland, Milroy notes that the connections of work, kin, and friendship were the most valuable (Milroy 1987:107).[9] She goes on to claim that the solidarity function (as exposed in network analyses) is often so strong as to influence linguistic behavior regardless of social status or sex (1980:84). She shows, for example, that in one section of Belfast men tend to use more vernacular variants, but some women are unusually high users of those same variants. It turns out that just those women whose local solidarity is greatest are those who make greatest use of the vernacular forms.[10] Labov's respondents in Martha's Vineyard who used the old-fashioned island vowels also turned out to be those who felt the greatest solidarity with island life and culture.

Solidarity or lack of it may be one of the principal determiners of the *distance* (3.5.1) in a given interaction.

Most specifically, solidarity would appear to be the principal explanatory factor in some groups' evaluating a surrounding standard variety high in areas of competence but a regional or nonstandard variety high in integrity and social attractiveness. The importance of solidarity helps account, at least in part, for the persistence of such varieties in the face of prestige forms:

> Standard accents and dialects usually connote high status and competence; regional, ethnic, and lower-class varieties are associated with greater speaker integrity and attractiveness. *The trust and liking apparently reflected in such varieties may be related to conceptions of ingroup solidarity.* (Edwards 1985:149; emphasis added)

Admittedly, however, the patterns of solidarity versus competence may be more complex. Ryan, Giles, and Sebastian (1982) show that both majority and minority groups may rate the standard or nonstandard higher for solidarity (table 3.1). In type A, both groups prefer the majority variety for both status and solidarity; in early studies of French-speaking Canadian responses to French and English (Lambert et al. 1960), it is assumed that the inferiority feelings of French speakers were so great that the majority language (in this case, English) was rated high for both competence and solidarity. In type B, minority speakers prefer their own variety for solidarity but not competence, but in type C each group prefers its own variety on both counts. This is likely to be true in areas with 'emerging' ethnic or regional standards. In type D, a superposed standard (e.g., RP) spoken naturally by none may be rated high only for competence.

*Table 3.1*   Preference for status and solidarity varieties by majority and minority group raters

| | Judges | | | |
|---|---|---|---|---|
| | LV1 speakers | | LV2 speakers | |
| Type of preference | Status | Solidarity | Status | Solidarity |
| A   Majority group | LV1 | LV1 | LV1 | LV1 |
| B   Majority group for status; in group<br> for solidarity | LV1 | LV1 | LV1 | LV2 |
| C   In-group | LV1 | LV1 | LV2 | LV2 |
| D   Majority group for status;<br> minority group for solidarity | LV1 | LV2 | LV1 | LV2 |

LV1 majority language
LV2 minority language
*Source*: Ryon, Giles, and Sebastian 1982:9

As a factor in SLA, solidarity operates at both societal and individual levels. Where large numbers of solidary NNSs use an L2, particularly when they may have historical and/or current reasons to feel that solidarity with NSs is unlikely, they may begin to develop an NNS variety. The five propositions which Ball and Giles (1982) identify as major contributors to likely failure in SLA, though stated in terms of individual responses, all refer to cases in which one group is in an unlikely position to form a solidary relation with another (2.1.3). It is not surprising, then, that intraethnic and emerging national solidarity, particularly in post-colonial societies, has produced NNS varieties (e.g., Kachru 1982b).

Solidarity as an explicit factor has not been the focus of research in SLA, though a number of studies have included factors which might be so reinterpreted. Beebe (1985) lists a large number of studies which were sampled to show variation in learners' preferences for a model (in both SLA and second variety acquisition). She suggests in five out of six circumstances that solidarity will be the unmarked choice (table 3.2). Only 'higher prestige over lower prestige' indicates a (possibly) nonsolidary unmarked choice as a model. Though it would be unreasonable to suggest that only solidary models of language be supported by teachers, materials, and programs, it is fair to suggest that analyses of natural and classroom SLA attend to the degree of solidarity learners may or may not feel (or can be brought about to feel) for speakers of the model. Recall, however, that not all SLA research has found that positive affective feelings for the L2 speakers (indications of an 'integrative' motivation – 2.1.3) predict success. In natural language learning settings, however, particularly among lower status immigrant groups, the

*Table 3.2*   Target language model preferences

| Unmarked choice | Marked choice |
| --- | --- |
| *Peers over teachers*<br>Labov (1972b) Black gang's<br>  BEV over SE<br>Stewart (1964) Black children<br>Milon (1975) Japanese child,<br>  HCE and SE of peers<br>Wolfram (1973) Puerto Ricans'<br>  BEV | *Teachers/parents/adults/own ethnic*<br>*group over peers*<br>Labov (1972b) lames<br>Wolfram (1973) lames<br>Subjective reaction tests<br>LaFerriere (1979) own ethnic Chinese<br>  group over Irish peers |
| *Peers over parents*<br>Hewitt (1982) British Black<br>  youths of Caribbean origin<br>L1 loss in second and third<br>  generation immigrants<br>Labov (1972b) New Jersey<br>  middle class White children<br>Stewart (1964) Black children<br>  learning BEV in Washington,<br>  DC<br>Poplack (1978) Puerto Ricans<br>  learning BEV despite low<br>  contact | |
| *Own social group over other*<br>*social group*<br>Labov (1972b) Black gang's<br>  BEV<br>Fishman (1966) language<br>  loyalty<br>LaFerriere (1979) ethnic<br>  stratification in Boston<br>Beebe (1981) Chinese Thai<br>  ethnic identity markers<br>Hewitt (1982) Black<br>  adolescents<br>Benton (1964) Maori child | *Other social group over own social group*<br>Wolfram (1973)<br>Reinstein and Hoffman (1972)<br>Poplack (1978)<br>Hewitt (1982) White using Black creole |
| *Friends over nonfriends*<br>Poplack (1978) Puerto Rican<br>  6th graders<br>Milroy (1980) social networks<br>  in Belfast<br>Labov (1972b) Black gangs<br>Hewitt (1982) White using<br>  Black creole of friends | *Nonfriends over friends*<br>Poplack (1978) nonreciprocal friendship<br>Labov (1972a) influence despite hostility |

*Table 3.2   continued*

| Unmarked choice | Marked choice |
| --- | --- |
| *High contact over low contact*<br>Wolfram (1973) Puerto Rican<br>  adolescents<br>Reinstein and Hoffman (1972)<br>  Puerto Rican 4th graders<br>Taylor, Meynard, and Rheault<br>  (1977) French Canadian<br>  university students | *Low contact over high contact*<br>Poplack (1978) Puerto Ricans learning<br>  BEV over SE |
| *Higher prestige over lower*<br>French preference for English<br>  over 'American' language<br>Subjective reactions tests<br>Labov (1972b) lames<br>Day (1980) SE over Hawaii<br>  Creole | *Lower prestige over higher prestige*<br>Labov (1972b) Black gangs<br>Poplack (1978) Puerto Rican's BEV<br>Wolfram (1973) Puerto Rican's BEV |

BEV = Black English Vernacular
SE = Standard English
HCE = Hawaiian Creole English
*Source*: Beebe 1985:406

highest indicator of SLA success is often the amount of interaction with NSs (e.g., Klein and Dittmar 1979, Werkgroep Taal Buitenlandse Werknemers 1980), surely a solidarity factor.

Another level of solidarity that is beginning to be investigated operates in the social world of the classroom itself. Although numerous discourse and input analyses of classroom interaction have been done, the treatment of the classroom as a setting for complex social and individual relations is relatively new (e.g., Breen 1985). Diary studies of classroom language learners reveal, for example, that solidarity among learners may emerge:

> One of the tangents we got off on today actually involved one student and the teacher, as near as I could tell. At least there were a few people who I noticed were looking around bored, annoyed, or laughing at the somewhat ridiculous questions this person tends to come up with regularly. This same person has the annoying (not just to me I believe) habit of exclaiming out loud in a 'whiny' tone, 'No-oo-o' when someone in class gives the wrong answer – a tone which seems to say, 'How *could* you say *that*!' Until today I thought I was the only one who reacted this way to her, but I noticed a comrade or two sharing my look of irritation and smiling at me in recognition. (Lynch 1979:44)

Bailey (1983:82) suggests that the word *comrade* in this entry is particularly rich in connotative power, implying, one must imagine, the beginnings of solidarity within this classroom setting, though, as in this case, not all solidarity springs from simple appreciation for others. In fact, it would be easy to imagine classroom situations in which the solidary front presented by students against the teacher (or by groups of students against one another, based, perhaps, on such natural distinctions as age, sex, status, and so on) impedes normal classroom activities.

Most generally, solidarity as a concept in SLA seems to have been considered for larger societal levels, informing such theories as Giles's intergroup model and Schumann's acculturation model (2.1.3) and the recognition of developing NNS standards in such areas as Singapore, West Africa, and India (for English).

In quantitative sociolinguistics, on the other hand, solidarity, when explicitly studied, is more often related to nonglobal aspects of language performance.

Though one might claim that any number of studies of affective variables in SLA have touched on themes which might be reinterpreted as solidarity, correlation of lower-level performance features in the developing interlanguage with solidarity singled out as a specific feature might add further information to the dispute over the role of just such variables.


### 3.3.2 *Network*

The number and type of relations an individual has to others make up his or her *network*; groups of such interrelated individuals are *social networks*. Bloomfield (1933:46) suggests that linguistic diversity and similarity is a direct result of speaker connections.

> Imagine a huge chart with a dot for every speaker in the community, and imagine that every time any speaker uttered a sentence, an arrow were drawn into the chart pointing from his dot to the dot representing one of his hearers. At the end of a given period of time, say seventy years, this chart would show us the density of communication within the community. Some speakers would turn out to have been in close communication: there would be many arrows from one to the other, and there would be many series of arrows connecting them by way of one, two, or three intermediate speakers. At the other extreme there would be widely separated speakers who had never heard each other speak and were connected only by long chains of arrows through many intermediate speakers. If we wanted to explain the likeness and unlikeness between various speakers in the community, or, what comes to the same thing, to predict the degree of likeness for any two given speakers,

our first step would be to count and evaluate the arrows and series of arrows connecting their dots. (1933:46–7)

In more recent quantitative sociolinguistic research, network has proved important in two respects: (1) the place of an individual speaker within a network may help explain his or her deviation from norms expected on the basis of such other factors as status, age, sex, and so on; and (2) the identification and use of social networks facilitates fieldwork.

A visual representation of a network may be very complex. Figure 3.6 shows the network relations (determined by 'hang-out' patterns) among a Black street gang known as the Jets. The strong, dark lines indicate members who named each other in response to the question 'Is there a bunch of cats you hang out with?' Dotted lines (with arrows) indicate a nonreciprocal naming. Stan, named most often, is a central figure. He belongs both to a group of six who are the best fighters (Deuce, Vaughn, Larry, Jesse, and Ronald) and to a group of five who keep and fly pigeons from roof-tops (Hop, Rednall, Doug, and Rel). Smaller circles indicate members more on the periphery of the gang, and the boxes indicate *lames*, individuals who only marginally participate in the street life of the gang (2.2.5). In one such gang Labov showed that both rule frequency and rule ordering may be predicted by network position. For example, postvocalic (r) before vowels (e.g., '... here in ...') occurs only 4 percent of the time in the use of T-Bird gang members but 21 percent of the time in the use of lames associated with the same gang. Gang members weight their final t/d deletion rule so that a following nonvowel (e.g., '... missed by ...') promotes operation of the rule most strongly and no preceding morpheme boundary (e.g., 'mist') promotes it only secondarily. The lames, however, have reversed that order, letting a lack of a morpheme boundary before the (t/d) variable promote its deletion more strongly than a following nonvowel does (Labov 1972b:226f.). Such explanations due to network position account for otherwise puzzling discrepancies in frequency scores between individuals of the same age, sex, ethnicity, and status.

Milroy (1980) has similarly shown that the degree of integration into a variety of local networks may account for linguistic differences. In Belfast, Northern Ireland the variable (a) refers to the retracting and raising of [æ] in the local vernacular. Milroy assigns scores ranging from 100 (standard [æ] to 500 (the most retracted and raised version – [ɔ³]). Figure 3.7 shows the scores for (a) for younger and older men and women in three areas of the city – the Hammer, the Clonard, and Ballymacarrett. As might be predicted from findings discussed so far (especially in 2.1.2), women in general and younger women in particular adhere more to the standard form. This is not true, however, of the younger women of the Clonard, whose vernacular (a) use is actually higher than young men's and nearly as high as older men's. Milroy shows, however, that the network scores for young women in the Clonard are

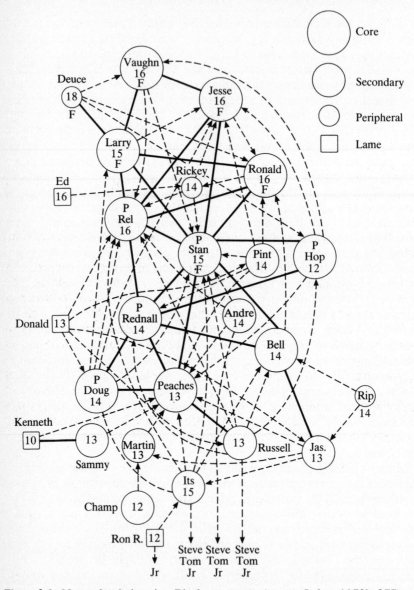

*Figure 3.6*  Network relations in a Black street gang (source: Labov 1972b: 277)

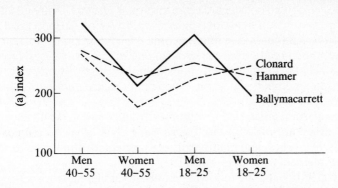

*Figure 3.7*   Age and sex variation of (a) in Belfast, Northern Ireland (source: Milroy 1980: 124)

exceptionally high, predicting their use of the local vernacular form (1980:152f.).

How are such network scores computed, and what general expectations might one have about them? Networks may be *anchored* in a single individual as a focal point, and the lines of personal contacts which connect that individual directly to others form the cluster of *first order zones*. Connections to other individuals through the first order zone contacts create a layer of *second order zones*, weaker than the first, but important in social networks in many areas of social life.

Networks may be *dense*, a notion which measures the number of linkages among people who are linked to the focal point. In figure 3.8, the first order zone network is an example of a relatively dense one; many of the persons connected to X, the focal point, are also connected to one another. The second order zone, however, is an example of a sparely connected network;

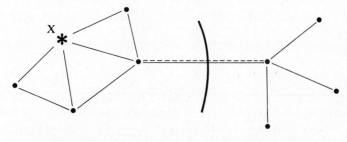

First order zone                    Second order zone

*Figure 3.8*   Network relations (source: Milroy 1980: 48)

three points are connected to a single one but not to each other (Boissevain 1974). Areas of high density are often known as *clusters* (Milroy 1980:50).

Another measure of network type is its *multiplexity*. An individual may be connected to another in one function only – friend or kin or workmate, and so on – and such relations are known as *uniplex*. In many cases, however, a person is related to another in more complex ways – workmate, church member, club member, and so on – such relations are *multiplex* (Boissevain 1974).

In general, rural areas tend to multiplexity and denseness and urban areas, with the exception of long-standing working class areas, to uniplexity and spareness. Denseness and multiplexity are particularly important settings for norm enforcement (e.g., Boissevain 1974).

Milroy (1980) used the following criteria to assign network scores to her respondents in Belfast, Northern Ireland:

1  Membership of a high-density, territorially based cluster.
2  Having substantial ties of kinship in the neighbourhood (more than one household, in addition to his own nuclear family).
3  Working in the same place as at least *two* others from the same area.
4  The same place of work as at least *two* others of the same sex from the area.
5  Voluntary association with workmates in leisure hours. This applies in practice only when conditions 3 and 4 are satisfied. (141–2)

Network scores are then assigned individuals along the range 0 (none of the above factors applied) to 5 (all the above factors applied). It is now possible to associate network scores with some of the groups in figure 3.7, where it was seen that the younger women from the Clonard, unexpectedly, used a higher percentage of a vernacular norm (the (a) variable) than the young men did:

| Age | Sex | Network score |
|---|---|---|
| 18–25 | F | 4.75 |
|  | M | 3.00 |
| 40–55 | F | 1.00 |
|  | M | 2.50 |

Although the usual higher network score for men is evident in the older group, the relation is reversed for the younger respondents. Since the maximum score is five, the 4.75 for the Clonard young women is very high indeed. Milroy explains that many Clonard men are unemployed, removing several of the possibilities for network connections; moreover, all the younger Clonard women were employed, and several of them were employed in the same place and spent a good deal of leisure time with one another, developing the sorts of dense, multiplex contacts often associated with men. Network density and type, then, provide another opportunity to observe how other factors may overcome linguistic stereotypes usually assigned on the basis of sex (2.1.2).

In an even more elaborate use of network analysis (and one which has more relevance for SLA), Bortoni-Ricardo (1985) studied the urbanization of the speech of rural Brazilian (Caipira) speakers who immigrate to urban areas. She uses the relationship, drawn explicitly by Milroy (1982), of network to concepts introduced by Le Page concerning the *diffuseness* and *focusing* of language varieties (Le Page 1978). A focused dialect community is one in which all the members of a group are most alike and in which there is little contact with outside influences. A diffuse group, on the other hand, has the opposite properties – differentiation among members, openness to outside influences, more loosely defined norms of behavior.[11] Bortoni-Ricardo argues that if a migrant from a rural area

> switches from an insulated network [focused, multiplex, dense] of kinfolk and fellow-migrants into a larger network [diffuse, uniplex, spare] of new acquaintances, some of whom are more advanced in the process of urban culture acquisition, he will tend to take the latter as models for his verbal and nonverbal behaviour. He will then commit himself to an effort towards the assimilation of more prestigious ways of speaking, which represents a movement away from the vernacular. (Bortoni-Ricardo 1985:119)

To relate linguistic performance to this hypothesis, each respondent in the Bortoni-Ricardo study was given an *integration index* score and an *urbanization index* score. The integration score is computed from a statistical program which assigns a quantitative value based on each group member's being asked to name three persons with whom he or she most frequently interacts:

> The higher the migrant's integration index, the more advanced s/he is likely to be in the process of transition from an insulated into an integrated network, and consequently, the more diffuse her/his rural dialect will tend to be. (Bortoni-Ricardo 1985:167–8)

To add another dimension to this simple quantitative measure, an average of each respondent's peers' scores on seven variables which indicated the degree of exposure to the urban setting was also taken. The variables included level of schooling, type of work, spatial mobility, participation in urban events, exposure to media, political awareness, and the domain in which a link with a peer was made (Bortoni-Ricardo 1985:169–70).

When these network findings are applied to linguistic facts, a typical pattern occurs: the more focused, dense, multiplex relations typical of rural areas predict retention of Caipira forms (or a slower acquisition of urban norms); the more diffuse, uniplex relations of an urban setting indicate increased use of prestige forms. An especially stigmatized Caipira form results when the palatal lateral [ʎ] is vocalized (e.g., *milho* 'corn,' pronounced [miʎu] in standard Brazilian Portuguese, is pronounced [miʲu] in rural varieties). A rank-order correlation test (male scores only, with certain atypical scores deleted) of integration scores with lateral vocalization scores yielded a significance of 0.001, and the correlation of this same variable with the urbanization score was significant at the 0.005 level. On the other hand, the correlation of palatal lateral vocalization for women with integration and urbanization scores showed no significance for integration and only limited significance (vocalization in only one linguistic environment – following vowels other than [i]) for urbanization, i.e., 0.034. More interestingly, Bortoni-Ricardo shows that the two indices themselves negatively correlate (at a 0.05 level of significance) for women while they positively correlate for men. The conclusion is that a numerical characterization for men is as sufficient as an account of urban contacts in explaining the diffusion of their rural speech patterns. For women, however, a high integration index score may be simply a reflection of associations with large numbers of kin, premigration contacts, and close neighbors, none of whom would serve as diffusion models. The frequency score of integration, then, does not really assess for women the degree of their assimilation to the urban setting. Bortoni-Ricardo suggests that they, in fact, do not go to urban life but that urban life comes to them, particularly through husbands and older children who make a more rapid accommodation to the urban setting. When such factors are considered (revealing a high urbanization index for some women) urban prestige variants also seem to increase in their speech (190).

More refined network analyses, then, which make use of culturally appropriate measures may provide satisfying accounts of individual variation in linguistic change.

Network analysis, as suggested above, has also informed fieldwork procedures in sociolinguistics. *Friends of friends*, as second order zone individuals are called in the literature (figure 3.8), are very often those who arrange for things to be bought wholesale, for traffic tickets or other minor legal difficulties to be taken care of at little expense or embarrassment, and so on (Boissevain 1974, Boissevain and Mitchell 1973). Milroy (1980) has made specific use of this network relationship in her collection techniques in Belfast, Northern Ireland. In dense networks, first order zones tend to be bounded; therefore, second order zone persons are extremely important in negotiating the sorts of goods and services which people in the first order may need but are not able to provide among themselves. A friend of a friend is, therefore, an established and useful sort of contact. In many cases Milroy's role as a fieldworker was not even mentioned in introductions since that had become secondary to her role as friend of a friend (Milroy 980:54). She notes further that such a relationship, particularly after obligations to her had been established by favors she rendered members of the group, allowed for the development of spontaneous speech styles in recordings (in contrast to the interview style so common in such settings). Though there is no claim that these recordings are of 'natural' speech, there is every indication that they are not characterized by the guiding of the interviewer or by a question-answer format (Milroy 1980:62–3).

Network analysis has, then, in addition to providing explanatory social variables for linguistic variation, allowed fieldworkers to identify and assess the social fabric more carefully by gaining entry to groups and being able to evaluate the subsequent performances for both their authenticity and type.

Studies of network position have not been specifically carried out in SLA settings, though a good many surveys which have been done may be reinterpreted along those lines. In particular, European studies of migrant worker communities appear to have been sensitive in both practice and planning to network-like relations among respondents and between respondents and the NS community (e.g., Perdue 1984, Heidelberger Forschungsprojekt 'Pidgin-Deutsch' 1975). In the Heidelberg study of Italian and Spanish migrant workers in Germany, the two social facts which best correlated with NS-like syntactic performance were (1) contacts with Germans in leisure time, and (2) contacts with Germans at work (Klein and Dittmar 1979:208). Such factors are clearly very like the sorts of considerations Milroy (1980) used in designing her network index for respondents in Belfast, Northern Ireland; nor are they very different from the sorts of scores used by Bortoni-Ricardo in characterizing the degree of urbanization of Brazilian Caipira migrants. An SLA community, at least in natural language learning settings, might be directly investigated in terms of its network properties. In the case of European migrant workers, many come from dense, multiplex, focused rural areas and move to urban areas where network connections are the opposite. One must ask, however, whether or not the sort of continuing network relations (of the sort some Brazilian women kept up even after migration, according to Bortoni-Ricardo) are possible in such situations. That is, are there sufficient kin and workmates available to maintain a dense, multiplex, focused community of speakers? Perhaps the answer will differ from site to site, depending both on quantity of immigrants and on the life style adopted by those who came earlier.

Network relations of classroom learners might be directly investigated as well. In some classrooms, the students come from heterogeneous backgrounds; the classroom network is decidedly uniplex, for students know one another only as students. In others, however, students are often related to one another in many other ways. The density and multiplexity of their relations might serve to impede language acquisition, if the model antagonizes or threatens the group in any way. On the other hand, classroom network solidarity might enhance language acquisition if the model could somehow become a part of the norms of the group. Since dense, multiplex networks impose norms with considerably more force than spare, uniplex ones do, that would be obviously desirable; since they resist new norms, however, it will be more difficult. Studies that focus on language learning communities which permit isolation of such factors might reveal the degree to which network relations play a role in language acquisition and suggest ways in which network manipulation might allow applied linguists avenues for curricular, syllabus, and teacher preparation modification.

### 3.3.3 *Power*

A great deal has already been said about the influence of power on linguistic forms, particularly in 2.1.2 and 3.3.1. What was often referred to as 'women's speech' is reinterpreted by some scholars to be 'powerless speech' and is characterized by hedging, politeness, and the like. Additionally, powerful speech is often associated with majority group performance, the variety often judged most competent in language attitude surveys (1.2.6 and 2.1.4). At the most concrete level, language and power are nearly synonymous in some cultures but not closely connected in others:

> Among the Araucanians of Chile the head of a band was its best orator, and his power dependeds upon his ability to sway others through oratory. Among the Abipon of Argentina no desired role or status depend upon skill in speaking; chiefs and members of the one prestigious men's group were selected solely on the basis of success in battle. The Iroquois value eloquence in chiefs and orators as much as bravery in war; the two are usually mentioned together and with equal status. A chief could rise equally quickly by either. (Hymes 1972:42)

Several approaches to language as power and uses of language to control, manipulate, and coerce are provided in Kedar (1987).

Recent research in social interaction emphasizes the negotiation of control in conversation rather than the function of absolute power (as seen in job interviews in 3.2.3). The negotiation of turn-taking in conversation, for example, has already been shown to be an important element in establishing control for that limited interaction, but, through that establishment, redefining (or reaffirming) relations among interlocutors.

At the level of linguistic forms, power, as it is represented in prestige varieties, may have a considerable influence on linguistic change. Although linguists have generally disregarded prescriptivism, such facts as middle class hypercorrection (2.2.3), among others, do not allow sociolinguistics to take that position. Kroch and Small (1978) show, for example, that prescriptive influences, realized as what they term *grammatical ideology*, cause more status aware speakers to avoid particle movement and *that*-deletion.

Sociolinguistic data collection must also be sensitive to the distribution of power in interviews. Although the sociolinguistic fieldworker may see the interview situation as one in which the interviewee is to provide the expertise and information, the interviewee may have a more traditional picture of the interview, one, in fact, more like that of the job interview described in 3.2.3, in which the interviewer is invested with considerable power and the structure of the interview itself is expected to follow a question and answer format. Wolfson (1976) suspects that the interviewee's perception of power and role distribution in the interview is so strong that the interviewer cannot effectively lower the stylistic level and place him or herself in the lower status position of the seeker of information. She suggests that confusion may result from such attempts and cites the following interchange among a fieldworker (Int), a restaurant owner, and a waitress:

> *Owner*: Let me ask you something. Are you from Philadelphia?
> *Int*: Yes
> *Owner*: Where were you born?
> *Waitress*: (laughs) Now he's gonna question you
> *Int*: Second and the Boulevard
> *Owner*: Second and the Boulevard. Uh huh. Do you find Philadelphia different?
> *Int*: Yeah
> *Owner*: You do? In what respect?
> *Int*: I think people used to be a lot friendlier
> *Owner*: Well, I think conditions have made it that way
> (Wolfson 1976:197–8)

The interviewee has here felt that the structure of the interview is inappropriate and has seized the interviewer's role (as is immediately recognized by the waitress). Wolfson argues that such pitfalls in interviewing are unavoidable and naturally emerge from the structure of the genre itself. She notes that even if an interview is 'successful' (if the roles are kept straight, presumably) it does not, as a result of its unique genre structure, provide the same sort of data that could be gleaned from conversational settings (1982:62).

In spite of these drawbacks, attention to network patterns (3.3.2) and careful considerations of the norms and expectations of the speech community (what Baugh 1979 calls *ethnosensitivity*) have allowed interviews to yield considerable quantities of important vernacular data. Though it is important to remember that the genre of the collection setting itself will have an influence on the interviewee's performance, modification of that genre, particularly through redefined relationships between the interviewee and interviewer, is not impossible to achieve.

Though usually connected explicitly to sex, nativeness, or some other factor, power has often been an underlying consideration in SLA research. Most generally, power is implicit in the patterns of language *choice*, *accommodation*, and *assimilation* as described by Giles for interethnic linguistic contact (2.1.4), and, although there are metaphoric and solidarity reasons for preserving and using minority varieties, the underlying assumption in many such general theories rests on the *power* of the so-called *dominant* group. In such models, the degree of tolerance for the distribution of social roles and linguistic functions in the face of asymmetric social relations appears to have considerable predictive value for SLA as well as for language maintenance.

Specific studies of that asymmetric relation have tried to show what influence it has on learner performance. Beginning with the general assumption that the NS has power by virtue of his or her linguistic ability alone, a number of studies, many already cited, have tried to show how that superiority is expressed in NS performance and how it influences NNS performance. Woken and Swales (to appear), for example, show that an 'expert' NNS dominates in a tutorial setting, even if the interlocutor is an NS (3.2.3). Zuengler (to appear) treats this theme even more explicitly when she shows that NNSs may be dominated by NSs, even in areas of NNS expertise, if the L2 proficiency of the NNS is particularly low. On the other hand, she found that NNS 'experts' dominated NSs in an interaction in *amount* of speech (3.1.3), but not in such other areas as interruption. The different results in her study and that of Woken and Swales might, however, be attributed to the different genres involved.

In some cases, cross-cultural examination of power as an influence on language choice suggests that L1 patterns may carry over into L2 performances. Beebe and Takahashi (to appear) study the degree to which the stereotype of Japanese deferential behavior is matched in actual performance and find that the transfer effect is quite strong. Japanese learners of English are a good deal more deferential (through indirectness) to more powerful interlocutors than NSs of English are. In contrast to the general stereotype, the same learners are a good deal less deferential to less powerful interlocutors than NSs of English are, suggesting, perhaps, that a *power*-rather than *solidarity*- based system is primary for Japanese and that that system is transferred into English. On the other hand, Fiksdal (to appear) shows that NNSs from a variety of L2 backgrounds are less direct with NSs in a more powerful role than NSs of English would be, suggesting that indirection is a general ploy for NNSs, a position also taken by Blum-Kulka and Olshtain (1986) in their study of the greater use of *external modification* (and, therefore, more elaborate deference) in NNS requests. Attitudinal surveys of NS reactions to NS and NNS deferential and nondeferential performances would appear to be an important next step in determining the effectiveness of this apparently rather general NNS strategy, although the influence of proficiency and other variables make such research more complex than simpler studies of reactions to such factors as degree of accentedness (e.g., Rey 1977 and other studies cited in 2.1.3).

## 3.4  Functions

What one wants to get done with speech is an important area of variability; the assumption that message-giving and getting is the only (or in some cases, even the principal) function of language misses a great deal. Similarly, to assume that even simply stated messages stand in a one to one relationship with their intended meanings is linguistically naive. Differences in realizing *illocutionary* and *perlocutionary* intents, alternative ways of coding what is meant, and the different uses various forms are put to, give variationists and SLA researchers alike interesting areas to investigate.

### 3.4.1  *Purpose*

What one wants to get done with a sentence is most directly exposed in its *illocutionary force* (1.2.5), i.e., whether it is an act of forgiving, promising, ordering, and so on. Such considerations would be unnecessary if it were the case that sentences had a one to one fit between form and function – 'I request that you give me a match.' But the same purpose may be fulfilled by a number of forms – 'I don't have any matches,' 'Do you have a match?,' 'I need a match' – none of which, in its surface syntax and the semantics derived from or associated with it, may be straightforwardly interpreted as a *request*. It is an old (and tired) joke, for example, to pretend to answer the request 'Do you have a match?' as if it were only a request for information.

Since direct illocutionary acts themselves might have only minor coding differences from one language or variety to another, a principal focus for research has been on indirection. Do languages use the same grammatical means to realize indirect speech acts? Are operating principles (which allow interpretation of indirect speech acts, e.g., Grice's maxims – 1.2.5) universal? Goffman (1976) suggests that any communication system has *system constraints* which are invariable but that individual systems have *ritual constraints* which may differ widely from one language or variety to another. For example, Ochs-Keenan (1976) claims that Grice's maxim 'Be informative' does not hold for men in Malagasy society (2.1.2), but it may still be argued that the maxim itself is universal (a system constraint) and that one must seek its inapplicability to men in Malagasy society in some special ritual constraint which holds there.

What may be most subtly nonuniversal are those conventionalized indirect speech acts which, as a result of their frequency, strike members of the culture as not indirect at all. Fraser (1983:29) reminds English speakers that

'How are you?' may count as a greeting but not as a leave-taking and that 'Can you pass the salt?' is most often a request, while the (apparently) synonymous 'Are you able to pass the salt?' is not. Such formulaic indirect speech acts are so much a part of general conversational routine that their direct inter-pretations seem almost bizarre or comic. Richards (1980:418) shows the confusing result of an NNS (B) not taking a yes-no question as a con-ventionalized request in a telephone call setting:

*A*: Hello, is Mr Simatapung there please?
*B*: Yes.
*A*: Oh . . . may I speak to him please?
*B*: Yes.
*A*: Oh . . . are you Mr Simatapung?
*B*: Yes, this is Mr Simatapung.
(418)

An NS might have answered 'Yes, speaking' or 'This is he.' Although the conventional indirection (a yes-no question standing for a request) is misinterpreted by the answerer, it would be premature to take this as evid-ence that the answerer's L1 does not have indirect speech acts or even that it does not have indirect acts of precisely this shape. A failure to attend to indi-rection may be a by-product of the overactive processing strategies NNSs must use to decode all messages on the one hand or of their tendency as bilinguals to avoid indirection in general by sticking to the more elaborate code on the other.

The most ambitious attempt to show that indirectness is a universal phenomenon, that it involves the same motives, and that it makes use of even similar grammatical realizations across cultures is Brown and Levinson (1978). In their model, a person may choose to perform an act or not; if action is chosen, the act may be *on record* or *off record*. 'I don't have any matches,' for example, is an off-record request since it puts a hearer under no obligation. If the speaker goes on record, the choice is between *baldly on record* or *face-saving* activity. 'Give me a match' is an example of the former. If one chooses face-saving politeness, either *negative* or *positive* strategies may be selected. Positive politeness emphasizes the relations among people, predicts or even assumes cooperativeness, and uses in-group or endearing forms – 'Let me have your matches dear.' Negative politeness uses con-ventionalized forms, hedges, and does not place a burden of cooperation on either the speaker or hearer – 'Could you spare a match?' Brown and Levinson claim that a good part of indirectness in speech owes its very existence to the universal need to be polite, to save face in the presence of the need to get others to act for us, to acknowledge our misdeeds, to approve our requests, and so on. What will differ, then, from one language and culture to another are such things as the specific structures used for particular indirection and the distribution of various strategies according to settings, interlocutors, and so on.

In a study of the distribution of politeness strategies for requests, Olshtain and Blum-Kulka (1985:310) try to show that bald on-record speech acts and positive politeness are preferred in Hebrew. They offered judges the choices of two negatively oriented requests (N), two positively oriented ones (P), one bald on-record request (D), and one distractor, as in the following example:

*Situation 1: Asking for a loan*
Ruth, a friend of yours at the university, comes up to you after class and tells you that she has finally found an apartment to rent. The only problem is that she has to pay $200 immediately and at present she only has $100. She turns to you and says:
(a) How about lending me some money? (P)
(b) So, do me a favor and lend me the money. (P)
(c) Do you want to lend me the money? (distractor)
(d) I'd appreciate it if you could lend me the money. (N)
(e) Could you possibly lend me the money? (N)
(f) Lend me the money, please. (D)

The samples were given in Hebrew and English. American judges rated negative politeness strategies as most appropriate and were intolerant of both positively polite and bald on-record strategies. NS Hebrew raters, however, accepted the informal positive politeness of (a) but rejected the presumptuousness of the positively oriented (b). They accepted, as did the English NSs, the conventionally indirect negative strategy of (d) but rejected the hedged formality of (e). Finally, NS Hebrew raters were not nearly as intolerant of the bald on-record strategy (f). Though indirectness appears to be an admired strategy in the face-threatening environment of requesting, the preferred strategies differ from one language and culture to another.

From a comprehension point of view, however, indirection may be less culture specific. In a study of NNS ability to correctly interpret indirect speech acts, Carrell (1979:301) shows that indirectness causes only slightly more difficulty for NNSs than directness or even uncooperativeness. ESL students from several different cultural backgrounds and from several different levels of ability in English responded to situations such as the following:

Bob comes up to Ann in the Study Center. Bob says: 'Did you go to the movies last night?' Ann says: 'I had to study last night.'
(a) Ann went to the movies last night.
(b) Ann did not go to the movies last night.
(c) I have not idea at all whether (a) or (b).

Jim and Henry are talking about a party they went to the night before. Jim says: 'Did you drink whiskey?' Henry says: 'All I drank was beer.'

James and Harold are discussing Harold's grandmother in Texas. James says: 'Did you write her a letter?' Harold says: 'I received a letter from an old friend of mine last week.'

Each selection was followed by the three-way choice exemplified for only the first item above. In the first, since Ann's remark about studying must be made relevant to the question (through, for example, some such strategy as that suggested in Grice's maxim – 1.2.5), the indirection is resolved, and one may conclude she did not go to the movies. In the second, since Henry drank only beer, direct linguistic evidence shows that he drank no whiskey. In the third, it is difficult, given no other information, to make Harold's response relevant to the question. Although NNSs were more accurate in interpreting direct and unrelated responses, they were not more or less adept at interpreting indirection on the basis of L1 or general English proficiency. Additionally, their difference from NS ability in interpreting indirectness was not particularly great. This experiment suggests that, as with production, devices for interpreting indirectness are universal but that actuation of them may be linked either to culture specific types or to some more general NNS strategy of avoiding indirection in general. Whatever the case, additional research both in attitudinal responses and in production and interpretation abilities will help isolate the culture specific and linguistically general characteristics of indirect speech act behavior.

Indirect speech acts, though universal, appear to be underutilized in even advanced interlanguage varieties, and this may be so for both sociopsychological and psycholinguistic reasons. NNSs may avoid indirection in L2 for the same reasons they avoid slang, metaphor, and obscenity. The language contact environment may militate against such usage both from the point of view of the NSs (who feel their system is being invaded) and the NNSs (who may feel such culture specific performance is both an infringement on NS territory and a symbol of the loss of identity provided by L1). Again, considerations of the language contact environment as specified by Giles and his associates are relevant here (2.1.4).

In FL learning situations, particularly when instructors are also NNSs, learners seem to take great delight in learning and using slang, obscenity, and metaphor; they are even given to mimicking phonological stereotypes of a variety they are studying (e.g., exaggerating the retroflex [ɹ] of some varieties of American English). In a study of fluent L2 learners in a setting which permitted only limited contact with NSs, Marton and Preston (1975) show that, on affective dimensions, NSs of British and American English gave lower rankings to those Polish university students who had learned the NS rater's variety. Since proficiency level and content (a reading passage) were held constant and since no specifically British or American lexical, morphological, or syntactic units were used, one may assume that the negative (or less positive) reactions were based on pronunciation alone, and interviews with the NS judges revealed, in nearly every case, that what was not appreciated was the exaggerated quality of some feature of the American or British pronunciation. Those exaggerations were noticed only by NSs. British and American judges alike felt that the NNS representations of the other variety were both pleasant and authentic. Perhaps FL learners' insensitivity to NS reactions to certain sorts of performances and the home base security of their learning environment allow them the luxury of experimenting with NS territory which the competent bilingual in the L2 setting would not invade, for both public and private reasons. In short, when learners move to an L2 setting or when learners acquire exclusively in the L2 culture, sensitivity to NS negative reactions and/or fear of anomie may curtail just those aspects of linguistic performance which are most negatively perceived and which threaten identity. Experiments with NS varieties and anecdotal evidence add considerable weight to the use of *accommodation theory* in SLA, a connection discussed in 2.1.3 and drawn specifically in Beebe and Zuengler (1983).

Psycholinguistically, however, one might argue that indirection is a natural consequence of a learner's *transparent* style, the desire to make one's L2 performance as simple and direct as possible. Kasper (to appear) suggests that NNSs may use more elaborate (apparently overpolite) external modification in certain face-threatening situations (as suggested, for example, in Blum-Kulka and Olshtain's 1986 study of NNS requests – 3.1.3) because such strategies involve constructions which have a better fit between surface syntax and semantic interpretation. For example, a person who makes a request by saying 'I am sorry to bother you, but will you help me with this problem' has explicitly encoded the fact that he or she is aware of the imposition a request places on an interlocutor. The point here is not that the NNSs do not know conventional or indirect means for politeness but that they more often choose directness since it obeys the more general language learning norms perhaps best expressed in the first two of four 'charges' to language: (1) be clear, and (2) be humanly processible in ongoing time (Slobin 1977). These charges are not at all unlike Naro's *factorization principle* for pidgin-creole varieties (1.2.3) or Gumperz's suggestion that elaborated code use is appropriate when extensive background knowledge is not shared.

The clever reader has seen a chicken or egg question developing all along with the problem of the competent bilingual and the impression he or she gives the NS (and, perhaps, other NNSs). Does the putative NS demand that NNSs identify themselves in some linguistic way derive from NS stinginess concerning certain aspects of the L2, or is it a by-product in NSs of having grown accustomed to and therefore expecting NNS learning strategies (e.g., the preference for transparent constructions) and inabilities (e.g., adult failure to acquire perfect L2 phonology) to persist in all NNS performances? From the other perspective, does NNS performance which is strikingly not native result from a (perhaps covert) sensitivity to NS negative reactions to certain culturally private areas of the language, from a desire to retain some residue of L1 identity, or from a simple carry-over of learning strategies into later competence, suggesting a fossilization in certain areas when some internal mechanism is satisfied that competence is achieved?[12] Though these issues are not uniquely a part of speech act research in SLA, the frequency of indirect versus direct acts and the variability of indirect acts highlight their relevance.

From one point of view, much of what has been discussed here may not concern direct or indirect speech acts in the illocutionary framework at all, for some speech act analysts would claim that 'be polite,' 'be aggressive,' 'be condescending,' and so on are *perlocutionary* not illocutionary acts (1.2.5). They help establish the *tenor* (3.5) of an interaction rather than determine the specific purposive action of the speaker. Unfortunately, the distinction often seems to be one of unresolvable levels. If the statement 'You are a wimp' is taken as an insult, should one assume that 'to insult' is an illocutionary act? Wouldn't it be better to group a set of utterances which serve such purposes together under the heading *expressives* (as, for example, Searle 1976 does)? From another perspective, however, 'You are a wimp' is, quite simply, a statement, perhaps for the speaker one as much of fact as 'The sun rises every morning.' That last interpretation, however, would set all speech act research back, for it would disclaim any importance for the speaker's purpose and allow as utterances only those paucal grammatical interpretations based on form – imperatives, interrogatives, declaratives.

Research by those interested in SLA has taken a healthy attitude to such unresolvable questions by sensing the importance of a speaker's intent or purpose in determining the status of utterances as units in learning and teaching. A formal theory, for example, would consider only those perlocutions which were intended by a speaker (e.g., Bach and Harnish 1979:17), but one could argue that it is precisely those unintentionally aroused perlocutionary effects in hearers which are of greatest concern in SLA. That is, where the likelihood of miscommunication is great, the perlocutionary *uptake* of the hearer must be considered along with the speaker's perlocutionary intent. All the following let a speaker of English know that he or she has been invited to a party; in every case, assume that the perlocutionary intent of the speaker is simply to 'appear polite in the normal illocutionary task of inviting.'

1   You come. My house. Tomorrow. Drink. Dance. Fun.
2   You will come to my house tomorrow for a party.
3   Would you like to come over to my place tomorrow at about 7.00? A few of us are getting together to drink, dance, listen to some music.
4   If it doesn't impinge on your own busy schedule too much, I wonder if it would be possible for you to consider spending some little time at my place tomorrow evening. It will be just a little affair, nothing so grand as

you are used to, I'm afraid, but we will have something to drink and there will be dancing. You might enjoy yourself, and I would be honored to have you.

No matter what the speakers' perlocutionary intent, the perlocutionary uptakes are wildly different. Unless 1 wants to be thought of as a marginal speaker of English (a Tarzan figure perhaps) with whatever caricatures of intelligence and so on that inevitably brings, the expression is astray. Invitation 2 strikes many NSs as cheeky; and 4 is satisfactory only if the speaker is in an obsequiousness contest. Unfortunately, 2 and 4 represent, as many who have dealt with NNSs of English know, not wildly imagined data. Type 2 is especially troublesome, for it appears to be a polite form in some emerging NNS standards of English and will, undoubtedly, take its place among cases of cross-cultural misunderstanding.

Illocutionary forces, in spite of Richards's (1980) Mr Simatapung, seem less often misunderstood and more easily repaired. What the perlocutionary effects of speech act theory have provided SLA research with is a basic understanding of the sorts of variable units which create unintended effects in hearers. Which specific locutions serving which illocutionary and perlocutionary intents are likely to cause negative reactions? That is an empirical question which can be studied in matched guise attitude experiments, in appropriateness ratings of different forms, and in a variety of other observational and experimental settings.

Finally, though not least important, it must be recognized that speech act research is one of the strong motivating factors in the establishment of notional-functional syllabuses (1.2.5, 3.2.1). Interestingly enough, the major influence on such language teaching activity seems to derive from the illocutionary side of speech act research (how to perform certain language functions), while the major influence on SLA research has been from the perlocutionary side (what forms, particularly in indirect speech acts, do not arouse suspicion, annoyance, or even hostility in the hearer).

From a pedagogical point of view, speech act theory obviously influences such a list of language functions as the following, specified for the Council of Europe's Unit/Credit System at the *threshold level* by V. C. Van Ek: (1976: 37–9):[13]

1 *Imparting and seeking factual information*
   1.1  identifying
   1.2  reporting (including describing and narrating)
   1.3  correcting
   1.4  asking
2 *Expressing and finding out intellectual attitudes*
   2.1  expressing agreement and disagreement
   2.2  inquiring about agreement or disagreement

2.3 denying something
2.4 accepting an offer or invitation
etc.
3 *Expressing and finding out emotional attitudes*
3.1 expressing pleasure, liking
3.2 expressing displeasure, dislike
3.3 inquiring about pleasure, liking, displeasure, dislike
3.4 expressing interest or lack of interest
etc.
4 *Expressing and finding out moral attitudes*
4.1 apologizing
4.2 granting forgiveness
4.3 expressing approval
4.4 expressing disapproval
etc.
5 *Getting things done (suasion)*
5.1 suggesting a course of action (including the speaker)
5.2 requesting others to do something
5.3 inviting others to do something
5.4 advising others to do something
etc.
6 *Socializing*
6.1 to greet people
6.2 when meeting people
6.3 when introducing people and when being introduced
6.4 when taking leave
etc.

Speech act theorists will be critical of such categories, for many are much too specific, but their specificity often grows out of the experience applied linguists have had in elaborating situational and grammatical syllabuses. Speech act analyses, such practitioners believe, provide them with a more realistic starting point for language lesson development, not necessarily a limiting catalog of functions. Testing such ideas in classrooms will determine the importance of their contribution, but even if the specific notional-functional approach to language teaching and learning is not a panacea, sociolinguistic and SLA research on the sorts of language functions indicated in this area of concern should continue along with other pragmatic considerations which contribute to cross-cultural and learner variation. In fact, a large number of SLA investigations of what might loosely be termed speech acts has already shown important cross-cultural differentiation. Beebe, Takahashi, and Uliss-Weltz (in press) investigate refusals in NS English, NS Japanese, and Japanese English; Cohen and Olshtain (1981), Olshtain (1983), and Olshtain and Cohen (1983) focus on apologies, and Blum-Kulka

(1982) studies requests. Blum-Kulka and Olshtain (1984) review work on apologies and requests in Israel, Europe, the United States, Canada, and Australia, especially within the framework of the CCSARP (Cross-Cultural Speech Act Realization Project). Wolfson and her associates have studied a variety of speech acts (invitations, compliments, greetings, partings), often collecting only base line NS data in English (Manes 1983, Manes and Wolfson 1981, Wolfson 1981, 1983a, b, Wolfson, D'Amico-Reisner, and Huber 1983, Wolfson and Manes 1980). Expressions of gratitude have been looked at by Eisenstein and Bodman (1986).

### 3.4.2 Outcome and goal

Both *outcome* and *goal* owe their labels to Hymes (1972). An outcome is the resolution of an event; whether it matches the goal of any participant may be irrelevant. In many societies a compromise is a most satisfactory outcome for an argument or arbitration; compromise is generally, however, not the goal of either participant in the conflict. Outcomes are culture- or group-centered; goals are individual-centered.

Some outcomes of language use are very general indeed. Malinowski (1923), for example, identifies the *phatic communion* function of language, use which simply signals the presence of interlocutors and establishes their common human bonds. Much small talk or chit-chat or the ubiquitous talk about the weather may be examples of phatic communion. More specifically, the outcome of language use may signal facts rather far from any goals or purposes of speakers. In the Vaupés region of Colombia, several different mutually unintelligible language groups occupy the same territory. Men may not marry women who speak the same language; therefore, any language use by a male in his father language will display what language aggregate group he belongs to and what women he may or may not court. The latter outcome is surely not the goal of every utterance of any man in the area no matter how eager he may be for life-long companionship.

Such results of language use in general, however, are not central to Hymes's concern for this category. His emphasis is on the outcome of bounded activities – speech events. The Black verbal contesting known as *playing the dozens* (3.2.3) is an activity in which community outcomes and individual goals may be separate. For individual players, it is a game of one-upmanship. Who can insult more subtly, more artfully, more outlandishly, and, by so doing, *cap* or *get* the other player? The moves of the contest play on themes of physical appearance, clothing, food, poverty, sexuality and the family, race, bizarre behavior, and so on. In the course of a session, there is immediate feedback on the success or failure of a contribution.

*Junior:* Aww, Nigger Bell, you smell like BO. Plenty.
*Bell:* Aww, nigger, you look like – you look like Jimmy Durante's grandfather.

*Stan:* Aw, tha's phony [bullshit] . . . Eh, you woke me up with that phony one, man . . .

*Bell:* Junior look like Howdy Doody.

*Stan:* That's phony too, Bell. Daag, boy! . . . Tonight ain't your night, Bell.

(Labov 1972b:326)

Some ineffective contributions may change the game from its ritual nature to a more personal tone. When this occurs the interpretation of statements as real rather than imaginary makes the game threatening, emotionally charged, and potentially dangerous. When Boot and David are engaged in a contest, David, the less effective player, resorts to a personal characterization of Boot's father's stuttering, which takes the game off its ritual track.

*Boot:* Your father look like a *grown pig*. (Boot, Money, and Ricky laugh).

*David:* Least my – at least my father don't be up there talking uh-uh-uh-uh-uh-uh!

*Boot:* Uh – so my father talks stutter talk what it mean? (Roger: He talk the same way a little bit.) At least my father ain't got a gray head! His father got a big bald spot with a gray head right down there and one long string . . .

*David:* Because he' old he's old, that's why! He's old, that's why! . . .

*Boot:* . . . and one long string, that covers his whole head, one, one long string about that high, covers his whole head (Roger: Ho Lord, one string! Money, Boot laugh).

*David:* You lyin' Boo! . . . You know 'cause he old, tha's why!

*Ricky:* Aw man, cut it out.

(Labov 1972b:332–3)

David has already begun to cry after Boot continues the 'one long string' remark. Although Boot's friend Roger supports him, Ricky objects to the tack the game has taken. The obscene and personal references lead to the outcome expected only so long as they are outlandish, exaggerated, or obviously untrue (or involve a sort of group factuality which would be as true of one player's family as another's). When David sounds on Boot's father's stuttering, he breaks the rules and opens the possibility for another outcome (a fight, hurt feelings). Although the goal of the players never changes (to best the opponent), failure to observe one of the game's rules results in a radical change of potential outcomes.

Even when goals are shared, the means of realizing them may be so different that miscommunication results. The difficulty a North American wife and Greek husband had in determining whether the other wanted to attend a party or not is discussed in 2.1.2. Marlos (1981) and Varonis and Gass (1985) show how interlocutors' failure to accurately perceive others' goals leads to specific misunderstandings of purposes (at the illocutionary level) and to unsatisfactory outcomes in both NS-NS and NNS-NS communication. Studies of alternative styles in different language and culture groups as regards individual goals and social outcomes will be important to SLA, both in research and application.

One mismatch between sociolinguistic reality and applied linguistic advice has its source in considerations of purpose, goal, and outcome, but cross-cultural difference is not the source of the difficulty at all. A great deal of modern language teaching advice assumes that learning profits from meaningful activity, tasks which promote actual communication. Some positions taken on this point are quite strong:

> A case can be made ... for reorienting 'language' teaching towards communication practice, not just because the eventual product aim is 'communication', but because communication practice can be expected to develop linguistic skills. (Allwright 1979:170)

Many discourse analyses of classroom interaction reveal, however, a great deal of noncommunicative activity, even in NS settings. Before the following exchange, a teacher has just played a videotape in which a speaker uses an especially 'posh' or upper status variety of British English (RP); the teacher's goal is to provide background for a discussion of attitudes towards language differences.

> *Teacher*: What kind of person do you think he is? do you – what are you laughing at?
> *Pupil*: Nothing.
> *Teacher: Pardon?*
> *Pupil*: Nothing.
> *Teacher*: You're laughing at nothing, nothing at all?
> *Pupil*: No.
> It's funny really 'cos they don't think as though they were there they might not like it. And it sounds rather a pompous attitude.
> (Sinclair and Coulthard 1975:30)

The pupil has misunderstood the teacher's 'What are you laughing at?' as a reprimand and offered the traditional student answer, for that is what the structure of the situation (classroom) would predict. In fact, the teacher was using the the pupil's authentic communicative response (laughter) to trigger further discussion of the accent the class had just heard. Given the setting, it was obviously difficult for the pupil to arrive at the ordinary direct speech act interpretation (request for information) of the teacher's utterance. On the other hand, it is too easy to deplore the general setting of classrooms which makes ordinary communication difficult and appreciate this sensitive teacher's attempt to use real communication, for, in fact, the direct speech act interpretation of the teacher's question still requires classroom understanding. If a group of individuals who share values and stereotypes experience something as distinct as a different accent, it would be perverse, outside a classroom situation, for one member of the group to ask another for clarification of what must be common knowledge. Teachers' rights, therefore, to ask questions which have obvious answers are the same as their rights to ask questions to which they already know the answer. In ordinary interactions, the following interchange would be strange.

> $A$: What time is it?
> $B$: Quarter to four.
> $A$: Yes, you're right.

It may be rightly objected that some of the special communication activities of classrooms exist elsewhere (e.g., job interviews – 3.2.3) and that the skills learned in them may be transferred. That is, the long-range outcome (language learning) is partially helped along by the short-range teacher and student goals of conducting classroom business. On the other hand, a great many important language behaviors are not ordinary outcomes of traditional classroom activities and will need to be specially prepared for. Sociolinguistic analyses of just those differences will allow applied linguists to make the sorts of recommendations which will bring, so far as possible, the goals of students and teachers in their daily activities in line with the expected general outcome of language acquisition itself.[14]

## 3.5 Tenor

The tone or mood of an interaction is, in some ways, the most difficult to characterize; nevertheless, sociolinguists and SLA researchers have found ways to operationalize some of these factors and have made them important factors in the study of language variation. The most discussed, *style* (here *distance*), has, from its operational sociolinguistic origins, even spawned complete theories of SLA (5.1), but other considerations of tenor have not drawn similar attention.

### 3.5.1 *Distance*

A number of personal and interactional characteristics conspire to require patterns of language use which have usually been characterized along some such dimension as degree of formality. It is important to distinguish between the description of such stylistic levels and the psycholinguistic importance attributed to them. Linguists and nonlinguists alike know that even speakers of only one language are not monostylistic, and the most generally discussed area for single-speaker variation is this so-called stylistic one. Once informality and incorrectness were seen as distinct (e.g., Kenyon 1948), the door was opened for consideration of a continuum of styles, the different levels of which were more or less appropriate to a variety of situations, personnel, and relations among personnel. Joos (1962), for example, tried to describe this sort of situational appropriateness by inventing five levels – the intimate, casual, consultative, formal, and frozen.

Such descriptive analyses of styles, often based on intuition rather than on an empirical study of written and/or spoken texts, were not nearly as significant for linguistic theory in general as Labov's claim that the lower levels of the stylistic continuum revealed the most systematic individual use of an internalized rule system (e.g., Labov 1972a). That is, a speaker's casual, unmonitored use (the *vernacular*) is the most important data for linguistic analysis. Since higher levels of the continuum allow and even demand speaker awareness and offer the opportunity of feedback into performance of learned rules, such data may exhibit a hodge-podge of misapplication of rules only partially learned or lapses in monitoring due to inattentiveness or other psycholinguistic processing factors. The vernacular became, therefore, for sociolinguists the object of data collection (1.1).

Irvine (1984) suggests that style is a complex of factors and proposes four components which may be universal: (1) the formal code is more structured; (2) the formal code is more consistent in application; (3) the formal code indicates positional rather than personal identity; and (4) the formal code is selected in more focused interactions.

At first, point (1) would seem to deny Labov's contention that the vernacular is the most consistent variety. What Irvine means by structured, however, is precisely the sort of monitored structuring Labov has in mind when he suggests that the formal end of the stylistic continuum requires more speaker attention. Irvine suggests that the formal code involves 'extra rules or conventions,' presumably just those sorts of special rules which require memorization or careful application since they are likely to involve exceptions and/or marked forms. It is not paradoxical, then, to suggest that the formal code is more structured but that the informal is more systematic.

Similarly, asserting that the formal code shows greater consistency might at first seem odd, but Irvine has in mind the consistency of its application, not its internal construction. Violations of stylistic consistency are much more likely to occur at levels which allow humor, metaphoric shift, irony, sarcasm, and so on (3.5.2). The seriousness of more formal exchanges requires a monotonic selection of forms. In informal settings among close acquaintances, for example, forms of address might vary among nicknames, terms of endearment, first and last names, comic use of titles, and so on. In a more formal setting even close friends might restrict themselves to first names, and in symbolically formal settings the same persons might use title plus last name in spite of their relationship.

That use of titles illustrates the contribution of formal usage to positional identity. Formality accompanies one's identity as a professor, church member, chairperson, and so on – positional and public identities. Informality accompanies one's identity as a parent, spouse, friend, and so on – personal identities.

Finally, formal language is chosen on occasions in which a single topic is invoked. Even people of the same social rank and relations discussing the same topic, for example, would use more formal language if that topic had been nominated for a *discussion* than if it had emerged in a *chat*.

What is most likely is that the stylistic continuum as it is evidenced in form is a response to the entire range of *individual* and *interactional* factors which are the subject matter of chapters 2 and 3 of the present work. The term chosen here for this relationship between code shape and contextual factors is *distance*, a notion perhaps most directly related to Bell's concept of *audience design* (1984:151):

> Variation on the style dimension within the speech of a single speaker derives from and echoes the variation which exists between speakers on the 'social' dimension.

Although the so-called 'social' dimension includes variables other than status (as Bell himself notes), it is that dimension which he pursues in validating this claim. For example, it is rare for the style-shifting done by any single group to outstrip the range of the most differentiated style on the social dimension. This is obviously the case in figure 1.1. The middle middle class has an (ng) index of (roughly) five in formal style; the lower working class has an index of one hundred for the same variable in the same style, yielding a range of ninety-five. The upper working class, the stratum which indulges in the most dramatic style-shifting, ranges, however, from an index of (roughly) five in word list style to (roughly) eighty-eight in casual style, a range of eighty-three, well within the boundaries set by status group variation in the most divergent style (in this case, formal).[15]

Status (and, it is argued here, the entire range of *participant* and *interaction* variables) provides the impetus for stylistic variation. This claim is not inconsistent with Bickerton's that variation may have its origins in form–function differentiation, for variables may acquire status associations after their initiation and then impose adjustment requirements (stylistic variation) on speakers more generally. It is a view also compatible with Kroch's, which views linguistic differentiation arising from the effort and/or symbolic importance marked and irregular forms have for higher status groups. Once initiated, such forms influence stylistic decisions in the wider speech community. By highlighting the adjustment of language form along a stylistic dimension to the larger context, the more limited view of style as a reflex of attention is relegated to its proper position as one of the variables of psycho-linguistic processing. Whether attention to form is greater or lesser in conjunction with certain tasks and in certain environments is then a part of a larger question concerning the influence of variables in language use which are not part of the general context or of the linguistic context in a narrow (perhaps superficial) sense.

Bell notes two exceptions to his *style axiom*. First, in hypercorrection, the stylistic shift of a class (usually the lower middle class in United States research) may outstrip the range of the status groups. In figure 2.13, for example, the lower middle class's use of (r) in the most formal styles is higher than the use of the upper middle class, and the lower middle class's style-shift range (approximately seventy-five) far outstrips the status range at its widest point (approximately fifty-five). Second, exceptions may exist where the elicitation devices cause a sharp break in the continuum (as, for example, reading styles do in a study of Teheran Persian in Modaressi 1978).

Bell's work, like much other recent work in sociolinguistics, suggests that multivariate analyses are most likely to be productive. The cultural relativity and individual variation in respondents' completion of certain tasks (e.g., interviews, reading) make attention to form the sort of processing or psycholinguistic variable which might be best manipulated within a very stringent setting, holding potential variables constant while trying to mani-pulate one feature (e.g., complexity of a reading passage) which might more specifically trigger different levels of attention to form. Regardless of these criticisms, the similarity of reading style to more formal conversational styles and the sensitivity of elicitation devices to different stylistic levels in inter-views have produced a considerable body of sociolinguistic data which illustrate the distance dimension. Its relation to such other frequently studied variables as sex, age, and status have already been focused on in 2.1.1, 2.1.2, and 2.2.3.

First notice of the specific parallelism between stylistic differentiation in NS and SLA data is generally attributed to Dickerson (1974). A typical example is shown in figure 3.9. A score of 100 indicates exclusive use of the native-like English [ɹ]; a score of 0 indicates exclusive use of a number of flapped NNS (Japanese) variants. What has attracted SLA researchers to such results is the fact that the increase in accuracy is in the same direction as increase in the use of prestige forms found in monolingual studies: the more formal (or attended to) the variety, the more accurate the performance.

The essential question concerning this parallelism is not that accuracy (in SLA) and formality (in NS performance) seem to accompany those modes which allow for greater planning time. A great deal of research shows this is true. The question is whether or not a stylistic dimension (*distance*) is being realized in both cases. The answer appears to be both yes and no. If one attaches a great deal of importance to the notion 'attention to speech,'

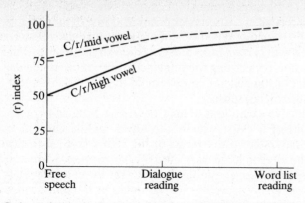

*Figure 3.9* Style variation in Japanese learners' realization of English (r) in two linguistic environments (source: Dickerson and Dickerson 1977: 21)

assuming that it is the cause of stylistic differentiation, the answer is clearly yes. Those few cases which show greater transfer (and therefore less accuracy) in formal style (e.g., Schmidt 1977, Beebe 1980) do not reflect the general tendency.[16]

If, on the other hand, one attaches greater importance to the range of tasks and interlocutors which trigger adjustment to situation, the answer is less clear. Forms themselves carry symbolic value by having been associated with certain interactional and participant settings, and, certainly at lexical levels, their formality cannot be completely explained by their marked or irregular nature. That is, though phonological, morphological, and even syntactic phenomena associated with lower status and less formal use may have their eventual source in regularity, they are synchronically associated with the situations in which they are appropriate. This conventional association of form with situation is very clearly what is not happening in much SLA data which show so-called stylistic differentiation. The ability to shift style according to situation is called *registral* shift (by Tarone 1983), and does not occur in the interlanguage style-shifting data she reviews. From this perspective, then, the shift in SLA data (at least at early stages) may be attributed to attention to form and is not parallel to the symbolically significant shifting of fluent speakers.

On the other hand, across a large number of languages and cultures, less careful attention to linguistic form will accompany a number of similar, presumably more casual, settings and tasks. If reduction from full forms, failure to use idiosyncratic forms, and similar strategies symbolize casualness cross-linguistically, there is no need to talk of the transfer of a stylistic dimension; it is universal. To that extent, of course, the answer to the above question is still yes; the NS stylistic dimension is like the so-called interlanguage stylistic continuum, and one would not expect NSs or NNSs to be overtly aware of the minor adjustments in frequency along the continuum. On the other hand, one would expect appropriate responses to such frequency modulation, and it is odd that such experiments which have been conducted with NSs (1.2.6) have not been duplicated with NNS. Additionally, one might expect (not exclusively at the most advanced levels) that so-called stylistic variation might have some of its source in the NNSs attempt to retain and/or display ethnic identity (2.1.3).

The operational characterization of stylistic differentiation in quantitative sociolinguistics has, therefore, a strong parallelism in SLA: the attention to form which results in an increased use of prestige items in monolingual settings leads to an increased use of L2 or more advanced interlanguage forms in SLA settings. To the extent that all languages evidence reduction, regularization, and use of less marked forms in more casual settings, there may even be a social as well as psycholinguistic dimension to such shift (e.g., Kroch 1976), though attitude tests of NNSs to such forms in L2 are required to add empirical backing to that suggestion.

Assuming that the style continuum as a reflex of attention to form is accurate, [17] what can be said about style as *distance*, that is, as an adjustment of form to context? Although work on NS–NNS and NNS–NNS interactions has been done, most studies have focused on NNS sensitivity to indirect speech acts and the amount and type of their conversational or interactive work. Measures of developing differentiation within the distance continuum and studies of the acquisition of the meanings attached to the continuum itself are lacking.

Distance (as planning) and style-shift (as creation of a variety space) are considered at greater length in 5.1.


### 3.5.2 *Manner*

A number of principally affective characteristics, particularly those associated with the speaker, seem to cooccur with specific parts of the distance continuum. Labov's selection of such topics as *the danger of death* and *childhood games* to promote less formal speech in interviews shows the operational use that has been made of this dimension in attempting to control distance.

In a study of three Hawaiian children's code-switching behavior, Purcell (1981) identifies a Hawaiian English (HE) dominant child, a General American English[18] (GE) dominant child, and a child who had greater fluency along the continuum between those two extremes (MR). The pattern of shift to HE in particular is marked by manner characteristics:

Beth [a strongly GE dominant child] and Avis [a strongly HE dominant child] tend to stick to their respective unmarked styles with minor modifications, but on occasion shift markedly to HE or more intense HE. These marked shifts coincide with short bursts of high emotion or humor, or with speech event boundaries, independent to a great extent of the code of the addressee. By contrast, Danny [an MR speaker] much more consistently adapts his speech towards that of his addressee, with somewhat less consistent coincidence with shifts in emotion, humor, and speech event boundaries. (Purcell 1981:511)

Purcell notes that Danny's shifting may be principally defined by a theory of *accommodation* (2.1.3) but calls Beth's and Avis's *marking*, a term used by Ervin-Tripp (1973a:270) to refer to *metaphorical shifting*.

In SLA studies, Selinker (1972) is quite specific about the role of emotion in the occurrence of *fossilized* (i.e., persistent interlanguage) forms.

Many of these phenomena reappear in IL [interlanguage] performance when the learner's attention is focused upon new and difficult intellectual subject matter or when he is in a state of anxiety or other excitement, and strangely enough, sometimes when he is in a state of extreme relaxation. (178)

Apparently, the degree to which emotional involvement distracts a speaker from attention to form is reflected in backsliding for language learners but in vernacular performance for NS. To the extent, however, that the rules fallen back on in such emotional moments represent the NNS vernacular, the parallelism with NS patterns is still strong (3.5.1). Lantolf and Ahmed (to appear) show decreasing L2 accuracy in an Arabic learner from interview style to conversational style, indicating that the respondent was emotionally engaged in the conversation topic, which he nominated himself at the end of a data gathering session. Eisenstein and Starbuck (to appear) also found greater L2 inaccuracy in respondents' emotionally invested conversations.

At a much different level, ethnographers and anthropologically oriented sociolinguists have been interested in the linguistic cues of emotional states and the degree of their universality (e.g., Irvine 1982, Shweder and LeVine 1984). In fact, role, situation, status (and, no doubt, other variables) predict type and occurrence of emotional display.

Of the Wolof low ranks, it is especially the griots – a bardic caste of professional speechmakers, musicians, historians, and message-bearers – who most appropriately display high affect. Actually, it might be more accurate to say not that the griots are most free to express feeling, but that they are expected to display it (whether they feel it or not) and to display it on the behalf of others as well as themselves. This contrast between griots and higher-ranking persons was sharply illustrated for me on an occasion when a woman in a village where I worked attempted suicide by throwing herself down a well. Among the other women who witnessed this act there were two griot and several high-ranking (noble) women; but only the two griots screamed. Now, the fact that only they screamed does not mean that only they were shocked. The point is, rather, that the emotional level attributable to a person cannot be read directly off his or her affective display; there is no simple one-to-one correspondence between the behavioral form and its pragmatic effect (here, the attribution of emotion of some particular type and intensity). (Irvine 1982:36)

A particularly appropriate study for review here is Ochs' (1986) investigation of emotional transparency in Samoan and of children's acquisition of the system. She notices a great deal of talk about emotion in caretaker interviews and concludes that communication of affective states must be particularly important. In investigating the adult language, Ochs (1986:262–3) finds affective markers at nearly every level:

Women weaving and talking about the funeral of another woman's mother
F: uhmm [pause] sa'o ā      le     mea ga
                right emph ART thing that
ka    popole ai   le    lo'omakua le    tagi
I-dear worry  PRO ART old woman ART cry
'It's true that the thing poor me worried about was the old woman crying'
L: Kagi kele  si           lo'o/ /makua
    cry   much ART-dear old woman
'The old woman cried a lot'
                    F: Kagi ia       le
                        cry   emph. ART
                        lo'oma/ /kua
                        old woman
                        'The old woman really
                        cried'
                    L: Kalofa e! sh!
                        pity    emph.
                        'What a pity!'

In the first line, F refers to herself with the first person sympathy pronoun ka ('poor me'); the word for the woman whose mother has died is another sympathy reference term (lo'omakua, 'dear old woman'); the phonological register with /t/ is more emotional than that with /k/, and in F's first line, she uses tagi ('cry') rather than the unmarked kagi (as in, e.g., L's first utterance); lengthening (indicated by / /) is another marker of affect; and si is even an 'endearing' article (in L's first utterance). In this short stretch of speech, then, special linguistic forms are used to convey the emotional content. Though one may argue that any language may show sympathy (or any other emotion), this example from Samoan makes it clear that the grammaticalization of such emotional states may be radically different from one language to another.

Description as well as expression of emotional states may vary from culture to culture. In a study of Oriya (Bhubaneswar, Orissa, India) and United States respondents, Shweder and Bourne (1984) find the Indian respondents prefer a style which concretizes the description of emotion. For example, Oriya respondents are likely to say 'she brings cakes to my family on festival days' while the United States respondents, given the same task, are likely to say something like 'she is friendly.' Similarly, the Indians are likely to indicate that a person is hostile and aggressive by saying 'he shouts curses at his neighbors'; the Western respondents might simply say 'he is aggressive and hostile' (Shweder and Bourne 1984:178). Though the authors are careful to show that the Oriya are not more concrete thinkers in general due to some sort of putative code or cultural *restrictiveness* (as opposed to *elaborateness*, e.g., Bernstein 1972), a cross-cultural account of the preferences for the description of emotion will surely play a role in the study of the acquisition of such practices in a new language.

Emotional expressiveness may be measured in part by extroversion and, from that point of view, could be considered as much an individual aspect of personality (2.2.5) as one of cultural stereotype. In studies of extroversion in SLA settings, however, there does not appear to be an advantage for one trait or the other (e.g., Naiman et al. 1978, Swain and Burnaby 1976, but see Rossier 1976 for a correlation between oral fluency and extroversion).

Though the emotional states brought about by anxiety might vary, anxiety itself seems, in general, to inhibit SLA (e.g., Carroll 1963, Gardner, et al. 1976, Naiman, et al. 1978, Oller, Baca, and Vigil 1977, and several studies reported in Pimsleur, Mosberg, and Morrison 1962). Chastain (1975), however, reports a correlation between high anxiety and achievement in Spanish and German (for English learners taught by traditional methods). Dulay, Burt, and Krashen (1982) suggest that some anxiety may be more appropriate for learning (the conscious mode) as opposed to acquisition (53).

The more general emotional adjustment to situations and a new culture which result from emerging bilingualism is not treated in depth here, though the influences such factors have on learners were reviewed from a social psychological perspective in both 2.1.3 and 2.1.4. The general emotional adjustment of bilinguals is discussed in McLaughlin (1978a:178–81).

It is odd, however, that specific studies of SLA data to determine the effectiveness of performance and understanding of emotional states are lacking. Some monocultural research has been conducted on the ability to identify expressions of disgust, happiness, interest, sadness, and so on on a *facial meaning sensitivity test* (Morain 1978:8). The use of verbal as well as nonverbal indicators of such states could provide interesting data on misunderstanding and on acquisition of this important aspect of communicative competence. From the instructional perspective, notional-functional syllabuses have devoted considerable space to learning how to express affective states (3.4.1), though impressive lists of what is to be taught appear not to be based on careful investigation either of NS (or competent bilingual) performances on the one hand or of learner data on the other (e.g., Moskowitz 1978:242–80).

Tonal characteristics, clued by gestural, phonological, or other phenomena, must play a large part in determining knowledge of when to realize speech acts as *ironic* or otherwise not serious. Myers (1977) notes that a driver who says to a passenger in his or her own car

I love people who signal

after nearly colliding with a car whose driver gave no signal before a turn must be interpreted as saying something which is generally true but ironic in this context (172). Though here the physical context is a clue for the ironic interpretation of the driver's remark, clues are often more subtle, depending on specific knowledge of the culture, the speaker's knowledge (or even personality), and the like. To say someone is 'as dumb as a fox' requires only that the hearer know that foxes are proverbially clever in English and that the remark is not insulting (unless it suggests guile). To say someone is 'as smart as Margaret Thatcher,' however, will require hearers to know the speaker's beliefs in determining whether insult or compliment is intended.

Such matters highlight a specific area of tenor, here referred to as *tone*. Interactions have a degree of seriousness, and a number of language characteristics may, at least in part, be predicted by an interaction's position on such a scale. Ordinarily news reporting involves serious topics and serious delivery. When a 'light' piece appears, it is often assigned to another reporter for delivery or there is some clear break between it and other reports (e.g., a commercial break). When a news item is unintentionally funny, it is difficult for the announcer to maintain a serious tone:

In the wonder of science, the Hayden Planetarium has heard from a Minnesota man who claims that the shape of the aurora borealis can be changed by flapping a bed sheet at it from the ground. The Planetarium doubts this but the man says he did successfully flap sheets in his backyard one midnight, although his wife kept hollering at him to cut out the foolishness and get back in the house! . . . [The announcer gives up trying to maintain a newscasting register, breaks up with laughter, and then, barely containing himself, attempts to continue.] This Sunday evening be sure to hear Drew Pearson on ABC. Pearson has received many awards for his work, and one of his treasures is the *Saturday Revoo of Literature* ... [The last error is too much and he floods out again, a few moments later regains enough composure to continue on, and finishes with a mock slip.] ... This is ABC, the American *Broad Company.* (Goffman 1981:308–9)

What is especially notable here is that the announcer finally resorts to intentional error. Perhaps unprepared for the sheet flapping item, he finds it impossible to shift back to his normal news announcing tone and even introduces error into his announcement on purpose to indicate a continuation of the mood established by his earlier laughter. Inconsistency of tone, revealed through rapid shifts in degree of distance, is a common source of humor, and a number of linguists have exploited just such shifts to illustrate the importance of consistency in distance features. Perhaps the best-known is Ervin-Tripp's

> How's it going, Your Eminence? Centrifuging okay? Also, have you been analyzin' whatch'unnertook t'achieve? (1971:38)

Ervin-Tripp calls the rules broken here ones of *cooccurrence* and suggests they are of two types. *Vertical* rules govern the consistency of linguistic forms in a given text type. The learned item 'analyzing' is inappropriately realized with an alveolar nasal ('in') in the -ing ending. *Horizontal* rules refer to consistency through time. The casual greeting 'How's it going' does not belong with the reverential 'Your Eminence.' The entire effect is comic, even bizarre.[19] Language learners, many of whom have learned more formal varieties of the distance spectrum, sprinkle newly learned slang and colloquialisms in their performances with the risk of similar effect. On the other hand, creolized varieties and emerging new Englishes often contain items which are inappropriately analyzed as indications of another distance level. In much of the English-speaking Caribbean, for example, the item 'vex,' as in 'He make me vex' for 'He made me angry,' is normal. It strikes nonlocals as a very fancy word, appropriate only to very formal occasions, or, for some speakers, literary modes.

Tonal shifts are apparently most likely in what Crystal and Davy (1969) call conversational style:

> The informality of the conversation situation is also reflected in the fact that any kind of language can occur, without its being necessarily inappropriate, including such extreme examples as complete switches in accent or dialect for humorous effect (cf. the professional use of the technique by comedians), or the introduction of recognisable (albeit artificial) dialect forms to indicate familiarity or intimacy. It is significant that in an informal language situation, very formal language may be used from time to time, as in argument or humour, without its

being out of place, whereas the reverse is not true. It is this juxtaposition of usually separated linguistic features which is a major characteristic of conversation. (104)

This apparently innocent claim is seriously problematic for sociolinguistics. If ordinary conversation, surely a realization of the vernacular, is filled with greater stylistic shifting than superordinate (nonvernacular) styles, how can the primacy of the vernacular with its touted consistency of rules be maintained? The answer lies in the greater incidence of metaphoric shifting in less formal situations, indicating that much more careful identification of just such shifts must be made. On the other hand, if the vernacular is characterized by just such shifts, how can the frequencies which arise from their implementation be ruled out? It is horrible to imagine theoretically oriented sociolinguists demanding data from the *ideal native speaker-hearer's vernacular*, but that is one possible resolution of this paradox.

On a more down to earth level, the sorts of shifts, whether for tone, stance, solidarity, or other matters, which occur in natural, casual conversation are rarely seen in language learning materials. In fact, a consistency of level is usually sought in such models, so-called 'conversational style,' but NS and competent bilingual performance in casual styles is full of metaphoric shift, and, at some level, SLA research and language teaching must attend to that fact. From an accommodation point of view, for example, how much of such shifting is necessary for competent bilinguals to present an optimum picture of themselves to NSs? How much must be avoided? For comprehension, should materials provide more emphasis on the inconsistency of levels apparent in ordinary conversational styles?

Some language teaching texts include specific material on humor, and some are sensitive to the possibility of cross-cultural differences. A text specifically prepared for learners of United States English is Claire (1984), and, although it is anthropologically unsophisticated, it contains many interesting activities to help NNSs understand what may be funny in otherwise puzzling situations. In general, however, humor is incidental in language teaching, though of course, those methods and models which stress learner relaxation often refer to it. Most specifically, models which note the interference the learner's self-consciousness may impose on learning are likely to spawn activities and techniques which play on humor and other means of lightening the atmosphere of learning (e.g., Oller and Richard-Amato 1983: Part VI).

Another topic which has received some attention in the general area of tenor is that of *stance* – the degree of speaker certainty. In some languages, for example, there is even grammaticalization of hearsay. Figure 3.1 shows that speakers of Hopi must choose different verb forms to report what hearers have seen along with speakers and what only speakers have seen (in past time).

More directly pertinent to stance, however, is the use of so-called *hedges*, a number of devices which weaken the assertiveness of speech. Many such hedges are associated with women's language (or 'powerless' language – 2.1.1) and involve such devices as qualifiers ('so,' 'maybe,' 'I guess,' and so on), tag questions ('This tastes good, doesn't it?'), statements with final rising intonation ('When would you like to leave? In an hour?'), and others (e.g., Lakoff 1975). Lower assertiveness in requests, however, is simply an indication of politeness in many cultures, and the use of modal verbs, greater length (3.1.3), and other devices may be used to verbally symbolize that demands are not being imposed on the hearer. The use (and misuse) of such devices within and across language groups has already been discussed in several places (particularly in 3.4.1).

SLA speech act studies have touched on the sorts of perlocutionary uptakes (whether intended or not) NNS and NS performances evoke, but adjustment of such findings to the tenor of an interaction, particularly the affective characteristics here called *manner*, have not been thoroughly investigated in either experimental or ethnographic settings.

## 3.6  Participation

It is easy to show that language acts consist of senders (speakers, writers, and signers) and receivers (hearers and readers), but, as Hymes (1972:54) has shown, the status of participants in speech requires more specification than that:

> Even if such a schema is intended to be a model, for descriptive work it cannot be. Some rules of speaking require *three* participants – addressor, addressee, hearer (audience), source, spokesman, addressees, etc.; some of but *one*, indifferent as to role in the speech event; some of *two*, but of speaker and audience (e.g., a child); and so on. In short, serious ethnographic work shows that there is one general, or universal, dimension to be postulated, that of *participant*. The common dyadic model of speaker–hearer specifies sometimes too many, sometimes too few, sometimes the wrong participants.[20]

Goffman (1976:260) goes one step further in identifying participation types of those who experience talk:

> Observe now that, broadly speaking, there are three kinds of listeners to talk: those who *over*hear, whether or not their unratified participation is inadvertent and whether or not it has been encouraged; those (in the case of more than two-person talk) who are ratified participants but

are not specifically addressed by the speaker; and those ratified participants who *are* addressed, that is oriented to by the speaker in a manner
to suggest that his words are particularly for them.[21]

In the grammatical system itself, English appears to formalize speaker (first
person), addressee (second person), and others (third person), complicating
this with number (singular and plural), although the second person (you) is
not formally marked (except in some regional and social varieties, e.g., 'you
all,' 'youse,' 'you'uns,' 'you guys'). The world of participants is more elaborately marked in Palaung where inclusion and exclusion of the addressee is
indicated and a dual number is added. (NB: 'you' always means 'you alone' in
the following translations.)

| Speaker included | Hearer included | One person | Two persons | More than two persons |
|---|---|---|---|---|
| X | X | | ar (you and I) | ɛ (you, I and others) |
| X | 0 | ɔ (I) | yar (I and another but not you) | yɛ (I and others, but not you) |
| 0 | X | mi (you) | par (you and another) | pɛ (you and others) |
| 0 | 0 | ʌn (he/she) | gar (he/she and another but not you) | gɛ (he/she and others but not you) |

(Wardhaugh 1986:225, based on Burling 1970:14–17)

Palaung avoids, then, the sort of participation clarifications which are common in English and other languages with less fully differentiated systems:

Where are you going?
Do you mean just me or all of us?

What should we do?
Do you mean just you and me or all of us?

On the other hand, participation status (or even identity) may shift with
certain communication needs. In a presidential debate, Jimmy Carter said
'The American people want a government which will be responsive to us'
(McKay 1980:293). Imagine Carter's dilemma; in a debate one must address
two sorts of ratified hearers – the fellow debaters and the audience. (In fact,
since such debates are broadcast, there are millions of unseen ratified
addressees as well.) Reference to 'the American people' must have struck
Carter as stand-offish, and, desiring to close the distance between himself

and his audience (and, perhaps, distance himself from his opponent), he switched to the first person, but an interpretation that the 'us' refers to the debaters is absurd. By his switch, Carter gives the impression of being a spokesperson for the group 'the American people' rather than a distant figure who refers to them. Literature presents similar difficulties when the narrator wants the reader to 'hear' a character but does not want to break the flow of the passage by resorting to quotation. McKay notes the following interesting example from Huck Finn, where the third person narrator shifts to first (plural):

Well, by and by the King he gets up and comes forward a little, and works himself up and slobbers out a speech, all full of tears and flapdoodle, about it being a sore trial for him and his poor brother to lose the diseased, and to miss seeing diseased alive after the long journey of four thousand mile, but it's a trial that's sweetened and sanctified to us by this dear sympathy and these holy tears, and so he thanks them out of his heart and out of his brother's heart, because out of their mouths they can't, words being too weak and cold, and all that kind of rot and slush, till it was just sickening; and then he blubbers out a pious goody-goody Amen, and turns himself loose and goes crying fit to bust. (Cited by McKay 1980:293)

From a larger perspective, many of the concerns already addressed in this work cooccur with participation status. Ervin-Tripp (1973b), although focusing on length of turn (3.1.3), indicates some of the richness of this interaction:

In informal small-group conversation the roles of sender and receiver may alternate; in a sermon the sender role is available only to one participant; in choral responses in a ritual, or in question period following a lecture, the role of sender is allocated at specific times. A second, related, determinant of the amount of talking is the role the participant has in the group and his social and physical centrality. He may be a therapy patient, chairman, teacher, or switchboard operator, so that his formal role requires communication with great frequency; he may informally play such a role, as in the case of a raconteur, or an expert on the topic at hand. . . . Because relative frequency of speaking is steeply graded, not evenly distributed, in a large group the least frequent speaker may get almost no chances to speak. The 'receiver' role is also unequally distributed even in face-to-face groups, being allocated to the most central, the most powerful, those with highest status, the most frequent speakers, and under conditions where agreement is desired, the most deviant. (241)

Participation status is, in large part, determined by the very factors of *individual* and *interaction* considered in chapters 2 and 3 of this work. All these factors may interact in interesting ways to cause miscommunication among participants or confusion across language and cultural boundaries. Even who (or what) may be addressed (and is qualified as a potential addressor) may radically differ:

> An informant told me that many years before he was sitting in a tent one afternoon during a storm, together with an old man and his wife. There was one clap of thunder after another. Suddenly the old man turned to his wife and asked, 'Did you hear what was said?' 'No,' she replied, 'I didn't catch it.' My informant, an acculturated Indian, told me he did not at first know what the old man and his wife referred to. It was, of course, the thunder. The old man thought one of the Thunder Birds had said something to him. He was reacting to this sound in the same way as he would to a human being, whose words he did not understand. The casualness of the remark and even the trivial character of the anecdote demonstrate the psychological depth of the 'social relations' with other-than-human beings that becomes explicit in the behavior of the Ojibwa as a consequence of the cognitive 'set' induced by their culture. (Hallowell 1964:64)

Members of post-technological societies who might feel superior to those who talk to thunder might recall conversations they have had with machines (computers, automobiles, telephone answering devices), prayer to intangible beings, and at least one-way talks with rocks, doors, and other offending objects.

What obligations and rights various participants have, including rights of nonparticipation, are of interest. Women's rights in public to being addressed on personal matters (e.g., attractiveness) have not traditionally been the same as men's:

> As I walked past them it began.
> 'Shore would like to have that swing in my backyard.'
> 'You want me to help you with your box, li'l lady?'
> 'Hesh up, Alvin, that ain't nice. Don't you talk to her like that.'
> 'I just want to help her with her box, thass all.'
> An explosion of mirth followed this riposte but it was quickly shushed by the man who had appointed himself my protector. . . .
> 'Shucks, ma'am, he didn't mean to insult you. He just thinks yore mighty sweet, thass all.' (King 1974:79)

Since the woman does not know the men and the site is a public place, she should have the participation rights of a stranger, of whom one might make undemanding requests ('Do you have the time, please?'), usually mitigated with politeness features. Any other establishment of participation roles in public (outside transactional encounters where some participant status is pre-established by one's role as clerk, driver, and so on) are usually associated with emergencies. In this interaction, however, the participation status of the woman is controlled by the group of men who use her sex as their right to involve her. The first line, a comment on the swaying of the woman's hips during her walk, is said with both the woman and other men as audience, though she may be treated, ironically, as an unratified participant (perhaps so the offending remark might be disclaimed as something she should not have been listening to; compare 'loud-talking,' described below). The second male remark, however, is especially interesting, for the offer is mock, and although it appears to be directly addressed to the woman, it is still primarily directed to the other men as audience. The man who remonstrates Alvin, however, is directly addressing him, though he, no doubt, has a continuing awareness of the woman as audience as Alvin certainly does with his response. The woman is finally addressed directly again, though the last part of the remark makes it clear that the speaker is still aware of the male audience.

Similarly, Blacks in the United States often create an audience with a device known as *loud-talking*.

> The term 'loud-talking' is applied to a speaker's utterance which by virtue of its volume permits hearers other than the addressee, and is objectionable because of this. Loud-talking requires an audience and can only occur in a situation where there are potential hearers other than the interlocutors. (Mitchell-Kernan 1972:329)

A student who has finished a test and is reading a novel notices that a classmate has turned his paper over and is copying from it. He says to her, loud enough for everyone to hear, 'What are you doing, girl?' She responds, 'You didn't have to loud-talk me,' meaning, of course, that others need not have been involved (Mitchell-Kernan 1972:330). Loud-talking need not be directed at shaming the interlocutor; it may as well be directed against the audience, but since the audience can be reanalyzed as an unratified overhearer, the loud-talker may pretend to be indignant. Abrahams and Gay (1972:205) develop the following scenario for what might happen after a teacher had heard a student make a critical remark about him or her in loud-talk to another student:

> *Teacher*: What did you say?
> *Student*: (With impatient anger) I wasn't talking to you.
> *Teacher*: But I heard you say something.
> *Student*: I didn't say anything.

*Teacher*: I'm almost sure I heard you saying something about me.
*Student*: (does not answer the teacher directly but murmurs – i.e., loud-talks) If you hadn't been listening you wouldn't have heard.

In short, unratified overhearers have no right to object to what they have heard, and some such reasoning even has legal status in some cultures:

A writes a letter to B containing defamatory statements about C. He puts the letter in his desk and locks it up. A thief breaks open the desk and reads the letter. A has not published a libel. (American Law Institute 1974:101)

Participation in its more usual senses, however, indicates obligations to construct communication which is reasonable for the particular interaction at hand.

The most far-reaching consideration of participant relations in general sociolinguistic theory is Bell's (1984) theory of *audience design* (3.5.1). Bell arranges participants on a scale of distance from the speaker – speaker, addressee, auditor, overhearer, eavesdropper (159). After claiming that interspeaker variation is a reflection of intraspeaker variation, Bell makes two specific claims about the relationship of stylistic alteration and participant status:

If a linguistic variable shows style variation according to any audience role, that presupposes variation according to all other roles closer to the speaker.
The effect on linguistic variation of each role is less than the effect on the role next closest to the speaker. (160)

The first point qualitatively establishes an implicational relationship. For example, a speaker who shifts style according to, say, overhearers, will, by definition, shift on that same variable in relation to auditors and addressees. In short, style-shifting does not leap over participant roles in its influence.

The second point makes a quantitative claim. If a speaker adjusts performance to an addressee, that adjustment will be stronger than any adjustment he or she makes for an auditor, and so on down the line (although, of course, speakers do not adjust to overhearers, since, by definition, their activity is unknown). Bell shows this relationship to be true for addresses and auditors by citing data from a Northern Irish experiment in which two subjects were recorded in a conversation with peers, and in a conversation with a peer and an English outsider. Taking the peer interaction as a base score, Bell indicates the percentage of increase towards standard [ŋ] over that base score (a) when the English outsider is an auditor, that is, when the two Northern

Irish peers are addressing one another, and (b) when the English outsider is an addressee:

|  | Percent increase of standard (ng) |
|---|---|
| Speaker C | |
| (a) Auditor effect | 18 |
| (b) Addressee effect | 22 |
| Speaker E | |
| (a) Auditor effect | 37 |
| (b) Addressee effect | 61 |

(Adapted from Bell 1984:174, who cites
Douglas-Cowie 1978: tables 1, 3, 4, and 12)

In both cases, as Bell's quantitative hierarchy suggests, the effect of the addressee is stronger than that of the auditor.

Although Bell's observations of speaker adjustment to participants are valuable for SLA research, the foundation of his theory does not apply. Since intraspeaker variation is confined by interspeaker variation, he claims that 'If a variable has no interspeaker variation, it will have no intraspeaker variation' (158). That, of course, cannot be the case for SLA variables, for many individual learners have a much wider range of variability than that evidenced by the input, even if one assumes it comes from NNSs as well as NSs, for there are processing and interference sources, to name only two, behind learner variation.

Although SLA acquisition research has paid a great deal of attention to the difference between production and comprehension, the bulk of that research concerns itself with psycholinguistic questions, not with the status of participants.[22] Some classroom research has focused on the special participant status imposed by student and teacher roles, but the more general concerns of participation have not been addressed. In experimental (e.g., Gass and Varonis 1986) and observational (e.g., Wong-Fillmore 1976) SLA research, either dyadic interaction or the special setting of the classroom are the norms for investigation. Some recent work on the training of NNS teaching assistants in university settings (e.g., Rounds 1987) deals with NNSs in a participant role different from those usually focused on, but, in general, that research does not elaborate on the participant status of the interlocutors.

The reader will surely have noticed by now a snowball effect. At the beginning of chapter 2 it was relatively easy to focus on one particular aspect of sociolinguistic concern and its relevance to SLA. Now that many have been surveyed, their interaction is overwhelming, and it is impossible to mention one without showing its involvement with others. That difficulty in organization, however, is surely nothing more than a reflection of the facts.

The various components of *individuals* and *interactions* surely influence one another in dramatically complex ways. Pretending that one may be isolated without the most careful experimental planning does not take this into account. On the other hand, clumping several together under the rubric of an *ad hoc* label does not advance the cause of understanding either.

Although chapter 4 takes a brief look at issues in general linguistics and the sociology of language which are relevant here, it returns to this theme of interaction and tries to wind many different strands of spaghetti around one fork. It is perhaps pretentious to call a taxonomic approach to sociolinguistic concerns a theory or a model, but it may have practical and pretheoretical values which will not be ignored in the final sections of this work.

# 4

# A taxonomy of language variation

This chapter summarizes and adds to areas of sociolinguistic concern, elaborating them into a taxonomy of components essential to the study of language variation. The taxonomy is then applied to an example of typical sociolinguistic data (language switching) and a sample of SLA research.

## 4.1 More categories

### 4.1.1 *General linguistics*

The language itself is what varies in sociolinguistics, and the smallest and largest elements have been most focused on. That odd couple may be explained by the two principal approaches to language variation. The first, in which the most significant work has been done in phonology and morphology, is essentially quantitative. It usually assumes that sociolinguistic variants are alternatives for delivering the same message. When speakers of United States Black English vernacular vary their realization of the final t/d of a consonant cluster (table 1.1), there is no semantic import to that variation. Only the fact that the variable (t/d) is not pronounced distinguishes 'He miss' school yesterday' from 'He missed school yesterday.' Everything else about the meaning of the two sentences remains the same, although some sociolinguists and ethnographers have included the social information encoded by such variation under the label 'meaning.' The quantitative sociolinguist, however, is interested in determining the social and contextual predictors of a variable's frequencies in an attempt to account for the status of the variant in the speech community, its usefulness as an indication of linguistic change, and its position and shape in the rule system of the individual.

At the other end of the scale, anthropologists, ethnographers, and conversational analysts have been more interested in the variation of text types, genres, participation strategies, and conversational structures. Neither approach has been pure; accounts of phonological variables have been qualitatively couched, and studies of conversational elements (turn-taking, interruptions, length of turn) have been quantitatively oriented. Practical and philosophical considerations have influenced the growth and style of research in both camps.

On the quantitative side, the difficulty of investigating larger units has been that of frequency. In a very short interview, a respondent will produce numerous examples of phonological items, and it is easy to provide reading passages and word lists which elicit the feature under investigation without focusing the respondent's attention on it. In work with larger units there are simply not enough incidences of the feature the researcher is investigating to provide a sample amenable to quantitative analysis. The ploys of word lists and reading passages, effective in eliciting phonological variables, will not elicit variation at all at higher levels.[1] Conversations, however, are rich in some of the sorts of information ethnographers want to observe (e.g., turn-taking) but may go on for hours without evidencing others (e.g., a particular genre).

From a theoretical rather than practical point of view, sociolinguists have been criticized for looking at any variation above the phonological and morphological levels (e.g., Lavandera 1977, and, within SLA, Young, to appear), for if there are semantic differences, then variation among equivalent forms does not exist. Labov (1978), however, argues that the elusive semantic difference between variables in syntax is precisely the sort of information variationist techniques may help discover and clarify. In the same way that different phonetic environments may promote more (or fewer) applications of a phonological rule, certain meanings seem to select certain syntactic forms with greater (or lesser) frequency rather than categorically determining them. The following 'one-question traffic survey' was carried out on the streets of Philadelphia:

It's about cops and jay-walkers. This happened in Milwaukee, where it's a big issue. This man came to a corner. The light was against him. There was a cop on the corner. And there were no cars coming. And he crossed the street
    and he got arrested.
      *or*
    and he was arrested.
      *or*
    and he got arrested to test the law.
      *or*
    and he was arrested to test the law.
Do you think that was the right thing to do? (Labov 1978:9)

Each respondent was given only one of the four final lines of the narrative. The question is ambiguous between whether it was the right thing for the man to do (cross the street) or for the policeman to do (arrest the man). If the 'he' of the test sentences is interpreted as the agent of an inchoative sentence, then answers such as 'No, because he was just asking for trouble' will be given. If, on the other hand, the 'he' of the sample sentences is analyzed as the patient of a passive sentence, then such responses as 'No, because I cross the street myself that way all the time' are more likely (Labov 1978:9–10). The 'get' and 'be' forms were clearly differentiated (with 'get' as inchoative and 'be' as passive) when 'to test the law' was added; without that addition, the respondents did not differentiate the 'get' and 'be' forms.[2]

Such a study allows specification of a syntactic form more or less rather than categorically determined by a semantic reading,[3] and it might be argued that the study of social and stylistic influences on such higher-level forms is valid only when there is no such preference, but even a form which varies in part due to the meaningful differences it signals may still be a candidate for social and stylistic variability. There is no reason to exclude investigations of socially and interactionally relevant frequencies of such semantic-syntactic preferences, particularly since the developing grammatical, discoursal, and pragmatic rules of an interlanguage could not be treated from a variationist standpoint if this kind of exclusion were adopted.

Perhaps one reason why some linguists have resisted this approach to larger units stems from the misuse of such information. If it is discovered, for example, that a group uses less of one sort of construction, particularly one associated with some such cognitive operation as 'hypothesizing,' some have claimed that the code may be restricted, perhaps even in need of applied linguistic remediation (e.g., Bereiter and Engelmann 1966, Bernstein 1972).

There is another apparent restriction on the use of variable rules. Labov (e.g., 1973) suggests that the linguistic constraints on a rule are similar for an entire speech community. Table 1.4, for example, shows four linguistic constraints on the deletion of (t/d). The constraint values for all classes are not significantly different from the values shown in table 1.3 for the upper middle class only:

|  | All classes | Upper middle class |
|---|---|---|
| Following vowel | 0.25 | 0.23 |
| Following consonant | 0.75 | 0.77 |
| Morpheme | 0.31 | 0.33 |
| Nonmorpheme | 0.69 | 0.67 |

On the other hand, the social constraint values (here, class) are quite distinct:

| | |
|---|---|
| Upper middle class | 0.29 |
| Lower middle class | 0.42 |
| Upper working class | 0.60 |
| Lower working class | 0.69 |

In other words, although considerable class stratification exists, the linguistic norm of the community, expressed in the values of the linguistic constraints, is the same. It is also the case, though it has not been discussed in the literature, that in many such VARBRUL analyses, the range of values of the social or stylistic constraints falls within the boundaries formed by the range of the values of the linguistic constraints.[4]

Labov notes, however, that there are cases in which the linguistic constraint norms are dissimilar (e.g., 1973). One possible conclusion is that different speech communities are involved and that the respondents were inappropriately grouped. Guy (1980) shows that the effect of following pause on consonant cluster reduction is significantly different for New Yorkers and Philadelphians, providing a quantitative justification for putting the two communities in different 'dialect areas.'

It is not just in different dialect areas, however, where there appear to be different linguistic constraint values for different groups. In a study of (l) vocalization in Philadelphia, Ash (1982) discovered linguistic constraint values which ranged from 0.17 (an unreduced vowel following (l), but with stress placed neither immediately before or after the variable, e.g., 'relocation') to 0.77 (the lexical item 'Philadelphia'). Sex, ethnicity, and class constraints all exhibited ranges which fell well within that established by the linguistic constraints. Age, however, showed a more severe pattern:

| Age group: | VARBRUL constraint |
|---|---|
| under 10 | 0.16 |
| 10–19 | 0.41 |
| 20–29 | 0.78 |
| 30–39 | 0.60 |
| 40–49 | no data |
| 50–59 | 0.80 |
| 60 and over | 0.27 |

The striking fact about these data is that the range established by linguistic constraints is exceeded on both ends. A lower frequency of (l) vocalization than that determined by the most constraining linguistic factor is predicted in the use of children under ten, and a higher frequency than that of the most promoting linguistic feature may be observed in the 20–29 and 50–59 age groups. Ash concludes that this is a typical case of change from below corrected by change from above. The (l) vocalization apparently arose in the current 50–59 age group (probably in the working class) and began to spread but was 'corrected from above' and is now marginal among the youngest groups. Such complex patterns of change are likely to show different linguistic norms among groups which, it must still be maintained, are from the same speech community. Kay (1978) claims that the stability of constraint values must be set aside in instances of change which are initiated and/or led dramatically by one social group or another within a speech community.

The implications for the processing and interpretation of SLA data in this format seem especially promising as a sensitive means of determining the weight of various influences on interlanguage development. Since Guy's (1980) study of influences on deletion in New York and Philadelphia found no difference between the two communities in the ranking of probabilities contributed by following consonants, liquids, glides, and vowels, it may be possible to distinguish between such 'natural' influences as those and such learned matters as pause, for which the two communities were distinct. Such procedures might help piece out the various interpretations given 'markedness' in SLA research by providing quantitative substantiation to invariant (universal) and variant (learnable) factors as well as distinguishing among the influences of individual and nonlinguistic contextual factors. Application of the VARBRUL 2 program to SLA data is exemplified in 1.2.1, 4.2, and 5.1.2.

The distinction between variable rules (or implicational scales) as devices for describing the shape and/or relationship of grammars (synchronically and diachronically) and such rules as only a way of capturing social and stylistic fluctuation is an important one. If the sociolinguistic contribution is only the latter, its relevance to much SLA research is limited to upper-level learners whose responses to social and situational contexts influence their performance. If the former, however, then sociolinguistic devices, due to their sensitivity to the variability of the grammar (or, in a dynamic paradigm, to various grammars – lects), are excellent means of capturing synchronic and diachronic aspects of interlanguage systems, no matter what the source of variation. This book cannot deal with all those implications, for many are outside the scope of sociolinguistics in its more general sense. SLA scholars who have looked at the development of formal versus functional operations in interlanguage have found implicational scales handy representational devices; those who have looked at the transfer and (possibly) universal effects on a developing interlanguage phonology may find the variable rule format useful. In short, models for the description of language variation, so-called sociolinguistic rules, are useful even if the source of variation is not one of the social or stylistic areas caricaturistically associated with sociolinguistic research. To the extent that a developing interlanguage is a natural language, it will require the sorts of descriptive apparatuses made available by a variationist grammar. This point is even better made by referring to such devices as 'variationist,' since it highlights the general and descriptive importance of accounting for differences in individual and group language shape rather than the influence of so-called nonlinguistic contextual forces suggested by the label 'sociolinguistics.'

Interactionist and ethnographic approaches to language variation also go beyond socially sensitive descriptions, often maintaining that meaning itself is created through interaction. This implies that the linguistic forms which are used for social creativity are not simply handed over from an autonomous linguistic component, for L1 acquisition studies (recently extended to SLA) suggest, as shown in 2.1.1, that syntax itself may develop from interaction.

Perhaps there is a cycle of social-stylistic and interactionist uses of and linguistic influences on variables. Once contextual influences are associated with linguistic forms (and it seems inevitable in any society that they will be), the potential for nonreferential use is multiplied by the associations previously formed. For early SLA research, linguistic contexts will dominate, and if sociolinguistic ways of representing grammars and relations among them did not help at this level, they would have little relevance to those concerned with SLA at the early stages. Emerging bilinguals at higher levels will, as suggested in many places in chapter 3, copy from and bring their own unique meanings to the representation of the social and stylistic dimensions of a new language.

The linguistic levels which need to be considered in the contribution of sociolinguistics to SLA are not just those smallest units which vary with no apparent consequence for referential meaning. Variability in form with reference to function is central to SLA research, and it has sufficient justification in sociolinguistic representations to allow a variety of accounts of variability to serve in general linguistic research of any sort. To be added to the catalog of individual and interactional factors, then, are the pieces of language itself, and in the account which follows, linguistic units from phone to genre will be considered fair game. They represent, however, not just dormant units waiting to gain social significance from use in a speech community but forms which may have, at least in part, taken their shape from such use itself.

1   Phonology (including intonation, pause, stress)
2   Morphology (including morphophonemic alteration)
3   Lexicon (including both meaning and control and response to structure)
4   Syntax
5   Semantics (including speech act interpretation and pragmatic concerns)
6   Discourse and text (including interactional structure, interpretation, and classification).

### 4.1.2   Sociology of language

The various positions (1) different languages hold among their neighbors and (2) different subparts of a single variety hold among one another cannot be ignored in a sociolinguistic approach to SLA.

An attempt to deal with some of the largest questions of language and variety status was developed by Stewart (1972), who identifies four language *attributes* and shows how they can be used to distinguish among several different communication system types (table 4.1).

*Table 4.1*    Attributes of language and variety status

| Attributes | | | | | |
| --- | --- | --- | --- | --- | --- |
| Standardization | Autonomy | Historicity | Vitality | Type | Symbol |
| + | + | + | + | Standard | S |
| + | + | + | − | Classical | C |
| + | + | − | − | Artificial | A |
| − | + | + | + | Vernacular | V |
| − | − | + | + | Dialect | D |
| − | − | − | + | Creole | K |
| − | − | − | − | Pidgin | P |

*Source*: Stewart 1972:573

*Standardization* refers to a language's range of acceptance and its association with a set of regulations which govern 'correct' usage. Writing systems
often indicate that a language has been standardized. The complex of factors
involved in standardization are listed in Garvin and Mathiot (1956) and
Garvin (1959) and more recently summarized in Downes (1984:32–8).
Kloss (1986) warns of confusing 'standard' with 'official' or 'national'
language.[5]
   A language has *autonomy* if its speakers (and/or speakers around it)
believe it is cut off from other varieties. This separation may be natural
(*abstand*); linguistic differences between two systems may be so great (e.g.,
English and Hungarian) that it is impossible to consider one a nonautono-
mous offspring or relative of the other. On the other hand, languages may be
separated in the minds of speakers by *ausbau* or 'effort.' Two linguistic
systems may, in fact, be very similar, but tribal, religious, or nationalistic
identities may cause speakers to regard them as distinct languages. In Spain,
Catalán is considered an autonomous variety in Catalonia (and particularly,
one would expect, by Catalonian nationalists) but is widely considered a
variety of Spanish elsewhere in the country. The *ausbau* effect may work in
reverse, piling together distinct varieties. So-called dialects of Chinese
(Cantonese, Mandarin, and so on) are as linguistically distinct as Spanish,
Portuguese, and Italian, but their existence in one country, the perception of
their similarity by non-Chinese, and the confusion of the writing system
(which is the same for all) with language itself (even among the Chinese!)
gives rise to the notion 'Chinese language.'
   *Historicity* is a belief in the natural development and origins of languages
over time, including folk accounts. Folklorists and anthropologists have
recorded a large number of beliefs in which birds teach language to humans,
and that fact is not unrelated to the folk etymological association of *pidgin*

with *pigeon* in many regions, although the recency of creation of pidgin and creole varieties and their specific origins in other known languages often make them lack a strong historicity. The Judeo-Christian account of the diversity of language based on the Tower of Babel myth is part of a widespread historicity of language diversity in general. Although some well-educated speakers may have little or no distinction between historicity and *source* (the scientific account of a language's roots and development), that does not remove the influence of beliefs about language origins from the speech community at large.

Finally, languages are dead or alive, dying or revivifying, or, in some cases, preserved in extremely limited use (e.g., Latin in religious and academic contexts); these concerns are indicated by the label *vitality*. For a language to be vital, it must be supported by a community of native speakers. If it is not, though it may appear vital for one generation, its existence is most likely doomed (at least on this dimension) since it will not be passed on as the native language of the next generation (e.g., a pidgin).

As shown in table 4.1, a *standard* language has all these attributes; its standardization is often guaranteed by an academy or body of scholars, and its rules of use may be promulgated in schools. A *classical* language is simply a dead (nonvital) standard (or one, like Latin, preserved for limited use).

An *artificial* language is not vital in the second sense outlined above. It has no continuing community of native speaker users, and it has no historicity (although it is not impossible to imagine an artificial language's acquiring some aspects of historicity – e.g., myths about its originator).

A *vernacular* has every aspect except standardization, although it is important to recognize that most sociolinguists do not use the term this way:

> At times, it refers to the most localized form of speech associated with the lowest socioeconomic group (e.g. Milroy's 1980 'Belfast vernacular') or ethnic group (e.g. Labov's BEV or Black English Vernacular), while at others it has been used to refer to the most informal speech style of an individual (cf. Labov 1972a). And elsewhere, Labov [1984:29] refers to the vernacular as that mode of speech that is acquired in pre-adolescent years; those between the ages of 9 and 18 are said to speak the most consistent vernacular. (Romaine 1984:20)

Although no field needs more jargon, it is certainly the case that precision in the labeling of varieties is weak in sociolinguistics. To suggest solutions only for the confusions listed by Romaine, local varieties should be referred to as *dialects* (perhaps in this particular case an *urban dialect*); if complicated by social status, the term *sociolect* might be appropriate; if by ethnic group, *ethnolect*. Stylistic and age dimensions need to be specified as well. (A long list of combinations with *-lect* is horrible to imagine, but *genderlect*, for example, has some currency.)

Nonattention to form is the dominating concern (at least of Labov's) in characterizing the vernacular, and to the extent that the stylistic dimension's more casual ranges are represented in unselfconscious talk, the use of *distance* to characterize the vernacular is central. On the other hand, claims that one's vernacular is acquired at a certain period or that the vernacular styles (distance modes) of upper classes share frequencies in the use of some features with the formal uses of lower classes are all empirical ones and require further investigation.[6]

All these vernaculars, however, are not what Stewart has in mind. Table 4.1 shows that vernaculars are autonomous and are, therefore, simply languages not standardized, not nonstandard (or other) varieties of autonomous languages, the category reserved in table 4.1 for *dialect*. Unfortunately, that term in Stewart's system is not limited to geographically diverse varieties but includes those which differ according to class, ethnicity, and so on.

Pidgins lack everything, but creoles, since they acquire native speakers, have vitality.

The concern for such facts as Stewart's attributes (and the language types they define) in SLA is more powerfully evident in language planning, language instruction policies, and so on, but they are not without importance to individuals, teachers, materials, and classrooms, particularly in terms of the social psychological effects which arise as a result of the relationships between the groups involved (2.1.3, 2.1.4). Only learners with strong academic or religious motivation may prove successful with nonvital languages; learners from strongly standardized languages may not be able to understand the descriptive rather than prescriptive status of rules they are taught in, say, a vernacular or creole. On the other hand, students without a standard may reject prescriptive rules on political or other grounds. Many of these concerns have been elaborated on in discussions of multilingualism, language contact, language shift, language loyalty, language loss, language planning, and the bilingual education movement. (Some 'classics' in these areas include Andersson and Boyer 1978, Fishman 1975, Fishman 1966, Fishman, Ferguson and Das Gupta 1968, Fishman et al. 1971, Le Page 1964, Weinreich 1953, Whiteley 1971, and UNESCO 1953, but this work does not pretend to deal deeply with the content or bibliography of this vast domain.)

In addition to these attributes which discriminate among system types, there are lower-level ones which discriminate within systems and address matters of both use and evaluation.

Along with historicity and source, languages have other temporal concerns – *currency*, *duration* and *frequency*. Parts of a language may be fully current, obsolescent, or obsolete (though the last, like entire nonvital languages, may be preserved in special contexts – e.g., the *thee*, *thou*, *thy*, and *thine* familiar second person singular pronouns of older English in prayer and other religious settings). In language teaching and learning based on literary texts, it is often the case that learners acquire a great deal of noncurrent language. Texts and materials, often prepared by those same learners in their later professional capacities, need to be updated for currency.

Items may last (have *duration*) in a language or they may be ephemeral. Unless there are specific reasons for learning and teaching short-lived items (e.g., specialization), they might be avoided since many are precisely those sorts of units which may elicit negative reactions from NSs, particularly if they are regarded as slang, popular culture references, or folk speech.

Finally, for temporal matters, items may be classified according to *frequency*, and 2.2.2 and 3.2.3 have already illustrated how language learning materials in specialized courses draw on frequency for authenticity of the model and economy of items to be acquired. Learners whose experiences have been with literary texts or with acquisition of only formal ranges of a language often use low frequency items in ordinary conversation.

In a belletristic tradition, *value* is granted to poems, plays, novels, and other genres, but outside that tradition, a great many items such as slang and folk speech are valued. Proverbial expressions are often integrated into ordinary usage, but they signal a playfulness, artistry, or desire to bring attention to form as well as content (*foregrounding*). Such expressions are distinct from ordinary language use because they constitute 'performance,' either in a larger nonvalued setting or as part of a larger valued structure (e.g., a joke). Bauman (1977:16) lists the following characteristics of valued language:

Special codes
Figurative language
Parallelism
Special paralinguistic features
Special formulae
Appeal to tradition
Disclaimer of performance

It is important to note that language is not valued by virtue of its structure alone, for different cultures value vastly different genres and patterns. Bauman agrees with Pratt (1977) who notes that the value assigned any level of usage is derived from the cultural tradition surrounding it. Even though Bauman's list emphasizes internal characteristics of valued language, they are, nevertheless, incidental to the cultural valuation itself, indicated in his list in 'appeal to tradition.'

There has been little attention to valued language in SLA studies, though old-fashioned language teaching focused on literary texts and more recent methodologists have commented on the role of literature in the language teaching syllabus (e.g., McConochie 1985). Texts which are 'valued' in a scientific tradition (Bley-Vroman and Selinker 1984) do not really have value of the sort under discussion here.

In a few studies, however, slang and proverbialisms have formed the basis for interesting investigations of language transfer. Kellerman (1977) asked learners of English in The Netherlands to judge the grammaticality of correct and incorrect English sentences rich in idiom, slang, and proverbialisms. Respondents tended to judge as incorrect those which had corresponding forms in their native language, suggesting that language specific items do not transfer. Irujo (1986), however, found that similar idioms in the first language aided production and comprehension of those in the second but also encouraged interference. Since nonvalued idioms (e.g., to run a risk, to open his eyes) were mixed with valued ones (e.g., to kill two birds with one stone; to swallow it hook, line, and sinker) in both studies, there may have been conflicting experimental results precisely because this different status of items was not taken into account. If such items are important indicators of language transfer, then a classification of their value status will be necessary to insure that only one dimension is being investigated.

Since slang and proverbialisms are intimately bound to the cultural groups which invest them with value, it is not surprising to find competent bilinguals selecting carefully among them. Ethnographic studies of the bilinguals' use of valued language items in their L2s could be very revealing of how such sensitive systems are formed precisely in relation to particularly symbolic language units.

Some language units have very special status – they are *magic* or *taboo*. The former is not at all composed of mumbo-jumbo:

> Each magical expression, taken by itself, can be seen to highlight some attribute of the experienced world, which serves as a model for the spell's desired outcome; each suggests a variety of associations that relate the practitioner, his objective milieu, and his immediate goals. (Rosaldo 1975:178)

Though metaphoric content of Ilongot magical spells is the focus of Rosaldo's work, what she says of the use of 'commonplaces' in magical languages appears to be a cultural universal. How one wants the world to be is the hope of magic; representing it linguistically in that way is the homeopathy that makes words magic:

> The ritual of the garden begins when the earth is prepared for the planting of the seed yams and continues until the harvesting. The planting charms describe the yams planted as of huge varieties and already grown. The charms required during the early growth period picture the twining of the vines under the image of the web-spinning of the large spider kapali:

>       Kapali, kapali,
>       twisting around,
>       he laughs with joy.
> I with my garden darkened with foliage.
> I with my leaves.
>       Kapali, kapali,
>       twisting around,
>       he laughs with joy.
> (Benedict 1934:134–5)

It is not surprising to find no references to magic language in either the research or pedagogical literature on language teaching and learning. One would expect, however, under the general rubric of the development of communicative competence, that learners should be aware of common magic language practices, their distribution in the speech community, and the degree of belief attached to them.

*Taboo* must first be distinguished from inappropriateness. Children talking like adults, men like women, scholars like street people are all examples of inappropriate language use, but none involves a taboo which emerges from a cultural restriction on the language itself, though any one might be a candidate for such restriction. For example, in some south Bantu tribes, women may no longer use the consonants which occur in the family name of their in-laws, and they develop sound substitutions to avoid breaking this regulation. Similarly, in a great many cultures, certain religious language is not only inappropriate to certain members of the speech community, but specifically forbidden except for select practitioners. Unfortunately, while a number of sophisticated accounts of linguistic taboo exist for small, isolated cultural groups, there are no professional, unprejudiced accounts of the types and functions of linguistic taboo in modern, technologically developed societies. The journal *Maledicta* revels in revealing elaborate taboo, but it offers little to further an understanding of its functions in society. Other accounts (Hartogs 1967, Legman 1968, 1975, Montagu 1967, and Sagarin 1962) are either not the result of any empirical research or have hand-wringing axes to grind. The collection of obscene words has fared better (e.g., Spears 1981, Wentworth and Flexner 1975), but dictionaries do little to describe use.

Topics which produce linguistic taboos are similar in many cultures (religion, body parts and functions, animals), but it is the linguistic item not the referent which is taboo, as the following pairs of words make clear – *piss* vs *urine* and *prick* vs *penis*.

Cross-cultural obscenity, intended and unintended, is a source of much folk humor. Jiménez (1965) reports on a joke telegram circulated in Mexico which pretended to be a news flash about the Japanese occupation of Saigon during World War II. The generals of the occupying army were listed; the names all appear to be Japanese, but a careful reading of them reveals that many are Spanish obscenities. General 'Nojoda Migata,' for example, is 'Don't fuck my cat' (86). Haas (1957) tells of some inventive Thai students in America who noticed that their word for pepper (phríg) sounded like English 'prick.' Since they used the word frequently when dining out, they avoided it by substituting the elegant Thai word for penis – 'lyŋ,' derived from Sanskrit *lingam*.

It is an often reported fact that beginning language learners are intrigued with the new language's slang and obscenity. Preston (1982) suggests, in a study of a group of English learners' concern for and inventive play with obscenities while acquiring Polish, that such items are highly symbolic for beginning learners of a level of competence far beyond their reach, but, in fact, no serious SLA accounts of taboo language exist.

Concern for the learner's knowledge of taboo language so that he or she may avoid embarrassment is well-known. Claire (1980) is an attempt to advise learners of English and actually includes some situational suggestions. Although it is unique in the area it covers, it appears to be based on the author's intuitions and does not count as an ethnographically sound presentation of this interesting area. For example, it makes no mention of the fact that solidarity (rather than insult and anger) is an important function of obscenity in many languages, nor does it indicate that this is an area rich in language play.

Finally, parts of languages or entire languages may have limited *publicity*. Of course, taboos may be limited in their publicity, but that is not a necessary condition. For example, the south Bantu women who do not use the consonants of the in-laws' names nevertheless know those consonants and hear others use them. On the other hand, some prayers and incantations may be ineffective if they are heard by restricted persons; in this case, taboo and publicity are both at work.

There are language uses, however, which are not meant for public consumption but do not constitute taboos. There are any number of veiled language practices, ranging from the highly developed secret codes of war and espionage to children's Pig Latin (regular phonological alterations of the native language). Most so-called secret languages or criminal argot turn out to function more for the purposes of in-group solidarity than public deception. Futrell (1981) notes that the United States scholar who knew most about underworld argot, David Maurer,

> has put to rest the myth that criminals' argots are secret languages used primarily to deceive. Argots, while secret or semisecret, are mainly used as a means of identification by members of the in-group who have knowledge of the sociolect of the subculture. (11)

SLA studies are not concerned with this particular aspect of language restrictiveness, but there is another aspect of linguistic parochialism which may, indeed, have affective repercussions for learners. Some languages (e.g., English, Spanish, French) are not only widespread but are spoken by ethnically diverse groups. Their publicity is most extensive; other languages, though spoken by millions, are unusual targets for learners (e.g., Hungarian, Turkish, Norwegian). Although these second languages are fully public and are taught, they are spoken by more-or-less ethnically homogeneous populations, and NS reactions to NNS knowledge of them ranges from shock to delight. Some isolated and tribal languages are taught only in specialist (anthropological and linguistic) settings, and speakers of them might even have taboos against teaching the language to outsiders. It would be wrong, however, to associate a language's degree of publicity with the attitudes of its NSs to learner performance. While English and French have equal status for publicity, the French, at least anecdotally, have always demanded a higher level of performance. Such recent entries in the world language learning and teaching community as Japanese may support, even in the face of technological and economic ascendancy, older beliefs about the uniqueness of the linguistic system and the impossibility of foreigners' mastering it. In ethnically homogeneous communities, notions of the relation of language and culture help sustain such attitudes. The research which has been done on the degree to which the presence of L1 and L2 in the larger world arena influences acquisition has generally taken place within the context of emerging NNS standards (e.g., Kachru 1982b). It appears to be the case that languages of greater publicity offer more opportunities for successful learning even with an instrumental (2.1.3) orientation (e.g., Lukmani 1972). Social psychological studies which include discussions of dominant and dominated groups (2.1.3, 2.1.4) provide another framework for further consideration of such matters.

In summary, aspects of the sociology and status of languages, varieties, and their units, although only briefly touched on here, include:

1  Standardization (codification of linguistic norms; writing system)
2  Autonomy (a language's independence, whether from linguistic distance [abstand] or speaker conception [ausbau])
3  Historicity (the folk concept of a language's origin and development)
4  Source (the scientific account of a language's origins and development)
5  Vitality (current use; acquisition as a native language by a next generation of speakers)
6  Currency (period of use [e.g., Old High German] and status [e.g., obsolescent] of entire language or any part)
7  Duration (length of existence of a language or any part of it)
8  Frequency

9   Value (the special status ['foregrounded'] assigned some linguistic units
    by their culture
10  Magic (making the world match words)
11  Taboo (codified restrictions on language use and participation)
12  Publicity (the spread and exposure of a language or any part of it).


### 4.1.3 *Media*

In addition to their status, form, and function, languages have a physical
reality, and the types of that realization are important influences on variation.

In many media contexts, participants may be seen, and studies of the
contribution of the body to communication is a long-standing concern (e.g.,
the pioneering work by Birdwhistle 1970 and E. T. Hall 1959, and 1966).
The physicality of participants includes presence, posture, attire, facial
expression (3.5.2), eye contact ('gaze' – 3.1.3), gesture, motion, and relation
to objects and others (including, specifically *proxemics* and *haptics* – rules
governing how close one may be to another and conditions for touching
another, respectively). Both inter- and intracultural uses and varieties of such
*body language* or *nonverbal communication* have been studied; only a few
samples can be given here.

Observations on the relativity of such matters has ranged from Darwin's
'naturalist' (1872) and Eibl-Eibesfeldt's 'innatist' positions (both summarized in Eibl-Eibesfeldt 1974) to the completely relativist position held by
Birdwhistle:

> Insofar as we know, there is no body motion or gesture that can be
> regarded as a universal symbol. That is, we have been unable to
> discover any single facial expression, stance, or body position which
> conveys an identical meaning in all societies. (1970:81)

Ekman and his associates occupy a middle ground, suggesting that many
expressions carry the same meaning in all cultures, but that each society has
its own 'display rules' which indicate whether it is appropriate to use an
expressive behavior or not (Ekman, Friesen and Ellsworth 1972:179).
Similarly, pan-cultural gestures may be modified by local specifics:

> Though the emblem for eating always involves a hand-to-mouth
> pantomime, in Japan one hand cups an imaginary bowl at about chin
> level, while the other scoops imaginary food into the mouth; but in New
> Guinea, where people eat sitting on the floor, the hand shoots out to
> arm's length, picks up an imaginary tidbit, and carries it to the mouth.
> (Davis 1975:77)

One of the early observations of body use in communication settings is Hall's (1966) description of proxemics – the comfortable distances among what he calls middle class American interlocutors:

1 *Intimate distance* From body contact to a separation space of 18 inches. An emotionally charged zone used for love making, sharing, protecting, and comforting.
2 *Personal distance* From 18 inches to 4 feet. Used for informal contact between friends. A 'small protective sphere or bubble' that separates one person from another.
3 *Social distance* From 4 to 12 feet. The casual interaction distance between acquaintances and strangers. Used in business meetings, classrooms, and impersonal social affairs.
4 *Public distance* Between 12 and 25 feet. A cool interaction distance used for one-way communication from speaker to audience. Necessitates a louder voice, stylized gestures and more distinct enunciation. (117–25)

Hall notes that Latin American distances are much different:

In Latin America the interaction distance is much less than it is in the United States. Indeed, people cannot talk comfortably with one another unless they are very close to the distance that evokes either sexual or hostile feelings in the North American. The result is that when they move close, we withdraw and back away. As a consequence, they think we are distant or cold, withdrawn and unfriendly. We, on the other hand, are constantly accusing them of breathing down our necks, crowding us, and spraying our faces. (1966:209)

Touch carries cultural meaning as well. Jourard (1966) observed couples in cafés in San Juan, Puerto Rico; Paris; Gainesville, Florida; and London. The number of times the couples touched one another ranged from 180 per hour in San Juan, through 110 in Paris, to 2 in Gainesville and 0 in London.[7] Intimacy in these several cultures obviously puts different requirements on body contact.

The dramatic cross-cultural results of such research have brought them to the attention of language teachers, particularly those who encourage the acquisition of communicative as well as linguistic competence (e.g., Green 1971, Morain 1978, and Pennycook 1985, which contains a review and bibliography of both the research and pedagogical literature).

Another strain of investigation in the physical aspect of communication concerns *paralinguistics*,[8] which, although the definition is by no mean well-agreed on, is here taken to mean physical aspects which accompany speech and interaction in a more direct way than the more independent characteristics of stance, gesture, and so on. Research in this area suggests that body motion provides a sort of rhythmic accompaniment to speech:

> When a person is speaking, his head and often other body parts move to mark the stresses in his speech, and his gestures or body movements mark off phrases, sentences, and even longer units. (Byers and Byers 1972:9–10)[9]

There may be a synchrony of body and conversational units as well.[10] Kendon (1967) shows that a speaker tends to look away from an addressee at the beginning of an utterance but gaze rather steadily as the utterance nears completion. At that point, the addressee, who has tended to look at the speaker, looks away. When the transition occurs, the new speaker is, appropriately, looking away from the addressee.[11]

Fiksdal (to appear) records NS – NNS differences in the uses of body shift and gaze which accompany 'uncomfortable moments' in an academic interview setting, suggesting, among other things, that the NSs of English in her study make more postural shifts at uncomfortable moments than do NNSs.

One language teaching method (Total Physical Response), though related to psychological rather than sociolinguistic or conversational analysis findings, suggests that recall is enhanced when verbal activity is accompanied by motor activity (e.g., Asher 1977).

More pertinent to the discussion here are efforts (1) to study the sorts of nonverbal communication which take place in classrooms, particularly between teachers of one cultural background and students of another, and (2) to recommend and devise suggestions for teaching (for both production and understanding) nonverbal behavior (Pennycook 1985). Morain (1978:13) warns, however, that

> some native speakers – perhaps in a display of kinesic territoriality – feel that it is offensive to see members of a foreign culture using imperfectly the gestural system of a culture that is not their own.

It will be maintained here that this notion might be strengthened by suggesting that a competent bilingual may form a body language system which differs from the NS's even if his or her competence allowed *perfect* use of the system.

Another feature of medium is *voice*, including all the characteristics which are not included in the regular features of the phonological system. Southerners in the United States have a 'drawl' (e.g., Feagin 1987), and such vocal qualities as 'creaky,' 'nasal,' and 'harsh' are shown to distinguish groups (e.g., dialects, sociolects, languages) as well as individuals (e.g., Easling

1981). Short-term use of such characteristics indicate emotional (anger) and physical (fatigue) states. Culturally rather than biologically induced differences in men's and women's speech as regards pitch was mentioned in 2.1.2, and a number of such inter- and intracultural differences in voice and vocal characteristics are reviewed in Laver and Trudgill (1979).

As with body motion, however, vocal phenomena are perhaps more interesting as clues to interactive organization and even discourse type. Gumperz (1982) notes the following shift:

> This incident was recorded at the end of a helicopter flight from a Bay Area suburb to San Francisco airport. The cabin attendant whose seat was squeezed in among the half dozen passengers all grouped together in the center of the aircraft picked up the microphone and addressed the group:
> We have now landed at San Francisco Airport. The local time is 10.35. We wish to thank you for flying SFO Airlines, and we wish you a happy trip. Isn't it quiet around here? Not a thing moving. (162–3)

The last two sentences of this announcement, although still spoken through the microphone, were marked by lower pitch, increased tempo, and wider intonational contours. These features (along with facts of lexicon and structure) identify a personal remark, and the passengers responded (as they had not earlier) by nodding; one passenger inquired why it was so quiet and was told by the attendant that the baggage handlers were on strike. A failure to use such appropriate vocal accompaniment in cross cultural settings often results in misunderstanding:

> The incident took place in London, England, on a bus driven by a West Indian driver/conductor. The bus was standing at a stop, and passengers were filing in. The driver announced, 'Exact change, please,' as all London bus drivers often do. When passengers who had been standing close by either did not have money ready or tried to give him a large bill, the driver repeated, 'Exact change, please.' The second time around, he said 'please' with extra loudness, high pitch, and falling intonation, and he seemed to pause before 'please.' One passenger so addressed, as well as others following him, walked down the bus aisle exchanging angry looks and obviously annoyed, muttering, 'Why do these people have to be so rude and threatening about it?' (Gumperz 1982:168)

British English speakers expect a rising intonation on 'please,' a politeness signal. When they heard a falling intonation (coupled with the other features of pause and loudness) they interpreted it as an indication of the speaker's annoyance with their actions.

Voice may maintain certain aspects of organization in an interaction. Amplitude, for example, may mark a speaker's *affiliation* to the preceding utterance (Goldberg 1978). A speaker tends to shift amplitude downward if an utterance is related to the one which precedes it; it is shifted upwards if it is not. One possible function of this signaling is that it advises the hearer to take what is said in terms of what has preceded or not (207–8). Such subtle differences as these have not been the focus of SLA research and instruction though they rather obviously suggest interesting possibilities.

Another concern of medium is communication *mode*. A language may be spoken, signed, or written. The spoken and some signed systems might be paired on one level, in that they are autonomous systems, not secondary representations of another. Other sign systems (e.g., finger spelling) may be paired with writing systems since they are derived and use visual rather than auditory stimuli.

Certainly too much was made in linguistics in times gone by of the secondary nature of writing systems (e.g., Lyons 1968:38–42). Any society with a long-standing literary tradition will have developed types and genres which are unique to writing or which only partially overlap with speech varieties. Some speakers of English would congratulate a friend with a phone call but send that same person a letter of condolence. More generally, since a writing system is a sign of language standardization, the written language may be viewed as the 'correct' language, and such attitudes need to be taken into account in applied linguistics planning.

Within writing itself variation ranges from the level of genre choice, through the sorts of organization and strategies such higher level choices impose on the written product, to the levels of lexical and syntactic variation. Applied linguists have been particularly active in their research on the organization of what one might call practical genres – research articles, business communications, medical reporting, and so on. Chiu (1972) and White (1974), for example, have already been discussed in 2.2.2 in connection with their studies of the frequency of lexical types in different writing tasks, and Swales (1981), as shown in 3.2.3, exemplifies a study of written genre structure.

The variation of organizational patterns and structural and lexical types in written forms has been studied in greater depth, however, than by simply referring to frequency. Lackstrom, Selinker, and Trimble (1970), for example, show how the variation of tense and aspect in technical writing reflects the level of generality. The past tense is used when the reporter knows of only one instance of what he or she is describing; the present perfect is likely in cases when a few instances are known, and the present when many instances are known and no future exceptions are seen (109):

1   A plant to convert cellulose of pine sawdust into a fermentable sugar and that into ethyl alcohol *failed* because a sawmill *couldn't*

    sell as much lumber as plans *called for*, and thereby *curtailed* the alcohol plant's raw material supply.

2  Plants to convert cellulose of pine sawdust into fermentable sugar and that into ethyl alcohol *have failed* because sawmills *haven't been able* to sell as much lumber as plans *have called for*, and thereby *have curtailed* the alcohol plant's raw material supply.

3  Plants to convert cellulose of pine sawdust into fermentable sugar and that into ethyl alcohol *fail* because sawmills *can't* sell as much lumber as plans *call for*, and thereby *curtail* the alcohol plant's raw material supply.

Although applied linguists have been leaders in the analysis of texts, using their results to inform materials preparation in particular, the trend in first language studies of writing (and in recommendations to its teachers) has been on the process of composition itself. Such research refers to textual analysis as a 'product' view and offers alternative approaches, although Connor (1987) believes that a writer's composing process can be completely studied only in conjunction with an understanding of the product. In general, process oriented approaches to writing focus on the writer's inventiveness, consideration of audience, purpose, and revision styles. Such research foregrounds the variation in text which derives from the difference between reader and writer; a text is 'constructed' on the basis of a reader's identity, information and background, motive for reading, and so on. A reader 'reconstructs' a writer's intentions through a set of inferences about what the writer intended. Both reading and writing, from this point of view, are dynamic processes, and there is ample room in such a view for consideration of precisely those variable contexts and identities which have been the subject of chapters 2 and 3 of the present work.

Other recent pedagogical claims are not at all unrelated to some of the variationist interests of this work. It is not a strange argument at all to suggest that emphasizing minor text problems introduces a kind of absurd organizational variation into texts. Schwartz (1984) asked students whether they thought a professor would prefer a clear but dull text or a clever and creative one which contained numerous lower-level text errors. Students, safely, chose the first.

Reading what has been written down rather than producing writing is the other obviously large issue in the category of mode. Gregory (1967) is careful to point out that not all writing is to be read the same way; there is writing to be read silently, writing to be read aloud as if it were written language, writing to be read aloud as if it were careful spoken language, and even writing to be read aloud which is supposed to sound like spontaneous language (e.g., drama). The source of variety does not stop, however, with the writer's intention of how the reader is to perform. Since the reader is active in reconstructing the text,[12] the variety of meanings and understandings between writer and audience may be considerable. Recent SLA studies of reading comprehension stress the need to distinguish between the reader's ability to get meaning from a text based on its actual content as opposed to what he or she is able to reconstruct from general knowledge (e.g., Steffensen 1986).

Language must have a *channel*. Spoken language may occur in face-to-face interaction, over a telephone, on a sound system accompanying an image on a movie or television screen, and so on. The written language may be carved in stone, printed in a book, or scribbled on a note. In many cultures, what is officially printed carries much greater weight than other channels. I once asked a group of students to cross out a mistake in a textbook. When I looked up the students had their pens poised, looking at one another, but none had dared to be the first to deface the text. It was, after all, one of the texts from the English Language Institute of the University of Michigan and the names of Lado and Fries were on the cover, but one suspects that a less well-known text might have received the same respect.

Of course, some channels impose restrictions (e.g., the inability to observe physical reactions to what is said or to question a writer about his or her meaning), and others pose very special requirements due to physical or technological facts (e.g., the new rhythm and turn-releasing procedures which must be established for long-distance conversations due to the time lag).

More interesting than such mechanical matters, however, are the cultural and conventional variation imposed on language by different channels. Recall that in France one must speak at considerable length to a person who answers the phone if he or she is known to the caller, even though the call is to another (3.1.3). Several early studies of the organization of conversation focused, in fact, on telephone conversations. Schegloff (1979), for example, elaborates an algorithm for the opening of telephone conversations (1.2.5).

Although little research attention has been paid to the use of different channels in SLA, some attention has been given them in practical, peda-gogical work.

In general, both sociolinguists and SLA researchers have not focused sufficiently on the differences triggered by changes in media, assuming in many cases a simple cline of formality. The range of details covered in chapters 2 and 3 should suggest that various media will be responsive to a much vaster array of concerns than simply a cline of processing (attention) or style (distance).

The concerns of media, then, include

1  Body
2  Voice
3  Mode (spoken, written, signed)
4  Channel.

## 4.2  Applications

This section combines the concerns of general linguistics (4.1.1), of the sociology of language (4.1.2), and of media (4.1.3) with those of identity (chapter 2) and of interaction (chapter 3) to provide a taxonomic application of sociolinguistic categories to variable data.

Hymes (1972) calls his SPEAKING mnemonic an attempt to outline a set of *etic* categories pertinent to the ethnography of speaking, but even those categories (and those of many other taxonomies – surveyed in Preston 1986a) assume too much about the structure of the interaction among users, codes, and settings. The taxonomy here hopes to avoid prejudice, particularly rejecting as too dense (i.e., composed of too many lower-level units) such constructs as 'domain,' 'speech event,' and 'speech activity.'

In that same spirit, the notion 'distance' (3.5.1) – though preferable to 'style' for the dimension indicated by Joos' terms 'intimate,' 'casual,' 'consultative,' 'formal,' and 'frozen' – is also not used here. It would be difficult to justify 'distance' as an etic category. What, for example, is not completely predicted about the distance of an interaction if all other identities and interactional relationships are known? What is the single dimension it measures? Only when a great deal of research identifies configurations of influencing variables with great consistency could an emic unit be identified and made use of in future research. Such procedures as Fishman's (e.g., 1964) which derive a concept such as 'domain' from the consideration of 'topic,' 'setting,' and 'participant roles' are on the right track but, perhaps, by limiting the consideration of the potential input to the higher-level construct to such a few items, miss important contributing factors. Of course, one of the purposes of an etic-level taxonomy is to provide the sort of exhaustiveness which allows more thorough identification.

On the other hand, categories which have ethnographic validity must not be excluded. It would not occur to lexicographers to omit 'pikeperch' or 'walleye(d) pike' from a dictionary on the grounds that it (*Stizostedion vitreum*) is not really a pike (i.e., does not belong to the genus *Esox*). On the other hand, considerable ethnographic research in the metalinguistic terminology of nonlinguists is not necessary to discover that a principal meaning for *slang*, at least in United States English, is 'nonstandard, uneducated usage.' Modern dictionaries (after citing the older senses of 'argot' and 'jargon'), however, prefer the linguist's relativistic assessment of slang as 'colloquial,' 'informal,' 'metaphoric,' and 'inventive.' Although raciness, figurativeness, and casualness are important elements in the folk as well as professional definition of slang, a principal sense for laypersons is simply that of poor, nonstandard, uneducated usage; the failure to give that nontechnical use an important position in the dictionary may come, at least in part, from the oddity of language specialists writing about nonlinguists' use of language terms.

More importantly, does a taxonomy have the necessary range of etic units? I hope those outlined in chapters 2 and 3 (with the additional elements from 4.1) are detailed enough to identify the components of folk units on the one hand ('joke,' 'chat,' 'bull session,' 'cussing') and to provide a distinctive feature set of elements for larger constructs (e.g., 'domain') which may emerge from analysis on the other.

### 4.2.1  *A sociolinguistic application*

An illustration of the application of this taxonomy (table 4.2) is drawn from the English to Spanish switch cited in 1.2.4 and given here in its larger context:

*Boss*:  Carmen, do you have a minute?
*Secy*:  Yes, Mr Gonzalez.
*Boss*:  I have a letter to dictate to you.
*Secy*:  Fine. Let me get my pen and pad. I'll be right back.
*Boss*:  Okay.
*Secy*:  Okay.
*Boss*:  Okay, this is addressed to Mr. William Bolger.
*Secy*:  That's B-o-r-g-e-r?
*Boss*:  B-o-l.
*Secy*:  Oh, oh, I see.
*Boss*:  Okay. His address is in the files.
*Secy*:  Okay.
*Boss*:  Okay. Dear Bill, Many thanks for telling me about your work with the Science Research Project. The information you gave me ought to prove most helpful.
*Secy*:  That was 'The information you gave me ought to prove most helpful?'
*Boss*:  Correct.
*Secy*:  Okay.
*Boss*:  Okay, ah. I very much appreciate the time you gave me. Never mind, strike that out. Ah, enclosed are two of the forms that you let me borrow. I'll be sending back the data sheets very soon. Thanks again, I hope that your hospital stay will be as pleasant as possible and that your back will be soon in top shape. Will soon be in top shape. It was nice seeing you again. Sincerely, Louis Gonzalez.
*Secy*:  Do you have the enclosures for the letter, Mr Gonzalez?
*Boss*:  Oh yes, here they are.
*Secy*:  Okay.
*Boss*:  Ah, this man William Bolger got his organization to contribute a lot of money to the Puerto Rican parade. He's very much for it. ¿Tú fuiste a la parada?

(Did you go to the parade?)
*Secy*: Sí, yo fuí.
(Yes, I went.)
*Boss*: ¿Sí?
*Secy*: Uh huh.
*Boss*: ¿Y cómo te estuvo?
(And how did you like it?)
*Secy*: y, lo más bonita.
(Oh, very pretty.)
*Boss*: Sí, porque yo fuí y yo nunca había
(Yes, because I went and I had never
participado en la parada y este año me
participated in the parade and this year
dió curiosidad por ir a ver como era y
I became curious to go and see how it was
estuvo eso fenómeno. Fuí con me
and that was a phenomenon. I went with my
señora y con mis nenes y a ellos
wife and my children and they
también le gustó mucho. Eh, y tuve
also liked it very much. And I had
día bien agradable. Ahora lo que me
a pleasant day. Now what
molesta a mi es que las personas cuando
bothers me is that people when
viene una cosa así, la parada
something like this comes along the Puerto
Puertorriqueña o la fiesta de San Juan,
Rican parade, or the festival of San Juan
corren de la casa a participar porque es
they run from the house to participate because it is
una actividad festiva, alegre, y sin
a festive activity, happy, and
embargo, cuando tienen que ir a la
then, when they have to go to
iglesia, o la misa para pedirle . . .
church or to mass, to ask . . . )
*Secy*: (Laughter)
*Boss*: A Diós entonces no van.
(God then they don't go.)
*Secy*: Sí, entonces no van.
(Yes, then they don't go.)
*Boss*: Pero, así es la vida, caramba.
(But that's life, you know.)

Do you think you could get this letter out today?
*Secy*:  Oh yes, I'll have it this afternoon for you.
*Boss*:  Okay, good, fine then.
*Secy*:  Okay.
*Boss*:  Okay.
(Fishman 1972a:30–2)

The point investigated here is the language switch at 'He's very much for it.
¿Tú fuiste a la parada?' The column marked 'Switching' in table 4.2 allows
identification of the large number of factors which may have helped
determine this language choice. An X in the column means that the switch
implies an important change (putting aside, for the moment, the more
difficult determination of cause and effect) in that component. Even where
items are not marked, there may be cross-cultural implications. For example,

*Table 4.2*    A taxonomy of language variation

| Components | | Text section | Switching | Research |
|---|---|---|---|---|
| I | **Individual** | 2 | | |
| A | *Ascribed* | 2.1 | | |
| 1 | Age | 2.1.1 | | (X) |
| 2 | Sex | 2.1.2 | | (X) |
| 3 | Nativeness | 2.1.3 | (X) | (X) |
| 4 | Ethnicity | 2.1.4 | X | (X) |
| 5 | Region | 2.1.5 | (X) | (X) |
| B | *Acquired* | 2.2 | | |
| 6 | Role | 2.2.1 | (X) | |
| 7 | Specialization | 2.2.2 | X | (X) |
| 8 | Status | 2.2.3 | | (X) |
| 9 | Fluency | 2.2.4 | (X) | X |
| 10 | Individuality | 2.2.5 | | X |
| II | **Interaction** | 3 | | |
| A | *Setting* | 3.1 | | |
| 11 | Time | 3.1.1 | | X |
| 12 | Place | 3.1.2 | | (X) |
| 13 | Length | 3.1.3 | | |
| 14 | Size | 3.1.4 | | |
| B | *Content* | 3.2 | | |
| 15 | Situation | 3.2.1 | (X) | |
| 16 | Topic | 3.2.2 | X | (X) |
| 17 | Genre | 3.2.3 | X | (X) |
| C | *Relations* | 3.3 | | |
| 18 | Solidarity | 3.3.1 | (X) | (X) |
| 19 | Network | 3.3.2 | | X |
| 20 | Power | 3.3.3 | (X) | (X) |

*Table 4.2   continued*

| Components | Text section | Switching | Research |
|---|---|---|---|
| D   *Functions* | 3.4 | | |
| 21   Purpose | 3.4.1 | X | X |
| 22   Outcome | 3.4.2 | X | X |
| 23   Goal | 3.4.2 | X | X |
| E   *Tenor* | 3.5 | | |
| 24   Emotion | 3.5.2 | | X |
| 25   Stance | 3.5.2 | X | X |
| 26   Tone | 3.5.2 | X | |
| F   *Participation* | 3.6 | X | (X) |
| III   **Language** | 4.1 | | |
| A   *Levels* | 4.1.1 | | |
| 27   Phonology | 4.1.1 | (X) | |
| 28   Morphology | 4.1.1 | | |
| 29   Lexicon | 4.1.1 | | X |
| 30   Syntax | 4.1.1 | X | |
| 31   Semantics | 4.1.1 | | |
| 32   Text | 4.1.1 | | X |
| B   *Types* | 4.1.2 | | |
| 33   Standardization | 4.1.2 | | |
| 34   Autonomy | 4.1.2 | | |
| 35   Historicity | 4.1.2 | | |
| 36   Source | 4.1.2 | | |
| 37   Vitality | 4.1.2 | | |
| 38   Currency | 4.1.2 | | X |
| 39   Duration | 4.1.2 | | X |
| 40   Frequency | 4.1.2 | | X |
| 41   Value | 4.1.2 | X | (X) |
| 42   Magic | 4.1.2 | | |
| 43   Taboo | 4.1.2 | | |
| 44   Publicity | 4.1.2 | | |
| C   *Media* | 4.1.3 | | |
| 45   Body | 4.1.3 | | |
| 46   Voice | 4.1.3 | | X |
| 47   Mode | 4.1.3 | | |
| 48   Channel | 4.1.3 | | |

Switching: English–Spanish switch (author's application)
  X = important change in taxonomic component
  (X) = change assumed or requires clarification
Research: Chinese plural marking (Young to appear)
  X = taxonomic component not considered by Young
  (X) = component partially considered, or interpretation doubtful

the sexes in this dyad are obviously the same before and after the language switch, but that does not mean that male-female relationships are the same in North American English and Caribbean Spanish cultures. In such cases, however, where there seems to be little possibility that that changed relationship could have been a motivating factor for the switch itself or there is simply not enough evidence to go on, an X is not used. That should not limit consideration of the point, or even reconsideration of it as a motivating factor. Xs in parentheses indicate that the point is assumed or requires clarification.

Little is known about *age* for either the boss or secretary, though they are both obviously in their working years, and Gonzalez has young children. Such factors might, indeed, influence some of the considerations developed here, but they are too speculative to indulge in. They do not use inappropriate language from this perspective in either English or Spanish, although that is not an unusual suggestion. My Hungarian is not only old-fashioned, nonstandard, nonfluent, and markedly regional, it is also wildly inappropriate for my age. Since I used it only to get to the toilet, get goodies from the kitchen, and play with my grandparents, that is understandable.

The relationship between married male boss and female secretary is caricaturistic in both English and Spanish settings, although there is nothing in this transcript to comment on from either point of view, and that is not the more important perspective from which *sex* differences need to be considered. Louis completely dominates the conversation on both work and nonwork topics; although one cannot tell if that domination is the result of his *power* (see below) or his sex, he holds the floor for the interaction. In addition, Carmen questions Louis only on business matters (spelling, enclosures), but he feels free to question her about her nonbusiness activities. In the nonwork section of the interaction, Carmen responds briefly, laughs, and repeats ('Sí, entonces no van') but does not nominate topics or even expand on those suggested by Louis, who feels free to talk about his family and about his personal feelings concerning the religious shortcomings of his fellow citizens. Although one may note that some of Carmen's activity is supportive of the interaction, providing the sorts of *back-channel* cues which keep it moving along, her status in the interaction is clearly subservient. From a purely lexical point of view, Carmen's response to the parade is stereotypically female – 'Ay, lo más bonita' – although that caricature needs to be explored more carefully from a cross-cultural perspective. The role sex may play in this example is developed further below in the discussion of *power*.

There is some little evidence that neither Carmen nor Louis is a perfectly disguised bilingual and that their English is marked by NNS characteristics. First, he corrects his 'will be soon in top shape,' a typical NNS error, to 'will soon be in top shape.' Second, though more subtle, Carmen confuses his pronunciation of the letter 'l' with 'r.' If his English pronunciation is good, his postvocalic /l/ will be dark – [ɫ], not cleanly articulated, as a Spanish [l] would be, perhaps causing Carmen to confuse it with the equally indistinctly articulated English [ɹ], which contrasts strikingly with Spanish trilled or flapped /r/. These characteristics suggest marking *nativeness*, assuming that, if the English of either speaker is nonnative in any small way, their Spanish might not be so marked. Of course, that interpretation could be wrong. Louis and Carmen might be fully native in English and weak in Spanish, still requiring a mark at nativeness. One strong predictor of language switching, of course, might be lack of full control of the other system.

It is presumed that both speakers are Puerto Rican and do not hide their background. That will be marked in *ethnicity*. Since the topic near the point of shift involves a discussion of topics closely related to that ethnicity, it, too, might be an important factor in the switch.

There might be *regional* (*area*) distinctions in both Louis's English (Metropolitan New York City?) and Spanish (Puerto Rican Spanish?), but neither fact would result in a mark at this component unless there were a curious mismatch between the status of the varieties. Imagine, for example, that his English is *not* typical of New York City and, naturally, evokes from listeners no stereotypes associated with that variety. His Puerto Rican Spanish might, however, be an urban or rural variety and might evoke carica-tures from listeners who supported such finer distinctions in Spanish (as his secretary fairly obviously would). On the other hand, if, as suggested above, Louis's Spanish is weak, he may have the full range of New York City speech characteristics, evoking the array of attitudes to that performance, and speak a variety of Spanish which, due to its NNS-like quality, might evoke only the broadest ('Caribbean') regional stereotypes. If he is an ordinary speaker of urban New York City English but a speaker of rural (*Jíbaro*) Puerto Rican Spanish, then the switch between English and Spanish would carry a great deal of dialectal as well as ethnic and language information. In a monolingual situation, it would correspond to a speaker's moving from RP, Hochdeutsch, or Parisian French to a rural variety. Since Spanish and English in New York City are in a diglossic (1.2.4) relationship, with English = H and Spanish = L, the switch would symbolize that relationship between language systems (discussed more fully below), and if Louis's Spanish is areally marked (e.g., rural) a sort of double diglossia would result. That is, the symbolism of the switch would be more radical than between the H and L of a diglossic inter-pretation. Where Ls (or Hs) have known internal varieties, triglossia (or even greater complications) might exist.

When Louis changes topics from business to a discussion of Bolger's support of Puerto Rican affairs (which might be considered a sort of 'aside' to the earlier work-related talk and, at the same time, a transitional device) and then to asking about the secretary's participation in the parade, he seems to shift *roles* from 'boss' to 'acquaintance,' perhaps 'friend,' though one would need to know more about the appropriateness of such personal questions in those roles in this environment before suggesting that too strongly. Does this dyad maintain employer-employee role relationships in non-work related conversations on a regular basis? If so, is that typical of speakers from their cultural backgrounds?

Items such as *dictate*, *pad*, and *enclosure* suggest the *specialization* ('business'), but nothing in the Spanish part of the interaction is specialized. Specialist lexicon is here taken as an indication of one of the characteristics of the speaker, not of the situation. On the other hand, the topic 'business' can be discussed by non-specialists who might or might not know appropriate specialist language, and specialists might choose non-specialist language in discussing their field with outsiders. It is often the case, however, that specialist lexicon in one language does not carry over into another. Many modern Polish linguists report that discussions of current linguistic theory must be carried out in English or, at the very least, require many English borrowed items since so many of them were trained in their subject matter in that language rather than their native one. In the case under consideration, the association of specialized activity with one language and non-specialized with another might be one of the clues to language switch, imposing an even stronger requirement than topic change.

*Status* does not obviously influence this particular switch, though more detailed information about the participants could make any or all of these categories relevant. Of course, one might attribute some of the domination and responsibility for the shift to Louis' higher status, but that is more directly addressed below in the discussion of *power*. On the other hand, one might find that in some situations switching itself is a status-marked activity. That is, language switching (and particularly mixing) might be associated with lower status; the switch which occurs here, then, could be a strong indication that Carmen and Louis are close enough for him to risk that interpretation of his usage.

If, as suggested above, there are minor disfluencies in the English abilities of both speakers (e.g., Louis' syntactic blunder during dictation), there would be a contrast with the language after the switch (Spanish), for there are no such indications of a lack of *fluency* there.

Such a short text does not permit serious consideration of *individuality*.

If more were known about *time*, perhaps issues which arose in the discussion of role could be resolved. Is this interaction during ordinary business hours, or have the secretary and boss stayed after work to get out an urgent mailing? If the latter, perhaps boss-employee roles are maintained in those less structured time periods even though the choice of topics is much freer. In normal work time, Spanish may be less open to extraneous and/or personal topics, and even friends are more likely to pursue such matters at designated periods (e.g., breaks). If that is true, Spanish would be an inappropriate language for personal matters in a work setting and might occur only if other factors dominated. Such considerations as these may lead to the discovery of *knockout* conditions, influencing factors which invariably promote or inhibit even high-level functions such as language switching exactly as those which invariably influence phonological realizations (1.2.1).

Nothing is known, as well, about the *place* of this interaction. Is the work done in an office setting, or are Louis and Carmen working at home on the weekend? Many Hispanics would find that alternative most implausible. *Place* will have to be treated with the same considerations as those given *time*, and, unfortunately, the details are unknown. In what follows, normal work time in an office will be assumed.

The *length* of the total interaction and its Spanish and English parts is not significant, though it might be, but here the entire interaction is about half English and half Spanish. Length of turn, however, as suggested above, may be particularly important as a clue to other factors. Louis dominates length in this interaction, in both the 'business' and 'Puerto Rican' segments and in both English and Spanish. The amount of either language's use, then, is dependent on his performance.

The *size* of the interaction is particularly important. That a dyad rather than even three or four participants is involved may impose powerful dynamics on such matters as language choice. Many bilinguals who have learned one variety at home may feel discomfort in using that language in larger groups or, put the other way around, may simply feel it is a language appropriate only to small-group interaction. Given this sample, one cannot be sure if English serves Louis principally as a language of public and large-group use. If so, such a speaker might have considerable difficulty in more intimate contexts in English, although the level of the specialized and everyday registers might be deceptively fluent. Although the size of this interaction does not change, its dyadic shape may be a powerful part of the general conditions for switching.

The *situation* is a culturally recognizable one in both Spanish and English when the interaction begins– office routine. If, however, the situation were seen only for those moments during the interchange concerning Puerto Rican concerns, would an observer (in either language) have made that assessment? Even if the segment in Spanish were viewed in its larger context, would observers from the two language backgrounds agree about the labeling? For example, if what was said above about the greater flexibility of English work situations is true, perhaps speakers of English would notice no situational shift; that is, the situation 'office routine' is flexible enough to permit moderate intervention of personal and nonwork related discussion. That may not be the case in Spanish, and NS Spanish observers may have seen two situations where NSs of English saw only one. Of course, such speculation must be validated by a variety of ethnographic techniques. One would assume that the boundaries of an identifiable situational change would provide a richer environment for language switching.

There is no doubt that *topic* changes. 'Letter' changes to 'Bolger's contribution' which, in turn, moves on to 'the parade,' and terminates with a return to 'letter.' Louis has been dictating a letter to William Bolger, and it is Bolger's company's contribution to the parade which makes the association with Puerto Rican matters, but he still feels the need for an indication of transition, supplied here by his 'Ah.' From just this evidence, one would be tempted to say that the stronger topic break lies between Carmen's 'Okay' and 'Ah, this man . . .,' for there is no such verbal indicator between '. . . for it' and '¿Tú fuiste . . .' where the actual language switch occurs. Topic is an important consideration in this switch, but it is not the sole contributor, for the topic before and after the switch is generally the same (the parade), though other factors change.

It is difficult to identify the *genre* characteristics of this interaction. What precedes the first major shift in topic (up to the 'Ah') is the sort of instrumental talk which accompanies work, and it resumes at the end. It would be easy to say that what follows the switch is 'conversation,' 'small talk,' or 'chatting,' but, in fact, as indicated above, it is completely dominated by Louis, and a considerable part of it may be better characterized as a 'monologue.' Again, verification from the speech community, particularly concerning the amount of floor domination by one speaker which conversational genres can tolerate, is needed.

One at first suspects *solidarity* between Louis and Carmen, for he addresses her with the solidary *tú*, rather than with *Usted*. Unfortunately, she never addresses him in Spanish, so it cannot be determined if she would have reciprocated or not, but in English their relationship would appear not to have that status, for he calls her 'Carmen,' while she addresses him as 'Mr Gonzalez.' Figure 3.5 shows that employer–employee relations (at least nonsolidary ones) should require the V form (here *Usted*); solidary relations (where power is unequal) – represented by 'master–faithful servant' in figure 3.5 – should show reciprocal T. If Carmen's Spanish performance is like her English, however, the form which accompanies 'Señor Gonzalez' will certainly be *Usted*. From this, one might conclude that a power relationship exists between them, but there is considerable variation in English-speaking offices, and, as has been suggested above, sex differences may play a role not taken into account by Brown and Gilman; that is, a male–female solidary relationship in a work setting might allow a superficial use of power pronouns, derived from sexual caricature. Ervin-Tripp (1971) provides an American address system chart (figure 4.1) to help guide consideration of this point. Louis enters the chart from the left, knows Carmen is an adult, and surely does not treat the office as a status-marked setting in which such rigidly controlled systems of address as 'Your honor' and 'Mr President' are required (Ervin-Tripp 1971:19).[13] He clearly knows Carmen's name, and it will be assumed they are not kin. Louis then goes to the 'Friend or colleague' diamond, chooses plus, and decides that the alter (other participant) is of lower rank. It is then assumed that Carmen is not fifteen years or more older than him, and that leads to the parallelogram marked 'FN' (first name), which

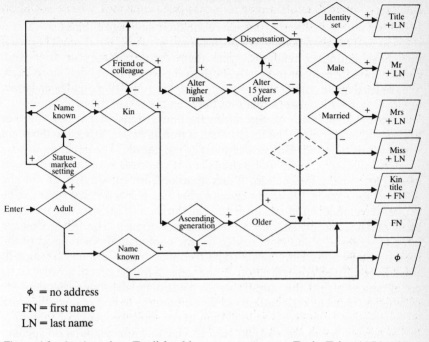

φ = no address
FN = first name
LN = last name

*Figure 4.1*   An American English address system (source: Ervin-Tripp 1971: 18)

is exactly how he addresses her. Carmen, however, goes through the same system but arrives at the choice for 'Alter higher rank' and must choose the plus, which leads her to a diamond marked 'Dispensation.' If dispensation has been granted, she may call him 'Louis' ('Luis'?), but, apparently, it has not, and she must stick with 'Mr Gonzalez.' (He apparently does not satisfy any 'Identity set' features which would qualify him for such titles as 'Dr' or 'Reverend'; since he is male, only 'Mr' + last name remains, and that is what Carmen uses.)

Although it is tempting to maintain that *power* is the dominating factor in the name and pronoun choices, the intricacies of role relationships and sex, as suggested above, make that observation risky. It is important to notice, however, that the language decisions are always Louis's. When he wants a letter taken, he asks in English, and Carmen answers in English; when he inquires about Carmen's going to the parade, he asks in Spanish, and she responds in suit. Finally, when he asks, again in English, if the letter can be gotten out today, again, Carmen responds in the language he has selected. Even when she asks about the spelling of Bolger's name, a fact which could have much more easily been taken care of in Spanish, she sticks to the language which has been determined by Louis. Whether from the sex, role, or power differences, or, as is more likely, a combination of all of them, the indication, at least here, is that dominating interlocutors are in charge of switching, and that other participants echo their language choices.

Louis and Carmen belong to a professional *network*, but it is not known if they have multiplex relations, tying them through family or friendship connections, directly or indirectly. Perhaps he would have been more likely to have used names rather than 'my wife and children' if there had been family or closer nonwork network relations between the two of them.

*Purposes* significantly change during the interaction and may hold another key to language choice. The English talk is *transactional*, at least to the point where Louis mentions Bolger's support of the parade. The general purpose of such language is to get things done, and it contrasts with the purposes of other parts of the interaction. When he asks Carmen whether or not she attended the parade, Louis may be exploring whether or not that topic can be further developed, although, from what has already been observed, it is more likely that he is simply announcing what the new topic will be. While Bolger's identity serves as a sufficient bridge for the comment about support of the parade, Louis apparently needs some feedback from Carmen on which to base his continued concentration on the topic. After he gets it, however, one could almost regard the purpose of his remaining talk about attending the parade and church going patterns of the community to be *excogitative*, more closely related to thinking out loud than to conversation. Any consideration of *perlocutionary* matters would lead too far into speculations on speaker intention.

*Goals* of business talk are usually straightforward though one may distinguish between employers and employees if the latter are not a part of the general planning of an operation. For example, Louis's goal in the dictation may be 'communicating with Bolger'; Carmen's might be something like 'successfully taking a letter.' The *outcome* from a management position may be vague or specific; he will have communicated with Bolger and fulfilled certain business obligations. The outcome from a secretarial point of view might be fulfillment of a task during the workday. These goals and outcomes, as well as the purposes of the lower-level elements, are in sharp contrast to those of the nontransactional part of the interaction. In fact, excogitative language and small talk seem nongoal oriented, fulfilling, more often than not, only the outcome of human interaction called *phatic communion* by Malinowski.

Of course, one might invent perlocutionary-like goals for both participants. Perhaps Carmen says so little and comments only on the attractiveness of the parade because she does not want to be drawn out on the matter of her sympathy for Puerto Rican matters, but wild speculation shows only how important it is to 'ground' such ethnographic work in comments by the participants themselves. Here, however, no matter what else might be uncovered, the goals and outcomes of the nonbusiness part of the interaction, largely conducted in Spanish, are very different from those of the business parts, suggesting another motive for language switch.

The *tenor* of this interaction is also varied. It is not marked by *emotional* coloring of any noticeable sort, but the *stance* is interesting. Although there is ample opportunity for hedging or indicating that what is given is an opinion, Louis never does so. He does not 'guess' that his wife and children had a good time at the parade, nor does he 'suggest' that people 'often' or 'more usually' go to festivals than to church. There are two reasonable interpretations for this relatively unusual force on what would appear to be clearly matters of opinion. First, one might assume this is Louis's style, that it is 'masculine,' perhaps culturally appropriate. Second, however, one could suggest that such unqualified talk is an indication of a closer relationship between Louis and Carmen than previously suspected. Perhaps they are such good friends that, typically, qualification is not a normal part of their interactions. Other indications, discussed above, make this interpretation unlikely. In addition, Louis's behavior in English is conventionally polite, both when he asks her to take dictation and when he asks if the letter can be sent today. If Louis and Carmen have a more solidary relationship, one not requiring extensive verbal qualification, all that part of the interaction is in Spanish, and the stance he takes may be another clue to the language switch. There is no evidence that Louis's Spanish is so weak that he does not command conventional politeness or hedging mechanisms.

The *tone* of the interaction obviously moves from the flat, serious manner of doing business to one which is lighter, for Carmen laughs at Louis's accusation of his fellow citizens for their love of festivals and neglect of church. This 'small talk,' or whatever genre it is, is, therefore, light. That, too, could be a motivating principle for language switch. Irony, sarcasm, humor in general are often more likely to be strongly associated with one variety or another, even in the styles of rather well-balanced bilinguals.

*Participation* status also reveals an interesting alteration during the interaction. During the transactional or business part of the conversation, Carmen, although she does not say as much, is a member of a dyad with rights as speaker as well as hearer. She initiates matters (pen and pad, enclosures) and interrupts, although all these things are done within the framework of the purposes and goals of the work situation. In the Spanish section of the interaction, however, Carmen is more like an audience member than a hearer who can get the floor when the situation requires it. Of course, that is just the point, when work is not being done, there is no reason for Carmen to take the floor, and she does not. She responds to direct questions, repeats, and laughs, but she does not share participation status as she does during the English segment. The goals and purposes of the interaction types, therefore, may be correlated with participation status.

The *language* levels are just those units which have been noticed in the analysis to this point. It is important to note, however, that both small and large units are being considered. Phonology and syntax played a role in identifying some of the considerations at nativeness, but no less valuable were the larger clues of size, turn-taking, and so on. In an attempt to provide a large-scale framework for analysis, it is important to exploit the complete inventory of linguistic dimensions.

In language *status*, both are *standardized*, *autonomous*, have conventional *historicities* and *sources*, and are alive. As suggested above, if there were, say, phonological clues which suggested the influence of a regional or social variety with some other status, that would be an interesting factor, but it cannot be determined. Both parts of the interaction are characterized by *frequent*, *current*, and *long-lived* linguistic elements, but Louis uses a proverbialism in Spanish ('así es la vida') and an exclamation ('caramba'). Although one might argue that his expression 'top shape' is casual, it is not a *valued* construction as proverbialism and slang (along with larger narratives) are. *Magic* and *taboo* are not considerations here, though one may note that 'Diós' and religious names are available for a wider range of use in Spanish. Louis may have said something like 'go to church to pray' if he had spoken in English, perhaps sensitive (or oversensitive) to that different distribution.

Spanish and English have considerable *publicity*, though all the things said about status might be revised if Louis's Spanish is nonstandard or otherwise restricted.

Nothing can be said about *body*, but an analysis of gaze, posture, and so on might reveal interesting things about this interaction. For example, what were the physical characteristics of speaker and hearer at the times of the language switch? Similarly, *voice* cannot be commented on, but it, too, might have revealed interesting facts. Do the vocal qualities (including pitch, paralinguistic characters, and so on) of these interlocutors change with language switch?

The *mode*, however, is spoken (not written or signed) language, but that is the same for both languages. In addition, the performance in both languages is of authentic spoken English and Spanish, so one does not feel that switching has provoked a spoken style which imitates writing in either variety. Since the *channel* is face-to-face, certain rules of speaking which would be necessary for, say, a telephone conversation are not evident here, and it might be the case that switches in face-to-face interaction have a different structure, frequency, and so on than those sent through other channels.

The upshot of this long walk through all these variables is a simple one. Whether experimental or ethnographic, sociolinguistic research deals with such obviously complex phenomena and is such a young science that careful consideration of all the forces which might be at work should precede speculation about either specific causes or labeling of bundles of causes ('emes') which always seem to interact. If a parallel from strictly quantitative sociolinguistics may be drawn, Labov has often suggested that learning which variables to enter into a variable rule program is the real solution to a problem at that level of sociolinguistic work. In other words, the dumping of masses of quantitative data into a machine will not result in a well-formed analysis. In exactly the same way that intuition and previous research findings would guide the search for an influencing phonological variable, some sociolinguistic variables in the larger-level study of language switching just carried out were identified as crucial and others were rejected, and the analyst's intuitions, familiarity with the data, experience, and findings from previous work were important guideposts. To treat such a taxonomy as this as a mechanical discovery procedure for sociolinguistic research would be as big a mistake as taking all combinations of distinctive features from a phonological inventory and, ignoring everything known about phonological processes, dumping them into a massive 'study' of environmental constraints.

At a more ambitious level, such elements may lead to 'emic' discoveries. As one finds that *power*, for example, is predicted by *role* in a certain group and in certain sorts of interactions, higher-level categories may be invented to cover such facts. Not all such sociolinguistic categories emerge directly from an appeal to NSs. Although reflection and intuition by NSs may indicate items in the folk repertoire which need to be accounted for, that procedure will not exhaust the possibilities for classification. It is also necessary to group various folk identified units together by function and restricted occurrence, and those groups are perhaps hidden from the conscious attention of members of the speech community.[14]

It would be difficult to ignore a large number of variables in accounting for the language switch just reviewed. Although such variation is often explained by an appeal to 'topic' (at the lowest level) or 'domain' (at the highest), a much more detailed consideration of influences is required.

### 4.2.2  An SLA application

SLA research which considers variation must also take into consideration a similar range of influences. Young (to appear) argues that excluding a number of potentially influencing factors and failing to pay proper attention to a variety of environmental differences has resulted in claims that behavior has varied in situations falsely identified as equivalent. He uses Hymes' SPEAKING mnemonic to provide a richer texture for the investigation of plural marking in the English interlanguage of Chinese respondents and lists the following specific variables considered in his research:

S    *Setting* Interviews were conducted in private homes, usually those of the respondent.
P    *Participants* Seven female and five male respondents from the

People's Republic of China and Taiwan between the ages of 26 and 65 of lower and higher English proficiency and of a variety of educational backgrounds; Chinese and English NS interviewers, an NS English investigator, and friends and family of the respondents.

E    *Ends* The purpose of the interview was to talk about any subject which arose; no outcome was expected or discerned.

A    *Art characteristics* Both the interviewer and the respondent were aware that they were 'performers' (as a result of the arrangement for the interview, microphone, recording equipment, and so on).

K    *Communicative key* The nature of the interview was light, friendly, humorous.

I    *Instrumentality* Face-to-face speech, with appropriate gesture, kinesic, and eye-contact characteristics, was the channel; the code was predominantly English, although, with the non-native interviewer, some switching to Chinese occurred.

N    *Norms* Those of a spontaneous interview applied, influencing such matters as turn-taking, back-channel cues, and exclusion of non-ratified participants.

G    *Genre* The genre is called a 'spontaneous interview.'

(Young to appear)

Young's use of a wider range of variables than is usually considered in such research is productive, and some of the results will be reviewed in 5.1. Here, however, it will be shown that attention to the even greater range of variables just reviewed would have made his study even more comprehensive.[15] Table 4.2 provides a column ('Research') for consideration of Young's work. A component marked with an X indicates that he has not considered it; a parenthesized X indicates that he has given it partial consideration or that there is some disagreement between his interpretation and the one given here.

Since the *age* of the respondents ranges from 26 to 65, it is a surprising oversight that such variety was not taken into consideration, particularly in light of the importance of this variable in both sociolinguistic and SLA research (2.1.1). Perhaps the greater focus in SLA on the pre-adolescent versus post-adolescent division caused this possibly significant factor to be overlooked.

Although there were seven females and five males and in spite of the considerable attention given *sex* as a variable in sociolinguistic studies (2.1.2), Young does not separate the data for these two groups. This appears to be a common failure in SLA work, with only a few exceptions (e.g., Selinker 1969, Gass and Varonis 1986).

*Nativeness* (2.1.3) is the variable in the interviewer and respondents which

Young manipulates. Although all the interviews were conducted in English, each respondent was interviewed twice, once by a native speaker of English and once by a native speaker of Chinese. The respondents were divided into groups of high (above 470 on the TOEFL test) and low (below 410 on the TOEFL) English language proficiency.[16] An important variable which Young does not mention, however, is the degree of English proficiency of the NNS interviewer. This is especially unfortunate, since, as discussed below, Young suggests that accommodation towards the ethnic Chinese interviewer will produce more noun plurals with no plural marker. If, however, the Chinese interviewer is a nearly flawless speaker of English, accommodation in his or her direction would result in greater use of the plural ending.

*Ethnicity* (2.1.4) varies, as indicated immediately above, only for the interviewer, but it would have been possible to hold that variable constant by using an ethnically Chinese native speaker of English. In some circumstances, particularly among emerging new NNS-based standards, the distinction between nativeness and ethnicity will need to be more carefully attended to. Along participant identity lines, then, Young does not carefully separate these two concepts. He is, however, sensitive to some of the social psychological concerns which might be raised in connection with both nativeness and ethnicity. He devises, for example, an 'identification scale' and hypothesizes that the respondent will accommodate more towards the interviewer the greater their similarity along the dimensions of ethnicity, age, sex, educational attainment, occupation, and place of origin. Accommodation, however, is a reflection of much more  complex behavior than adjustment to the speech of another on the basis of similarity. One factor which determines accommodation strategies is the degree to which one speaker wants to gain the approval of the other (2.1.3). Are Young's respondents more eager to gain the approval of the English or Chinese interviewer? A good deal more about the social situation of the respondents in general and of the character of each dyad would need to be known before one could address these questions in detail. On the other hand, Young's attempt to deal with this issue is important, and it does allow him to consider some of the dimensions of participant identity (e.g., sex, age) which, perhaps, ought to have been separate at the more general level of the investigation.

Although the Standard Mandarin of the People's Republic of China and Taiwan (and the resultant attitudes towards language and language learning) may vary in interesting ways, *region* is not treated as an important variable, although it is mentioned. The areal varieties of the interviewers, however, are not characterized.

Young notes that the respondents had been prepared for their *role*, and the interviewers had obviously been trained. There is no doubt, then, that the roles of 'provider' and 'elicitor' of data, respectively, dominate, although a number of other characteristics will call that strict identification into question.

No comments are made about the *specialization* of either the respondents or the interviewers. A fuller characterization of the respondents' individual characteristics would have enhanced confidence in their homogeneity. Since the investigator was present (attending to the recording but not participating in the interview), one may still imagine that his specialty as 'language expert' had some influence on the general context (along with the physical evidence of his profession provided by recording devices and so on). It is interesting to note that even in large-scale sociolinguistic surveys, fieldworkers have (e.g., Trudgill 1974) and have not (e.g., Labov 1966) identified themselves as linguists.

Although the respondents' and interviewers' *status* could partially be determined from the characteristics used to construct the 'identification scale,' it would have been better to have attended to this factor within the general design of the experiment.

*Fluency*, at least in the sense discussed here, is not characterized for the interviewers and respondents (although one would suspect that the interviewers were skilled in promoting and responding to talk, and the characterization of the interactions suggests that). There is no indication that the respondents were not able to fulfill their linguistic roles, although Young notes a few occasions when they lacked sufficient English skills to carry out a certain part of the interaction and would, with the NNS interviewer, resort to Chinese. It is unfortunate that just those stretches (although they might have provided no useful morphophonological information, the focus of this study) were, in a sense, lost. From another point of view, the topics and content of those switches might prove very interesting.

*Individuality* is often given brief mention in SLA research, suggesting that a subject is outgoing or shy, aggressive or taciturn, but Young does not comment on the individual respondents or the interviewers from this perspective. Since there was only a small number of respondents, this would have been possible. An ethnographic thumb-nail sketch of each respondent would be an attractive addition to such investigations.

Young does not indicate at what *time* these interviews were conducted, and that does not appear to be a pertinent issue, although in some cases, one might suspect certain genres or other matters to be influenced by just this component.

The *place* of data collection is the respondent's home or the home of a friend. Of course, it would have been better not to have introduced that variation, but it seems trivial. On the other hand, Young indicates that the interviewer and respondent usually sat next to one another on a couch. Although this factor will have more ramifications for later components, it is worth pointing out here that, at least in experimental settings, similar physical arrangements for interlocutors ought to be provided. An interview conducted over a kitchen table with respondent and interviewer in a face-to-face position might produce different norms of interaction. On the other hand, if the aim of collection is to provide a setting for spontaneous, natural talk, freedom of physical arrangement and motion should be allowed respondents.

The *length* of each interaction (one hour) was held constant, and the amounts of participation by the respondent and the interviewer were imbalanced, the respondents being responsible for the majority of the talk while the interviewer provided appropriate back-channel cues (except for identifying questions at the beginning of the session and leading and drawing-out questions as it progressed).

Young is careful to indicate that, although dyads were created for the inter-view situation, the *size* of the group included, at least, the investigator, and, often, family members and friends. Unfortunately, a particularly unnatural ignoring of the surrounding participants was encouraged; luckily it occurred only a small number of times in the actual data collection. One wonders if other cultural groups were involved whether this ploy would not have led to disaster. Group size and identity is a powerful instigator of language variety (3.1.4), and even when overhearers are not ratified participants in the conversation (although that notion needs clarification in an interview situation), they, no doubt, influence the interaction.

The *situation* is an interview, and both the interviewer and respondents referred to it with that term. Although there are a number of signals that the tone, genre, and other components are more relaxed or friendly or intimate than that identification would suggest, there is no reason to assign another classification to this larger situational context. Young indicates that con-versation did go on after the recording was completed, and the participants (or observers) might assign some other label to that situation.

*Topics* are not accounted for in this study, and they might have been a guide to variation even at the level studied here. Labov's use of 'the danger of death' and 'childhood games' illustrates how topic manipulation has been used to elicit variety in respondents' performances. Young does indicate that the interviews often included respondents' accounts of personal and family history topics, but there is no use of topic shift or identification in the analysis.

Young conflates *genre* and *situation* by labeling 'spontaneous interview' an example of the former, and many such combinations are appropriate. The name of a speech genre might coincide with the identity of a situation, so that a 'joke session' would pretty clearly contain a large number of jokes (though it would be a bizarre one without some other material). In this case, Young notes that many of the respondents tell personal and family *narratives*, although he mentions this fact in his discussion of 'Ends.' Narrative genres are quite distinct from interactive or conversational ones, and the failure to separate them and perhaps others as distinct performance types illustrates the danger of using higher-level taxonomies as checklists against which to measure the components of a research design.

*Solidarity* seems to arise from ethnic similarity, for Young notes the following behaviors of the interviewer and the respondents:

> They often touched as they talked and all the interviews contained some laughter, this being especially noticeable on the occasions when the interlocutor was a fellow Chinese. (Young to appear)

Other indications (forms of address) are not discussed as possible clues to the relationship between the interviewers and the respondents.

In addition, it is not known if any of the respondents were known to either the interviewers or the investigator before the data collection. Even if they were known to persons known to the investigator or the interviewers, they would fit the category 'friend of a friend' shown to have significant influences on interview and data collection results (3.3.2). In short, the *network* characteristics among respondents and between respondents and collectors should be characterized.

There are not many ways of determining the *power* relationship in these interviews. Characteristics of age, sex, solidarity, ethnicity, nativeness, and so on will have an influence on this category in general. Young mentions, however, that some of the respondents were paid a small fee for their cooperation. The power relationship between the research team and the paid respondents is rather different from that between them and the unpaid ones, for payment of a fee provides the researchers the right to place certain demands on those who have been paid. Again, since such linguistic cues of deference or hedging are not discussed, it is impossible to give a full account of this dimension.

The functional characteristics of this research are most difficult to characterize. Young suggests that the 'end in view' (Hymes's term) was 'to talk about any topic which they found of interest,' but that seems unlikely. At the level of *purpose*, the interviewer wants to promote the respondents' speech (through leading questions, attractive topic suggestions, and so on) and sustain it (through back-channel cues, attentiveness, appropriate responses, and so on). The respondents' purpose is even more difficult to characterize. In many sociolinguistic interviews, particularly with unskilled fieldworkers but often even in the face of expert handling, the respondents' purpose for some period appears to be a discovery procedure. They try to find out what is expected of them and even answer direct questions, for example, with rising intonation patterns, indicating that they want reassurance from the investigator that they are fulfilling their role properly. As interviews become more comfortable, both the interviewer and the respondents may employ a greater variety of purposes, the ones natural to exchanging interesting and pertinent information, opinions, and so on.

Young observes that there is no particular *outcome* to this interview, but that is surely not the case. For the researchers, the interviews provide an appropriate body of data, an instrumental outcome which is attached to any linguistic fieldwork. For the respondents, there is, at least, the completion of a task related to academic or research activities, regardless of how vague or incomplete their notion of the specific uses of it might be.

The *goals* of the interaction for the research team members are not distinct from the purposes which guide their turn-level utterances. They want to keep the respondents talking and promote, as much as possible, a type of performance which is not stilted or overinfluenced by the other contextual variables which push it in the direction of formality. The respondents' goals are, certainly at first, to provide the researchers with what they are after, although, as indicated above, they may develop a set of more natural communicative goals as the interaction develops and as a dominating awareness of the intended outcome of the interview is lost sight of.

By breaking down the interlocutors' functional attitudes to their respective performances, there is a better chance of explaining aspects of the interview which would otherwise challenge interpretation. It might be argued, in particular, that an understanding of goals, purposes, and outcomes is especially helpful in identifying variation in genres, though such understanding will contribute to a much wider range of concerns.

No *emotional* coloring is discussed in connection with this research, and, perhaps, it is not necessary. Certainly if there are segments of interviews which are characterized by anger, sadness, mirth, and so on, they should be taken into consideration. Young characterizes the 'communicative key' as 'light, friendly, and humorous.'

No information about the *stance* taken in these interviews is provided. It is important that interviewers do not make pronouncements or speak authoritatively on subjects which are being elicited from the respondents; from the description of the tenor of the interviews, that appears not to be the case. On the other hand, the degree of authority shown by respondents might provide an important clue to a certain segment of a performance. Interlanguage performances, particularly in amount of talk and other interactional characteristics, might vary according to degree of assertiveness.

The *tone* is light and friendly, and one assumes that the degree of seriousness of the interactions is reflected in that description. If there is variation along this dimension, however, perhaps clued by laughter or other paralinguistic devices, it should be considered.

*Participation* has already been characterized in some of the other comments. There are two interlocutors who do not have equal rights as speakers; the respondents know that it is their performance which is sought, and the interviewers participate with that purpose and goal in sight. There are also family members and friends nearby who are curiously not permitted participation status. They are known listeners, and one might wonder about the degree to which some of the respondents' performance is directed towards them. Although setting, topic, and identity of the participants should make these others qualify for participation, the situation (interview) rules them out. There is, then, a sort of curious mismatch between the setting (and a number of other components) and the distribution of participation status. Familiar surroundings may enhance one aspect of an interview but strangely distort others. The investigator is also an odd participant; undoubtedly the respondent must be aware of his presence. A number of these difficulties are raised in Young's description of the 'nonparticipants':

> One norm which was particularly apparent was that the interview was limited to only two participants – the informant and the interlocutor. This was made clear when the norm was violated on occasions when the informant would try to involve the investigator in the conversation, or other family members present in the room would try to join in. In the former case the investigator always sat out of line of sight of the two participants with his back turned and refused to acknowledge remarks which the participants addressed to him. In the latter case, the inter-locutor managed to skillfully acknowledge the contribution from outside by means of a gesture or smile but made no attempt to respond. (Young to appear)

This norm appears to be one imposed by the investigator and his interviewer, not one which developed naturally from the situation. If absolute dyadic interactions were considered a necessary part of the research, then settings which would not open themselves to these incredibly unnatural perform-ances and reactions should have been chosen.

The linguistic components of this investigation will make up both the dependent variable (a morphophonological target) and various linguistic environments which may influence its realization.

Young checks the influence of phonological context by looking at the presence or absence of preceding and following vowels and noun stem final sibilants. As suggested earlier, the selection of influencing linguistic factors for VARBRUL investigation is not done by appealing to a large number of arbitrarily selected features. In this case, Young is justified in his selection, for the intervocalic environment, as opposed to others, is likely to promote the occurrence of a consonant (here the noun plural marker) to preserve CVCV structure, a universally less-marked structure and one which predominates in Chinese. Final sibilants are likely to retard the addition of the noun plural marker in English since the plural marker is a sibilant itself. The rule which inserts a vowel to separate the two similar sounds (wish → wishes) is more likely to be acquired in advanced stages of acquisition. Although either or both of these hypotheses might be attacked, both are reasonable and are drawn from information about the status of syllable structure, previous SLA research, L1 acquisition data, and so on.

Similarly, Young investigates the influence of the NP's function (adverbial, subject, object, 'be' complement) and the noun's role in the NP (head or prenominal modifier) to account for syntactic influence, and he singles out animacy and definiteness of NP as semantic features which may contribute to the presence or absence of plural marking. These features are, as well, based on the researcher's knowledge of previous work, including, in this case, information from pidgin-creole studies, contrastive features of Chinese, and morphophonological details of English (i.e., confusion between the plural and the possessive).

Two descriptive considerations are noticeably absent. There is both older dialectological evidence (2.1.5) and more recent work in both sociolinguistics (e.g., Harris 1987) and SLA (e.g., Kellerman 1986) that lexical items themselves may form significant groups in patterns of variation. If some words participate earlier in the applicability of morphological adjustment or syntactic privileges (from the point of view of either restriction or expansion), that might explain a great deal of variation in just such a study as the one under analysis here.

Second, the linguistic environments of text or position in discourse are not considered as one of the independent variables which might influence plural marking. Are items 'embedded' in narrative (long turns) distinct from ones which are part of short answers or more rapid give-and-take segments? Classification along these lines might reveal interesting patterns, particularly if one believes in interactionist models of language acquisition (2.1.1).

The *media* of these interactions are pretty well accounted for. In several places Young describes eye-contact, touch, proximity, gesture, and movement, giving some importance to the factors here called *body*. Such details might be given even greater prominence in a finely tuned investigation of the degree to which such matters accompany variables. Fiksdal (to appear) accounts for the difference between NS and NNS motion and gaze in interactions, but work on the synchronicity of such matters and variable elements has not taken place.

The *voice* characteristics of these interviews are not recorded, and, unless there is something remarkable about them, they probably do not need to be.

The *mode* of these interactions is clearly speech, and the *channel* is face-to-face. All that is accounted for.

The larger characteristics of the sociology of the language are not of particular importance here. Both languages are *standardized*, *autonomous*, and *vital* (unless, again, there are social or regional features of some respondents which should be outlined in greater detail). Both have fully accounted for folk *historicities* and scientific *sources*. Of course, these categories might not always be irrelevant. Learners of (or from) creoles, learners of (or from) nonstandardized languages or of developing NNS-based standards, and so on would require more careful characterization along these dimensions.

Since transcripts of these interactions were not studied, the smaller temporal aspects of lower-level units of the language are unknown. Is *current* language employed? Is there slang or other ephemeral items (in terms of *duration*), or is everything long-standing English? What is the distribution of high, medium, and low *frequency* vocabulary, constructions, and so on? More importantly, if there are distinctions along any of these dimensions, do they predict anything about the variation under study here? For example, the earlier remarks concerning the diffusion of a variable through a set of lexical items might be based on word frequency.

Young regards *art characteristics*, specifically 'performance,' as the respondents' awareness that they are being recorded and that their contributions are being treated as linguistic data. From the point of the present work, that does not constitute *value*. The awareness of the special uses of the interaction is amply described in the considerations of situation, specialization, genre, and other components.

Nothing can be said about *taboo* or *magic*; if such forms occurred, they might not even require comment considering the focus of this study, though they might provide insights into other components (e.g., solidarity).

Chinese and English are languages conspicuously subjected to great *publicity*.

It is important to stress that this second trip through the taxonomy was not meant to display shortcomings in Young's work. His research is a model of careful consideration of a wide range of topics rarely looked at and even more rarely made a part of a multivariate statistical investigation.[17]

Application of such a fuller range of considerations will reassure researchers that they have attended to the variety of concerns which ought to be brought to bear on studies which focus on variability. On the other hand, this taxonomy, although etic-level, does not automatically provide the content from each component which needs to be considered. Chapters 2 and 3, and to a lesser extent the information in section 4.1, summarize earlier findings for these components and suggest some new directions. More importantly, the components that warrant consideration at all cannot be predicted for any given piece of research. The SLA researcher's experience, expertise, and intimate knowledge of subjects and data will be the best guides in the selection of variables for emphasis in a given study. This long list is not meant to discourage those who would study language variation in any setting; it is intended as a friendly reminder of the complex set of forces at work.

# 5

# Sociolinguistics and the learning and teaching of foreign and second languages

This chapter briefly summarizes those aspects of models or theories of SLA which have direct links to the study of language variation and suggests a model more consistent with the variety of sociolinguistic components outlined above. Psycholinguistic concerns of these models not directly connected with variation are not discussed. Finally, a few comments on concerns in the teaching of foreign and second languages are made.

## 5.1 Variationist theories of SLA

Models of SLA begin their modern period with the rejection of the strong version of the *contrastive* hypothesis. Many of the differences between a learner's performance and L2 were attributed to interference from the learner's L1. These transfer phenomena were not discussed in variationist terms because the learner language itself was not considered a system.

Although the introduction of the notion of the learner's language as a system – an *interlanguage* (Selinker 1972), *approximative system* (Nemser 1971), or *idiosyncratic dialect* (Corder 1971) – did not do away with the notion that the learner's L1 influenced (positively or negatively) SLA, it focused attention on the substance which falls between NS-like performances in L1 and L2 and suggested other sources than interference for the difference between the learner's performance and the shape of the target language (Richards 1974). Some of these sources allowed researchers to claim that SLA had an internally driven creative dimension as well as an externally determined one (Corder 1967), perhaps one which followed a natural or developmental order (Dulay and Burt 1973).

Emerging interlanguages were said to be no different from other human languages, although Adjemian (1976) points out that they must be more 'permeable,' for they are more subject to change. At the time, the prevailing linguistic model was an early generative-transformational one based on intuited data (presumably reflecting an *ideal native speaker-hearer's* competence), and it made use of categorical rules exclusively (1.2.1). Learner language seemed so far from the fiction of the ideal, however, and open to introspection in such an oddly different way, that very shortly concern for its variation developed. Tarone, Frauenfelder, and Selinker (1976), admitting to having discovered a great deal of variation in the speech of individual speakers at one time, called such variation *unsystematic*. Variation over time was referred to as *instability*. Although they show that both progress and *backsliding* necessarily involve instability, they never explicitly connect the movement from one stage of the interlanguage to another with the variable behavior at a given stage. For them, lack of systematicity requires only specification of the error involved, although they suggest that such error might be explained by the researcher on the basis of its 'psychological, social or stylistic factors' (98). The variable rule, particularly one sensitive to linguistic factors and capable of characterizing variable systematicity in the interlanguage, is not employed (although they are clearly aware of Dickerson 1975). That variation in an interlanguage might be systematic did not seem a possibility, and instability in the system caused some to ask (James 1974): 'How can a system remain a system if it is in flux?'

At this stage of SLA theory, then, although sociolinguistic procedures for handling data (i.e., Tarone, Frauenfelder, and Selinker 1976:102) were used, variation itself did not play an important role. Researchers had not yet widely employed sociolinguistic mechanisms for describing systematic variation, and they seem not to have sensed that synchronic variation might be connected in some direct way to diachronic variation.

L. J. Dickerson (1974, 1975) showed that interlanguage performance could be characterized by variable rules in terms of both linguistic and task oriented environments, and W. B. Dickerson (1976) drew the parallelism between developing interlanguages and the use of variable rules and/or the dynamic paradigm to characterize language change. Faerch (1980) criticizes this view by suggesting that SLA is more 'targeted' than historical change, but, if one adopts a sociolinguistic view, that is not a valid objection, for the mental end-products for the individual in the process of monolingual change may be as clear (or as fuzzy) as those of a language learner. In addition, the informal learner may be no more conscious of those targets than the monolingual involved in historical change.

Although most of the early work in SLA variation made use of Labov's notion of the stylistic continuum and the variable rule, Bickerton and Bailey's dynamic paradigm was not ignored. Gatbonton (1978) showed the development of interlanguage phonology in an implicational rule format, and considerable research in that mode followed.

At the end of the 1970s, the stage seemed set for a rich cooperation between SLA researchers and sociolinguists interested in the quantitative representation of language data and its importance to language change. SLA and applied linguistic recognition of ethnographic and interactionist research was soon to follow.

Instead of testing mutually interesting hypotheses, however, particularly those concerned with finely tuned mechanisms of contextual variation and language change, SLA researchers turned their attention to psycholinguistic model building, and many sociolinguists continued to pay little attention to the psycholinguistic ramifications of a variable grammar.

### 5.1.1 A dual competence model

Krashen's *monitor model* (e.g., Krashen 1981) is, at least in terms of its use of variationist thought, the simplest model. It states that a language is *acquired* (by use, in natural settings, unconsciously) and *learned* (in classrooms, through the study of the grammar, consciously). The function of learned language is to monitor performance, and that can only occur when there is sufficient time for focus on message rather than meaning. Learning advances only through *comprehensible input* at a level which is i+1, i.e., intelligible to the learner through various clues but slightly beyond his or her competence. Input may be disrupted by activity of the *socioaffective filter*, which stands between the learner and the input (Dulay and Burt 1977) and is characteristic of the sorts of sociopsychological concerns discussed in 2.1.3.

Evidence for this model comes, in particular, from a number of studies which show a natural order of acquisition of morphemes by learners from different L2 backgrounds and by L1 learners, particularly of English (e.g., Krashen 1977). Since some such settings as tests, writing, and carefully planned speech show different orders from the natural one, Krashen concludes that they allow the monitor to operate, and this is evidenced by the fact that simple grammatical items ('learnable' ones) move up in their order on the natural, developmental scale.

The principal focus on variation in this model is the distinction between monitored and unmonitored performance. There does not seem to be room for partial monitoring (it is either on or off), and Krashen maintains that the monitor is not widely used even in conditions where it might be. Tarone (1983) calls the monitor a 'dual knowledge' model, suggesting that there are two, discrete levels of attention rather than a continuum of attention to form. Krashen notes, however, that the monitor applies along a continuum associated with attention to form (e.g., Krashen 1987:104–12). In other words, there is no incompatibility between Krashen's monitor and models which suggest that there is a variability of SLA performance along such a continuum. More attention to form simply means more use of the monitor. While it is true that the monitor is dichotomous (on or off), it is possible that it is only one of the constructs which might be brought to bear while one is attending to form. The difficulty is, of course, with the term *monitor*. 'Attention to form' and 'monitoring' could be taken to be synonymous, but the first refers to a continuum derived from crude attempts to operationalize the careful versus noncareful (and, by implication, the vernacular versus nonvernacular) dimension of sociolinguistic concerns. The monitor, on the other hand, is a psycholinguistic construct, referring primarily to the way in which linguistic information is learned and only secondarily to the conditions under which that knowledge is used (i.e., in situations when form is attended to). The most dramatic proof that Krashen does not intend monitoring to be synonymous with attention to form comes from evidence that some who attend to form cannot monitor simply because they have not learned:

> *Interviewer:* (When you write a composition) ... do you think of grammar rules? Do you think 'Should I have used the present tense here or would the present continuous be better or ...'
> *V:* I don't refer to the books and all that, you know. I just refer it to this, uh, my judgment and ... sensing if I'm writing it right or wrong. Because I really don't know ... what where exactly how ... the grammatical rules work out.

(Stafford and Covitt 1978)

V has not monitored here since a condition for monitoring according to Krashen is 'know the rule.' Tarone and others are correct, then, in criticizing the monitor for providing a paucal account of variation, for there is no doubt that V's performance will show the variation discovered in all other studies which focus on attention to form through such operationalized constructs as writing versus free speech. The monitor simply applies to performance in those rare moments when a learned rule is applied.[1]

On the other hand, the monitor model may be incorrect, and rules and other linguistic information both consciously and unconsciously acquired may apply across a wide range of attended and unattended occasions of language use (Bialystok 1981). Whether or not the monitor model has psycholinguistic validity is, therefore, not a concern for a variationist look at SLA. It does not attempt to account for such variation and it cannot. Whether it has any general validity as a construct in accounting for SLA has been discussed thoroughly elsewhere (e.g., McLaughlin 1978b, Gregg 1984, Spolsky 1985).

### 5.1.2  *A continuous competence model*

Tarone (1979, 1982, 1983) has developed a model of SLA based on the operational continuum of attention to form used by Labov and a number of quantitatively oriented sociolinguists to test variation along the so-called stylistic dimension. Her work leads to the following:

The vernacular style of the interlanguage is:
1  most systematic in the sense of its impermeability (to both L1 and L2 influences) but not in its relation to the superordinate norm
2  most open to natural, universal, and developmental restructuring

3  more likely to be elicited in settings which require the respondent to pay less attention to form.

Tarone supports the first point by citing the large number of studies which show greater approximation to L2 norms in tasks which require more attention to form (e.g., Dickerson 1974, Gatbonton 1978, LoCoco 1976, Dickerson and Dickerson 1977, Schmidt 1980, Fairbanks 1982). A smaller number of studies indicate that attention to form also attracts influence on the interlanguage from prestige elements of L1 (e.g., Schmidt 1977, Beebe 1980) and aberrant forms (e.g., Felix 1977).

The second part of that first point, however, is more problematic. If the interlanguage vernacular is not more systematic in the sense 'contains less variation' than the target norm, it contradicts Labov's understanding of a vernacular:

> *The vernacular*  Not every style or point on the stylistic continuum is of equal interest to linguists. Some styles show irregular phonological and grammatical patterns, with a great deal of 'hypercorrection.' In other styles, we find more systematic speech, where the fundamental relations which determine the course of linguistic evolution can be seen most clearly. This is the 'vernacular' – the style in which the minimum attention is given to the monitoring of speech. Observation of the vernacular gives us the most systematic data for our analysis of linguistic structure. (1972a:208)

How are Tarone's and Labov's notions of the vernacular the same, putting aside for the moment the questionable practice of using attention to form as the exclusive guide to either's identity and/or elicitation? Quantitative sociolinguists do not trust the hypercorrection and other oddities of more carefully monitored styles, for they do not reflect change from below (2.2.3). Tarone is justified, then, in hoping to examine the interlanguage vernacular, for, if it is like the ones studied in quantitative sociolinguistics, it will provide, as Labov suggests, the clearest indications of the path of linguistic change.

It is odd that Tarone and others do not connect 'change from above' and 'change from below' with Krashen's monitor, for the parallelism is striking. A form, usually contributed by lower middle class or upper working class users, enters the speech community below the level of conscious awareness ('change from below'). It may work its way into variability and complete the entire cycle of change, becoming categorical, never the object of public notice. On the other hand, it may come to the attention of the speech community and trigger correction from above – a conscious attempt to eliminate a form seen as an intruder on local norms. Change from below is very much like 'acquisition' and change from above like 'learning.' An interlanguage vernacular style is, therefore, more open to change from below (like ordinary vernaculars) and might respond to change from above only by way of superordinate styles.[2]

What are the parallel sources for change from above and below in SLA? The second point above, a minor one in Tarone's work and not as fully developed as stated above, may provide part of the answer, and it is not at all inconsistent with Kroch's (1976) notion that vernaculars are more influenced by natural, unmarked, universal categories. A great deal of recent work on universally based preferences by learners, whether from pidgin-creole, typological, or theoretical parameter setting sources, suggests that the interlanguage continuum is subject to such influences (e.g., Rutherford 1984, Cook 1985, Gass 1984, Felix 1984). Additionally, those few studies which show L1 prestige influence on the interlanguage superordinate (carefully monitored style) involve the transfer of marked elements (r-like forms in Beebe 1980 and interdentals in Schmidt 1977). Finally, though no less important, the interlanguage vernacular is surely open to modification on the basis of developing functions, and they, of course, may be graded in priority in terms of their centrality or peripherality from some universalist or bio-programmatic point of view (e.g., Huebner 1983a).

To add psycholinguistic depth to Tarone's characterization of a stylistic continuum in SLA, then, it is suggested that the interlanguage vernacular is open to change from below of essentially the same sort suggested by Kroch (1976). Universal, general, unmarked, core, bioprogram forms (all admittedly controversial) influence the interlanguage vernacular, and it is obviously not impermeable to such factors. The interlanguage superordinate (the more carefully monitored style) is open to both aberrant forms and L1 and L2 forms which deviate from the normal and/or developmental shapes suggested above.

Tarone's own work suggests that some restatement of the style-shifting continuum in interlanguage studies must be made. In her study of several morphological and syntactic variables (1985), she suggests that forms will increase in accuracy (target language shape) as they move away from the vernacular style of the interlanguage (376). She found, however, that, while this was true for the third person singular verbal morpheme, the opposite was true for the article and the direct object pronoun *it* (385).

Tarone's third assertion about the elicitation of the interlanguage vernacular on the basis of attending to form, already criticized in several places in the present work, may have been one of the difficulties in this research, and that is discussed here not only as a possible explanation for the data which emerge in this particular study but also in connection with her third general assumption outlined above.

Tarone examines what she calls the stylistic continuum of the interlanguage by (1) giving the respondents a written grammatical test in which they were to identify incorrect forms and supply corrections, (2) having the respondents tell a narrative suggested by a series of pictures to an NNS so that he or she could select the correct picture sequence, and (3) interviewing the respondents on academic topics with an NS interviewer. The test was assumed to elicit the least vernacular variety and the interview (especially since it was with an NS) was also thought to be at some distance from the vernacular. Since the listeners to the narration task had to solve problems, it was taken to be more communicative, and, therefore, closer to the vernacular. The narrative task was also assumed to be closest to the vernacular due to earlier researchers' success in eliciting the vernacular with such tasks and to its relative simplicity.

It should be unnecessary to go through the list of components provided in chapter 4 to show what an incredible array of variables is involved here. Media, participation, ethnicity, goals and purposes, genres, and many others vary; what is surprising is not that two variables did not arrange themselves along this putative continuum as suggested but that any did.

Tarone, however, does not reject the use of attention to form outright, although she admits (1985:374–5) it is problematic and seeks other explanations for the surprising shape of her data on articles and direct object pronouns. After determining that the grammar test did, indeed, test knowledge of the items (by subjecting it to NSs), Tarone rejects the explanation which might emerge from Krashen's assertion that some forms might be learned and others acquired. The third singular and article, two forms studied by Tarone, are also ranked in the order of acquisition studies Krashen uses to bolster monitor theory. He claims the third person singular of verbs is simple and, therefore, can be learned. That is consistent with Tarone's study, for it is that form which improves as it moves towards the end of the continuum where form is more attended to. Similarly, the article, subject to a set of complex regulations and occupying a low place in the natural acquisition scale, is not learnable and actually exhibits fewer target language forms as attention to form increases, perhaps an indication that the monitor has no rule to apply, and, being thwarted, produces the sort of hypercorrection and odd performances seen in superordinate styles in monolingual situations.

Tarone rejects Krashen's monitor as an explanation for these data (1) because the direct object pronoun is, according to her, a simple rule but shows the same pattern of correctness as the article and (2) the decrease in accuracy for the article and direct object pronoun in the test setting cannot be accounted for by the monitor. If, she claims, the rule has been acquired, there is no reason for it not to surface in situations which normally elicit learner behavior (1985:390). One might argue, however, that rules acquired are not open to use in the sorts of tasks which elicit learned behavior. The NSs Tarone gave the tests to, for example, did not score perfectly, yet it would be difficult to claim that any of them did not possess these simple rules of English. In addition, it would be safe to suggest that they had all acquired and not learned them. A monitor model, however, is not required to explain that variability, for a number of observations suggest different performances based on, for example, planned versus unplanned language use (Ochs 1979), cognitive awareness by adult learners (e.g., Cook 1977), and controlled versus automatic processes (e.g., Schneider and Shiffrin 1977, McLaughlin 1978b, Sharwood-Smith 1981, Bialystok 1982, 1984). Moreover, Krashen's characterization of some rules as simple (e.g., the third singular) obviously fails to attend to markedness, pidgin-creole hypotheses, and other theoretical concerns which find nothing simple about simplicity.

Tarone's eventual account of the discrepancies in the increase and decrease of target-like forms between the third person singular on the one hand and the article and direct object pronoun on the other comes close to the position taken above which suggests that universal, unmarked, and/or functionally relevant forms are likely to have a stronger influence on the interlanguage vernacular. Although she does not appeal to this position directly, she notes that the article and object pronoun forms are more target-like in tasks which require greater textual cohesiveness. The narrative requires the longest stretches of connected speech and the grammar test requires none, with the other tasks ranging somewhere in between those two extremes. Articles and pronouns are two structures particularly important in marking cohesiveness (e.g., Halliday and Hasan 1976), but, more pertinent to the proviso added here to Tarone's stylistic continuum in interlanguage studies, tasks which require connected discourse also require the use of functionally appropriate markers of such matters as definiteness (or specificity, knowledge, or old information) and anaphora. On the other hand, connected speech modes would require least of all the redundant marking of the third person singular indicative of the verb. Perhaps the explanation is a little deeper than the assertion that different tasks will elicit different orders in the developmental sequence (Larsen-Freeman 1975) or different patterns of occurrence in the stylistic continuum of the interlanguage (Tarone 1985). I will tentatively claim that the vernacular of the interlanguage is more open to universal and functional elements. Although work already done does not contradict this, it is an empirical claim that ought to lend itself to specific investigation. Major's work in interlanguage phonology (e.g., Major 1986) which claims that lenition is more likely to operate in casual styles and fortition in more formal ones strongly supports this position.[3]

Further consideration of Tarone's 1985 study is given in 5.1.4.

### 5.1.3 A variable competence model

Ellis (1984, 1985a, 1985b, 1987a, to appear) develops a *variable competence* model of SLA. He adopts the dynamic paradigm as better suited to SLA interests and finds in variability itself the source of interlanguage development.

Ellis carries over many of the principal findings reported for the vernacular and superordinate varieties of the interlanguage as discussed by Tarone, and those matters will not be repeated here. He tries, however, to be a good deal more precise about the various sources of interlanguage variability, elaborating the different effects linguistic environment, processing, interaction, genre type, and sociolinguistic status have on the learner's performance. Most importantly, he distinguishes what he calls free from systematic variation and notes that free variation is the clue to development. He suggests that the restructuring in environments which leads to change goes through a period of unsystematic or free application of competing rules (or, if he is to be true to Bickerton's concept) competing rule systems. Therefore, for example, Canadian French acquirers of English /ð/, as shown in table 1.8, are applying rules in free variation when they use both NS and NNS forms (symbolized by '1,2'). They are the speakers who occupy the vertical dimension of the S-curve of figure 1.5, and there is no doubt that such implicational scales are apt representations of the growth of an interlanguage, especially as regards dimensions above the level of phonology (e.g., Adamson 1980).

Unfortunately, Ellis misrepresents both Bickerton's criticism of Labov and the status of variable rules in the attempt to establish free variation as the basis for interlanguage development. He is fond of quoting the following comment of Bickerton's, assuming it highlights the primacy of linguistic matters in language change:

> While, with the help of a little hindsight, a plausible contextual explanation can be given for many stylistic shifts, there are many more that operate in quite unpredictable ways. (1975:183)

What Bickerton is actually criticizing here is the position that low-level variation as seen in the performance of the individual speaker can be related to external (social) variables:

> Choice of style is governed, not by any intersubjective and objectively perceptible features in the situational context, but by the autonomous and fluctuating feelings of the speaker himself or herself. Obviously situations affect people's feelings, but they do so in puzzlingly different ways for different individuals, and in any case it is not the situation as objectively perceived by the observer, but the situation as subjectively perceived by the actor, which constitutes the operant factor – and only one among several at that. (184)

What Ellis is after is Bickerton's criticism of social influences on linguistic change, not the difficulty of accounting for situational variety shifting:

> A further argument against the incorporation of social or contextual constraints in grammars is that any such procedure reverses the laws of cause and effect. The somewhat misleading title of Labov's seminal

paper on sound change (Labov 1963) is worth noting in this respect. In fact, the phenomenon of diphthong-centralization therein described does not represent a sound change *sensu stricto*. Centralized /ai/ antedated the social conditions responsible for its rapid contemporary spread; what happened was not that the influx of outsiders *caused* native Martha's Vineyarders to *introduce* a change, rather that they selected for intensification a feature that already existed as a variable in island speech and then generalised it to /au/ by dropping the original [-back] constraint.

This argument applies *a fortiori* in a creole setting. The complex layers of the grammar we have tried to unravel in the two preceding chapters represent an apparatus far more complex than could possibly be required to carry social or contextual information. However, it can be, and is, exploited by local speakers for purposes of that kind. (184–5)

The inconsistency in Bickerton's position will be put aside, but if speakers make use of linguistic variation for social purposes, then they must be capable of recognizing the situations when such use is suitable, and that may constitute an area of considerable interest to sociolinguists who are not concerned with change. Moreover, that such use itself may trigger further stages of development seems, in light of Labov's and others' work on change from below, uncontroversial.

Ellis, however, (especially Ellis to appear) uses Bickerton's claims that (1) social contexts are nearly impossible to calculate in synchronic use by an individual speaker and (2) that linguistic material is not contributed to language change by social groups as evidence that the use of two forms with the same meaning in the same context are in free variation. Ellis (to appear) outlines the following requirements for free variation:

Free variation can be held to exist when:
1   the two forms occur in the same situational context
2   the two forms perform the same illocutionary meaning
3   the two forms occur in the same linguistic context
4   they occur in the same discourse context
5   there is, in the manner of their production, no evidence of any difference in the amount of attention paid to the form of the utterance.

This list is a good characterization of stable linguistic variation, i.e., of a socio-linguistic indicator, but not of 'free variation.' Figure 2.12, illustrating the distribution of Norwich (a:), shows a feature which is sensitive to social class differences but hardly at all to stylistic differences (attention to form). Usually such a form is stagnant and not noticed by the surrounding community; it may constitute a sort of residue of a previous change or minor influences from surrounding varieties. The important fact, however, is that in all social classes there is considerable variation along the 0 to 200 scale. That is, only the lower working class in its most casual style approaches categorical use.

The issue is whether or not such a feature can be captured by any systematic account of variation, and it is just such features which are open to variable rule analysis. Why does Ellis call such variation 'free'? The answer lies in his misunderstanding of the nature of a variable rule:

> If it is accepted that learners perform differently in different situations, but that it is possible to predict how they will behave in specific situations, then the systematicity of their behaviour can be captured by means of *variable rules*. These are 'if . . . then' rules. They state that if *x* conditions apply, then *y* language forms will occur. (1985a:9)

Those conditions describe perfectly the operation of a *context-sensitive* rule, but miss by a wide mark the ones required for a variable rule. In 1.2.1 a rule was offered which showed that my mid-front lax vowel [ɛ] is raised to high-front lax [I] before nasals. Such rules are ordinary in generative phonology and, moreover, capture no variability. That is, my raising of [ɛ] before nasals is categorical. On the other hand, it is clearly an 'if . . . then' rule; [ɛ] is raised if, and only if, a nasal segment follows. No wonder Ellis rejects the variable rule as he understands it as a mechanism for the display of variation. Context-sensitive rules, in fact, display only categorical linguistic facts.

If Ellis's misunderstanding of free variation ran only as deep as a technical error about what a variable rule is, it would be easy to disregard. The rest of his proposals which are related to free variation could be evaluated by suggesting that he means to investigate forms which are in flux, especially ones where multiple functions are signaled by one form but are challenged by newly learned forms which seem to split apart that older multifunctional representation into two new formal classes and redistribute the load of form–function relationships, a position few would argue with. But Ellis admits items into the realm of free variation intuitively:

> I sometimes say /dɑtə/ and sometimes /deitə/, sometimes /ɒfn/ and sometimes /ɒftn/, sometimes /skedju:l/ and sometimes /ʃedju:l/. . . . To the best of my knowledge I alternate quite haphazardly between 'who' and 'that' as subject relative pronouns with human references in non-restrictive relative clauses. (1985b:121)

Just those sorts of choices which go on below the conscious level are practically the entire subject matter of quantitative sociolinguistics. Arm-chair sociolinguistics might yield as much free variation, if that is the object of the investigator, as it might patterned variability. One cannot trust, therefore, any case of so-called free variation in Ellis's work, for it potentially has a complex, systematic variable relationship to a number of factors.

It is unfortunate that Ellis misunderstands what sociolinguists mean by variation, for his work is sensitive to the very large number of psycholinguistic and processing factors which might influence variability in an interlanguage, and he attempts to draw them into line with the dynamic paradigm. Since so much of the data he examines, however, is asserted to be in free variation (e.g., Wagner-Gough 1975, Eisenstein, Bailey, and Madden 1982, and even Huebner 1981), one must be very careful in considering his relating psycholinguistic to sociolinguistic claims.

Ellis calls the product of language use the continuum of styles ranging from planned to unplanned discourse (an attempt to get around the difficulty of attention to form). The process of language use, however, employs both knowledge (*competence*) and the ability to apply it (*capacity*) (Widdowson 1984). Note, by the way, that a device which moves from rules to use is particularly contrary to the monitor model. The variable product results, then, according to Ellis (1985a:267) from

1 A variable competence, i.e., the user possesses a heterogeneous rule system
2 Variable application of procedures for actualizing knowledge in discourse.

The heterogeneity of the rule systems derives from the fact that there are two dimensions to it – analyzed versus unanalyzed and automatic versus nonautomatic (Bialystok 1982). Although competence might contain analyzed and unanalyzed material, it is difficult to see how access to that material (automatic or nonautomatic) is a part of the variable rule competence. It surely, as Bialystok intended it, refers to a method for gaining access to competence, a processing consideration.

Ellis goes on to suggest (1985a:268–9) that primary processes are those used in unplanned discourse and make use of the unanalyzed and automatic while secondary procedures are those used in planned discourse and make use of the analyzed and nonautomatic aspects of competence. Each process can be broken down into its discourse-level aspect and its cognitive aspect; that is, discourse controls the form of the output but is related to the conceptual rationale for producing that shape at that time.

The variability of language use is a by-product of the use of different sets of processing types, and development is a direct result of the acquisition of new rules which emerge from participation in a variety of discourse types, eventually allowing newly formed items to be accessed by the procedures appropriate to unplanned discourse.

In the long run, then, Ellis comes to the same conclusion as that drawn above, though it is stated rather differently since it begins from a psycholinguistic perspective. The vernacular of the interlanguage (unplanned discourse) is most open to influence from processes which are unanalyzed. These will be taken to be those natural, bioprogrammatic, universal, unmarked items which were suggested as the most likely candidates for invasion of the interlanguage vernacular above. Ellis' addition of an interactive and discourse setting for the acquisition of new rules is perhaps unnecessarily elaborate, for surely new items may come into the system in any number of ways, but it does help explain how marked or nonuniversal material might make an early appearance, contrary to the expectations raised so far. If an interaction (or series of them) highlights a form, i.e., gives it greater salience through frequency or other prominence of function, it may go rather more directly to the interlanguage vernacular, through some sort of special dispensation routing which allows the learner to overlook experimentation with unmarked forms first. This is, perhaps, the necessary adjunct to Gass's (1984) claim that speakers will fall back on L1 and L2 structures (or, presumably, other devices) only after the most reasonable universal characteristics of a new form are explored. That might be true if only the vernacular of the interlanguage were on the lookout for new items. Since it is sensitive to change from below, it will be the prime experimenter with such universal material. Superordinate forms of the interlanguage, however, sensitive to other sorts of information, may send some emergency messages to the acquirer, indicating that frequency or saliency demands attention, even from the more stable vernacular.

Such reasoning is consistent with recent work on form versus function in acquisition. Bailey (to appear) notes that -ing forms, formally indistinct in the present and past in English, serve, however, radically different functions. In the present, the -ing forms signal, primarily, the universally important distinction punctual versus nonpunctual while the formally simple present covers complex temporal relations (e.g., iteration, continuity, and so on). The past progressive, equally simple in form, however, carries complex discourse backgrounding information. The plain past is a complex form (in English) with considerable irregularity, but carries the simple temporal information +past. In order of acquisition, Bailey and others find that the present progressive, simple in form and function, and the plain past, complex in form but simple in function, are acquired relatively early. In terms of what has been suggested here, the unmarked necessity of a simple past function has required the vernacular to open itself up to the superordinate's attention to the complexity of the English plain past form. On the other hand, even though the plain present is simple in form, the vernacular has not taken to it, for it represents no unmarked, universalist, early developmental temporal meaning. Similarly, the past progressive, in spite of its simplicity of form, does not get to the vernacular since it does not cover a functional unmarked, universal area. Apparently, however, early learning of the present progressive influences earlier acquisition of the past progressive than need for its functions would indicate, providing introduction of a variable past form in the vernacular which will not develop its appropriate function for quite some time.

Ellis's work and such form–function studies as Bailey's open the possibility for relating the psycholinguistic concerns so traditionally associated with SLA to the concerns of variability of sociolinguistic research. In so doing, they will seek not only to verify such psycholinguistic claims as have been made by sociolinguists, but also to contribute to the development of such thought.

The theories of SLA which are principally built on accommodation strategies or other sociopsychological foundations are not reviewed here since they are treated at some length in 2.1.3. Moreover, many are not complete theories and often find a place (e.g., Krashen's use of the 'socio-affective filter') in more general accounts. When they are elaborated to cover the specific acquisition of linguistic material, as Schumann's acculturation theory is, particularly as revised by Andersen under the rubric 'nativization,' they reflect greater concern with strictly psycholinguistic matters than socio-linguistic ones. On the other hand, to the extent that Schumann's and Andersen's theories reflect work on pidgin-creole studies, they deserve mention here, and they have been reviewed above, particularly in 1.2.3.

Much recent work in SLA suggests that an L2 develops according to the plan of interaction it follows. Such ideas range from far-reaching proposals which suggest that syntagmatic functional relations in sentences are reflexes of so-called vertical relationships in discourse (e.g., Hatch 1978) to relatively detailed accounts of how such matters as turn-taking, correction, and simplification of input influence and guide SLA (e.g., Gass and Madden 1985, Pica 1987, Pica, Young, and Doughty 1987).

Discourse and interactionist scholars outside SLA often ally themselves with sociolinguists. That affinity has been established principally through the work of such sociolinguists as Hymes and Gumperz, who have looked at the larger aspects of communicative competence rather than the lower-level characteristics of variable rules and dynamic paradigms. Since that work covers so much territory it is impossible to review all of it, and the avowed prejudice of this book is quantitative. Moreover, reviews such as Gass and Madden (1985) and Day (1986) make research and theory in this area available to SLA specialists.

Finally, and reluctantly, there is simply not space to explore every SLA model's relation to variationist thought. Those thoroughly rooted in the psycholinguistic and processing sources of interlanguage are not inconsistent with variationist representation; moreover, it is hoped that the review of those theories described above which are more directly derived from socio-linguistic concerns provides a sufficient model for the consideration of others.

### 5.1.4  *A sociolinguistic model*

How may the sociolinguist's concern for variation in the speech community, including its intimate relationship to language change, be specifically related to the general concerns of SLA? Krashen's monitor model suggests that language is acquired in two radically different ways and that 'learned' material does not penetrate into ordinary, rapidly processed language systems. While 'monitor' may be a handy term for the attention paid to form during more planned language activities, it is clear from numerous studies in sociolinguistics that change from above does influence speech communities, and, therefore, individual competence; leakage from learned to acquired is well-substantiated.

Tarone suggests that the cline of attention to form or of planned to unplanned accounts for considerably more variation, but her work (1985) shows that performance at the superordinate or less vernacular ends of the interlanguage continuum are not always more accurate or target-like. Even when accuracy is understood to mean closer approximation to the next historical stage of the interlanguage rather than L2 correctness, the variability is not all accounted for. In fact, Tarone (1985) shows that characterizations of the interactional factors discussed in chapter 3 in the present work, particularly as they are related to the incidence of certain grammatical forms, must be included.

Ellis's proposals go further in identifying and clarifying the numerous sources of variability, including ones of both interaction and individual, but his eventual proposal, which accounts for interlanguage growth on the basis of free variation, makes his work diametrically opposed to either a dynamic or quantitative sociolinguistic account which finds instability and/or patterned variation where he finds random occurrences of one form or another.

Before developing a more comprehensive model of sociolinguistic interlanguage development, a review and reanalysis of some exemplary data is in order.

At the level of phonology, sociolinguistic strategies seem particularly well-suited to the study of SLA, and several studies suggest that interlanguage phonology is sensitive to monitoring or style – the more attention, the more target-like the pronunciation. Research also suggests that interlanguage phonology is synchronically/developmentally sensitive to linguistic context; that is, environments influence the proportion of target-like forms at one stage in the developing interlanguage, and those environments with the greater influence are most likely to have an even greater (perhaps eventually categorical) influence at a next or later stage.

Figure 3.9 illustrates that Japanese learners' realization of target-like (English) /r/ is both sensitive to phonological environment (before a mid or high vowel) and to attention to form (here elicited through 'free speech,' 'dialogue reading,' and 'word list reading'). Figure 1.2 shows that Japanese learners of English pronounce a nearly target-like /z/ before vowels (V) and noncoronal consonants (C), but consistently less target-like forms before pauses (#) and coronals (T). Both synchronic and diachronic variation may be inferred from the data displayed in table 1.8, Gatbonton's (1978) study of

French Canadians' realization of English /ð/. One group of subjects (lect 1, $N=3$), shows categorical use of nontarget-like substitutes, but a second group (lect 2, $N=7$) shows variable use of target-like /ð/ after vowels (the 'heaviest,' i.e., most influential environment). In group lect 9 ($N=1$), even the lightest environment (a preceding voiceless stop) promotes variable realization of the target-like form.

As suggested in the discussion of Tarone's work (5.1.2), however, the notion 'target-like' form rather than 'L2' form stresses the need to know what the learner's perception of the next stage of development is. Perhaps he or she is exploring possibilities which lead to a use unlike the L2 norm but consistent with a mental representation. Such 'developmental errors' are common in L1 as well. For example, very young children acquiring English as L1 may mimic the noises of both 'foot' and 'feet.' After they have learned the '-s' plural rule, however, they may produce 'foot' and 'feet' (singular) and 'foots' and 'feets' (plural). (Later concern with the irregular nature of the form may even lead them to such forms as 'footses' and 'feetses.') The 'foots' and 'feets' forms would, in spite of their distance from the adult model, be considered 'more target-like.'

It has also been shown that greater attention to form may result in more or less target-like forms depending on the status (social and/or linguistic) of parallel forms in the L1. For example, Thai respondents showed less accuracy in pronouncing initial English /r/ in elicitation environments which promoted greater attention to form (word lists). Beebe (1980) notes that a nontarget-like trilled /r/ in initial position in Thai has high prestige value, and Major (1986) shows that an English-like /r/ is more frequent in initial position in more casual speech in Thai. Major (to appear c) shows how L1 phonological processes alternate in yielding target-like and then nontarget-like results for Brazilian Portuguese learners of English. In the pronunciation of words such as 'meadow,' careful speech will yield a target-like realization of the final vowel. The pronunciation may change to [u] in casual environments, however, due to the Portuguese rule /o/ → [u] at the end of words. On the other hand, careful pronunciation of Brazilian Portuguese /il/ and /iu/ is normally [iw], but in casual speech, [yu]. The pronunciation of such an English item as 'cute,' therefore, will, in careful speech, receive the non-L2–like treatment [kiwt], but in rapid or less formal speech, it will occur as [kyut].

Fossilization which occurs at the phonological level for physical-developmental reasons (e.g., Scovel 1969) is not especially interesting from a language variation point of view, although the results may be important to sociolinguistic studies of reactions to interlanguage performance ('foreign accent').

More importantly, fossilization (particularly early fossilization, usually at some distance from L2 norms) may occur for reasons which have to do with the social and psychological make-up of the learners, their relationship to other, especially shared L1, learners, and their feelings toward and reception in the new speech community. Some adolescent learners under peer-pressure, for example, make no public progress in the pronunciation of noises which would gain them no respect; adults who find no welcome in the speech community (e.g., Schumann's Alberto) are also alienated speakers who gain usually only enough proficiency to carry out basic instrumental needs. I will call this phenomenon *social fossilization*.

At the other end of fossilization from a sociolinguistic perspective, however, is the competent bilingual, whose fossilized forms represent a more subtle construction of the variability which characterizes his or her identity in the speech community. Although such a learner's pronunciation may not be perfectly L2–like due to a number of factors (age, learning opportunities and style, L1, length of residence), it may also not be L2–like because the speaker is *not* a native member of the L2 speech community. It is likely that the optimum performance for such a speaker will be a variable, nearly L2–like interlanguage which carries, nevertheless, fossilized evidence of the eventual non-L2 identity of the speaker. The diary entry of a Japanese learner of English and experimental styles of optimum accommodation (carried out by Giles and his associates) reported in 2.1.3 help substantiate this second more subtle part of this proviso. Quantitatively, this interpretation is supported by such studies as Beebe (1977a, b) which show that Chinese-Thai children and adults increase and decrease the proportion of target-like forms on the basis of the ethnic identity of their interlocutors. Accommodation, then, must be considered in characterizing the variation in interlanguage phonology.

This sort of symbolic variability, which I shall call *sociolinguistic fossilization*, may be seen most dramatically in a creole continuum (1.2.3) in which some apparently receding variants are preserved for their in-group value, resulting in forms which have been called mesolectal and basilectal. Stable variation in a relatively homogeneous, monolingual population is possible as well, and in many cases carries social class meaning (e.g., figure 2.12).

At the morphological and syntactic levels, these generalizations given for phonology require reconsideration. Unfortunately, Young's (to appear) study of Chinese learners of English, which focuses on noun plurals, does not make a 'formal' versus 'informal' or 'planned' versus 'unplanned' distinction in its data elicitation strategies. If 'high convergence' versus 'low convergence' (based on shared characteristics of the respondent and inter-viewer) could be interpreted as yielding less formal performance in the 'high convergence' environments, then the general trend found in phonological areas is reversed:

| | |
|---|---|
| High convergence with an NS | 0.62 |
| High convergence with an NNS | 0.57 |
| Low convergence with an NNS | 0.43 |
| Low convergence with an NS | 0.38 |

These VARBRUL probabilities clearly indicate that high convergence promotes greater L2–like accuracy. Moreover, it shows that high convergence is more powerful than ethnic identity, at least for this group of respondents. On the other hand, if high convergence is reinterpreted as a precondition for accommodation, the scores relating to NSs show the extremes of the scale: accommodation is highest (most L2–like) when there is high convergence with an NS, lowest when there is not. These results point out the need for the consideration of variables other than the stylistic continuum when considering complex interlanguage data, as suggested in several places throughout this work. These data are even more revealing when the low proficiency and high proficiency groups are separated:

|  | Low proficiency | High proficiency |
|---|---|---|
| High convergence with an NS | n/s | n/s |
| High convergence with an NNS | n/s | 0.59 |
| Low convergence with an NNS | n/s | n/a |
| Low convergence with an NS | n/s | 0.26 |

n/s = not significant; n/a = insufficient data

It is only high proficiency speakers who contribute to the significance of variation on this social variable, and the strongest influence is the degree to which the lack of  convergence with an NS causes target-like forms to decrease. These findings fit well with conclusions reached about accommodation, and they suggest another reasonable generalization concerning variable development in an interlanguage: the appearance of socially sensitive variable behavior is most likely met in respondents at higher levels of proficiency; linguistic environments are more likely to be powerful among groups of lower proficiency.

Young's data as regards linguistic environments not only support the generalization that interlanguage variability is synchronically sensitive to environment but also strengthen the notion that linguistic rather than social environments are more powerful influences for lower proficiency groups:

|  | Low proficiency | High proficiency |
|---|---|---|
| Function |  |  |
| Adverb | 0.70 | 0.58 |
| Complement | 0.51 | 0.60 |
| Subject | 0.40 | 0.40 |
| Object | 0.38 | 0.42 |
| Stem final segment |  |  |
| Stop | 0.73 | n/s |
| Vowel | 0.69 | n/s |
| Nasal | 0.63 | n/s |
| Sibilant | 0.47 | n/s |
| Lateral | 0.10 | n/s |

Redundant marker

| | | |
|---|---|---|
| Numeral | 0.70 | 0.61 |
| Demonstrative | 0.50 | 0.67 |
| Quantifier | 0.45 | 0.49 |
| Partitive | 0.45 | 0.38 |
| No marker | 0.39 | 0.35 |

n/s = not significant

Although both high and low proficiency learners' use of noun plural marking is sensitive to the function of the noun itself, the range of sensitivity is greater for the low proficiency group (0.38 to 0.70 as opposed to 0.40 to 0.60 for the high proficiency group). For the next feature, sensitivity to the nature of the final segment of the noun stem, the distinction is even more dramatic; the higher proficiency learners' results were not significant at all, but the low proficiency group shows a considerable influence on noun plural marking based on this phonological environment. On the other hand, both groups show sensitivity to other marking of plurality in the noun phrase, although the exact items which show the greatest influences are not the same for both groups.

Tarone (1985) provides more evidence on the question of morphological variability (5.1.2). A VARBRUL 2 treatment of her data for noun plurals reveals the following:

| | |
|---|---|
| Japanese | 0.50 |
| Arabic | 0.50 |
| Grammar test | 0.45 |
| Interview | 0.54 |
| Narrative | 0.51 |

Neither ethnolinguistic group nor elicitation environment is significant in characterizing this variation. That is, Japanese and Arabic learners of English apparently belong to the same 'speech community' as regards this feature, and it is not sensitive to elicitation environments. These results, and the results from Young's high proficiency respondents, might lead one to reject for morphology the first generalization cited for phonology – that greater attention to form will elicit more target-like behavior. However, Tarone's respondents do not seem to confirm that conclusion in their performance on the third singular indicative marker:

| | |
|---|---|
| Japanese | 0.63 |
| Arabic | 0.37 |
| Grammar test | 0.63 |
| Interview | 0.48 |
| Narrative | 0.39 |

The influence of the least formal elicitation environment ('narrative') is less than that of the more formal 'interview,' and the most formal environment ('grammar test') actually promotes target-like performances. A regression analysis of these data show, however, that the contribution made to this model of variation by the elicitation environments is not significant. That is, the variation here is best characterized by the two ethnolinguistic groups. That in itself is an important conclusion, showing statistical confirmation of the importance of L1 in L2 progress (*transfer*). Recall that Japanese and Arabic learners did not perform differently on noun plural marking.

On the other hand, the generalization that increased attention to form promotes increased frequency of target-like forms is weakly confirmed in this sample and cannot be rejected.

At the lexico-syntactic level, data from Tarone (1985) is again the best for reanalysis. In the same study she investigates the frequency of target-like forms for direct object pronouns and the article. A VARBRUL 2 analysis of the article shows the following weights:

| | |
|---|---|
| Japanese | 0.42 |
| Arabic | 0.58 |
| Grammar test | 0.23 |
| Interview | 0.56 |
| Narrative | 0.72 |

Again, the two ethnolinguistic groups are statistically different and should be considered different communities of learners on this item. The distinction among the elicitation modes, however, requires a closer look. The direction of increase of target-like forms appears to be just the reverse of that usually encountered in phonological data, and it is the same for both ethnolinguistic backgrounds. Before a new generalization (for morpho-syntactic or lexical data) is advanced, however, consider these additional VARBRUL data:

| | Error |
|---|---|
| Japanese | |
| Grammar | 6.197 |
| Interview | 0.548 |
| Narrative | 0.366 |
| Arabic | |
| Grammar | 6.001 |
| Interview | 0.436 |
| Narrative | 0.529 |

Any error score of over 1.5 (conservatively 1.0) is unacceptable; these figures reveal that the grammar test results are completely incompatible with the other two elicitation frameworks. That was not true of the noun plural or third singular indicative data, in which the grammar test figures (though not significant) were not rejected from the model by VARBRUL. A rerun of these data with the grammar test scores omitted shows a similar difference for Japanese and Arabic learners, but the following for elicitation environments: interview = 0.41; narrative = 0.59. Both ethnolinguistic background and elicitation environment are significant contributors to the variation, and the error scores are well within acceptable limits, indicating not only that the two elicitation environments form a continuum but, when considered collectively, that the appopriate variables were investigated to account for this variation:

|  | Error |
| --- | --- |
| Japanese |  |
| Interview | 0.006 |
| Narrative | 0.015 |
| Arabic |  |
| Interview | 0.008 |
| Narrative | 0.034 |

It is not strange to discover that a grammar test may not form a part of the stylistic continuum, but whether it does or does not is a matter of interpretation for each feature studied. Tarone's investigation of the direct object pronoun presence or absence focuses on an even more directly syntactic matter:

| Japanese | 0.33 |
| --- | --- |
| Arabic | 0.67 |
| Grammar test | 0.32 |
| Interview | 0.50 |
| Narrative | 0.69 |

These data strengthen what was hinted at in the weak (statistically insignificant) accuracy increase for the third singular and the unexpected order for the article: monitoring or attention to form does not so clearly influence morphological and syntactic phenomena in interlanguage behavior in the direction of target-like preference. The continuum of grammar test to interview to narrative is not rejected by VARBRUL 2 for this object pronoun data, but the direction of improved accuracy is dramatically opposed to that seen in the majority of phonological data studied.

These opposing forces can, however, be brought together by appealing to their linguistic status. The third singular indicative, like careful pronunciation, is open to monitoring and use by rule application, but object pronoun occurrence and article use are more subtle morpho-syntactic and semantic processes. Neither can have its rule for use stated easily, but both reflect unmarked, natural requirements for language use (e.g., reference and specificity, or information familiarity). Within this territory, however, why does a grammar test form part of the stylistic continuum for the object pronoun but not the article? Although both share natural (perhaps functional) language properties, object pronoun use is a grammatically local phenomenon. A test which provides only a sentence (e.g., 'The house which we lived in it last year was sold,' 'He took the ball and threw to Tom' – actual items from Tarone 1985) gives enough information to determine correctness. Although a clever tester may provide sentences which seem to demand article use (e.g., 'Jones received best grade in our physics class last semester' – also taken from Tarone 1985), the learner-user's strategy for determining appropriateness of article use is likely to be much less local in the syntactic sense; consideration of extrasentential data is required. That a grammar test might, therefore, provide good data on a stylistic continuum for the object pronoun forms but not for the article seems reasonable on just such grounds. That statistical analysis might help confirm the degree to which tests actually measure linguistic abilities (other than test-taking ones) has already been suggested (Tarone 1985).

Considering these more careful analyses of interlanguage variability, some tentative generalizations may be possible.

Figure 5.1 displays what are meant to be noncontroversial variable facts about interlanguage development.[4] In figure 5.1a, a feature which is just entering the system has a weak influence and, therefore, accounts for only about 5 percent of the occurrences. The receding form is still very strong and accounts for about 95 percent of the occurrences. Figure 5.1b shows what has happened when an entering form has nearly gone through the process of being incorporated into the system as a categorical rule, for the receding form

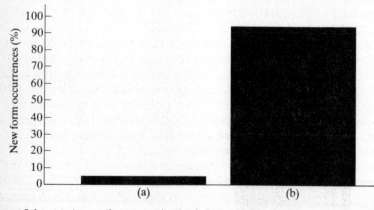

*Figure 5.1*   (a) A new form entering and (b) an old form leaving an interlanguage system

has now almost disappeared, surfacing in only about 5 percent of the occurrences.

The next stage of development is based on restructuring, hypothesizing, limited input evidence, limited memory capacity, and so on – all the things which do not allow the full-fledged L2 system to simply rush in. Even 'entering' and 'receding' forms are only long-range, hindsight labels. The balance will need to be recalculated at each step of development, and, from psycholinguistic perspectives, they may show a variety of interesting patterns. Assume that Bickerton is correct when he suggests that the earliest stage of untutored SLA is a simple relexification of the L1 grammar. Imagine, further, a fortuitous correlation (*positive transfer*) between elements of L1 and L2. All these high frequency items in the interlanguage might be called 'entering' only to discover that overgeneralizations or other (later) developmental factors will considerably reduce their frequency. Perhaps the earlier classification was not a mistake, for, eventually, since they are L2 constructions, they are likely to win out. That is not, however, the ultimate fate of all L2 features; some, in spite of earlier, fortuitous use, disappear or have only a low frequency of occurrence as the interlanguage *fossilizes*, at least as regards that item.

This ebb and flow of entering versus receding forms (and their identity at any point) is common in interlanguage systems, and specific patterns are recognized in, e.g., Kellerman's notion of U-shaped behavior (1979), in which marked forms, acquired in early stages, are rejected in more advanced ones, but reappear in advanced proficiency, or in Major's contention that transfer error gives way to developmental strategies as proficiency increases (1986, 1987, to appear a, b, c). All these re-evaluations of the status of items which enter, influence, and leave an interlanguage system may be represented in the model suggested in figure 5.1, which although providing for a specification of the system at a given moment, is obviously prejudiced towards representing its dynamic aspects, whether through cross-sectional or longitudinal studies.[5]

Figure 5.2 shows the typical variation which one discovers when interlanguage is investigated along a stylistic dimension, although this book has tried to make it clear that ways to elicit the unplanned (vernacular) and planned (superordinate) are controversial. Nevertheless, figure 5.3 shows that planned performance often reveals a higher frequency of entering forms. (In this figure and in those which follow, actual studies represent the generalizations, and percentages rather than VARBRUL weights are given.)

Figure 5.3 shows the unexpected reversal of the pattern of figure 5.2. These apparently contradictory patterns may be built into this model by assuming that the normal route for marked forms is like change from above and that their highest frequency realization usually occurs in planned speech behavior. On the other hand, the normal route into the interlanguage vernacular (unplanned) is through change from below, the acquisition device

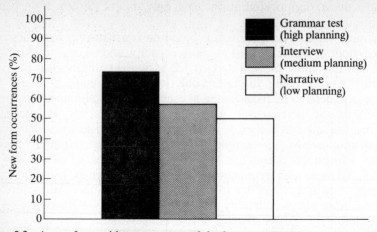

*Figure 5.2*   A new form with greater strength in the nonvernacular (source: percentages taken from Tarone's 1985 data for Japanese and Arabic students' use of the third person singular marker in English)

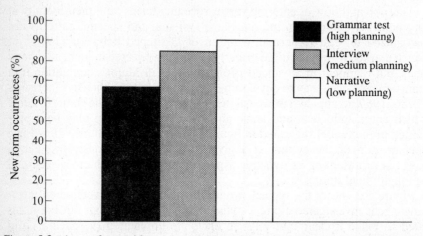

*Figure 5.3*   A new form with greater strength in the vernacular (source: percentages taken from Tarone's 1985 data for Japanese and Arabic students' use of object pronouns in English)

which is more likely to work on unmarked, universal forms. As indicated in 5.1.2, research in developing interlanguage systems does not seem to contain counterexamples to that position.

It is easy to misunderstand 'change from above' and 'change from below' to be synonymous with both the experiential and processing mechanisms which have to do with learning. They are related but distinct notions. Change from above and below refer to the levels of awareness of a form in the members of the speech community. In change from above, the form is commented on, speakers are aware of it, and it is often a specific reaction to another (undesirable) change. As Kroch (1976) suggests, change from above often disrupts change in universal, unmarked directions by imposing odd forms, and, in some sense, such forms require more effort both to acquire and maintain. Change from above does not suggest, however, that the mechanisms which eventually incorporate them into linguistic competence are different from those which incorporate those initiated by change from below. Although they have a greater frequency in planned behavior during their competitive period, if they win out, they may become categorical in the vernacular as well as in the superordinate. A complete outline of the stages of change from above and below is given in Labov (1972a:178–80).

It is tempting, as well, to suggest that classroom attention is synonymous with change from above, but it is as likely that, e.g., Tarone's respondents have been subjected to as much (or more) explicit instruction about the article and object pronoun forms as they have about the third person singular marker on the verb or the noun plural. To appear in the interlanguage vernacular, however, change from above, no matter how odd the forms it deals with, must have a clear plan of attack. The third singular allows that; as Krashen suggests, though marked in its paradigm, it is simple, and change from above can defeat, at least in planned discourse, the tendency not to use this redundant marking feature. Noun plurals might obey the same sort of regulation, although they show no significant variation in Tarone's study (1985). The article and object pronoun, though they may be the subject of class discussion and exercise, allow planned discourse to show that sort of instability marked by hypercorrection or other odd patterns. Their rules more clearly emerge in implementation in functional necessity, and that is the pattern of figure 5.3.[6] This sort of explanation provides an account of different sorts of variation within one setting which is not captured in the distinction between *pedagogic* and *social* norms proposed by Littlewood (1981).

On the other hand, these results require one to be particularly careful about the psycholinguistic status of marked versus unmarked forms. White (1987) catalogues the various meanings which might be assigned the notion markedness in SLA studies, and the generalization made here about the tendency for change from below to attach itself to unmarked forms is meant to be sensitive to that variety of interpretations.

What is the influence of the receding forms in relation to change and to planned and unplanned behavior? Figure 5.4 has the same relative shape as figure 5.2, but the perspective here is on the weight of influence not of the new form but of the receding one. This is the case reported in the great majority of quantitative SLA studies reviewed so far, particularly those in phonology. It is especially important here to note that the sources of these receding forms

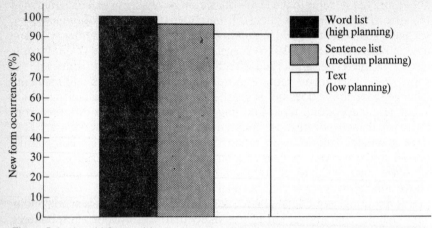

*Figure 5.4* An old form with greater strength in the vernacular (source: percentages taken from Major's 1986 study of lax vowel epenthesis in English consonant clusters by Brazilian learners)

may vary widely. Major suggests that beginners transfer a great deal into the system but, later on, incorporate more developmental items (e.g., Major to appear a). One might require the cross-linguistic identification of marked items in L1, then, to be suspended for early learners, expecting that, even in unplanned language behavior, transfer would have a particularly heavy influence.

Finally, figure 5.5 suggests that receding forms also have access to the superordinate variety, here the use of trilled /r/ in initial position in English by Thai learners.

These developmental processes in the interlanguage distribute themselves appropriately on the basis of effort, naturalness, or simplicity along the planned and unplanned dimensions and support Kroch's (1976) speculation about the linguistic character of sound change in monolingual environments.

In a full model, the planned–unplanned tri- and bifurcation of figures 5.2 through 5.5 must give way to a continuum; there will be a continuous horizontal dimension of 'planning,' but, in light of Young's work and the taxonomy presented in 4.2, future operationalizing of this dimension should be much more carefully done.

There are other aspects of the shape of the model which might be toyed with. The vertical dimension (the 'interlanguage system' itself) might be elongated through time to indicate increasing complexity (e.g., Corder 1977), though that would be most questionable as a representation of change outside SLA situations. If verticality simply represented system size, the dimension might be altered along the planned versus unplanned dimension as well (producing a sort of vertical parallelogram rather than an elongated

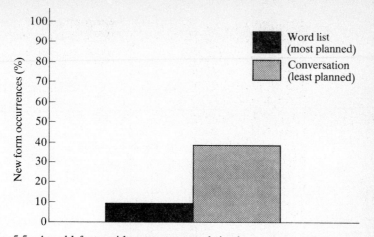

*Figure 5.5*   An old form with greater strength in the nonvernacular (source: percentages taken from Beebe's 1980 study of Thai learners' realization of initial English /ɹ/)

rectangle). That is, some learner systems might have considerably greater content on their planned sides (classroom learners? careful monitors?), while others might be much larger on their unplanned side (natural acquirers?).

So far, forms which come in and go out have been aligned with processing time, markedness, and so on, but have not been related straightforwardly to matters of individual or interactional identity. Variability, at least for native and fluent speakers, has depth. That depth is the apparently synchronic social use of diachronic facts. Although it would be an exaggeration to say that such symbolism is generally rooted in the planned–unplanned distinction, it would not be a bad guess. The caricatures of the who, to whom, when, where, what, and why of planned versus unplanned speech are strong in all societies. Whether that etiological interpretation is correct or not, the relative frequencies of entering and receding forms eventually reflect more than the surface plane of relative planning. They must be sensitive to dimensions which include the characteristics of individual and interaction.

Figure 5.6 shows the depth dimension of this model (and does away with the two-way planning distinction). Different frequencies for men and women, class distinctions, age differences, genres, relationships, and so on will provide a complex variation space which will be interesting to those concerned with the function and status of use. The relative frequency or weight of entering and receding forms in the variation space will identify the roles individuals and environments play in utilizing the variability created by linguistic change. Moreover, it is not necessary to resolve an apparent argument between Labov and Bickerton about the 'social' or 'linguistic' nature of variation. It is linguistic, but the symbolism attached to forms is

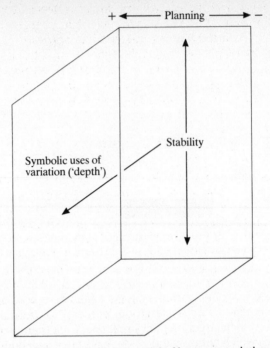

*Figure 5.6*   An integrated model of language variation

itself a part of the fluidity of this variation space. Its content is a part of the general structure of the system which, particularly for monolingual studies where external norms are rarely important, make up the background for the emergence of new influences.

Stability, from this point of view, may be achieved in two ways. On the surface dimension, either before new forms enter or after they have become categorical, there is an absence of variation. Stability may, however, establish itself in the depth dimension as well. Although the association of a greater or lesser frequency with a social or stylistic dimension may simply indicate the leaders (or resisters) of change, long-range association may halt or slow the movement of a feature. This symbolic stability is rather obviously the status of sociolinguistic indicators; its relation to fossilization in SLA needs to be more carefully explored.

Although this model unifies linguistic change for both SLA and mono-lingual settings, it does not destroy the ability to distinguish them, but the distinctions are matters of degree and subtlety, as those who have claimed that interlanguage systems are natural languages knew all along.

First, one must surely agree with those who find interlanguage systems in a greater state of instability than ordinary systems (e.g., Ellis and Roberts

1987), though it is surely an exaggeration to say as Beebe does that NSs have 'complete command' of their systems and that 'changes ... are minor' (1988:44). Perhaps 'instability' is a quantitative expression of the number of changing features which will need to be characterized for any given system. From the individual's point of view, this instability imposes much more powerful processing requirements, but the introduction of change from above and below in an early interlanguage will, generally speaking, come from the shallow surface of linguistic demands, not from the depth of symbolic use of forms.

Second, the journey of an entering form from onset to completion in an interlanguage system may be very rapid, and the realignment of emerging and receding forms may be even quicker. An interlanguage system, therefore, is not only more variable in the sense of the number of items which are involved in change but more variable in the sense of the rapidity of change. Since the L2 provides constant pressure, often in the form of change from above, such rapidity is to be expected; even monolingual systems which show the corrective influence of change from above show a more rapid change than those involved in the more surreptitious change from below (e.g., Ash 1982). It is in this sense, rather than a more general one, that Faerch's (1980) claim that interlanguage change is more targeted than L1 might be understood. Monolingual change is as surely targeted in the sense of the identity of entering and receding forms, but the trip to the target may be idle. Additionally, change is much more likely to be fossilized in a monolingual setting when variation itself gains a more or less stable symbolic association in the depth dimension. That sort of symbolic fossilization is less likely to occur in a developing interlanguage, although more must be said about the potential for arrested development.

Recall that fossilization may be 'social' or 'sociolinguistic.' The first is the result of a massive failure to accommodate to the new speech community; rejection, anomie, cultural conflicts of an institutionalized sort, and so on provide the social setting for dramatically arresting linguistic development. The sorts of concerns of 2.1.3 and 2.1.4 apply to this kind of fossilization, but a subtle variation model of the sort under discussion here is not an important factor in accounting for this sort of arrested development, for it often results in categorical performances and has only the simplest social depth: the speaker ends up with a system which excludes him or her from the speech community except for the grossest communication chores.

Sociolinguistic fossilization occurs along a wide range of phenomena and in response to the same sorts of identity and interaction factors which would affect NSs. Such fossilization may be general if there is a community of learners or it may appear in isolated examples. The concerns of identity, accommodation, nativeness, and so on require the competent bilingual to construct a variation space which is different from the NS's. For many speakers the apparently neuro-motor basis of phonological distinctiveness will allow an almost effortless symbolic use of phonological forms. It will be difficult to predict, however, what other variable items of the system a speaker will sociolinguistically fossilize, but the task of creating a system sensitive to identity and at the same time fully communicative will, doubtless, result in much fine tuning.

Finally, although less stable, the interlanguage system is smaller, particularly in the width of its planning dimension, but especially in the depth of its symbolic use of variation. One might argue, for example, that only the caricatures an early learner has of the planning dimension will have symbolic value, and there is no doubt that he or she will transfer a good deal of the L1 associations of formal versus informal speech along this dimension. Numerous studies characterized in this work have looked at such cross-cultural mismatches in the assignment of meaning to performance styles, although, it must be admitted, most dealt with the larger areas of speech acts and pragmatics rather than with those features which have been the mainstay of quantitative sociolinguistics.

This model hopes to give some meat to the tautological notion that change is the result of variation (e.g., Widdowson 1975) by making some specific claims concerning the onset and progress of forms in a developing interlanguage. The model for those claims comes from the consideration of not only the linguistic make-up of forms but also the social settings which both host their progress and provide them with the connotative accretion which is inevitable in human societies. In creole societies, for example, entire blocks of the developing system have become associated with social meaning. In some cases, the symbolism attached to a large number of forms has become so associated with groups in the community that they seem to reorient the entire set of likely emerging and receding forms. Labov, for example, has recently claimed that Black English may be diverging from the varieties surrounding it. In the model provided here, such divergence would be revealed by a realignment of emerging and receding forms, and, although the certain answer will not be known until the change has actually taken place, earlier work on the identification of leaders and sources of change may provide helpful clues. Use of the VARBRUL technique to determine whether or not subgroups stand outside the range of probabilities set by linguistic influences, as suggested in 4.1.1, might provide a helpful quantitative rule of thumb for such claims.

Will it be possible to develop more exact models of likely emerging and receding forms at various stages of the developing interlanguage? Where there is no real community of learners and no previous accretion of symbolic depth, such change will be more linguistically determined along the shallow, surface plane of the model proposed here, but one should not be too quick to dismiss the symbolic value even early learners may assign variation in developing forms. Rampton (1987), for example, suggests that nontarget forms are maintained in some interlanguage varieties to exhibit learner status, and there is a great deal of anecdotal evidence for such 'symbolic backsliding.' Breen (1985) reminds researchers of the classroom as a social context for its individuals as well as a setting for interactional research on classroom talk; the relations and identities which develop there provide another setting for symbolic variation.

How may one align, as was attempted briefly in 2.2.3 and in the development of the sociolinguistic model of SLA, the commonplaces of the two fields? What are the unified field equivalents of *overgeneralization* and *hypercorrection*? Are *fossilization* and *rule stagnation* the same? If the taxonomy of this effort has shortcomings and if the variationist model is flawed, perhaps raising the questions will promote closer work on problems which obviously concern both fields. Perhaps even more importantly, cooperation will lead to an even stronger forum for the use of authentic language data in conjunction with intuition in the continuing development of general linguistic theory.

## 5.2 Applied sociolinguistics

Throughout the book there have been references to the concerns of language teaching, syllabus design, materials preparation, and so on, for, in many cases, researchers and appliers have been the same person. Some research has gone on with very practical aims in mind. Such fields as language teaching for special purposes might be singled out as ones which have led in the description and definition of genres (e.g., Swales to appear), and classroom discourse and interaction analyses have contributed to general understandings of how to carry out such work (e.g., Sinclair and Coulthard 1975, Wong-Fillmore 1976).

One might tour the various schools of language teaching currently (and previously) in vogue, determining the degree to which they hit or miss the sort of sociolinguistic model described immediately above. There are reasons other than this book's running out of space not to do that. There are a number of excellent current reviews of such schools of teaching, even some (e.g., Richards and Rodgers 1986) apparently disinterested ones, and many practitioners who work in one school or another are bound to their approaches by required texts, determined supervisors, or personal tastes. The parts of the presentation here which fit and abet their work are more important than those which might rock its foundations. Although the point of view of this book is optimistic on the matter of the importance of information to teaching, there is enough truth in Chomsky's infamous claim (1966) that the proof of the pudding in teaching is the result, not the theory, that all who theorize are better off taking the position of offering information, results, and suspicions for what they may be worth rather than pontificating about how a language will or will not grow in the hothouse of the classroom. Even those

270 SOCIOLINGUISTICS AND SECOND LANGUAGES

who hold that no instruction at all provides the optimum setting for acquisition will be able to use this book for descriptions of the sorts of conditions which appear to be essential to SLA from a variationist perspective.

Those who intend to take information and test it in materials, classrooms, and so on, however, might want to consider the following more general ideas which emerge from this work.

*Selectivity*   The work of sociolinguists of all persuasions provides applied linguists with massive amounts of authentic language data of more circumscribed sorts than ever before available. The old-fashioned way to create a letter, dialog, joke, or phone call for pedagogical use was to rely on NS or fluent intuitions. That is no longer necessary. While it may be necessary to modify authentic material for pedagogical purposes, there is no need to risk the creation of inauthentic structures, moves, organizations, or levels of usage, particularly in areas of a selected text which are not the designer's focus for the lesson involved. If taxi drivers, young boys, or nuclear physicists are involved in an argument, discussion, or chat, then that language experience carries with it not only its structural elements (at every possible level) but also evidence of the synchronic, symbolic variety space which is being exhibited to the learner. His or her eventual positioning in that space depends on an evaluation of all experiences in the language. Applied linguists of different schools may believe they can or cannot guide that development directly, but all have a responsibility to provide the sorts of data which will give appropriate enabling clues to the learner's own reconstruction of the system and adjustment to it. One must reject Ellis's notion that development of the interlanguage is only movement towards categorical use (1987b:184). Neither the NS's nor the competent bilingual's system will result in non-variable use. A new rule might end up stagnant at a 50 percent level of frequency, for example, as the appropriate distribution of that form in the symbolic variety space of the learner and his or her group.

*Description*   Selectivity and authenticity carry with them another level of information for applied linguists who believe in the learner's conscious acquisition. They will want accurate descriptions of the authentic data described above, for data themselves do not bring with them analysis. The descriptions given in this work and in other principally sociolinguistic studies will not do for the vast majority of classrooms, but pedagogical grammars with sociolinguistic content are not strange ideals. When one provides authentic models, careful and insightful description might accompany them. There may be cases where that is not acceptable (some language teaching methods, work with young children), but, in the main, wherever teaching involves explanation as well as presentation, the findings of the sorts of research characterized in this book should be appropriate. Since careful, conservative surveys of the effects of instruction on learning do not dismiss its value, one risks much by ignoring it and little by attending to it (e.g., Long 1983c).

*Structuring* From the more theoretical perspective presented just above, it should be possible to arrange items on the basis of their position of entry into the learner's developing interlanguage. Ellis (1987b:186) makes such a claim when he notes that the learner's careful style is more permeable. Although that has been shown not to be the case for certain sorts of language entities and it may be influenced by the depth as well as the planning width of the system, the principle is a good one. What can one predict from the model of sociolinguistic competence outlined above about the likely timing and status of items as they advance into and through a developing interlanguage? Although many of the generalizations offered in the present work come from monolingual sociolinguistic studies, work on these questions in SLA is advancing. Young (to appear) shows, for example, that phonological environments constrain the accuracy of noun plural marking for Chinese learners of English in the early stages of acquisition but have no influence at all on more advanced learners. Quantitative analyses may be used as well to determine differences in learner groups and effectiveness of testing strategies, as illustrated in 5.1.4. If future research can combine such generalizations with the dimension of planning and the influence of identity and interaction from the emerging depths of interlanguage systems, even more elaborate suggestions about the ordering of linguistic units for syllabuses and materials for those who believe in structuring can be made. Even those who believe that such structured organization should not be a part of syllabus design will find these guideposts important in the evaluation of student progress, identifying, particularly, appropriate areas for instructional intervention.

*Conditions* When one finally considers the influence of identity and interaction on the development of forms, the large set of conditioning factors in the language teaching setting arises. Sociolinguistic research provides information from two levels. First, the identity factors of sex, age, ethnicity, and so on appear to interact with the changing system in specific ways. Female leadership in change, age-grading, male hypocorrection, lower middle class hypercorrection, and so on identify patterns of frequency realizations at the interface of identity and the competing forms in a language system. How are these conditions like those in SLA? When are they met in foreign versus second language acquisition settings? Are they powerful in classrooms? How may they vary by cultural background? Second, the larger-level analysis of the interface of interactional elements provides a further setting for the correlation between form and the symbolism given it in the depth of social reality. The frequencies of forms in genres, conversation types, and other larger elements provide another arena for the variable realization of features as they influence the total system. Which features are singled out (and at what stage of development) to accomplish politeness, deference, power, and so on? Does indirection realize itself more in certain media than others? Again, do cross-cultural matters influence this interface?

Much applied linguistics has taken an invariant attitude to goals and models in SLA, but L2, L1, interlanguages, and the most successful learners' competent systems are not invariant. Watching such systems grow and accounting for them is the goal of general sociolinguistics. Perhaps knowing more about how that happens will help those who would like to foster their growth.

# 6

# Summing up

This book has presupposed and/or developed the following themes.

*Linguistic theory*  Sociolinguistics is central, not peripheral, to general linguistic theory. One cannot understand how a first or second language is learned without consideration of variable rather than categorical matters, and one cannot account for language change without a similar account. In fact, one cannot give an accurate picture of synchronic performance without accounting for variation, but since many find competence rather than performance the key to general linguistics, that argument is not as telling. The misunderstanding of sociolinguistics as the field which simply describes the variables in language use for different sexes, classes, genres, media, and so on is a tempting one to adhere to, for it focuses on real distinctions in language use. It fails to capture, however, the dynamic role of identity, interaction, language status, and even media components in linguistic evolution. Those factors play a role in both long-term (historical) and short-term (language acquisition) settings. Of course, they are not the only factors to be considered, and this book does not deny the importance of matters of psycholinguistic processing and linguistic universals in SLA. In fact, the model elaborated in figure 5.6 hopes to show how societal factors interact with just such mechanisms, although, admittedly, the identity and characterization of those mechanisms is not elaborately treated here.

One upshot of this view is a reconciliation of the apparent disagreement between Labov and Bickerton over the role of 'linguistic' versus 'social' elements in variation and linguistic change. If an element of system restructuring, on its way to completion, is arrested (or retarded) by symbolic use from some component in the depth dimension of the variety space, one may agree with Bickerton that social use has been made of linguistic change. The fact is, however, that the partial restructuring due to these so-called social forces now constitutes part of the input which may bring about new influences on the total system. When they enter as 'linguistic items,' they carry with them, nevertheless, some of the accretion of their previous symbolic association. Labov's work on the history of New York City (r) is an excellent example of a variable's changing status as an emerging or receding form, its fluctuating status dependent on the values and associations it gains in the symbolic variety space of the speech community.[1] SLA work will focus on the linguistic aspects of system restructuring in early stages of acquisition (e.g., Huebner 1983b), but the dimension of planning will have to be considered early on as well, particularly its possible L1 associations. Ultimately, the participation of the components of identity, interaction, language status, and media will have to be studied as the emerging bilingual creates the associations which establish his or her variety space and contribute to the continuing development of the interlanguage.

*Levels of analysis*   Sociolinguistics is young, and its findings are as yet best seen as generalizations which can be made about its lower-level components, what were called in chapter 4 its 'etic' level units. At first that claim might seem anti-ethnographic, but it is consistent with the best ethnographic as well as quantitative sociolinguistic research, for the two schools simply begin at the opposite ends of the continuum of interests all sociolinguists share. Such a position reconciles the views of Hymes and Gumperz on the one hand with those of Labov on the other. A quantitative linguistic analysis begins with the characterization of variable frequencies of an item which has attracted the analyst's attention. The analysis may never proceed (and often does not) so far as including accounts of that variable within such larger contexts as situation type or genre, but nothing would prevent it from being so treated, and, one might argue, thorough studies of a speech community would demand it. From the other point of view, an ethnographic investigation observes relationships, task-like identities, cultural events and the speech which accompanies them. Though such research tries to provide an appropriate description and folk label to the larger units it considers, it must also characterize them in terms of their components, and such taxonomizing as Hymes (e.g., 1974) is an attempt to provide an account of lower-level constructs which allow for universal classification of such matters. The full cycle is made, of course, when the units determined from ethnographic investigation are related to the variable frequencies of the more familiar linguistic units of phonology, morphology, lexicon, and so on.

Both procedures apply to variation in SLA, but the ethnographic procedure, although it cannot be completely ignored, will surely not reveal much in the earliest stages of acquisition. Even when ethnographic or higher-level unit approaches to SLA (or language studies in general) are appropriate, one must guard against limited claims. Assume that a cultural event accompanied by speech has been identified through some appropriate ethnographic study procedure. While it may be tempting to report the frequencies of lower-level units which occur within the event, it will be important to determine the independent influence of smaller components, including, of course, those of the purely linguistic context. Ethnographic zeal, for example, might lead one to suggest that a higher frequency of this or that form obtained in a certain linguistic setting or situation. Closer examination might reveal that the variance of the form was almost completely characterized by the sex, status, or some other identity factor of the participants and that that same frequency emerged whenever participant identities were similar, regardless of the higher-level concerns. In fact, in terms of internal system economy, it is much more likely that a sort of front-line symbolism attaches itself to the most distinctive elements of the culture, although they may radically differ from one society to another. Such concerns as these make the depth component of symbolism even more complex than that suggested earlier. Consider the following possibility. A feature from the + side of the planning dimension attaches itself to gender in a given society; women more frequently exhibit an emerging element of the system which is more frequently realized in planned speech. As a result, planned speech (at least for that element) becomes symbolically attached to women's speech, although that symbolic attachment need not be known consciously by the speech community, for it could be a marker as well as an indicator. Imagine now a speech event which is dominated by women, a rhyme or chant, for example, which accompanies a traditional activity. At this point in the investigation of the variety space[2] of the speech community, the frequency of the feature in the chant is a direct outcome of the frequency of the feature in women's use in general. That is, identity of the participants in the speech activity (the chant) will fully account for the frequency of the linguistic unit; appeal to the activity as an explanation for the frequency is redundant, perhaps misleading. Suppose, however, that a new planning distinction (or a distinction from some other source) begins to replace the old one for just this linguistic unit and that women again are especially responsive to it, perhaps even freezing its frequency at such a high level that it is again associated with women's language use. Although there is a route for the new feature to penetrate the chant, it need not do so. The chant has a level of identity quite separate from that of +female. It may have a conservative position in the speech community which would cause it to resist new forms, although women in general would not. In the analysis of the speech community at this stage, then, one would want to identify the contribution of the speech event itself to the frequency of a particular form. Of course, other features from the taxonomy (e.g., 'value') might allow one to avoid reference to the specific event in characterizing the probability of a particular form.

It will normally not do, then, to mark out an area of figure 5.7 and label it as some 'domain,' or 'speech event' type. There is no doubt that interesting variation can be explained in such work, and SLA research has recently begun to attend to this important way of analyzing the distribution of form and symbolism in individuals (e.g., Selinker and Douglas 1985). So long as the relation between higher-level constructs and their components is fully investigated, the relationship between ethnographic and quantitative approaches will remain fruitful; ignoring either side may lead to misleading results.

*Attitudes and beliefs*   Sociolinguistic facts do not reveal themselves exclusively in linguistic products. No matter how thorough the research on frequencies is and how tempting it will be to attach symbolic importance to the greater use of this or that form by certain groups or in particular contexts, the subjective dimension must be taken into consideration. This position is the same as that taken against the purely empiricist position of Selinker (1972) in interlanguage studies. Schachter, Tyson, and Diffley (1976) argue that a look at the mental structure of the interlanguage system as well as an examination of its performance products is necessary. Similarly, in sociolinguistics, access to attitudes, stereotypes, and folk beliefs about language are necessary adjuncts to the assumed symbolic values extracted from the frequency counts of typical quantitative studies. The tradition of Lambert et al. (1960) is particularly strong in current social psychological studies. Howard Giles and his associates have carried out a number of interesting projects on attitudinal and adjustment concerns, and much of their work is cross-cultural and cross-linguistic. The status of the competent bilingual, one who constructs an eventually different but successful system, is largely determined by the affective and attitudinal matters uncovered through such research. Studies of folk attitudes and ethnographic concerns about language and language learning are not as common, but they will surely emerge as the techniques for them develop; at least, they should look at the range of issues suggested by Hoenigswald (1966).

*Larger units*   Conversational analysis, text analysis, discourse analysis, and other investigations of larger linguistic domains have provided sociolinguists with a new way of looking at further elements of linguistic structure. Viewed no longer as the static elements of genre or text type, units under consideration in the most recent studies constitute the dynamic process of on-going negotiation among interlocutors. To the extent that such negotiations include matters essential to language learning ('interactional' properties), they need to be examined and carefully described.

This book has tried to detail the components that must be involved in variety description, but it presupposes that sociolinguistics is essential to linguistics and that the resulting variable linguistics is essential to an account of SLA. To the extent that the characterization of variety in emerging L2 systems contributes to the general ability to describe language and build an efficient model of it, it belongs no less to the central concerns of the science.

# Notes

## Introduction

1 Neither of these samples corresponds to readily available empirical rankings of request strategies (e.g., Walters 1979), though Coffey's model reverses only 'would' and 'could.' Walters ranks request strategies in the following order (from most to least 'polite'):

| | | | |
|---|---|---|---|
| 1 | If you can... | 8 | I came to... |
| 2 | Could... | 9 | You have... |
| 3 | May... | 10 | You can... |
| 4 | Would... | 11 | Where... |
| 5 | Do... | 12 | You have to... |
| 6 | Will... | 13 | I want... |
| 7 | Can... | 14 | (Imperative) |

2 The idea that an NS model is the only appropriate one has been challenged from several points of view (e.g., Preston 1981a, b, Kachru 1982a).
3 A survey of the problems involved in questioning NSs about language use is given in Preston (1983, 1984).

## Chapter 1   The sociolinguistic background

1 Though the psycholinguistic reality of grammatical rules seemed headed for an early demise in the late sixties and early seventies, new claims have appeared (e.g., Berwick and Weinberg 1986).
2 Detailed reviews of types of variable rules may be found in Sankoff and Labov (1979) and Kay and McDaniel (1979); detailed instructions for running a micro-computer version of VARBRUL 2 is provided in Fasold (1985).
3 A clever reader may be fooled by taking the average of the probabilities and comparing it to the results in table 1.1. The input (0.60), upper middle class (0.29), following vowel (0.25), and nonmorpheme (0.69) probabilities would yield a mean of 0.46. Table 1.1, however, shows this deletion percentage to be 0.28 (extrapolated to a raw score of 28 deletions out of one hundred), and VARBRUL 2 predicted that there would be 30.61 deletions (an error of only 0.32, well within

the conservative limits of acceptability). Those mathematically inclined will want to substitute the following formula to check the predictability force of VARBRUL 2 since a simple mean of probabilities is not the correct strategy.

$$p = \frac{p_0 \times \ldots \times p_n}{[p_0 \times \ldots \times p_n] + [(1-p_0) \times \ldots \times (1-p_n)]}$$

Using the above figures,

$$p = \frac{0.60 \times 0.29 \times 0.25 \times 0.69}{[0.60 \times 0.29 \times 0.25 \times 0.69] + [(1-0.60) \times (1-0.29) \times (1-0.25) \times (1-0.69)]}$$

$$p = \frac{0.030015}{0.030015 + 0.06603}$$

$$p = \frac{0.030015}{0.096045}$$

$$p = 0.3125097$$

which is, of course, substantially the same as the 0.3061 probability which would be required to cause the expected 30.61 applications of the rule in this environment.

4  A coin flipping analogy was used in Kay and McDaniel (1979) to characterize different models of variable rules, but they suggested that each influencing factor was a toss.

5  'Scanning the linguistic surroundings' is quite a different concept from remembering (and/or predicting) the performance of variables. If the linguistic environment were not read, no context-sensitive rules could apply.

6  The coin flipping psycholinguistic version of the variable rule offered here represents the strongest version of what a speaker knows about variation (e.g., Wolfram and Fasold 1974:110–11).

7  A recent statement on the organization of language use based on identity is Le Page and Tabouret-Keller (1985).

8  Preston (1986a) surveys a large number of sociolinguistic variables and examines their use in more sensitive characterizations of environments for language shift.

9  Fasold (1973) provides a useful characterization of the place of implicational orderings within the wave theory model and concludes that systematic variation is not inconsistent with such a model.

10  Some recent research has shown nouns to be switched even more frequently than sentences (Berk-Seligson 1986:326).

11  But see, for example, Kontra (1985) for examples of Hungarian affixes on English loans into the Hungarian spoken by immigrants in the United States.

12  Text analysis is not discussed here since it is, perhaps, the least sociolinguistic of approaches to discourse. Katz and Fodor (1964:490) go so far as to say that 'discourse can be treated as a single sentence in isolation by regarding sentence boundaries as sentential connectives.'

13  Apparently ungrammatical sentences may be interpreted by providing elaborate

contextualization. A favorite, though the characters are changed here to reflect 1980's politics, is

\* Reagan reckons Preparation H

which is quite OK as a response to the question: 'What do some people think Ed Meese slicks his hair down with?'

14  A relatively principled way of arriving at indirect speech acts will be discussed below.

15  On this point, see Frawley (1987) for an attack on pragmatic, discourse, and conversation analyses which are done with no reliance on principled methods, though, to the credit of one of the fields represented here, he notes that especially valuable interactional analysis has been carried out by SLA researchers.

## Chapter 2   Individual characteristics

1  Large-scale investigations carried out since Krashen, Long, and Scarcella (1979) or not reported there have generally upheld the finding that age at onset of acquisition is an important factor (e.g. Heidelberger Forschungsprojekt 'Pidgin-Deutsch' (1978); but see Burstall et al. (1974), which shows that learners who began French at age eight and continued to thirteen did less well than those who began at ten and continued to fifteen).

2  Neither Krashen nor Schumann claims that adults cannot overcome these social psychological factors which retard long-range, high-level success in SLA; nor would either claim that this variable explains all the problems associated with age related variation in SLA. Hatch (1983) cautions that 'it is still too soon to make strong claims' (196), though she would seem to support, at least in spirit, this general emphasis on social psychological factors when she notes that

age-related variables change the possibilities for a good language learning prognosis. If there is to be an optimal age hypothesis at all, I think it must not be based on age or aging, but on age-related variables. (197)

3  The earliest formulation of age-grading is Hockett (1950).

4  A sociolinguistic variable is enclosed in parentheses ( ) to distinguish it from a phoneme, usually presented between slashes / /, and a phone, usually presented between square brackets [ ].

5  An alternative method would involve calculating the score for each individual:

|          | Speaker 1       | Speaker 2         | Speaker 3          |
|----------|-----------------|-------------------|--------------------|
| (e)–1    | $3 \times 1 = 3$ | $3 \times 1 = 3$  | $1 \times 1 = 1$   |
| (e)–2    | $4 \times 2 = 8$ | $6 \times 2 = 12$ | $0 \times 2 = 0$   |
| (e)–3    | $2 \times 3 = 6$ | $8 \times 3 = 24$ | $10 \times 3 = 30$ |
| Totals:  | 9   17          | 17   39           | 11   31            |

Dividing the score by the number of tokens, subtracting 1, and multiplying by 100 (as above for the entire group) yields (e) scores for each individual:

Speaker 1:  $17/9 = 1.89-1 \times 100 = 89$
Speaker 2:  $39/17 = 2.29-1 \times 100 = 129$
Speaker 3:  $31/11 = 2.82-1 \times 100 = 182$

A group score could be derived from this method by simply summing the scores and dividing by the number of subjects:

$89 + 129 + 182 = 400/3 = 133$

This is sufficiently close to the score derived from the group method above (135) to allow confidence that the two methods yield substantially similar results. Note, however, that the difference in individuals is highlighted in the second method.

6  Social class or *status* is a later topic (2.2.3), but it must be brought up here to clarify points about change from above and change from below.

7  Note, however, that the relationship between older and younger speakers in change from above for both prestige and stigmatized features is the same and that the same pattern would be observed again for a stable, prestige feature.

8  Labov calls features which are noted and commented on in the speech community *stereotypes*, not consciously noted features which show social and stylistic stratification *markers*, and not consciously noted variable features which may differentiate classes but are not sensitive to stylistic change (along some formal–informal dimension, for example) *indicators* (1972a:237–51). I have suggested (Preston MS) that stereotypes which become part of the folk repertoire of a community be called *caricatures*.

9  Of course, the contributions of status and sex (and other variables) to change are not highlighted here; see, particularly, 2.1.2 and 2.2.3.

10  When young adults and older adults are compared, the younger ones have an advantage. Brown (1985) shows that a number of discourse characteristics help explain this difference:

1  The older adults do not seem to focus on the input in language learning as much as the younger learners.

2  While the younger learners are more concerned about the amount of input they are responsible for, the older learners are more concerned about changing the kind of input they get.

3  While the older learners seem to make more individual requests for specific input, the total number of requests per class hour is not significantly different for the two groups.

4  The younger learners make significantly more requests than older learners for the input of specific vocabulary items. (280)

Seright (1985) suggests that younger and older adults be separated in instructional programs so that 'the older learners might be less inhibited and generally more at ease' (470).

11  There will be much more to say about conversation, input, and simplification in following sections; recall that the focus here is on age.

12  These suggestions are consistent with the findings of Cathcart-Strong (1986) who, in distinguishing between conversational learning which took place in child NNS and adult NS interactions and child NNS and peer NS interactions, determined

that NNS children require careful instructional preparation or some socio-linguistic advantage in gaining appropriate input from NS peers (525–6).

13  That richness cannot be reviewed here; a reader who wants guidance in the depth and breadth of these studies should consult the excellent annotated bibliography in Thorne, Kramarae, and Henley (1983).

14  The only striking contradiction, the male 017 and female 067 scores in casual style, may be explained by the fact that an extremely small number of tokens of (ng) occurred for male subjects in this style. Note, by the way, the possibility of arranging these data (separating male and female scores) in an implicational scale (see 1.2.2).

15  Assuming that the standard deviation is not high, for, in fact, such a score could represent a much more diverse combination of all four (eh) values. Unfortunately such statistical commonplaces were often not included in early sociolinguistic work.

16  Here (and elsewhere in this book) *folk* always means patterns of activity, thought, language, and construction which derive from traditional (nonacademic or non-professional) sources. It never refers to the practices (including language) of the so-called rustic, uneducated, or primitive, nor does it predict whether a folk concept or belief is correct or not. For example, *folk linguistics* refers to beliefs about language held by nonlinguists, regardless of their social class or general sophistication and regardless of the correctness of their beliefs.

17  An excellent review of folk linguistic beliefs about women's language is provided in Coates (1986: 16–34).

18  Interruptions may, however, support rather than disrupt a conversation by indicating that the listener agrees or wants the speaker to continue (Aleguire 1978).

19  Of course, questions may be a part of keeping a conversation moving along, not just indications of the questioner's inferiority or lack of information (Coates 1986:106).

20  Even the higher and lower pitched voices associated with male and female speakers respectively may be a partially learned fact rather than a purely bio-logically determined trait (Mattingly 1966; Sachs 1975).

21  Such studies as Saint-Jacques (1973), however, suggest that some gender differences are widespread in the world's languages, if not universal.

22  Such principally psycholinguistic studies may be of considerable interest to socio-linguists, and the division between monolingual and multi- or bilingual data bases may be artificial. An excellent monolingual study of the acquisition of a second dialect is Payne (1976, 1980). Where other social factors (e.g., ethnicity) interfere, sociolinguistics has a more respectable history of interest and research.

23  Some specific linguistic data from a nonacculturated, pidginized learner are shown (in a VARBRUL format) in 1.2.1.

24  Other social psychological theories of SLA (which give greater or lesser emphasis to components of the three already discussed) include H. D. Brown (1980), Clément (1980), and Gardner (1985).

25  In fact, this is the northern/north midland boundary of classical United States dialect studies.

26  There is surely, however, a point where selection from *any* variety would be non-productive, particularly in the construction of a rule-based phonology.

27  If they are not, considerations from 2.1.3 would apply.

28  Theoreticians will notice that the *parameter setting* notion of recent work in semanto-syntactic theory is just such an idea.

29  Of course, both variable rules and implicational scales can be used to indicate historical change; this characterization stresses only the superficial or apparent utility of those models.

30  Corder (1967) is the seminal work in error analysis.

31  Labov uses *hypercorrection* (and *hypocorrection*) to refer to high (or low) frequency of use of a form, not to the use of an unprecedented form (2.1.5).

32  It is also the case that Fillmore confuses fluency with artistry. A fluent speaker is one who has the communicative competence to acquit him or herself well linguistically in a wide variety of contexts, particularly those which are likely to occur as a result of roles an individual is likely to assume. A fluent speaker is not one who is regarded as having special linguistic abilities by the speech community; that *valued* sort of linguistic performance, the subject of much rich investigation in folklore, is discussed briefly in 4.1.2.

33  In the United States in particular the emphasis on differences in learning styles led to a movement to *individualize* foreign and second language teaching (e.g., Altman 1972).

## Chapter 3   Interactional factors

1  On the other hand, that such suggestions emerge from what are seen by some as principally sociolinguistic studies should not be surprising; the study of language in its social context should lead to basic understandings in general linguistics, and a bilingual sociolinguistics offers even greater opportunities to test and revise universalist hypotheses of precisely the sort discussed here.

2  That is itself a geographical term loaded with historical overtones of source or origin, for even westerners whose immediate origins are not in the East still go *back* there.

3  In a survey of comprehensive treatments of sociolinguistic topics (Preston 1986a), it was found that only Gregory (1967) mentions the number of participants in an interaction as an important variable.

4  See Sigman (1983) for a criticism of proposition-based identifications of topic, particularly for their failure to attend to a variety of just such sociolinguistic variables as those considered here. He goes on to suggest that the introduction of many topics serve *phatic* communicative purposes rather than informational ones and cannot, therefore, be related to the superficial information level of the text structure. On the other hand, he surely exaggerates two things: (1) Keenan and Schieffelin's claim that propositional content must be the same if topic is to remain the same, and (2) any number of conversational analysts' ignorance of implied topics.

5  *Topic* here includes that aspect of Fishman's *domain* which concerns what the conversation is about; that is, the characterization of a consistent 'school' domain as a conversation about a math problem with a teacher in a classroom could be broken down into *place* (3.1.2), *specialization* (2.2.2) – though 'teacher' might require considerably more specification, particularly in such interactional

categories as *power* (3.3.3), *distance* (3.5.1), *manner* (3.5.2), and *topic*. Finally, Gumperz's term *speech activity* (1977:205–6) is, like domain, a term which includes topic. Examples of such speech activities as 'discussing politics' and 'lecturing about linguistics' indicate that Gumperz combines topic with what is called here *genre* (3.2.3) since both 'lecturing' and 'discussing' are not topical, though there may be genres and topics which appear suited to one another ('chatting about last weekend's party') while others are not ('chatting about the end of the world').

6  Preston (1986a: 21–2) offers justifications for distinguishing among such genres as conversation and joke but does not suggest that they are different classes of linguistic objects.

7  Macro-level categories to which jokes and arguments might belong have been called *narratives* and *harangues*, respectively, by John Swales (personal communication).

8  On the other hand, task often refers to a variety of linguistic performances (e.g., free conversation, oral reading of continuous text, elicited imitation of short words and phrases) usually designed to elicit different stylistic levels (e.g., Sato 1985). Some of these performances would not be classified as examples of a genre.

9  There is independent evidence that these three areas produce relevant categories for social analyses (e.g., Argyle, Furnham, and Graham 1981:120–5).

10  Just as so-called women's speech characteristics turned out to be the speech of men and women who were inexperienced in a certain genre and setting – courtroom testimony (2.1.2).

11  Focused dialect groups are identified through a cluster analysis process which groups those individuals who are most similar. McEntegart and Le Page (1982) evaluates the use of such statistical techniques in a survey of two Caribbean creole communities.

12  All these positions, but especially this last one, allow for considerable individual variation.

13  Alternative lists are given in Wilkins (1976:44–54) and Finocchiaro and Brumfit (1983:65–6); the latter is the most recent and most thorough discussion of integrating the several components (situation, grammar, function) of a notional-functional syllabus and of implementing such a program in the classroom. An ESP oriented list of functions in Munby (1978) goes so far as to link functions with associated attitudinal stances of the speaker, indicating, in some cases, specific perlocutionary intent and, in others, emotional and other 'tonal' characteristics of the act (3.5).

14  This discussion focuses on the difference between communication activities inside and outside classrooms, not on the justification (or lack of it) for teaching about the language, a controversy touched on in 5.2 but left, for the most part, to psycholinguists for resolution. Teaching and talking about the language could provide considerable background for information related language use, no matter what role the information from such a topic plays in the process of SLA itself.

15  Status differentiation does not demand stylistic shift. Figure 2.12 illustrates an *indicator*, which shows social stratification but little or no stylistic shift (2.2.3).

16  In fact, both may be inaccurate, in either data presentation or interpretation. Major (1986) claims that Beebe's Thai speakers do indeed transfer a formal Thai feature for their realization of a variable (r) into English, one which happens to

result in inaccuracy. There is an informal Thai (r), however, which, fortuitously, corresponds phonetically to American English [ɹ]. Beebe's failure to mention this fact would make it appear that the formal level in NNS performance is more open to L1 interference (*transfer*). In fact, as Major shows, both ends of the stylistic continuum evidence transfer; the accidental correspondence of the Thai and English forms in the more informal ranges make it appear, however, that the formal style is more influenced by NS forms. Similarly, Schmidt's claim that the formality of realizing interdentals carries over from Arabic to English surely does not pay enough attention to the fact that such sounds are developmentally late (even in first language acquisition) and universally rare. One expects, then (following Kroch's claim concerning the appearance of lesser marked forms at the lower social strata and less formal styles), that the distribution of interdentals in Arabic and English will be the same, and transfer of stylistic preferences may be an unnecessary complication. These matters are treated further in 5.1.

17  Measurement of such attention is problematic, and selection of tasks which promote different degrees of it is an experimental difficulty (e.g., Sato 1985).

18  Though General American English is a dialectological fiction, Purcell here means specific differences between standard spoken English from all parts of the United States and such Hawaiian phenomena as *neva* ('never') for *didn't* and high-falling intonation for yes-no questions (opposed to the usual rising).

19  Silva and Zwicky (1975) is an interesting attempt to establish an implicational hierarchy of such relations, a study which ought to suggest to those who prepare language teaching materials that degrees of distance can be presented with some consistency. Ohashi (1978) is another attempt to provide a systematic account of differences among distance levels.

20  It is odd but not surprising that in varieties of linguistic research which pay no attention to social detail this dyad is taken as a given in the fiction *ideal speaker-hearer*. It would be admittedly difficult to say what an 'ideal overhearer' might be, although rules of communicative competence try to state the norms for behavior in just such roles.

21  Relationships among participants are developed even more elaborately in Goffman (1979), particularly in sections III through VII.

22  Being able to understand but not speak a language has sociolinguistic relevance, however. Sharp (1958), for example, reports on three language groups (Yir Yoront, Koko Bera, and Kut Taiori) in north Queensland in which it is typical for individuals to speak only the language of their own group but to understand one or even both of the others.

## Chapter 4   A taxonomy of language variation

1  This is not exactly true, of course, since fluent readers will often change items to match their own variety (or some other concept they have of what the text should be like), but the resultant variation from such chance occurrences is not usually what the student of language variation is after. In some cases, i.e., when the respondent's variety is far removed from the sample, even a spoken repetition task will result in syntactic alteration away from the model provided:

*Model*: I asked Alvin if he knows how to play basketball.
*Boot*: I ax Alvin do he know how to play basketball.
*Money*: I ax Alvin if–do he know how to play basketball. (Labov 1972b:228)

In addition, some elicitation questionnaires have been devised to get at grammatical elements:

IV Question inversion   This time, you're going to hear the man on the tape say two sentences. The lady is going to put them together. After you hear some examples, you will hear some sentences and we'll see if you can put them together in the same way.

| *Male voice* | *Female voice* |
|---|---|
| A   John told me this.<br>Roy was going home. | John told me that Roy<br>    was going home |
| B   John thinks this.<br>Mary is cute. | John thinks that Mary<br>    is cute. |
| C   John told me this.<br>Go home. | John told me to go<br>    home. |
| etc. . . . | |
| 3   John asked me this.<br>Did the mail come yet?<br>etc. | |
| 8   John asked him this.<br>Where did they go? | |

(Fasold 1972:243)

In this last example, the respondents are being tested to see if they have control of the embedded question inversion rule or will respond with Black English vernacular forms such as 'John asked me did the mail come yet' and 'John asked him where did they go.'

2  This sort of sociolinguistic work above the levels of phonology and morphology obviously appealed to such general linguists as Ross (e.g., 1973), who believed that items might more-or-less rather than categorically belong to a grammatical class such as noun or verb; hence, a noun like 'Carol' is 'nounier' than one like 'there' (as in 'There's a man in the other room') or 'it' (as in 'It's raining').

3  Similar sorts of tests have been carried out contrasting the variation in the learner's interlanguage with NS variation (e.g., Altman (1986), which studies the semantics of *should* and *had better*).

4  I investigated a fairly large number of VARBRUL studies; whenever a social or stylistic probability fell outside the boundaries of the range established by linguistic variables, the system under consideration was always undergoing dramatic change.

5  Kloss also provides minor revisions of Stewart's scheme and some additional classificatory labels.

6  To further confuse matters, dialectologists often refer to a sort of class-like continuum in differentiating among *cultivated*, *common*, and *folk* speech (e.g., Kurath 1949:7).

7  Nine-Curt (1983:43), who apparently believes North Americans are peculiarly

nontactile, sarcastically wonders if the two cases in Gainesville might not have involved Cubans.

8  It is not meant to suggest, however, that these physical characteristics exhaust the possibilities for paralinguistic features. For example, *voice*, discussed later, is obviously another.

9  Two studies of the synchrony of body and speech are Condon and Ogston (1967) and Kendon (1970).

10 A recent study of such synchrony in interaction is Erickson and Shultz (1982).

11 See 3.1.3 for an example of a speaker monitoring an addressee's gaze in determining the construction of a conversation.

12 Such more recent views of reading are discussed in, for example, Smith (1978).

13 Hispanic offices are more status-marked than those in English-speaking North America, but not so much as courtrooms, formal meetings, and so on.

14 This view is rather obviously at odds with Fishman's understanding of NS authority on emic units at every level (1972a:34).

15 In fact, Young does not accurately represent some of Hymes's categories, but that is not the major issue here.

16 Some of Young's respondents are from the People's Republic of China and some are from Taiwan. He may confuse some readers by suggesting that, therefore, some speak *Pǔtōnghuà* and others *Guóyǔ*, but these are simply People's Republic and Taiwanese terms, respectively, for Standard Mandarin. Of course, to the extent that regional differences exist, there might be some cause for concern, but those concerns would more likely have to do with educational experience and other factors than the details of the linguistic system itself.

17 This review comes from an article-length study by Young (Young to appear) which is derived from Young (1988), a much larger presentation that may include details about many of the issues raised here.

**Chapter 5   Sociolinguistics and the learning and teaching of foreign and second languages**

1  Spolsky (1985:274) suggests that there must be as many monitors as there are points on the continuum, but points on the continuum simply have heavier or lighter hands on the monitor control switch.

2  In fact, Tarone (1985) comes very close to articulating this parallelism, but she pays too much attention to Krashen's assertion that the monitor can learn only simple rules and does not notice the parallelism between acquisition and change from below.

3  Tarone now suggests that it was a mistake to state that the stylistically more formal end of the continuum would attract the greatest percentage of correct forms; it would attract the greatest percentage of forms which the learner *believed* to be correct, i.e., the ones stored in his or her superordinate interlanguage system (personal communication).

4  Apologies are made for introducing possibly further confusions of horizontal versus vertical dimensions in sociolinguistic and SLA studies.

5  Cross-sectional studies run the risk of overlooking individual patterns in interlanguage development.

6 Ellis (1987a) would have been an excellent test case to decide whether or not this pattern emerges in other areas since he contrasts regular and irregular past tense forms in English. Unfortunately, any value of this work for quantitatively oriented studies of SLA is vitiated by the fact that (1) he did not count occasions of over-generalization (e.g., *losed*), and (2) he counted only the first occurrence of each verb unless the first instance of it was deviant and the second correct. In this case it was counted twice. Therefore, if there were fourteen occurrences of *ride* + past as *rided*, they would not have been counted at all. Worse, if the verb *walk* occurred twelve times and only the first attempt was correct, the score would reflect categorical accuracy; similarly, if the verb *walk* occurred twelve times, the first time wrong and the remaining eleven correct, the second correct occurrence would have provided only a weight of 50 percent on the entire score.

**Chapter 6   Summing up**

1 This reconciliation does not, however, extend to the essentially psycholinguistic question of the shape of an individual's grammar vis-à-vis the social facts of variation; Bickerton still would argue for separate grammars arranged in an implication scale; Labov would still claim that the individual has an internal var-iable grammar. Guy's (1980) suggestion that one sort of rule or another may be appropriate to the distribution of items according to society type does not resolve the psycholinguistic dimensions of the issue.

2 I mean a somewhat more restricted use of 'variety space' than that given the term in, e.g., Dittmar, Schlobinski, and Wachs (1985).

# References

Abrahams, R. D. and Gay, G. 1972: Talking Black in the classroom. In R. D. Abrahams and R. C. Troike (eds), *Language and Cultural Diversity in American Education*, Englewood Cliffs, NJ: Prentice-Hall, 200–7.

Adamson, H. D. 1980: A study of variable syntactic rules: the interlanguage of Spanish-speaking adults. Washington, DC: Georgetown University PhD dissertation.

Adamson, H. D. 1988: *Variation Theory and Second Language Acquisition*. Washington, DC: Georgetown University Press.

Adjemian, C. 1976: On the nature of interlanguage systems. *Language Learning* 22, 297–320.

Agheyisi, R. and Fishman, J. A. 1970: Language attitude studies: a brief survey of methodological approaches. *Anthropological Linguistics* 12, 131–57.

Akinnaso, F. N. and Ajirotutu, C. S. 1982: Performance and ethnic styles in job interviews. In J. J. Gumperz (ed.), *Language and Social Identity*, Cambridge: University Press, 119–44.

Aleguire, D. G. 1978: Interruptions as turn-taking. Paper presented at the International Sociological Association Ninth World Congress, Uppsala University, Sweden.

Alexander, L. G. 1976: Threshold level and methodology. Supplement to J. A. van Ek, *The Threshold Level for Modern Language Learning in Schools*, London: Longman, 148–65.

Allen, H. B. 1973: Language variation and TESOL. *TESOL Quarterly* 7, 13–23.

Allen, H. B. and Linn, M. (eds). 1986: *Dialect and Language Variation*. New York: Academic.

Alleyne, M. C. 1980: *Comparative Afro-American: An Historical- Comparative Study of English-based Afro-American Dialects of the New World*. Ann Arbor, MI: Karoma.

Allwright, R. 1979: Language learning through communication practice. In C. J. Brumfit and K. Johnson (eds), *The Communicative Approach to Language Teaching*, Oxford: University Press.

Allwright, R. L. 1980: Turns, topics, and tasks: patterns and participation in language learning and teaching. In D. Larsen-Freeman (ed.), *Discourse Analysis in Second Language Research*, Rowley, MA: Newbury House, 165–87.

Altman, H. B. (ed.) 1972: *Individualizing the Foreign Language Classroom*. Rowley, MA: Newbury House.

Altman, R. 1986: Getting the subtle distinctions: *should* versus *had better*. *Studies in Second Language Acquisition* 8, 80–7.

American Law Institute 1974: Restatement of the law, second: Torts (tentative draft no. 20). Philadelphia: American Law Institute.

*American Speech* 1987: 62, no. 1.

Andersen, R. W. 1979: Expanding Schumann's pidginization hypothesis. *Language Learning* 29, 105–19.

Andersen, R. W. (ed.) 1983: *Pidginization and Creolization as Language Acquisition*. Rowley, MA: Newbury House.

Andersson, T. and Boyer, M. 1978: *Bilingual Schooling in the United States* (2nd edn). Austin, TX: National Education Laboratory.

Argyle, M., Furnham, A., and Graham, J. A. 1981: *Social Situations*. Cambridge: University Press.

Aries, E. 1976: Interaction patterns and themes of male, female, and mixed groups. *Small Group Behavior* 7, 7–18.

Ash, S. 1982: The vocalization of intervocalic /l/ in Philadelphia. *The SECOL Review* 6, 162–75.

Asher, J. 1977: *Learning Another Language through Actions*. Los Gatos, CA: Sky Oaks.

Atwood, E. B. 1950: 'Grease' and 'greasy': a study of geographical variation. *Texas Studies in English* 29, 249–60.

Austin, J. L. 1962: *How to Do Things with Words*. Oxford: Clarendon.

Bach, K. and Harnish, R. 1979: *Linguistic Communication and Speech Acts*. Cambridge, MA: MIT Press.

Bailey, C.-J. 1972: The integration of linguistic theory. In R. Stockwell and R. Macauley (eds), *Linguistic Change and Generative Theory*, Bloomington: Indiana University, 22–31.

Bailey, C.-J. 1973: *Variation and Linguistic Theory*. Arlington, VA: Center for Applied Linguistics.

Bailey, K. M. 1983: Competitiveness and anxiety in adult second language learning: looking *at* and *through* the diary studies. In H. W. Seliger and M. H. Long (eds), *Classroom Oriented Research in Second Language Acquisition*, Rowley, MA: Newbury House, 67–102.

Bailey, N. to appear: Theoretical implications of the acquisition of the English simple past and past progressive: putting together the pieces of the puzzle. In S. M. Gass, C. Madden, D. R. Preston, and L. Selinker (eds), *Variation in Second Language Acquisition, Volume 2: Psycholinguistic Issues*, Clevedon, Avon: Multilingual Matters.

Bailey, N., Madden, C., and Krashen, S. 1973: Is there a 'natural sequence' in adult language learning? *Language Learning* 24, 235–43.

Ball, P. and Giles, H. 1982: Do I choose to master your language? *Polycom* 30, 2–6.

Baugh, J. 1979: *Linguistic Style Shifting in Black English*. Philadelphia: University of Pennsylvania PhD dissertation.

Baugh, J. and Sherzer, J. (eds) 1984: *Language in Use: Readings in Sociolinguistics*. Englewood Cliffs, NJ: Prentice-Hall.

Bauman, R. 1977: *Verbal Art as Performance*. Prospect Heights, IL: Waveland.

Beebe, L. 1977a: Dialect code-switching of bilingual children in their second language. *CUNY Forum* 3, 141–58.

Beebe, L. 1977b: The influence of the listener on code-switching. *Language Learning* 27, 331–40.

Beebe, L. 1980: Sociolinguistic variation and style shifting in second language acquisition. *Language Learning* 2, 433–48.

Beebe, L. 1981: Social and situational factors affecting the communicative strategy of dialect code-switching. *International Journal of the Sociology of Language* 32, 139–49.

Beebe, L. 1985: Input: choosing the right stuff. In S. Gass and C. Madden (eds), *Input in Second Language Acquisition*, Rowley, MA: Newbury House, 104–44.

Beebe, L. 1988: Five sociolinguistic approaches to second language acquisition. In L. Beebe (ed.), *Issues in Second Language Acquisition: Multiple Perspectives*, New York: Newbury House, 43–77.

Beebe, L. to appear: *The Social Psychological Basis of Second Language Acquisition*. London: Longman.

Beebe, L. and Takahashi, T. to appear: Do you have a bag?: social status and patterned variation in second language acquisition. In S. M. Gass, C. Madden, D. R. Preston, and L. Selinker (eds), *Variation in Second Language Acquisition, Volume 1: Discourse and Pragmatics*, Clevedon, Avon: Multilingual Matters.

Beebe, L., Takahashi, T. and Uliss-Weltz, R. in press: Pragmatic transfer in ESL refusals. In R. Scarcella, E. Andersen, and S. Krashen (eds), *On the Development of Communicative Competence in a Second Language*, Rowley, MA: Newbury House.

Beebe, L. and Zuengler, J. 1983: Accommodation theory: an explanation for style shifting in second language dialects. In N. Wolfson and E. Judd (eds), *Sociolinguistics and Language Acquisition*, Rowley, MA: Newbury House, 195–213.

Bell, A. 1984: Language style as audience design. *Language and Society* 13, 145–204.

Benedict, R. 1934: *Patterns of Culture*. New York: Mentor.

Benton, R. 1964: *Research into the English Language Difficulties of Maori School Children, 1963–64*. Wellington: Maori Education Foundation.

Berdan, R. H. 1975: *On the Nature of Linguistic Variation*. Austin: University of Texas PhD dissertation.

Bereiter, C. and Engelmann, S. 1966: *Teaching Disadvantaged Children in the Pre-school*. Englewood Cliffs, NJ: Prentice- Hall.

Berger, C. R. and Bradac, J. J. 1982: *Language and Social Knowledge: Uncertainty in Interpersonal Relations*. London: Arnold.

Berkowitz, D. 1979: Grammatical intuitions of second language learners: implications for placement tests. Paper presented at the NYS ESOL/BEA Annual Conference, Buffalo, NY.

Berk-Seligson, S. 1986: Linguistic constraints on intrasentential code-switching: a study of Spanish/Hebrew bilingualism. *Language and Society* 15, 313–48.

Berman, R. A. 1986: A crosslinguistic perspective: morphology and syntax. In P. Fletcher and M. Garman (eds), *Language Acquisition* (2nd edn), Cambridge: University Press, 429–47.

Bernstein, B. 1972: A sociolinguistic approach to socialization; with some reference to educability. In J. J. Gumperz and D. Hymes (eds), *Directions in Sociolinguistics: The Ethnography of Communication*, New York: Holt, Rinehart and Winston, 465–97.

Berryman, C. L. 1980: Attitudes towards male and female sex- appropriate and sex-inappropriate language. In C. L. Berryman and V. A. Eman (eds), *Communication, Language and Sex*, Rowley, MA: Newbury House, 195–216.

Berwick, R. C. and Weinberg, A. S. 1986: *The Grammatical Basis of Linguistic Performance*. Cambridge, MA: MIT Press.

Bialystok, E. 1981: The role of linguistic knowledge in second language use. *Studies in Second Language Acquisition* 4, 31–45.

Bialystok, E. 1982: On the relationship between knowing and using forms. *Applied Linguistics* 3, 181–206.

Bialystok, E. 1984: Strategies in interlanguage learning and performance. In A. Davies and C. Criper (eds), *Interlanguage: Proceedings of the Seminar in Honour of Pit Corder*, Edinburgh: Edinburgh University Press.

Bickerton, D. 1971: Inherent variability and variable rules. *Foundations of Language* 7, 457–92.

Bickerton, D. 1975: *Dynamics of a Creole System*. Cambridge: University Press.

Bickerton, D. 1977: *Change and Variation in Hawaiian English. Volume II*. Final Report on NSF Grant GS-39748. Honolulu: Social Sciences and Linguistics Institute, University of Hawaii at Manoa.

Bickerton, D. 1981: *Roots of Language*. Ann Arbor, MI: Karoma.

Bickerton, D. 1983: Comments on Valdman's 'Creolization and second language acquisition.' In R. W. Andersen (ed.), *Pidginization and Creolization as Language Acquisition*, Rowley, MA: Newbury House, 235–40.

Bickerton, D. and Givón, T. 1976: Pidginization and syntactic change: from SXV and VSX to SVX. In *Papers from the Parasession on Diachronic Syntax*, Chicago: Chicago Linguistic Society.

Bickerton, D. and Odo, C. 1976: *Change and Variation in Hawaiian English, Volume I: General Phonology and Pidgin Syntax*. Final Report on NSF Grant GS-39748. Honolulu: Social Sciences and Linguistics Institute, University of Hawaii at Manoa.

Birdwhistle, R. 1970: *Kinesics and Contexts*. Philadelphia: University of Pennsylvania Press.

Bley-Vroman, R. and Selinker, L. 1984: Research design in rhetorical/grammatical studies: a proposed optimal research strategy. *English for Specific Purposes* 82/83, 1–4 (part 1); 84, 1–6 (part 2).

Blom, J.-P. and Gumperz, J. J. 1972: Social meaning in linguistic structure: code-switching in Norway. In J. J. Gumperz and D. H. Hymes (eds), *Directions in Sociolinguistics: The Ethnography of Communication*, New York: Holt, Rinehart and Winston, 407–34.

Bloomfield, L. 1933: *Language*. New York: Holt, Rinehart and Winston.

Blum-Kulka, S. 1982: Learning to say what you mean in a second language: a study of the speech act performance of learners of Hebrew as a second language. *Applied Linguistics* 3, 29–59.

Blum-Kulka, S. and Olshtain, E. 1984: Requests and apologies: a cross-cultural study of speech act realization patterns. *Applied Linguistics* 5, 196–213.

Blum-Kulka, S. and Olshtain, E. 1986: Too many words: length of utterance and pragmatic failure. *Studies in Second Language Acquisition* 8, 165–79.

Boissevain, J. 1974: *Friends of Friends: Networks, Manipulators and Coalitions*. Oxford: Blackwell.

Boissevain, J. and Mitchell, J. C. (eds) 1973: *Network Analysis: Studies in Human Interaction*. The Hague: Mouton.

Bortoni-Ricardo, S. M. 1985: *The Urbanization of Rural Dialect Speakers: A Sociolinguistic Study in Brazil*. Cambridge: University Press.

Bowen, J. D. 1975: *Patterns of English Pronunciation*. Rowley, MA: Newbury House.

Bransford, J. D. and Johnson, M. K. 1973: Considerations of some problems of comprehension. In W. G. Chase (ed.), *Visual Information Processing*, New York: Academic.

Breen, M. P. 1985: The social context for language learning – a neglected situation? *Studies in Second Language Acquisition* 7, 135–58.

Brennan, E. M., Ryan, E. B., and Dawson, W. E. 1975: Scaling of apparent accentedness by magnitude estimation and sensory modality matching. *Journal of Psycholinguistic Research* 4, 27–36.

Brouwer, D., Gerritsen, M., and Dettaan, D. 1979: Speech differences between women and men: on the wrong track? *Language in Society* 8, 33–50.

Brown, C. 1985: Requests for specific language input: differences between older and younger adult language learners. In S. M. Gass and C. Madden (eds), *Input in Second Language Acquisition*, Rowley, MA: Newbury House, 272–81.

Brown, G. and Yule, G. 1983: *Discourse Analysis*. Cambridge: University Press.

Brown, H. D. 1980: *Principles of Language Learning and Teaching*. Englewood Cliffs, NJ: Prentice-Hall.

Brown, P. 1980: How and why are women more polite: some evidence from a Mayan community. In S. McConnell-Ginet, R. Borker, and N. Furman (eds), *Women and Language in Literature and Society*, New York: Praeger, 111–36.

Brown, P. and Fraser, C. 1979: Speech markers of situation. In K. R. Scherer and H. Giles (eds), *Social Markers in Speech*, Cambridge: University Press.

Brown, P. and Levinson, S. 1978: Universals in language usage: politeness phenomena. In E. N. Goody (ed.), *Questions and Politeness: Strategies in Social Interaction*, Cambridge: University Press, 56–289.

Brown, R. and Gilman, R. 1960: The pronouns of power and solidarity. In T. A. Sebeok (ed.), *Style in Language*, Cambridge, MA: MIT Press, 253–76.

Brukman, J. 1975: Tongue play: constitutive and interpretive properties of sexual joking encounters among the Koya of south India. In M. Sanches and B. G. Blount (eds), *Sociocultural Dimensions of Language Use*, New York: Academic, 235–68.

Burling, R. 1970: *Man's Many Voices: Language in its Cultural Context*. New York: Holt, Rinehart and Winston.

Burstall, C., Jamieson, M., Cohen, S., and Hargreaves, M. 1974: *Primary French in the Balance*. Slough: National Foundation for Educational Research.

Byers, P. and Byers, H. 1972: Nonverbal communication and the education of children. In C. B. Cazden, V. P. John, and D. Hymes (eds), *Functions of Language in the Classroom*, New York: Teachers College Press, 3–31.

Candlin, C., Leather, J., and Bruton, C. 1976: Doctors in casualty: applying communicative competence to components of specialist course design. *International Review of Applied Linguistics* 14, 245–72.

Carrell, P. 1979: Indirect speech acts in ESL: indirect answers. In C. Yorio, K. Perkins, and J. Schachter (eds), *On TESOL '79: The Learner in Focus*, Washington, DC: TESOL, 297–307.

Carroll, J. 1963: The prediction of success in intensive foreign language training. In R. Glaser (ed.), *Training Research and Education*, Pittsburgh: University Press, 87–136.

Cathcart-Strong, R. L. 1986: Input generation by young second language learners. *TESOL Quarterly* 20, 515–30.

Cazden, C. B., John, V. P., and Hymes, D. H. (eds) 1972: *Functions of Language in the Classroom*. New York: Teachers College Press.

Chafe, W. 1986: Writing in the perspective of speaking. In C. R. Cooper and S. Greenbaum (eds), *Studying Writing: Linguistic Approaches*, Beverly Hills: Sage, 12–39.

Chambers, J. K. and Trudgill, P. 1980: *Dialectology*. Cambridge: University Press.

Chastain, K. 1975: Affective and ability factors in second language learning. *Language Learning* 25, 153–61.

Chen, M. and Hsieh, H.-I. 1971: The time variable in phonological change. *Journal of Linguistics* 7, 1–14.

Chen, M. and Wang, W. S.-Y. 1975: Sound change: actuation and implementation. *Language* 51, 255–81.

Chiu, R. K. 1972: Measuring register characteristics: a prerequisite for preparing advanced level TESOL programs. *TESOL Quarterly* 6, 129–41.

Chomsky, N. 1966: Linguistic theory. In R. G. Mead, Jr (ed.), *Reports of the Working Committees*, Northeast Conference on the Teaching of Foreign Languages.

Chomsky, N. 1981: *Lectures on Government and Binding*. Dordrecht: Foris.

Chomsky, N. 1982: *Some Concepts and Consequences of the Theory of Government and Binding*. Cambridge, MA: MIT Press.

Chomsky, N. 1986: *Barriers*. Cambridge, MA: MIT Press.

Claire, E. 1980: *A Foreign Student's Guide to Dangerous English*. Rochelle Park, NJ: Eardley.

Claire, E. 1984: *What's So Funny: A Foreign Student's Guide to American Humor*. Rochelle Park, NJ: Eardley.

Clément, R. 1980: Ethnicity, contact and communicative competence in a second language. In H. Giles, W. P. Robinson, and P. M. Smith (eds), *Language: Social Psychological Perspectives*, Oxford: Pergamon.

Coates, J. 1986: *Women, Men and Language*. London and New York: Longman.

Coffey, M. P. 1983: *Fitting In: A Functional/Notional Text for Learners of English*. Englewood Cliffs, NJ: Prentice-Hall.

Cohen, A. and Olshtain, E. 1981: Developing a measure of sociocultural competence: the case of apology. *Language Learning* 31, 113–34.

Condon, J. C. and Yousef, F. 1975: *An Introduction to Intercultural Communication*. Indianapolis, IN: Bobbs-Merrill.

Condon, W. C. and Ogston, W. D. 1967: A segmentation of behavior. *Journal of Psychiatric Research* 5, 21–35.

Connor, C. 1987: Research frontiers in writing analysis. *TESOL Quarterly* 21, 677–96.

Cook, V. 1977: Cognitive processes in second language learning. *International Review of Applied Linguistics* 15, 1–20.

Cook, V. 1985: Universal grammar and second language learning. *Applied Linguistics* 6, 2–18.

Cooper, C. 1985: Aspects of article introductions in IEEE publications. Aston, England: Aston University MSc dissertation.

Corder, S. P. 1967: The significance of learners' errors. *International Review of Applied Linguistics* 4, 161–70.

Corder, S. P. 1971: Idiosyncratic dialects and error analysis. *International Review of Applied Linguistics* 9, 147–60.

Corder, S. P. 1977: Language continua and the interlanguage hypothesis. In S. P. Corder and E. Roulet (eds), *Actes du 5ème Colloque de Linguistique Appliquée de Neuchâtel: The Notions of Simplification, Interlanguages and Pidgins and their Relation to Second Language Pedagogy*, Geneva: Droz, 11–17.

Coulmas, F. 1981: *Conversational Routines*. The Hague: Mouton.

Coulthard, M. 1977: *An Introduction to Discourse Analysis*. London: Longman.

Crow, B. K. 1983: Topic shifts in couples' conversations. In R. T. Craig and K. Tracy (eds), *Conversational Coherence: Form, Structure, and Strategy*, Beverly Hills: Sage.

Crystal, D. and Davy, D. 1969: *Investigating English Style*. London: Longman.

Darwin, C. 1872: *The Expression of Emotions in Man and Animals*. London: John Murray.

Davis, F. 1975: *Inside Intuition*. New York: Signet.

Davis, L. M. 1982: American social dialectology: a statistical appraisal. *American Speech* 57, 83–94.

Davis, L. M. 1983: *English Dialectology: An Introduction*. University, AL: University of Alabama.

Day, R. R. 1980: The development of linguistic attitudes and preferences. *TESOL Quarterly* 14, 27–37.

Day, R. R. (ed.) 1986. *Talking to Learn*. Rowley, MA: Newbury House.

Dickerson, L. J. 1974: *Internal and External Patterning of Phonological Variability in the Speech of Japanese Learners of English: Toward a Theory of Second-language Acquisition*. Champaign-Urbana: University of Illinois PhD dissertation.

Dickerson, L. J. 1975: The learner's interlanguage as a system of variable rules. *TESOL Quarterly* 9, 401–7.

Dickerson, L. J. and Dickerson, W. B. 1977: Interlanguage phonology: current research and future directions. In S. P. Corder and E. Roulet (eds), *Actes du 5ème Colloque de Linguistique Appliquée de Neuchâtel, The Notions of Simplification, Interlanguages and Pidgins and their Relation to Second Language Pedagogy*, Geneva: Droz, 18–30.

Dickerson, W. B. 1976: The psycholinguistic unity of language learning and language change. *Language Learning* 26, 215–31.

Dittmar, N., Schlobinski, P., and Wachs, I. 1985: *Studies in the Urban Berlin Vernacular*. Berlin: de Gruyter.

Dorian, N. 1980: *Language Death: The Life Cycle of a Scottish Gaelic Dialect*. Philadelphia: University of Pennsylvania Press.

Douglas-Cowie, E. 1978: Linguistic code-switching in a Northern Irish village: social interaction and social ambition. In P. Trudgill (ed.), *Sociolinguistic Patterns in British English*, London: Arnold, 37–51.

Downes, W. 1984: *Language and Society*. London: Fontana.

Duff, P. A. 1986: Another look at interlanguage talk: taking task to task. In R. R. Day (ed.), *Talking to Learn*, Rowley, MA: Newbury House, 147–81.

Dulay, H. and Burt, M. 1973: Should we teach children syntax? *Language Learning* 23, 245–58.

Dulay, H. and Burt, M. 1977: Remarks on creativity in language acquisition. In M.

Burt, H. Dulay, and M. Finocchiaro (eds), *Viewpoints on English as a Second Language*, New York: Regents, 95–126.

Dulay, H., Burt, M., and Krashen, S. 1982: *Language 2*. Oxford: University Press.

Dundes, A., Leach, J. W., and Özkök, B. 1972: The strategy of Turkish boys' verbal dueling rhymes. In J. J. Gumperz and D. H. Hymes (eds), *Directions in Sociolinguistics: The Ethnography of Communication*, New York: Holt, Rinehart and Winston, 130–60.

Easling, J. H. 1981: Methods in voice quality research in dialect surveys. In H. J. Warkentyne (ed.), *Methods/Méthodes IV*, Papers from the Fourth International Conference on Methods in Dialectology, Victoria, BC: Department of Linguistics, University of Victoria, 126–38.

Edwards, J. 1985: *Language, Society and Identity*. Oxford: Blackwell.

Eibl-Eibesfeldt, I. 1974: Similarities and differences between cultures in expressive movements. In S. Weitz (ed.), *Nonverbal Communication*, New York: Oxford, 269–90.

Eisenstein, M. 1982: A study of social variation in adult second language acquisition. *Language Learning* 32, 367–91.

Eisenstein, M. 1983: Native reactions to non-native speech: a review of empirical research. *Studies in Second Language Acquisition* 5, 160–76.

Eisenstein, M., Bailey, N., and Madden, C. 1982: It takes two: contrasting tasks and contrasting structures. *TESOL Quarterly* 16, 381–93.

Eisenstein, M. and Berkowitz, D. 1981: The effect of phonological variation on adult learner comprehension. *Studies in Second Language Acquisition* 4, 75–80.

Eisenstein, M. and Bodman, J. 1986: 'I very appreciate': expressions of gratitude by native and non-native speakers of American English. *Applied Linguistics* 7, 167–85.

Eisenstein, M. and Starbuck, R. to appear: The effect of emotional investment on L2 production. In S. M. Gass, C. Madden, D. R. Preston, and L. Selinker (eds), *Variation in Second Language Acquisition, Volume 2: Psycholinguistic Issues*, Clevedon, Avon: Multilingual Matters.

Eisenstein, M. and Verdi, G. 1985: The intelligibility of social dialects for working-class adult learners of English. *Language Learning* 35, 287–98.

Ekman, P., Friesen, W. V., and Ellsworth, P. 1972: *Emotions in the Human Face*. New York: Pergamon.

Ellis, R. 1984: *Classroom Second Language Development*. Oxford: Pergamon.

Ellis, R. 1985a: *Understanding Second Language Acquisition*. Oxford University Press.

Ellis, R. 1985b: Sources of variability in interlanguage. *Applied Linguistics* 6, 118–31.

Ellis, R. 1987a: Interlanguage variability in narrative discourse: style shifting in the use of the past tense. *Studies in Second Language Acquisition* 9, 1–20.

Ellis, R. 1987b: Contextual variability in second language acquisition and the relevancy of language teaching. In R. Ellis (ed.), *Second Language Acquisition in Context*, Englewood Cliffs, NJ: Prentice-Hall, 179–94.

Ellis, R. to appear: Sources of intra-learner variability in language use and their relationship to second language acquisition. In S. M. Gass, C. Madden, D. R. Preston, and L. Selinker (eds), *Variation in Second Language Acquisition, Volume 2: Psycholinguistic Issues*, Clevedon, Avon: Multilingual Matters.

Ellis, R. and Roberts, C. 1987: Two approaches for investigating second language acquisition in context. In R. Ellis (ed.), *Second Language Acquisition in Context*, Englewood Cliffs, NJ: Prentice-Hall, 3–29.

Elyan, O., Smith, P. M., Giles, H., and Bourhis, R. 1978: RP accented female speech: the voice of perceived androgyny? In P. Trudgill (ed.), *Sociolinguistic Patterns in British English*, London: Arnold, 122–31.

Erickson, F. and Shultz, J. 1982: *The Counselor as Gatekeeper: Social Interaction in Interviews*. New York: Academic.

Ervin-Tripp, S. M. 1971: Sociolinguistics. In J. Fishman (ed.), *Advances in the Sociology of Language I*, The Hague: Mouton, 15–91.

Ervin-Tripp, S. M. 1973a: Children's sociolinguistic competence and dialect diversity. In A. S. Dil (ed.), *Language Acquisition and Communicative Choice: Essays by Susan M. Ervin-Tripp*, Stanford: University Press, 262–301. Reprinted from I. J. Gordon (ed.), *Early Childhood Education: The Seventy-First Yearbook of the National Society for Education*, Chicago: University Press, 1972, 123–60.

Ervin-Tripp, S. M. 1973b: An analysis of the interaction of language, topic, and listener. In A. S. Dil (ed.), *Language Acquisition and Communicative Choice*, Stanford: University Press, 239–61. Reprinted from *American Anthropologist* 66, part 2, 1964, *The Ethnography of Communication*, eds J. J. Gumperz and D. H. Hymes, 86–102.

Ervin-Tripp, S. M. 1979: Children's verbal turn-taking. In E. Ochs and B. Schieffelin (eds), *Developmental Pragmatics*, New York: Academic, 391–414.

Espinosa, A. M. 1917: Speech mixture in New Mexico: the influence of the English language on New Mexican speech. In H. M. Stephens and H. E. Bolton (eds), *The Pacific Ocean in History*, New York: MacMillan, 408–28.

Faerch, C. 1980: Describing interlanguage through interaction: problems of systematicity and permeability. *Working Papers on Bilingualism* 19, 59–78.

Faggion, C. M. 1982. Atitudes em relacão a dialetos regionais. Porto Alegre: Instituto de Letras, Universidade Federal do Rio Grande do Sul, seminar paper.

Fairbanks, K. 1982: Variability in interlanguage. Minneapolis: ESL Program, University of Minnesota.

Fanslowe, J. F. 1977: Beyond *Rashomon* – conceptualizing and describing the teaching act. *TESOL Quarterly* 11, 17–39.

Fasold, R. W. 1972: *Tense Marking in Black English* Arlington, VA: Center for Applied Linguistics.

Fasold, R. W. 1973: The Bailey wave model: a dynamic quantitative paradigm. In R. W. Fasold and R. W. Shuy (eds), *Analyzing Variation in Language*, Washington, DC: Georgetown University Press, 27–58.

Fasold, R. W. 1984: Variation theory and langauge learning. In P. Trudgill (ed.), *Applied Sociolinguistics*, London: Academic, 245–61.

Fasold, R. W. 1985: Microcomputer VARBRUL 2 system: CP/M version, Washington, DC: Georgetown University, Department of Linguistics, unpublished manuscript.

Feagin, C. 1987: A closer look at the southern drawl: variation taken to extremes. In K. M. Denning, S. Inkelas, F. C. McNair-Knox, and J. R. Rickford (eds), *Variation in Language: NWAV-XV at Stanford*, Stanford: Department of Linguistics, Stanford University, 137–50.

Felix, S. 1977: How reliable are experimental data? Paper presented to the 11th Annual TESOL Convention, Miami Beach.

Felix, S. (ed.) 1980a: *Second Language Development: Trends and Issues*. Tübingen: Narr.

Felix, S. 1980b: The effect of formal instruction on second language acquisition. Paper presented to the Second Language Research Forum, Los Angeles, March.

Felix, S. 1984: Two problems of language acquisition: the relevance of grammatical studies in the theory of interlanguage. In A. Davies and C. Criper (eds), *Interlanguage: Proceedings of the Seminar in Honour of Pit Corder*, Edinburgh: Edinburgh University Press.

Ferguson, C. 1959: Diglossia. *Word*, 15, 325–40.

Ferguson, C. 1971: Absence of copula and the notion of simplicity: a study of normal speech, baby talk, foreigner talk, and pidgins. In D. Hymes (ed.), *Pidginization and Creolization of Languages*, Cambridge: University Press, 141–50.

Fiksdal, S. to appear: Framing uncomfortable moments in cross- cultural gatekeeping interviews. In S. M. Gass, C. Madden, D. R. Preston, and L. Selinker (eds), *Variation in Second Language Acquisition, Volume 1: Discourse and Pragmatics*, Clevedon, Avon: Multilingual Matters.

Fillmore, C. 1979: On fluency. In C. Fillmore, D. Kempler, and W. Wang (eds), *Individual Differences in Language Ability and Language Behavior*, New York: Academic, 85–101.

Finocchiaro, M. and Brumfit, C. 1983: *The Functional-Notional Approach: From Theory to Practice*. Oxford: University Press.

Fischer, J. 1958: Social influence in the choice of a linguistic variant. *Word* 14, 47–56.

Fishman, J. A. 1964: Language maintenance and language shift as fields of inquiry. *Linguistics* 9, 32–70.

Fishman, J. A. 1966: *Language Loyalty in the United States*. The Hague: Mouton.

Fishman, J. A. 1972a: *The Sociology of Language: An Interdisciplinary Social Science Approach to Language and Society*. Rowley, MA: Newbury House.

Fishman, J. A. 1972b (1971): The relationship between micro- and macro- sociolinguistics in the study of who speaks what language to whom and when. In A. S. Dil (ed.), *Language in Sociocultural Change: Essays by Joshua A. Fishman*, Stanford: University Press, 244–67. Reprinted from J. A. Fishman, R. L. Cooper, R. Ma, et al. (eds), *Bilingualism in the Barrio*, Bloomington: Indiana University Language Science Monograph Series, no. 7, 1971.

Fishman, R. L. (ed.) 1975: *Advances in Language Planning*. The Hague: Mouton.

Fishman, J. A., Cooper, R. L., Ma, R., et al. (eds) 1971: *Bilingualism in the Barrio*. Bloomington: Indiana University Language Science Monograph Series, no. 7.

Fishman, J. A., Ferguson, C. A., and Das Gupta, J. (eds). 1968: *Language Problems of Developing Nations*. New York: Wiley.

Fishman, J. A. and Greenfield, L. 1970: Situational measures of normative language views in relation to person, place and topic among Puerto Rican bilinguals. *Anthropos* 65, 602–18.

Fishman, P. M. 1978: What do couples talk about when they're alone? In D. Butturff and E. L. Epstein (eds), *Women's Language and Style*, Akron, OH: L & S Books, 11–22.

Fishman, P. M. 1980: Conversational insecurity. In H. Giles, W. P. Robinson, and P. M. Smith (eds), *Language: Social Psychological Perspectives*, Oxford: Pergamon, 127–32.

Forgas, J. P. 1976: The perception of social episodes: categorical and dimensional representations in two different social milieux. *Journal of Personality and Social Psychology* 34, 199–209.

Fox, J. J. 1974: 'Our ancestors spoke in pairs': Rotinese views of language, dialect, and code. In R. Bauman and J. Sherzer (eds), *Explorations in the Ethnography of Speaking*, Cambridge: University Press, 65–85.

Frake, C. O. 1972: 'Struck by speech': the Yakan concept of litigation. In J. J. Gumperz and D. H. Hymes (eds), *Directions in Sociolinguistics: The Ethnography of Communication*, New York: Holt, Rinehart and Winston, 106–29.

Francis, N. W. 1983: *Dialectology: An Introduction*. London: Longman.

Fraser, B. 1983: The domain of pragmatics. In J. C. Richards and R. W. Schmidt (eds), *Language and Communication*, London: Longman, 29–59.

Frawley, W. 1987: Review article of T. A. van Dijk (ed.), *Handbook of Discourse Analysis* (I–IV), Orlando: Academic. *Language* 63, 361–97.

Friedrich, P. 1972: Social context and semantic feature: the Russian pronominal usage. In J. J. Gumperz and D. H. Hymes (eds), *Directions in Sociolinguistics: The Ethnography of Communication*, New York: Holt, Rinehart and Winston, 270–300.

Futrell, A. 1981: Introduction. In D. W. Maurer, *Language of the Underworld*, Lexington: University of Kentucky, 1–12.

Gal, S. 1979: *Language Shift: Social Determinants of Linguistic Change in Bilingual Austria*. New York: Academic.

Gardner, P. M. 1966: Symmetric respect and memorate knowledge: the structure and ecology of individualistic culture. *Southwestern Journal of Anthropology* 22, 389–415.

Gardner, R. C. 1985: *Social Psychology and Second Language Learning: The Role of Attitudes and Motivation*. London: Arnold.

Gardner, R. C. and Lambert, W. E. 1959: Motivational variables in second language acquisition. *Canadian Journal of Psychology* 13, 266–72.

Gardner, R. C. 1972: *Attitudes and Motivation in Second-Language Learning*. Rowley, MA: Newbury House.

Gardner, R. C., Smythe, P., Clément, R., and Gliksman, L. 1976: Second language learning: a social-psychological perspective. *Canadian Modern Language Review* 32, 198–213.

Garfinkel, H. 1967: *Studies in Ethnomethodology*. Englewood Cliffs, NJ: Prentice-Hall.

Garner, W. R. 1962: *On Certainty and Structure as Psychological Concepts*. New York: Wiley.

Garvin, P. 1959: The standard language problem: concepts and methods. *Anthropological Linguistics* 1, 28–31.

Garvin, P. and Mathiot, M. 1956: The urbanization of the Guarani language: a problem in language and culture. In A. Wallace (ed.), *Men and Cultures*, Philadelphia: University of Pennsylvania Press.

Gass, S. M. 1984: The empirical basis for the universal hypothesis in interlanguage studies. In A. Davies and C. Criper (eds), *Interlanguage: Proceedings of the Seminar in Honour of Pit Corder*, Edinburgh: Edinburgh University Press.

Gass, S. M. and Madden, C. (eds) 1985: *Input in Second Language Acquisition*. Rowley, MA: Newbury House.

Gass, S. M. and Selinker, L. (eds) 1983: *Language Transfer in Language Learning*. Rowley, MA: Newbury House.

Gass, S. M. and Varonis, E. M. 1985: Task variation and NNS/NNS negotiation of meaning. In S. M. Gass and C. Madden (eds), *Input in Second Language Acquisition*, Rowley, MA: Newbury House.

Gass, S. M. and Varonis, E. M. 1986: Sex differences in nonnative speaker – nonnative speaker interactions. In R. R. Day (ed.), *Talking to Learn: Conversation in Second Language Acquisition*, Rowley, MA: Newbury House, 327–51.

Gatbonton, E. 1978: Patterned phonetic variability in second language speech: a gradual diffusion model. *Canadian Modern Language Review/La Revue Canadienne des Langue Vivantes* 34, 335–47.

Gauchat, L. 1905: L'unité phonetique dans le patois d'une commune. In *Aus Romanischen Sprachen und Literaturen: Festschrift Heinrich Mort*, Halle: Max Niemeyer, 175–232.

Giles, H. 1979: Ethnicity markers in speech. In K. R. Scherer and H. Giles (eds), *Social Markers in Speech*, Cambridge: University Press, 251–90.

Giles, H., Bourhis, R. Y., and Taylor, D. M. 1977: Towards a theory of language in ethnic group relations. In H. Giles (ed.), *Language, Ethnicity and Intergroup Relations*, London: Academic, 307–48.

Giles, H. and Byrne, J. L. 1982: An intergroup approach to second language acquisition. *Journal of Multilingual and Multicultural Development* 1, 17–40.

Giles, H. and Marsh, P. 1979: Perceived masculinity and accented speech. *Language Sciences* 1, 301–15.

Giles, H. and Powesland, P. F. 1975: *Speech Styles and Evaluation*. London: Academic.

Giles, H. and Smith, P. M. 1979: Accommodation theory: optimal levels of convergence. In H. Giles and R. N. St Clair (eds), *Language and Social Psychology*, Oxford: Blackwell, 45–65.

Giles, H., Smith, P. M., Ford, B., Condor, S., and Thakerar, J. 1980: Speech style and the fluctuating saliency of sex. *Language Sciences* 2, 260–82.

Godard, D. 1977: Same setting, different norms: phone call beginnings in France and the United States. *Language in Society* 6, 209–19.

Goffman, E. 1969: *Strategic Interaction*. Philadelphia: University of Pennsylvania Press.

Goffman, E. 1974: *Frame Analysis*. New York: Harper and Row.

Goffman, E. 1976: Replies and responses. *Language in Society* 5, 257–314.

Goffman, E. 1979: Footing. *Semiotica* 25, 1–29.

Goffman, E. 1981: *Forms of Talk*. Philadelphia: University of Pennsylvania Press.

Goldberg, J. 1978: Amplitude shift in conversation. In J. Schenkein (ed.), *Studies in the Organization of Conversational Interaction*, New York: Academic, 199–218.

Goldstein, L. M. 1987: Standard English: the only target for nonnative speakers of English? *TESOL Quarterly* 21, 417–36.

Goodwin, C. 1981: *Conversational Organization*. New York: Academic.

Green, J. R. 1971: A focus report: kinesics in the foreign-language classroom. *Foreign Language Annals* 5, 62–8.

Gregg, K. R. 1984: Krashen's monitor and Occam's razor. *Applied Linguistics* 5, 79–101.

Gregory, M. 1967: Aspects of varieties differentiation. *Journal of Linguistics* 3, 177–98.

Grice, H. P. 1975: Logic and conversation. In P. Cole and J. L. Morgan (eds), *Syntax and Semantics 3: Speech Acts*, New York: Academic, 41–58 (reduced version of William James Lectures, Harvard University, 1967).

Gumperz, J. J. 1972: Introduction. In J. J. Gumperz and D. Hymes (eds), *Directions in Sociolinguistics: The Ethnography of Communication*, New York: Holt, Rinehart and Winston, 1–25.

Gumperz, J. J. 1977: Sociocultural knowledge in conversational inferences. In M. Saville-Troike (ed.), *Linguistics and Anthropology*, Washington, DC: Georgetown University Press, 191–211.

Gumperz, J. J. 1982: *Discourse Strategies*. Cambridge: University Press.

Guy, G. 1980: Variation in the group and the individual: the case of final stop deletion. In W. Labov (ed.), *Locating Language in Time and Space*, New York: Academic, 1–36.

Haas, M. 1957: Interlingual word taboo. *American Anthropologist* 53, 338–41.

Hall, E. T. 1959: *The Silent Language*. New York: Doubleday.

Hall, E. T. 1966: *The Hidden Dimension*. New York: Doubleday.

Hall, R. A., Jr 1966: *Pidgin and Creole Languages*. Ithaca: Cornell University.

Halliday, M. A. K. and Hasan, R. 1976: *Cohesion in English*. London: Longman.

Hallowell, A. I. 1964: Ojibwa ontology, behavior and world view. In S. Diamond (ed.), *Primitive Views of the World*, New York: Columbia University, 49–82.

Halpern, G., MacNab, G. L., Kirby, D. M., Tuong, T. T., Martin, J. C., Hendleman, T. and Tourigny, R. 1976: *Alternative Schools Programs for French Language Learning.* Toronto: Ontario Ministry of Education.

Hancher, M. 1979: The classification of co-operative illocutionary acts. *Language and Society* 8, 1–14.

Harris, J. 1987: Towards a lexical analysis of sound change in progress. In K. M. Denning, S. Inkelas, F. C. McNair-Knox, and J. R. Rickford (eds), *Variation in Language: NWAV-XV at Stanford*, Stanford: Department of Linguistics, Stanford University, 183–96.

Hartford, B. S. 1976: Phonological differences in the English of adolescent Chicanas and Chicanos. In B. L. Dubois and I. Crouch (eds), *The Sociology of the Languages of American Women*, San Antonio: Trinity University, 73–80.

Hartogs, R. 1967: *Four-Letter Word Games: The Psychology of Obscenity*. New York: Dell.

Hatch, E. M. 1978: Discourse analysis and second language acquisition. In E. M. Hatch (ed.), *Second Language Acquisition: A Book of Readings*, Rowley, MA: Newbury House, 401–35.

Hatch, E. M. 1983: *Psycholinguistics: A Second Language Perspective*. Rowley, MA: Newbury House.

Haugen, E. 1956: *Bilingualism in the Americas: A Bibliography and Research Guide*. Gainesville, FL: The American Dialect Society. (reissued by the University of Alabama Press, 1964).

Heath, S. B. 1983: *Ways with Words*. Cambridge: University Press.

Heidelberger Forschungsprojekt 'Pidgin-Deutsch' 1975: *Sprache und Kommunikation ausländischer Arbeiter*. Kronberg (Ts): Scriptor.

Heidelberger Forschungsprojekt 'Pidgin-Deutsch' 1978: The acquisition of German syntax by foreign migrant workers. In D. Sankoff (ed.), *Language Variation: Models and Methods*, New York: Academic, 1–22.

Hellinger, M. 1980: 'For men must work, and women must weep': sexism in English language textbooks used in German schools. In C. Kramarae (ed.), *The Voices and Words of Women and Men*, Oxford: Pergamon, 267–75.

HELP (Hawaii English Language Program) 1979: Student journal. Honolulu: University of Hawaii at Manoa (cited in Preston 1981a and b).

Hewitt, R. 1982: White adolescent creole users and the politics of friendship. *Journal of Multilingual and Multicultural Development* 3, 217–32.

Hilpert, F. P., Kramer, C., and Clark, R. A. 1975: Participant's perceptions of self and partner in mixed-sex dyads. *Central States Speech Journal* 26, 52–6.

Hockett, C. F. 1950: Age-grading and linguistic continuity. *Language* 26, 449–57.

Hoenigswald, H. 1966: A proposal for the study of folk- linguistics. In W. Bright (ed.), *Sociolinguistics*, The Hague: Mouton, 16–20.

Holmes, J. 1984: Hedging your bets and sitting on the fence: some evidence for hedges as support structures. *Te Reo* 27, 47–62.

Huang, J. A. 1970: Chinese child's acquisition of English syntax. Los Angeles: UCLA MA-TESOL thesis..

Huebner, T. 1981: Creative construction and the case of the misguided pattern. In J. Fisher, M. Clarke, and J. Schachter (eds), *On TESOL '80: Building Bridges*, Washington, DC: TESOL.

Huebner, T. 1983a: *A Longitudinal Analysis of the Acquisition of English*. Ann Arbor, MI: Karoma.

Huebner, T. 1983b: Linguistic systems and linguistic change in an interlanguage. *Studies in Second Language Acquisition* 6, 33–53.

Hulstijn, J. and Hulstijn, W. 1984: Grammatical errors as a function of processing constraints and explicit knowledge. *Language Learning* 34, 23–44.

Hyaltenstam, K. 1984: The use of typological markedness conditions as predictors in second language acquisition. In R. Andersen (ed.), *Second Languages: A Cross-Linguistic Perspective*, Rowley, MA: Newbury House.

Hymes, D. H. 1971: *Pidginization and Creolization of Languages*. Cambridge: University Press.

Hymes, D. H. 1972: Models of the interaction of language and social life. In J. J. Gumperz and D. H. Hymes (eds), *Directions in Sociolinguistics: The Ethnography of Communication*, New York: Holt, Rinehart and Winston, 35–71.

Hymes, D. H. 1974: *Foundations in Sociolinguistics: An Ethnographic Approach*. Philadelphia: University of Pennsylvania Press.

Hymes, D. H. 1986: Discourse: scope without depth. *International Journal of the Sociology of Language* 57, 49–89.

Irujo, S. 1986: Don't put your leg in your mouth: transfer in the acquisition of idioms in a second language. *TESOL Quarterly* 20, 287–304.

Irvine, J. T. 1982: Language and affect: some cross-cultural issues. In H. Byrnes (ed.), *Contemporary Perceptions of Language: Interdisciplinary Dimensions* (Georgetown University Round Table on Languages and Linguistics 1982), Washington, DC: Georgetown University Press, 31–47.

Irvine, J. T. 1984: Formality and informality in communicative events. In J. Baugh and

J. Sherzer (eds), *Language in Use: Readings in Sociolinguistics*, Englewood Cliffs, NJ: Prentice-Hall, 211–28. Reprinted from *American Anthropologist* 81, 773–90, 1979.

Ito, K. 1980: Direction in Japanese and English: independent study paper. Honolulu: Department of English as a Second Language, University of Hawaii.

Jackson, B. 1987: *Fieldwork*. Urbana and Chicago: University of Illinois.

Jain, D. 1975: *A Sociolinguistic Study of Hindi Pronouns*. Philadelphia: University of Pennsylvania PhD dissertation.

James, C. 1974: Linguistic measures for error gravity. *AVLA Journal* 12, 3–9.

Janicki, K. 1985: *The Foreigner's Language*. London: Pergamon.

Janicki, K. 1987: An equalizer model of the native speaker's perception of the foreigner's language: a pilot study. Paper presented to the XIth University of Michigan Conference on Applied Linguistics: Variation in Second Language Acquisition, Ann Arbor, October.

Jefferson, G. 1978: Sequential aspects of storytelling in conversation. In J. Schenkein (ed.), *Studies in the Organization of Conversational Interaction*, New York: Academic, 219–48.

Jiménez, A. 1965: *Picardía Mexicana* (20th edn). Mexico City: Libro Mex.

Jingfu, P. 1987: Organizational features in chemical engineering research articles. *ELR Journal* 1, 79–116.

Jones, E. E. 1964: *Ingratiation*. New York: Appleton-Century-Crofts.

Jones, R. G. and Jones, E. E. 1964: Optimum conformity as an ingratiation tactic. *Journal of Personality* 32, 4–36.

Joos, M. 1962: The five clocks. *International Journal of American Linguistics* 28, part V.

Jourard, S. M. 1966: An exploratory study of body accessibility. *British Journal of Social and Clinical Psychology* 5, 221–31.

Judd, E. 1983: The problem of applying sociolinguistic findings to TESOL: the case of male/female language. In N. Wolfson and E. Judd (eds), *Sociolinguistics and Language Acquisition*, Rowley, MA: Newbury House, 234–41.

Kachru, B. 1982a: Models for non-native Englishes. In B. Kachru (ed.), *The Other Tongue: English Across Cultures*, Oxford: Pergamon, 31–57.

Kachru, B. (ed.) 1982b: *The Other Tongue: English Across Cultures*. Oxford: Pergamon.

Kaplan, R. B. 1966: Cultural thought patterns in inter-cultural education. *Language Learning* 16, 1–20.

Kaplan, R. B. 1986: Cultural thought patterns revisited. In U. Conner and R. B. Kaplan (eds), *Writing Across Languages: Analysis of L2 Text*, Reading, MA: Addison-Wesley.

Kasper, G. to appear: Variation in interlanguage speech act realization. In S. M. Gass, C. Madden, D. R. Preston, and L. Selinker (eds), *Variation in Second Language Acquisition, Volume 1: Discourse and Pragmatics*, Clevedon, Avon: Multilingual Matters.

Katz, J. J. and Fodor, J. A. 1964: The structure of a semantic theory. In J. A. Fodor and J. J. Katz (eds), *The Structure of Language: Readings in the Philosophy of Language*, Englewood Cliffs, NJ: Prentice-Hall, 479–518. Reprinted from *Language* 39, 170–210, 1963.

Kay, P. 1978: Variable rules, community grammar, and linguistic change. In D.

Sankoff (ed.), *Language Variation: Models and Methods*, New York: Academic, 71–83.

Kay, P. and McDaniel, C. K. 1979: On the logic of variable rules. *Language in Society* 8, 151–87.

Kay, P. and Sankoff, G. 1974: A language-universals approach to pidgins and creoles. In D. DeCamp and I. F. Hancock (eds), *Pidgins and Creoles*, Washington, DC: Georgetown University Press, 61–72.

Kedar, L. 1987: *Power through Discourse*. Norwood, NJ: Ablex.

Keenan, E. 1974: Norm-makers, norm-breakers: uses of speech by men and women in a Malagasy community. In R. Bauman and J. Sherzer (eds), *Explorations in the Ethnography of Speaking*, Cambridge: University Press, 125–43.

Keenan, E. and Schieffelin, B. 1976: Topic as a discourse notion: a study of topic in the conversations of children and adults. In C. Li (ed.), *Subject and Topic*, New York: Academic.

Keenan, E. L. and Comrie, B. 1977: Noun phrase accessibility and universal grammar. *Linguistic Inquiry* 8, 63–99.

Kellerman, E. 1977: Towards a characterization of the strategy of transfer in second language learning. *Interlanguage Studies Bulletin* 2, 58–145.

Kellerman, E. 1979: Transfer and non-transfer: where are we now? *Studies in Second Language Acquisition* 2, 37–57.

Kellerman, E. 1986: An eye for an eye: crosslinguistic constraints and the development of the L2 lexicon. In E. Kellerman and M. Sharwood Smith (eds), *Crosslinguistic Influence in Second Language Acquisition*, Oxford: Pergamon, 35–48.

Kendon, A. 1967: Some functions of gaze-direction in social interaction. *Acta Psychologica* 26, 22–63.

Kendon, A. 1970: Some relationships between body motion and speech: an analysis of an example. In A. Seigman and B. Pope (eds), *Studies in Dyadic Interaction: A Research Conference*, New York: Pergamon.

Kenyon, J. S. 1948: Cultural levels and functional varieties of English. *College English* 10, 31–6.

King, F. 1974: The good ole boy: a southern bell's [sic] lament. *Harper's*, April, 78–82.

Kiparsky, P. 1972: Explanation in phonology. In S. Peters (ed.), *Goals of Linguistic Theory*, Englewood Cliffs, NJ: Prentice- Hall, 189–227.

Kipers, P. S. 1987: Gender and topic. *Language in Society* 16, 543–57.

Klein, W. 1986: *Second Language Acquisition*. Cambridge: University Press.

Klein, W. and Dittmar, N. 1979: *Developing Grammars: The Acquisition of German Syntax by Foreign Workers*. Berlin: Springer.

Kloss, H. 1986: On some terminological problems in interlingual sociolinguistics. *International Journal of the Sociology of Language* 57, 91–106.

Kontra, M. 1985: Hungarian–American bilingualism: a bibliographic essay. *Hungarian Studies*, 1/2, 257–82.

Krashen, S. D. 1977: Some issues relating to the monitor model. In H. D. Brown, C. A. Yorio, and R. H. Crymes (eds), *On TESOL '77*, Washington, DC: TESOL, 144–58.

Krashen, S. D. 1981: *Second Language Acquisition and Second Language Learning*. Oxford: Pergamon.

Krashen, S. D. 1982: Accounting for child–adult differences in second language rate and attainment. In S. D. Krashen, R. C. Scarcella, and M. A. Long (eds), *Child–*

*Adult Differences in Second Language Acquisition*, Rowley, MA: Newbury House, 202–26.

Krashen, S. D. 1987: *Principles and Practice in Second Language Acquisition*. Englewood Cliffs, NJ: Prentice-Hall.

Krashen, S. D., Long, M. A., and Scarcella, R. C. 1979: Age, rate, and eventual attainment in second language acquisition. *TESOL Quarterly* 13, 573–82.

Krashen, S. D., Scarcella, R. C., and Long, M. A. (eds). 1982: *Child–Adult Differences in Second Language Acquisition*. Rowley, MA: Newbury House.

Kroch, A. S. 1976: Toward a theory of social dialect variation. *Language in Society* 7: 17–36.

Kroch, A. S. and Small, C. 1978: Grammatical ideology and its effect on speech. In D. Sankoff (ed.), *Linguistic Variation: Models and Methods*. New York: Academic, 45–55.

Kurath, H. 1949: *A Word Geography of the United States*. Ann Arbor: University of Michigan.

Labov, W. 1963: The social motivation of a sound change. *Word* 19, 273–309.

Labov, W. 1966: *The Social Stratification of English in New York City*. Arlington, VA: Center for Applied Linguistics.

Labov, W. 1972a: *Sociolinguistic Patterns*. Philadelphia: University of Pennsylvania Press.

Labov, W. 1972b: *Language in the Inner City*. Philadelphia: University of Pennsylvania Press.

Labov, W. 1973: Where do grammars stop? In R. Shuy (ed.), *Sociolinguistics: Current Trends and Prospects* (Monograph Series on Language and Linguistics, no. 25, 1972; 23rd Annual Round Table), Washington, DC: Georgetown University Press, 43–88.

Labov, W. 1978: Where does the linguistic variable stop? A response to B. Lavandera, Sociolinguistic Working Paper no. 44. *Working Papers in Sociolinguistics*. Austin: Southwest Educational Development Laboratory.

Labov, W. 1981: What can be learned about change in progress from synchronic description? In D. Sankoff and H. Cedergren (eds), *Variation Omnibus*, Carbondale, IL and Edmonton, AL: Linguistic Research, 177–99.

Labov, W. 1984: Field methods of the project on linguistic change and variation. In J. Baugh and J. Sherzer (eds), *Language in Use: Readings in Sociolinguistics*, Englewood Cliffs, NJ: Prentice-Hall, 28–53.

Labov, W. in progress: A study of cross-dialectal comprehension. National Science Foundation research project, Philadelphia: University of Pennsylvania.

Labov, W. and Fanshel, D. 1977: *Therapeutic Discourse*. New York: Academic.

Lackstrom, J. E., Selinker, L., and Trimble, L. 1970: Grammar and technical English. In R. C. Lugton (ed.), *English as a Second Language: Current Issues*, Philadelphia: Center for Curriculum Development.

LaFerriere, M. 1979: Ethnicity in phonological variation in change. *Language* 55, 603–17.

Lakoff, R. 1975: *Language and Woman's Place*. New York: Harper and Row.

Lambert, W. E. 1967: A social psychology of bilingualism. *Journal of Social Issues* 23, 91–109.

Lambert, W. E. 1974: Culture and language as factors in learning and education. In F.

E. Aboud and R. D. Meade (eds), *Cultural Factors in Learning and Education*, Bellingham, WA: Fifth Western Washington Symposium on Learning.

Lambert, W. E., Hodgson, R., Gardner, R. C., and Fillenbaum, S. 1960: Evaluational reactions to spoken language. *Journal of Abnormal Social Psychology*, 60, 44–51.

Lambert, W. E. and G. R. Tucker 1972: *Bilingual Education of Children: The St. Lambert Experiment*. Rowley, MA: Newbury House.

Lantolf, J. and Ahmed, M. To appear: Psycholinguistic perspectives on interlanguage variation: a Vygotskian analysis. In S. M. Gass, C. Madden, D. R. Preston, and L. Selinker (eds), *Variation in Second Language Acquisition, Volume 1: Psycholinguistic Issues*, Clevedon, Avon: Multilingual Matters.

Larsen, D. N. and Smalley, W. A. 1972: *Becoming Bilingual: A Guide to Language Learning*. New Canaan, CN: Practical Anthropology.

Larsen-Freeman, D. 1975: The acquisition of grammatical morphemes by adult ESL students. *TESOL Quarterly* 9, 409–20.

Lavandera, B. 1977: Where does the sociolinguistic variable stop? Sociolinguistic Working Paper no. 40. *Working Papers in Sociolinguistics*. Austin, TX: Southwest Educational Development Laboratory.

Laver, J. and Trudgill, P. 1979: Phonetic and linguistic markers in speech. In K. R. Scherer and H. Giles (eds), *Social Markers in Speech*, Cambridge: University Press, 1–32.

Legman, G. 1968: *Rationale of the Dirty Joke: an Analysis of Sexual Humor* (first series). Castle Books.

Legman, G. 1975: *Rationale of the Dirty Joke: an Analysis of Sexual Humor* (second series). New York: Breaking Point.

Lenneberg, E. 1967: *Biological Foundations of Language*. New York: Wiley.

Le Page, R. B. 1964: *The National Langauge Question*. London: Oxford University Press.

Le Page, R. B. 1978: *Projection, Focusing and Diffusion, or Steps towards a Sociolinguistic Theory of Language, Illustrated from the Sociolinguistic Survey of Multilingual Communities, Stages I: Belize (British Honduras) and II: St Lucia*. Society for Caribbean Linguistics Occasional Paper 9, Mimeo. St Augustine, Trinidad: School of Education, University of the West Indies. Reprinted in *York Papers in Linguistics* 9, University of York, Department of Language.

Le Page, R. B. and Tabouret-Keller, A. 1985: *Acts of Identity: Creole-Based Approaches to Language and Ethnicity*. Cambridge: University Press.

Li, C. (ed.) 1976: *Subject and Object*. New York: Academic.

Linde, C. and Labov, W. 1975: Spatial networks as a site for the study of language and thought. *Language* 51, 924–39.

Littlewood, W. 1975: Role-performance and language teaching. *International Review of Applied Linguistics* 13, 199–208.

Littlewood, W. 1981: Language variation and second language acquisition. *Applied Linguistics* 2, 150–8.

LoCoco, V. 1976: A comparison of three methods for the collection of L2 data: free composition, translation and picture description. *Working Papers on Bilingualism* 8, 59–86.

Long, M. H. 1980: Input, interaction and second language acquisition. UCLA PhD dissertation.

Long, M. H. 1983a: Linguistic and conversational adjustments to non-native speakers. *Studies in Second Language Acquisition* 5, 77–93.

Long, M. H. 1983b: Native speaker/non-native speaker conversation in the second language classroom. In M. Clarke and J. Handscombe (eds), *On TESOL '82*, Washington, D.C.: TESOL.

Long, M. H. 1983c: Does second language instruction make a difference? A review of the research. *TESOL Quarterly* 17, 359–82.

Long, M. H. 1985: Input and second langauge acquisition theory. In S. M. Gass and C. G. Madden (eds), *Input in Second Langauge Acquisition*, Rowley, MA: Newbury House, 377–93.

Long, M. H., Adams, L., McLean, M., and Castaños, F. 1976: Doing things with words – verbal interaction in lockstep and small group classroom situations. In J. Fanslowe and R. Crymes (eds), *On TESOL '76*, Washington, DC: TESOL, 137–53.

Lukmani, Y. M. 1972: Motivation to learn and learning proficiency. *Language Learning* 22, 261–73.

Lynch, B. 1979: The adult second language learner: an introspective analysis of an individual learning Spanish as a second language. San José: California State University, unpublished manuscript.

Lyons, J. 1968: *Introduction to Theoretical Linguistics*. Cambridge: University Press.

Macaulay, R. K. S. 1978: Variation and consistency in Glaswegian English. In P. Trudgill (ed.), *Sociolinguistic Patterns in British English*, London: Arnold, 132–43.

McConochie, J. 1985: 'Musing on the lamp flame': teaching a narrative poem in a college-level ESOL class. *TESOL Quarterly* 19, 125–36.

McEntegart, D. and Le Page, R. B. 1982: An appraisal of the statistical techniques used in The Sociolinguistic Survey of Multilingual Communities. In S. Romaine (ed.), *Sociolinguistic Variation in Speech Communities*, London: Arnold, 105–24.

McKay, J. H. 1980: Points of view on point of view: the free indirect style. In R. W. Shuy and A. Shnukal (eds), *Language Use and the Uses of Language*, Washington, DC: Georgetown University Press, 288–96.

McLaughlin, B. 1978a: *Second-language acquisition in childhood*. Hillsdale, NJ: Erlbaum.

McLaughlin, B. 1978b: The monitor model: some methodological considerations. *Language Learning* 28, 309–32.

Major, R. C. 1986: Paragoge and degree of foreign accent in Brazilian English. *Second Language Research* 2, 53–71.

Major, R. C. 1987: Phonological similarity, markedness, and rate of L2 acquisition. *Studies in Second Language Acquisition* 9, 63–82.

Major R. C. to appear a: A model for interlanguage phonology. In G. L. Ioup and S. L. Weinberger (eds), *Interlanguage Phonology*, Rowley, MA: Newbury House.

Major, R. C. to appear b: Foreign accent: recent research and theory. *International Review of Applied Linguistics*.

Major, R. C. to appear c: The natural phonology of second language acquisition. In A. R. Jams and J. Leather (eds), *Sound Patterns in Second Language Acquisition*, Dordrecht: Foris.

Malinowski, B. 1923: The problem of meaning in primitive languages. In C. K. Ogden and I. A. Richards, *The Meaning of Meaning*, London: Routledge and Kegan Paul.

Manes, J. 1983: Compliments: a mirror of cultural values. In N. Wolfson and E. Judd (eds) *Sociolinguistics and Language Acquisition*, Rowley, MA: Newbury House, 96–102.

Manes, J. and Wolfson, N. 1981: The compliment formula. In F. Coulmas (ed.), *Conversational Routine*, The Hague: Mouton.

Marlos, E. S. 1981: Why answer? a goal-based analysis of a speech event. In D. Sankoff and H. Cedergren (eds), *Variation Omnibus*, Carbondale, IL and Edmonton, AL: Linguistic Research, 553–64.

Marquez, E. and Bowen, J. D. 1983: *English Usage*. Rowley, MA: Newbury House.

Marton, W. and Preston, D. R. 1975: British and American English for Polish university students: research report and projections. *Glottodidactica* 8, 27–43.

Mattingly, I. G. 1966: Speaker variation and vocal tract size. *Journal of the Acoustical Society of America*, 39, 1219.

Milon, J. P. 1975: Dialect in the TESOL program: if you never you better. In M. Burt and H. Dulay (eds), *On TESOL '75: New Directions in Second Language Learning, Teaching, and Bilingual Education*, Washington, D.C.: TESOL, 159–67.

Milroy, L. 1980: *Language and Social Networks*. Oxford: Blackwell.

Milroy, L. 1982: Social network and linguistic focusing. In S. Romaine (ed.), *Sociolinguistic Variation in Speech Communities*, London: Arnold, 141–52.

Milroy, L. 1987: *Observing and Analyzing Natural Language*. Oxford: Blackwell.

Milroy, L. and Milroy, J. 1977: Speech and context in an urban setting. *Belfast Working Papers in Language and Linguistics* 2(1).

Mitchell-Kernan, C. 1972: Signifying, loud-talking, and marking. In T. Kochman (ed.), *Rappin' and Stylin' Out*, Urbana, IL: University of Illinois, 315–35.

Modaressi, Y. 1978: *A Sociolinguistic Analysis of Modern Persian*. Lawrence: University of Kansas PhD dissertation.

Montagu, A. 1967: *The Anatomy of Swearing*. New York: Collier.

Morain, G. G. 1978: *Kinesics and Cross-Cultural Understanding* (Language in Education no. 7, Theory and Practice). Arlington, VA: Center for Applied Linguistics.

Moskowitz, G. 1978: *Caring and Sharing in the Foreign Language Classroom*. Rowley, MA: Newbury House.

Munby, J. 1978: *Communicative Syllabus Design*. Cambridge: University Press.

Murray, T. E. 1985: On solving the dilemma of the Hawthorne Effect. In H. F. Warkentyne (ed.), *Methods/Méthodes V* (Papers from the Fifth International Conference on Methods in Dialectology), Victoria, BC: Department of Linguistics, University of Victoria, 327–40.

Myers, A, 1977: Toward a definition of irony. In R. W. Fasold and R. W. Shuy (eds), *Studies in Language Variation*. Washington, DC: Georgetown University Press, 171–83.

Naiman, N., Frohlich, M., Stern, H., and Todesco, A. 1978: The good language learner. *Research in Education Series 7*, Toronto: Ontario Institute for Studies in Education.

Naro, A. J. 1978: A study on the origins of pidginization. *Language* 54, 314–47.

Nemser, W. 1971: Approximative systems of foreign language learners. *International Review of Applied Linguistics* 9, 115–23.

Neto, S. da S. 1957: Breves notas para o estudo da expansão da língua portuguêsa em África e Ásia. *Revista de Portugal* 22, 129-47.

Neto, S. da S. 1970: *História de língua portuguêsa.* (2nd edn, augmented). Rio de Janeiro: Livros de Portugal.

Nine-Curt, J. C. 1983: Intercultural interaction in the Hispanic-Anglo ESL classroom from a non-verbal perspective. University of Puerto Rico, monograph.

O'Barr, W. and Atkins, B. 1980: 'Women's language' or 'powerless language'? In S. McConnell-Ginet, R. Borker, and N. Furman (eds), *Women and Language in Literature and Society,* New York: Praeger, 93-110.

Obler, L. to appear: Exceptional second language learners. In S. M. Gass, C. Madden, D. R. Preston, and L. Selinker (eds), *Variation in Second Language Acquisition, Volume 2: Psycholinguistic Issues,* Clevedon, Avon: Multilingual Matters.

Ochs, E. 1979: Planned and unplanned discourse. In T. Givón (ed.), *Syntax and Semantics, Volume 12: Discourse and Semantics,* New York: Academic, 51-80.

Ochs, E. 1986: From feelings to grammar: a Samoan case study. In B. Schieffelin and E. Ochs (eds), *Language Socialization across Cultures,* Cambridge: University Press, 251-72.

Ochs-Keenan, E. 1976: The universality of conversational postulates. *Language in Society* 5, 67-80.

Ohashi, Y. 1978: *English Style: Grammatical and Semantic Approach.* Rowley, MA: Newbury House.

Oliveira do Canto, M. L. 1982: Atitude de pessoas que moram em Santa Maria com relação à fala de outras regiões de estado. Porto Alegre: Instituto de Letras, Universidade do Rio Grande do Sul, seminar paper.

Oller, J., Baca, L, and Vigil, A. 1977: Attitudes and attained proficiency in ESL: a sociolinguistic study of Mexican-Americans in the Southwest. *TESOL Quarterly* 11, 173-83.

Oller, J. and Richard-Amato, P. (eds) 1983: *Methods that Work: A Smorgasbord of Ideas for Language Teachers.* Cambridge, MA: Newbury House.

Olshtain, E. 1983: Sociocultural competence and language transfer: the case of apology. In S. M. Gass and L. Selinker (eds), *Language Transfer in Language Learning,* Rowley, MA: Newbury House.

Olshtain, E. and Blum-Kulka, S. 1985: Degree of approximation: nonnative reactions to native speech act behavior. In S. M. Gass and C. Madden (eds), *Input in Second Language Acquisition,* Rowley, MA: Newbury House, 303-25.

Olshtain, E. and Cohen, A. 1983: Apology: a speech act set. In N. Wolfson and E. Judd (eds) *Sociolinguistics and Language Acquisition,* Rowley, MA: Newbury House, 18-35.

Patella, V. and Kuvlesky, W. P. 1979: Situational variation in language patterns of Mexican American boys and girls. *Social Science Quarterly* 37, 855-64.

Payne, A. C. 1976: *The Acquisition of the Phonological System of a Second Dialect.* Philadelphia: University of Pennsylvania PhD dissertation.

Payne, A. C. 1980: Factors controlling the acquisition of the Philadelphia dialect by out-of-state children. In W. Labov (ed.), *Locating Language in Time and Space,* New York: Academic, 143-78.

Pennycook, A. 1985: Actions speak louder than words: paralanguage, communication, and education. *TESOL Quarterly* 19, 259-82.

Perdue, C. (ed.) 1984: *Second Language Acquisition by Adult Immigrants: A Field Manual*. Rowley, MA: Newbury House.

Petyt, M. 1980: *The Study of Dialect: An Introduction to Dialectology*. Boulder, CL: Westview, and Oxford: Blackwell.

Pfaff, C. 1987: Functional approaches to interlanguage. In C. Pfaff (ed.), *First and Second Language Acquisition Processes*, Rowley, MA: Newbury House, 81–102.

Pica, T. 1987: Second-language acquisition, social interaction, and the classroom. *Applied Linguistics* 8, 3–21.

Pica, T., Young, R., and Doughty, C. 1987: The impact of interaction on comprehension. *TESOL Quarterly* 21, 737–58.

Pimsleur, P., Mosberg, L., and Morrison, A. 1962: Student factors in foreign language learning. *Modern Language Journal* 46, 160–70.

Planalp, S. and Tracy, K. 1980: Not to change the topic but...: a cognitive approach to the management of conversation. In D. Nimmo (ed.), *Communication Yearbook 4*, New Brunswick, NJ: Transaction.

Poplack, S. 1978: Dialect acquisition among Puerto Rican bilinguals. *Language in Society* 7, 89–103.

Poplack, S. 1980: 'Sometimes I'll start a sentence in Spanish y termino en español': toward a typology of code-switching. *Linguistics* 18, 581–618.

Porreca, K. 1984: Sexism in current ESL textbooks. *TESOL Quarterly* 18, 705–24.

Porter, P. A. 1986: How learners talk to each other: input and interaction in task-centered discussions. In R. R. Day (ed.), *Talking to Learn: Conversation in Second Language Acquisition*, Rowley, MA: Newbury House, 200–22.

Powell, D. R. 1966: American vs. British English. *Language Learning* 16, 31–9.

Prator, C. 1968: The British heresy in TESL. In J. Fishman, C. Ferguson, and J. Das Gupta (eds), *Language Problems of Developing Nations*, New York: Wiley, 459–76.

Pratt, M. L. 1977: *Toward a Speech Act Theory of Literary Discourse*. Bloomington: Indiana University Press.

Preston, D. R. 1981a: The ethnography of TESOL. *TESOL Quarterly* 15, 105–16.

Preston, D. R. 1981b: Separate but equal: a good deal for bilingual education. In R. Padilla (ed.), *Bilingual Education Technology* (Ethnoperspectives in Bilingual Education, Vol. 3), Ypsilanti: Eastern Michigan University, 265–80.

Preston, D. R. 1982: Lusty language learning: confessions on acquiring Polish. *Maledicta* 6, 117–20.

Preston, D. R. 1983: The unicorn and the virgin; the basilisk and the rabbit: an English language teaching and learning bestiary. *English Teaching Forum* 21, 2–7.

Preston, D. R. 1984: How to milk a native speaker: an essay in TES/FL husbandry. *English Teaching Forum* 22, 11–16, 23.

Preston, D. R. 1985: Mental maps of language distribution in Rio Grande do Sul (Brazil). *The Geographical Bulletin* 27, 46–64.

Preston, D. R. 1986a: The fifty some-odd categories of language variation. *International Journal of the Sociology of Language* 57, 9–47.

Preston, D. R. 1986b: Sociolinguistics and foreign language teaching and learning. In G. Nickel and J. C. Stalker (eds), *Problems of Standardization and Linguistic Variation of Present-Day English*, Heidelberg: Julius Groos, 5–24.

Preston, D. R. 1986c: Five visions of America. *Language in Society* 15, 221–40.

Preston, D. R. 1987: Domain-, role-, or network-specific use of language. In U. Ammon, N. Dittmar, and K. Mattheier (eds), *Sociolinguistics: An International Handbook of the Science of Language and Society*, vol. 1, Berlin and New York: Walter De Gruyter, 690–9.

Preston, D. R. MS: Talking Black and talking White: two studies in the ethnic ethnography of speaking. Ypsilanti, MI: Eastern Michigan University.

Preston, D. R. in progress: *The Perception of Language Variety*.

Purcell, A. K. 1981: Tracing variation in the stream of speech. In D. Sankoff and H. Cedergren (eds), *Variation Omnibus*, Carbondale, IL and Edmonton, AL: Linguistic Research, 505–12.

Putnam, W. B. and Street, R. L., Jr 1984: The conception and perception of non-content speech performance. *International Journal of the Sociology of Language* 46, 97–114.

Rampton, B. 1987: Stylistic variability and not speaking 'normal' English: some post-Labovian approaches and their implications for the study of interlanguage. In R. Ellis (ed.), *Second Language Acquisition in Context*, Englewood Cliffs, NJ: Prentice-Hall, 47–58.

Redlinger, W. 1976: Mother's speech to children in bilingual Mexican-American homes. In B. L. Dubois and I. Crouch (eds), *The Sociology of the Languages of American Women*, San Antonio: Trinity University, 119–30.

Reinstein, S. and Hoffman, J. 1972: Dialect interaction between Black and Puerto Rican children in New York City: implications for the language arts. *Elementary English* 49, 190–6.

Rey, A. 1977: Accent and employability: language attitudes. *Language Sciences* 47, 7–12.

Reynolds, A. G., Flagg, P., and Kennedy, W. 1974: Language study abroad: evaluation and prediction. Paper presented to the Northeastern Educational Research Association meeting. Ellenville, NY.

Richards, J. C. 1974: A non-contrastive approach to error analysis. In J. C. Richards (ed.), *Error Analysis*, London: Longman, 172–88.

Richards, J. C. 1980: Conversation. *TESOL Quarterly* 14, 413–32.

Richards, J. C. and Rodgers, T. S. 1986: *Approaches and Methods in Language Teaching*. Cambridge: University Press.

Robinett, B. W. and Schachter, J. (eds) 1983: *Second Language Learning: Contrastive Analysis, Error Analysis, and Related Matters*. Ann Arbor: University of Michigan.

Romaine, S. 1980: A critical overview of the methodology of urban British socio-linguistics. *English World Wide* 1, 163–98.

Romaine, S. 1984: *The Language of Children and Adolescents*. Oxford: Blackwell.

Romaine, S. 1988: *Pidgin and Creole Languages*. London: Longman.

Rosaldo, M. Z. 1975: It's all uphill: the creative metaphors of Ilongot magical spells. In M. Sanches and B. Blount (eds), *Sociocultural Dimensions of Language Use*, New York: Academic, 177–203.

Ross, J. R. 1973: A fake NP squish. In C.-J. N. Bailey and R. W. Shuy (eds), *New Ways of Analyzing Variation in English*, Washington, DC: Georgetown University Press, 96–140.

Rossier, R. 1976: Extroversion–introversion as a significant variable in the learning of oral English as a second language. Los Angeles: University of Southern California PhD dissertation.

Rounds, P. L. 1987: Characterizing successful classroom discourse for NNS teaching assistant training. *TESOL Quarterly* 21, 643–71.

Rubin, J. 1970: Bilingual usage in Paraguay. In J. A. Fishman (ed.), *Readings in the Sociology of Language*, The Hague: Mouton, 512–30.

Rutherford, W. E. (ed.) 1984: *Language Universals and Second Language Acquisition*. Amsterdam and Philadelphia: John Benjamins.

Ryan, E. B., Carranza, M. A., and Moffie, R. W. 1975: Mexican American reactions to accented English. In J. W. Berry and W. J. Lonner (eds), *Applied Cross-Cultural Psychology*, Amsterdam: Swets and Zeitlinger, 174–8.

Ryan, E. B. and Giles, H. 1982: *Attitudes towards Language Variation*. London: Arnold.

Ryan, E. B., Giles, H., and Sebastian, R. J. 1982: An integrative perspective for the study of attitudes toward language variation. In E. B. Ryan and H. Giles (eds), *Attitudes towards Language Variation*, London: Arnold, 1–19.

Sachs, J. 1975: Cues to the identification of sex in children's speech. In B. Thorne and N. Henley (eds), *Language and Sex*, Rowley, MA: Newbury House, 152–71.

Sacks, H., Schegloff, E., and Jefferson, G. 1974: A simplest systematics for the organization of turn-taking for conversation. *Language* 50, 696–735.

Sagarin, E. 1962: *The Anatomy of Dirty Words*. New York: Lyle Stuart.

Saint-Jacques, B. 1973: Sex, dependency and language. *La Linguistique* 9, 89–96.

Sankoff, D. and Labov, W. 1979: On the uses of variable rules. *Language in Society*, 8, 189–222.

Sato, C. 1985: Task variation in interlanguage phonology. In S. M. Gass and C. Madden (eds), *Input in Second Language Acquisition*, Rowley, MA: Newbury House, 181–96.

Saville-Troike, M. 1982: *The Ethnography of Communication: An Introduction*. Oxford: Blackwell.

Scarcella, R. C. 1983: Discourse accent in second language performance. In S. M. Gass and L. Selinker (eds), *Language Transfer in Language Learning*, Rowley, MA: Newbury House.

Scarcella, R. C. and Higa, C. A. 1981: Input, negotiation, and age differences in second language acquisition. *Language Learning* 31, 409–37.

Scarcella, R. C. and Krashen, S. D. (eds) 1980: *Research in Second Language Acquisition*. Rowley, MA: Newbury House.

Schachter, J. 1986: In search of systematicity in interlanguage production. *Studies in Second Language Acquisition* 8, 119–34.

Schachter, J., Tyson, A., and Diffley, F. 1976: Learner intuitions of grammaticality. *Language Learning* 26, 67–76.

Schegloff, E. A. 1968: Sequencing in conversational openings. *American Anthropologist*, 70, 1075–95.

Schegloff, E. A. 1972: Notes on a conversational practice: formulating place. In P. P. Giglioli (ed.), *Language and Social Context*, Harmondsworth: Penguin, 95–135. Reprinted from D. Sudnow (ed.), *Studies in Social Interaction*, New York: Free Press, 1971.

Schegloff, E. A. 1979: Identification and recognition in telephone conversation openings. In G. Psathas (ed.), *Everyday Language: Studies in Ethnomethodology*, New York: Irvington, 23–78.

Schegloff, E. A. and Sacks, H. 1973: Opening up closings. *Semiotica*, 8, 289–327.

Schmidt, M. 1980: Coordinate structures and language universals in interlanguage. *Language Learning* 29, 181–91.

Schmidt, R. W. 1977: Sociolinguistic variation and language transfer in phonology. *Working Papers in Bilingualism* 12, 79–95.

Schmidt, R. W. and Richards, J. C. 1980: Speech acts and second- language learning. *Applied Linguistics* 1, 129–57.

Schneider, W. and Shriffin, R. 1977: Controlled and automatic human information processing: 1. detection, search and attention. *Psychological Review* 84, 1–66.

Schumann, J. H. 1974: The implications of interlanguage, pidginization and creolization for the study of adult second language acquisition. *TESOL Quarterly* 8, 145–52.

Schumann, J. H. 1975: Affective factors and the problem of age in second language acquisition. *Language Learning*, 2, 209–35.

Schumann, J. H. 1978a: *The Pidginization Process*. Rowley, MA: Newbury House.

Schumann, J. H. 1978b: The acculturation model for second-language acquisition. In R. C. Gingras (ed.), *Second-Language Acquisition and Foreign Language Teaching*, Arlington, VA: Center for Applied Linguistics, 27–50.

Schumann, J. H. 1978c: Social and psychological factors in second language acquisition. In J. Richards (ed.), *Understanding Second and Foreign Language Learning*, Rowley, MA: Newbury House, 163–78.

Schwartz, M. 1984: Response to writing: a college-wide perspective. *College English* 46, 55–62.

Scollon, R. T. 1974: *One Child's Language from One to Two: The Origins of Construction*. The University of Hawaii PhD dissertation.

Scollon, R. T. and Scollon, S. B. K. 1979: *Linguistic Convergence: An Ethnography of Speaking at Fort Chipewyan, Alberta*. New York: Academic.

Scotton, C. M. 1976: Strategies of neutrality: language choice in uncertain situations. *Language* 52, 919–41.

Scovel, T. 1969: Foreign accents, language acquisition, and cerebral dominance. *Language Learning* 19, 245–54.

Searle, J. R. 1969: *Speech Acts*. Cambridge: University Press.

Searle, J. R. 1975: Indirect speech acts. In P. Cole and J. L. Morgan (eds), *Syntax and Semantics 3: Speech Acts*, New York: Academic.

Searle, J. R. 1976: The classification of illocutionary acts. *Language and Society* 5, 1–24.

Searle, J. R. 1979: *Expression and Meaning: Studies in the Theory of Speech Acts*. Cambridge: University Press.

Segalowitz, N. 1976: Communicative incompetence and the nonfluent bilingual. *Canadian Journal of Behavioural Science* 8, 122–31.

Seliger, H. and Long, M. (eds) 1983: *Classroom-Oriented Research in Second Language Acquisition*. Rowley, MA: Newbury House.

Selinker, L. 1969: Language transfer. *General Linguistics* 9, 67–92.

Selinker, L. 1972: Interlanguage. *International Review of Applied Linguistics* 10, 201–31.

Selinker, L. and Douglas, D. 1985: Wrestling with 'context' in interlanguage theory. *Applied Linguistics* 6, 190–204.

Seright, L. 1985: Age and aural comprehension achievement in francophone adults learning English. *TESOL Quarterly* 19, 455–73.

Sharp, L. 1958: People without politics. In V. F. Ray (ed.), *Systems of Political Control and Bureaucracy*, Seattle: University of Washington, 1–8.

Sharwood-Smith, M. 1981: Consciousness-raising and the second language learner. *Applied Linguistics* 2, 159–69.

Shweder, R. A. and Bourne, E. J. 1984: Does the concept of person vary cross-culturally? In R. A. Shweder and R. A. LeVine (eds), *Culture Theory: Essays on Mind, Self, and Emotion*, Cambridge: University Press, 158–99.

Shweder, R. A. and LeVine, R. A. (eds) 1984: *Culture Theory: Essays on Mind, Self, and Emotion*. Cambridge: University Press.

Sigman, S. J. 1983: Some multiple constraints on conversational topics. In R. T. Craig and K. Tracy (eds), *Conversational Coherence: Form, Structure, and Strategy*, Beverly Hills: Sage, 174–95.

Silva, C. M. and Zwicky, A. M. 1975: Discord. In R. W. Fasold and R. W. Shuy (eds), *Analyzing Variation in Language*, Washington, DC: Georgetown University Press, 203–19.

Silverman, D. 1973: Interview talk: bringing off a research instrument. *Sociology* 7, 31–48.

Sinclair, J. McH. and Coulthard, R. M. 1975: *Towards an Analysis of Discourse: The English Used by Teachers and Pupils*. London: Oxford University Press.

Slobin, D. I. 1977: Language change in childhood and history. In J. Macnamara (ed.), *Language Learning and Thought*, New York: Academic, 185–214.

Smith, F. 1978: *Understanding Reading* (2nd edn). New York: Holt, Rinehart and Winston.

Smith, P. M. 1985: *Language, the Sexes and Society*. Oxford: Blackwell.

Sole, Y. R. 1976: Sociocultural and sociopsychological factors in differential language retentiveness by sex. In B. L. Dubois and I. Crouch (eds), *The Sociology of the Languages of American Women*, San Antonio: Trinity University, 137–53.

Spears, R. 1981: *Slang and Euphemism*. Middle Village, NY: Jonathan David.

Spolsky, B. 1985: Formulating a theory of second language learning. *Studies in Second Language Acquisition* 7, 269–88.

Stafford, C. and Covitt, G. 1978: Monitor use in adult second language production. *ITL: Review of Applied Linguistics* 39–40, 103–25.

Stalker, J. C. and Stalker, J. W. to appear: The acquisition of rhetorical strategies in introductory paragraphs in written academic English: a comparison of NNSs and NSs. In S. M. Gass, C. Madden, D. R. Preston, and L. Selinker (eds), *Variation in Second Language Acquisition, Volume 1: Discourse and Pragmatics*, Clevedon, Avon: Multilingual Matters.

Stauble, A.-M. 1978: Decreolization as a model for second language development. *Language Learning* 28, 29–54.

Steffensen, M. 1986: Register, cohesion and cross-cultural reading comprehension. *Applied Linguistics* 7, 71–85.

Sternberg, S. 1963: Stochastic learning theory. In R. Luce, R. Bush, and E. Galanter (eds), *Handbook of Mathematical Psychology*, vol. II, New York: Wiley.

Stewart, W. A. 1964: Urban Negro speech: sociolinguistic factors affecting English teaching. In R. W. Shuy (ed.) *Social Dialects in Language Learning*, Champaign, IL: National Council of Teachers of English, 10–19.

Stewart, W. A. 1972: A sociolinguistic typology for describing national multilingualism. In J. Fishman (ed.), *Readings in the Sociology of Language*, The Hague: Mouton, 531–45.

Stiles, W. B. 1981: Classification of intersubjective illocutionary acts. *Language in Society* 10, 227–49.

Strother, J. B. and Alford, R. L. 1987: The relationship between L2 speakers' pronunciation and their ability to detect variations in dialects of American English. Paper presented to the 11th Michigan Conference on Applied Linguistics: Variation in Second Language Acquisition, Ann Arbor.

Stubbs, M. 1983: *Discourse Analysis: The Sociolinguistic Analysis of Natural Language*. Oxford: Blackwell.

Swacker, M. 1975: The sex of the speaker as a sociolinguistic variable. In B. Thorne and N. Henley (eds), *Language and Sex*, Rowley, MA: Newbury House, 76–83.

Swacker, M. 1977: *Attitudes of Native and Non-native Speakers toward Varieties of American English*. College Station: Texas A & M University doctoral dissertation.

Swain, M. and Burnaby, B. 1976: Personality characteristics and second language learning in young children: a pilot study. *Working Papers on Bilingualism* 11, 76–90.

Swales, J. 1981: Aspects of article introduction. *ESP Research Reports*, no. 1. Aston, England: Aston University.

Swales, J. 1983: *Episodes in ESP*. Oxford: Pergamon.

Swales, J. 1985: A genre-based approach to language across the curriculum. Paper delivered at the RELC Conference, Singapore.

Swales, J. to appear: *Genre Analysis and its Application to Research English*. Cambridge: University Press.

Takahashi, T. to appear: The influence of the listener on L2 speech. In S. M. Gass, C. Madden, D. R. Preston, and L. Selinker (eds), *Variation in Second Language Acquisition, Volume 1: Discourse and Pragmatics*, Clevedon, Avon: Multilingual Matters.

Tannen, D. 1979: *Processes and Consequences of Conversational Style*. Berkeley: University of California, Berkeley PhD dissertation.

Tannen, D. 1981: New York Jewish conversational style. *International Journal of the Sociology of Language*, 30, 133–49.

Tannen, D. 1982: Ethnic style in male–female conversation. In J. J. Gumperz (ed.), *Language and Social Identity*, Cambridge: University Press, 217–31.

Tarone, E. 1979: Interlanguage as chameleon. *Language Learning* 29, 181–91.

Tarone, E. 1982: Systematicity and attention in interlanguage. *Language Learning* 32, 69–84.

Tarone, E. 1983: On the variability of interlanguage systems. *Applied Linguistics* 4, 142–63.

Tarone, E. 1985: Variability in interlanguage use: a study of style-shifting in morphology and syntax. *Language Learning* 35, 373–403.

Tarone, E., Frauenfelder, U., and Selinker, L. 1976: Systematicity/variability and stability/instability in interlanguage systems. In H. D. Brown (ed.), *Papers in Second Language Acquisition* (*Language Learning*, Special Issue no. 4), 93–134.

Taylor, D. M., Meynard, R., and Rheault, E. 1977: Threat to ethnic identity and second-language learning. In H. Giles (ed.) *Language, Ethnicity and Intergroup Relations*, London: Academic, 99–118.

Taylor, D. M. and Simard, L. 1975: Social interaction in a bilingual setting. *Canadian Psychological Review*, 16, 240–54.

Thorne, B., Kramarae, C., and Henley, N. 1983: *Language, Gender, and Society*. Rowley, MA: Newbury House.

Troike, R. 1971: TESOL and Joos's five clocks. TESOL Quarterly 5, 39–45.

Trudgill, P. 1972: Sex, covert prestige and linguistic change in the urban British English of Norwich. *Language in Society* 1, 179–95.

Trudgill, P. 1974: *The Social Differentiation of English in Norwich*. Cambridge: University Press.

Trudgill, P. 1983: *On Dialect: Social and Geographical Perspectives*. New York: New York University.

Trudgill, P. 1986: *Dialects in Contact*. Oxford: Blackwell.

Tucker, G. R. and Lambert, W. E. 1969: White and Negro listeners' reactions to various American English dialects. *Social Forces* 47, 463–8.

Tyler, S. A. 1972: Context and alternation in Koya kinship terminology. In J. J. Gumperz and D. H. Hymes (eds), *Directions in Sociolinguistics: The Ethnography of Communication*, New York: Holt, Rinehart and Winston, 251–69.

Tyler, S. A. 1978: *The Said and the Unsaid*. New York: Academic.

UNESCO 1953: *The Use of Vernacular Languages in Education*. Paris.

Valdés-Fallis, G. 1978: Code-switching among bilingual Mexican-American women: towards an understanding of sex-related language alternation. *International Journal of the Sociology of Language* 17, 65–72.

Van Dijk, T. A. 1977: *Text and Context: Explorations in the Semantics and Pragmatics of Discourse*. London and New York: Longman.

Van Ek, J. A. 1976: *The Threshold Level for Modern Language Learning in Schools*. Longman: London.

Van Els, T. Bongaerts, T., Extra, G., Van Os, C., and Janssen-Vand Dieten, A.-M. 1984: Applied Linguistics and the Learning and Teaching of Foreign Languages. London: Arnold.

Varonis, E. M. and Gass, S. M. 1985: Miscommunication in native/nonnative conversation. *Language in Society* 14, 327–43.

Wagner-Gough, J. 1975: Comparative studies in second language learning. Los Angeles: UCLA MA-TESOL thesis.

Wagner-Gough, J. and Hatch, E. 1975: The importance of input data in second language acquisition studies. *Language Learning* 25, 297–308.

Walters, J. 1979: The perception of politeness in English and Spanish. In C. A. Yorio, K. Perkins, and J. Schachter (eds), *On TESOL '79: The Learner in Focus*, Washington, DC: TESOL, 288–96.

Wardhaugh, R. 1985: *How Conversation Works*. Oxford: Blackwell.

Wardhaugh, R. 1986: *An Introduction to Sociolinguistics*. Oxford: Blackwell.

Weinreich, U. 1953: *Languages in Contact*. New York: The Linguistic Circle of New York.

Weinreich, U. 1954: Is structural dialectology possible? *Word* 10, 388–400.

Weinreich, U., Labov, W., and Herzog, M. I. 1968: Empirical foundations for a theory of language change. In W. P. Lehmann and Y. Malkiel (eds), *Directions for Historical Linguistics*, Austin: University of Texas, 95–188.

316   REFERENCES

Weist, R. M. 1986: Tense and aspect. In P. Fletcher and M. Garman (eds), *Language Acquisition* (2nd edn), Cambridge: University Press, 356–74.

Wells, J. C. 1982: *Accents of English 2: The British Isles*. Cambridge: University Press.

Wentworth, H. and Flexner, S. B. 1975: *Dictionary of American Slang*. New York: Thomas Y. Crowell.

Werkgroep Taal Buitenlandse Werknemers 1980: Taalattitude, taalvaardisheid, en sociale omstandigheden van Marokkaanse arbeiders in Nederland: een verkennend onderzoek. In P. Muysken (ed.) *De Verwerving van het Nederlands door Buitenlandse Arbeiders*, Instituut Algemene Taalwetenschap Amsterdam #27, 49–106.

White, L. 1987: Markedness and second language acquisition: the question of transfer. *Studies in Second Language Acquisition* 9, 261–80.

White, R. V. 1974: The concept of register and TESL. *TESOL Quarterly* 8, 401–16.

Whiteley, W. H. (ed.) 1971: *Language Use and Social Change*. Oxford: University Press.

Whorf, B. L. 1940: Science and linguistics. *Technology Review* 42, 229–31, 247–8. Reprinted in and quoted from J. B. Carroll (ed.), *Language, Thought, and Reality: Selected Writings of Benjamin Lee Whorf*, Cambridge, MA: MIT Press, 207–19.

Widdowson, H. 1975: The significance of simplification. *Studies in Second Language Acquisition*, 1, 11–21.

Widdowson, H. 1984: *Learning Purpose and Language Use*. Oxford: Oxford University Press.

Wilkins, D. A. 1976: *Notional Syllabuses*. Oxford: University Press.

Williams, A. P. 1972: Dynamics of a black audience. In T. Kochman (ed.), *Rappin' and Stylin' Out*, Urbana, IL; University of Illinois, 101–6.

Williams, F. 1976: *Explorations of the Linguistic Attitudes of Teachers*. Rowley, MA: Newbury House.

Woken, M. and Swales, J. to appear: Expertise and authority in native–nonnative conversations: the need for a variable account. In S. M. Gass, C. Madden, D. R. Preston, and L. Selinker (eds), *Variation in Second Language Acquisition, Volume 1: Discourse and Pragmatics*, Clevedon, Avon: Multilingual Matters.

Wolfram, W. 1973: *Sociolinguistic Aspects of Assimilation: Puerto Rican English in New York City*. Arlington, VA: Center for Applied Linguistics.

Wolfram, W. and Fasold, R. W. 1974: *The Study of Social Dialects in American English*. Englewood Cliffs, NJ: Prentice-Hall.

Wolfson, N. 1976: Speech events and natural speech: some implications for sociolinguistic methodology. *Language in Society* 5, 189–209.

Wolfson, N. 1981: Invitations, compliments, and the competence of the native speaker. *International Journal of Psycholinguistics* 24.

Wolfson, N. 1982: *CHP: The Conversational Historic Present in American English Narrative*. Dordrecht: Foris.

Wolfson, N. 1983a: An empirically based analysis of complimenting in American English. In N. Wolfson and E. Judd (eds), *Sociolinguistics and Language Acquisition*, Rowley, MA: Newbury House, 82–95.

Wolfson, N. 1983b: Rules of speaking. In J. Richards and R. Schmidt (eds), *Language and Communication*, London: Longman, 61–87.

Wolfson, N., D'Amico-Reisner, L., and Huber, L. 1983: How to arrange for social commitments in American English. In N. Wolfson and E. Judd (eds), *Sociolinguistics and Language Acquisition*, Rowley, MA: Newbury House, 116–28.

Wolfson, N. and Manes, J. 1980: The compliment as a social strategy. *International Journal of Human Communication* 13, 391–410.

Wong-Fillmore, L. 1976: *The Second Time Around: Cognitive and Social Strategies in Language Acquisition*. Stanford: Stanford University PhD dissertation.

Young, R. 1988: Approaches to variation in interlanguage morphology: plural marking in the speech of Chinese learners of English. Philadelphia: University of Pennsylvania PhD dissertation.

Young, R. to appear: Ends and means: methods for the study of interlanguage variation. In S. M. Gass, C. Madden, D. R. Preston, and L. Selinker (eds), *Variation in Second Language Acquisition, Volume 2: Psycholinguistic Issues*. Clevedon, Avon: Multilingual Matters.

Zimmerman, D. H. and West, C. 1975: Sex roles, interruptions and silences in conversation. In B. Thorne and N. M. Henley (eds), *Language and Sex*, Rowley, MA: Newbury House, 105–29.

Zuengler, J. to appear: Performance variation in NS-NNS interaction: ethnolinguistic difference, or discourse domain? In S. M. Gass, C. Madden, D. R. Preston, and L. Selinker (eds), *Variation in Second Language Acquisition, Volume 1: Discourse and Pragmatics*, Clevedon, Avon: Multilingual Matters.

# Index

Bold type indicates principal discussion of a topic.